WAR OF WORDS

WAR OF WORDS
The Censorship Debate

Edited by George Beahm

Illustrated by Kenny Ray Linkous

Andrews and McMeel

A Universal Press Syndicate Company

Kansas City

Library of Congress Cataloging-in-Publication Data

War of words : the censorship debate /
edited by George Beahm.
p.   cm.
Includes bibliographical references.
ISBN 0–8362–8015–6 : $12.95
1. Censorship—United States.
I. Beahm, George W.
Z658.U5W37   1993
363.3′1—dc20   93–7765
CIP

See page 427 for continuation of copyright notice.

ATTENTION SCHOOLS AND BUSINESSES

Andrews and McMeel books are available at quantity
discounts with bulk purchases for educational, business, or
sales promotional use. For information, please write to:
Special Sales Department, Andrews and McMeel,
4900 Main Street, Kansas City, Missouri 64112

for Ned Brooks
and
Donna Martin

Contents

Introduction: The Nature of the Beast   *xiii*

Part 1: Books

1. Kurt Vonnegut: On Censorship   *3*
   Haynes Johnson: The Bill of Rights   *7*
2. Michael R. Collings: Censorship in the Renaissance:
   A Paradigm for Today?   *8*
3. Morris L. Ernest: "On Banned Books"   *16*
4. James A. Michener: "Are There Limits to Free Speech?"   *20*
5. John F. Baker: Book Banning Blues: A New Chorus   *25*
   On Banned Books Week   *27*
6. Anne Lyon Haight: The Political and Religious Control of Books   *28*
   Celebrate Freedom: Read a Banned Book Sweatshirt and T-shirt   *30*
7. Stephen King on Censorship   *31*
8. George Beahm: Stephen King's Scary Idea   *32*
9. Anthony Schulte: The Freedom to Read   *33*
10. Art Buchwald: Dirty Books   *36*

Fahrenheit 451

11. George Beahm: On *Fahrenheit 451:* A Cautionary Tale   *38*
12. Ray Bradbury: "Coda" to *Fahrenheit 451*   *40*

American Psycho

13. George Beahm: *American Psycho*—Censorship or Editorial Judgment?   *43*
14. Douglas E. Winter: Book Review, *American Psycho*   *45*

Nineteen Eighty-Four

15. George Beahm: *Nineteen Eighty-Four:* Another Cautionary Tale   *49*
16. Walter Cronkite: Preface to *Nineteen Eighty-Four*   *50*
17. Michael Shelden: An extract from *Orwell: The Authorized Biography*   *52*

Salman Rushdie

18. George Beahm: Notes from Underground   *54*
   A Rushdie Chronology   *56*
19. Perspectives on *The Satanic Verses*   *57*
20. Karsten Prager Interview: Salman Rushdie   *59*

21. Norman Mailer: A Folly Repeated *63*

22. Art Buchwald: The White House's Rushdie Brushoff *67*

23. Salman Rushdie: An extract from "A Pen Against the Sword:
In Good Faith" *69*

Part 2: Art and the NEA

24. An American Civil Liberties Union Briefing Paper: Artistic Freedom *75*
Samuel Walker: "The Boston Massacre" 80

25. John E. Frohnmayer: "Chairman's Statement":
The National Endowment for the Arts *81*
Shirley M. Green: The NEA: The White House Perspective 87

26. John E. Frohnmayer: The Art Your Tax Money Buys *88*
NEA Publications 91

27. John E. Frohnmayer: Raising Hell *92*

28. *USA Today* Interviews: "Let Clash of Ideas Determine the Truth"
Point: John E. Frohnmayer *97*
Counterpoint: Phyllis Schlafly *99*

29. Jesse Helms: Art, the First Amendment, and the NEA Controversy *102*
Perspectives: Patrick Buchanan, James J. Kirpatrick, William F. Buckley, Jr.   106

30. Pat Robertson: To the Congress of the United States *107*
Resolution No. 4: On Government Support of Obscene and Offensive Art   109

31. Emergency Committee for the Arts: An Open Letter to Congress *110*
Here's What Some U.S. Presidents Had to Say During Their Terms of Office   111

32. At Issue: Should Congress Restrict the Types of Art
That Can Be Funded by the NEA? *112*
Yes says Jesse Helms *112*
No says Wayne Lawson *113*

The Future of the NEA

33. *Newsweek* Interview: John Frohnmayer on Tough Times at NEA *115*
USA Today *Editorial (extract): Let's Stop Playing Politics with
Support of the Arts 117*

34. George Beahm: Dark Days—"Artists as Enemies, Ideas as Demons" *118*

Mapplethorpe

35. George Beahm: Robert Mapplethorpe: Persona Obscura *120*
Bound to Please: Mapplethorpe 122

36. Marcia Pally: Cincinnati: City Under Siege *123*

37. *USA Today* Interview: Dennis Barrie *132*

38. Irving Kristol: What Do Artists Want from Us? *135*

39. Garry Wills: In Praise of Censure *139*

40. Dave Barry: The Naked Truth *144*

Part 3: In the Schools

41. Jeff Meade: Battle over the Books: Grave Impressions   *149*

42. *USA Today* Editorial: "Don't Let Zealots Censor Kids' Books"   *159*

43. Washington Coalition Against Censorship:
Local Pro-Censorship Group Formation   *161*

44. Jerry Falwell: The Religious Right Must Guard American Values   *163*

45. American Library Association: Diversity in Collection Development:
An Interpretation of the Library Bill of Rights   *168*
Library Bill of Rights   *169*

46. Nancy Motomatsu and Jean Wieman: How Conflicting Values
Result in Challenges   *170*

47. Washington Coalition Against Censorship: Some Specific Objections
by Pro-Censorship Groups to Educational Materials   *174*
In the Eyes of the Beholder   *176*
"Freedom to Read"   *177*

48. Washington Coalition Against Censorship:
Common Questions and Answers   *178*
Perspectives: School Censorship   *180*

49. Greg R. Jesson: How Parents Can Refute the "Censor" Label   *181*

50. Phyllis Schlafly: Who Are the Real Censors?   *183*

51. Arthur J. Kropp: Using Parents as a Trojan Horse for School Censorship   *189*

In the Beginning

52. Henry M. Morris and Gary E. Parker: Evolution as Religion   *193*

53. Frederick Edwords: Scientific Illiteracy   *196*

54. Bill Moyers Interview: Isaac Asimov   *201*
Arthur C. Clarke on "The Menace of Creationism"   *203*

Part 4: Seduction of the Innocent

55. George Beahm Interview: Barry Hoffman   *207*
Gauntlet   *211*

Comics

56. Douglas E. Winter: Seeing Is Not Believing   *212*

57. George Beahm: Wertham's *Seduction of the Innocent*   *218*
Seduction of the Innocent: *Dust Jacket Copy*   *219*

58. Comics Magazine Association of America, Inc.: Comics Code   *220*

59. George Beahm: All in Color for a Dime   *223*
Fredric Wertham on Censorship   *226*

60. George Beahm Interview: Colleen Doran and David Weaver   *227*
A Distant Soil   *229*

The Movie Ratings Game

61. Gary L. Wood: The Censorship Game: Hype in Hollywood *230*

62. Jack Valenti: The Voluntary Movie Rating System *236*
    "Rated 'G'—For Gone?" *241*

63. American Library Association: Statement on Labeling:
    An Interpretation of the Library Bill of Rights *242*

Television

64. George Beahm: The Outer Limits—Network Program Standards *244*

65. Forrest Sawyer Interview: Madonna *247*
    Madonna's Sex *254*

66. Christopher M. Finan: The Rev. Donald E. Wildmon's Crusade
    for Censorship, 1977–89 *255*
    Television Programs Attacked by Wildmon Because of Their Content *269*
    *Corporations Criticized by Wildmon for Sponsoring Programs or
    Material Wildmon Has Opposed* *270*

The Music Industry

67. Parents Music Resource Center: A Brief Overview of Explicit Lyrics
    and State Legislation *272*

68. PMRC Mission Statement *275*
    Gwen Ifill: Beyond Voluntary Labeling *276*

69. Recording Industry Association of America: The Recording Industry's
    Voluntary Lyrics Labeling Program *277*
    Michael Cover: "One Vote in a Hot Spot" *278*

70. Frank Zappa: Mythical Beasts *279*

71. Mary Morello: Sound Off! *285*

72. George Beahm: Corporate Censorship—
    He Who Pays the Piper Calls the Tune *287*
    Perspectives on Ice-T's "Cop Killer" *288*

Part 5: Sex and Censorship

73. Morality in Media, Inc: Debunking Misinformation About Pornography
    and Obscenity Law *291*
    Obscenity Statute Utilizing Miller *Standard* *299*

74. Wendy Melillo: Can Pornography Lead to Violence? *300*

The Meese Commission

75. "This Week with David Brinkley": A Roundtable Discussion
    on the Meese Commission *308*
    Letter from the Attorney General's Commission on Pornography *321*

Contents

76. *Attorney General's Commission on Pornography Final Report:*
    "The Risks of Abuse"   *322*

77. Kurt Vonnegut: On the Meese Commission and the First Amendment   *326*

Sexuality: Different Voices

78. Anne Rice: On Women and Pornography   *328*

79. George Beahm Interview: William Margold   *330*

80. George Beahm: "Trampling Basic Rights"   *333*

81. George Beahm: The Devil Made Me Do It—The Bundy Bill   *335*

82. Mitch McConnell: Pornography Victims' Compensation Act   *339*
    S. 1521—Pornography Victims' Compensation Act   *343*

83. John Irving: Pornography and the New Puritans   *344*

84. Marcia Pally: *Sense and Censorship—The Vanity of Bonfires*   *352*

Appendices

1. Susan Arnold: Waldenbooks—A Position Statement   *381*

2. Project Censored: The Ten Best Censored Stories of 1992   *383*

3. Art Censors of the Year   *385*

4. Fighting Censorship: What You Can Do   *395*

5. Resources   *398*

   Bibliography   *419*

   Acknowledgments   *423*

   About the Editor and Artist   *425*

   Copyrights Extension   *427*

> ## Free speech is life itself.
>
> —SALMAN RUSHDIE, address to the Graduate School
> of Journalism at Columbia University, 1992

Introduction: The Nature of the Beast

> Congress shall make no law respecting an establishment of
> religion, or prohibiting the free exercise thereof; or abridging
> the freedom of speech, or of the press; or the right of the
> people peaceably to assemble, and to petition the
> Government for a redress of grievances.
>
> —Amendment 1, Constitution of the United States, 1791

The censorship battle," wrote *Newsweek*'s Peter Plagens, "won't go away in the 1990s, because it reflects a fundamental tension in our society."

A decade of division, the nineties has seen all the birds come home to roost: racism (black v. white), family values (traditional v. nontraditional), the economy (the haves and, increasingly, the have-nots), sexuality (heterosexuality v. pansexuality), and values (humanism v. fundamentalism).

The censorship battle—a component of what's commonly called the cultural wars—has always been a part of this country's history, but the nineties has seen it become a dominant issue.

The vexing question, of course, is, Who should decide what you read or view—the church, the state . . . or you?

On virtually every cultural front, censorship has made headlines in the nineties: attempts to ban books in public schools and libraries are on the rise, according to People for the American Way; controversial lyrics from rap singers are under attack from church groups and organizations like the Parents Music Resource Center (PMRC); controversial videos—especially X-rated, adult videos—are targeted by overzealous public prosecutors and church groups; and the visual arts have become a political debate, with the National Endowment for the Arts as its focal point.

An ongoing battle between point and counterpoint, censorship begins on an offensive front: a self-appointed arbiter of public morality, always citing the common good, seeks to impose his vision of the world on others. In response, anticensorship groups, defending their positions, go on the offensive.

And as with any war, there are inevitably casualties and collateral damage.

Frequently lost in this debate is the notion that "those who do not know their opponent's arguments do not completely understand their own," as the publishers of *Censorship: Opposing Viewpoints* explained.

This book is intended to be a starting point for the censorship debate. The diversity of voices representing both sides of the debate underscore the fact that things are rarely what they seem; the adage about considering the source is especially good advice when examining the censorship issue.

o   o   o

In *Censorship: Opposing Viewpoints,* we are told the story behind the word *censor:*

> In 443 BC, the Comitia Centuriata, one of the ruling bodies of the ancient Roman State, established the office of censor. Originally, the censor was charged with taking a census of all Roman citizens for purposes of taxation, voting, and military service. In time, however, the power and authority of the censor grew until eventually the person holding the office became the official arbiter of Roman manners and morals.

Eventually, we are told, the "authoritarian arm" of the censor reached "even the hallowed chambers of the powerful Roman Senate as certain senators found themselves removed from office, publicly ostracized and often banished from their beloved city."

Little, it seems, has changed since that time.

The practice of censorship has merely proved that the road to hell *is* paved with good intentions. For instance, no one can fault the *intent* of the Bundy bill, but if it were enacted into law, self-censorship would almost certainly become the order of the day.

Today's censors—wolves in sheep's clothing—are quick to point out their favorite dictionary definition of censorship: prior restraint of publication by the government. These disingenuous souls know that the majority of Americans, often disagreeing on content, do agree on one critical point: they—and not the government, not the church, and especially not self-appointed moral arbiters—should have the right to decide what to read and view. (Reading is fundamental, the bookselling community tells us, but the freedom to read, and view, is even more fundamental.)

The Random House Dictionary of the English Language offers a second, more useful, definition of *censor:* "any person who supervises the manners or morality of others." Not surprisingly, no one willingly stands up to term himself a censor; whatever his actions, he is likely to point out that he is only exercising his constitutional right to free expression, even if in the end it means silencing yours.

As Ray Bradbury explained in "Coda," a short essay in *Fahrenheit 451,* "There is more than one way to burn a book. And the world is full of people running about with lit matches. Every minority . . . feels it has the will, the right, the duty to . . . light the fuse."

o   o   o

In Britain, under police protection, a writer unwillingly lives in seclusion, fearing for his life. Salman Rushdie, author of *The Satanic Verses,* had the audacity to use his fiction as a vehicle to explore the human condition. Taking offense where none was intended, Islamic fundamentalists—kindred spirits to Christian fundamentalists—were outraged and charged him with blasphemy.

Four years later, despite international protests, Rushdie remains in hiding; the *fatwa* condemning him to death remains in effect.

It can't happen here, you say. Perhaps not—certainly not with such extreme measures. But though there is only one way to kill an author, there is more than one way to kill a book.

"Free speech is the whole thing, the whole ball game," said Rushdie in a rare U.S. visit in 1992, when he addressed Columbia University's Graduate School of Journalism. "Free speech," he reminded us, "is life itself."

Echoing Rushdie's words, Elie Wiesel wrote: "Any attack on you is directed at us all. Censorship in literature is the enemy of literature and death threats, addressed for whatever reason, if they succeed in silencing the author, would mean not only the end of literature but the end of civilization."

Part 1
Books

Don't join the book burners. Don't think
that you're going to conceal thoughts by
concealing evidence that they ever existed.

—DWIGHT D. EISENHOWER, speech at Dartmouth College, June 14, 1953

(from *Banned Books Week '91: A Resource Book* edited by Robert P. Doyle)

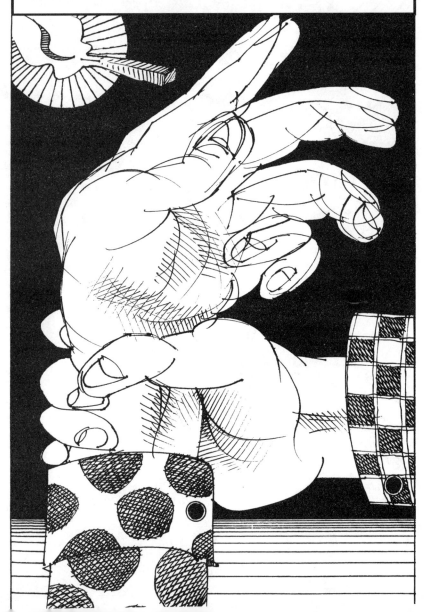

1

On Censorship

by Kurt Vonnegut

Chapter VII from Fates Worse than Death *titled "An Autobiographical Collage,"*
the piece that follows makes a reference to the previous chapter on requiems.
    In the piece, Vonnegut tells what he wanted to say to the Attorney General's
Commission on Pornography. Although it declined his request, he did get a chance
to deliver his comments in public, at a public information briefing on the Commis-
sion on Pornography, sponsored by the National Coalition Against Censorship, on
January 16, 1986.

And speaking of revered old documents that cry out for a rewrite nowadays, how about the First Amendment to the Constitution of the United States of America, which reads:

"Congress shall make no law respecting an establishment of religion, or prohibiting the free exercise thereof; or abridging the freedom of speech, or of the press; or the right of the people peaceably to assemble, and to petition the Government for a redress of grievances." What we have there is what should have been at least three separate amendments, and maybe as many as five, hooked together willy-nilly in one big Dr. Seuss animal of a nonstop sentence. It is as though a starving person, rescued at last, blurted out all the things he or she had dreamed of eating while staying barely alive on bread and water.

When James Madison put together the first ten amendments, the "Bill of Rights," in 1778, there was so much blurting by male property owners ravenous for liberty that he had 210 proposed limitations on the powers of the Government to choose from. (In my opinion, the thing most well-fed people want above all else from their Government is, figuratively speaking, the right to shoot craps with loaded dice. They wouldn't get that until President Ronald Reagan.)

I said to a lawyer for the American Civil Liberties Union that Madison's First Amendment wasn't as well written as it might have been.

"Maybe he didn't expect us to take him so seriously," he said.

I think there is a chance of that, although the lawyer was being wryly jocular. So far as I know, Madison did not laugh or otherwise demur when Thomas Jefferson (who owned slaves) called the Constitutional Convention in Philadelphia an assembly of demi-Gods. People two-thirds of the way to the top of

Mount Olympus might not take as seriously as some of us do the possibility of actually honoring among the squabbling mortals the airy, semi-divine promises of the Bill of Rights.

The ACLU lawyer said that I, as a writer, should admire Madison for making his amendments as unambiguous as a light switch, which can be only "on" or "off," by the strong use of absolute negatives: "Congress shall make *no* law . . . shall *not* be infringed . . . *No* soldier shall . . . shall *not* be violated, and *no* warrants shall issue . . . *No* person shall be held to answer . . . *no* fact tried by a jury . . . shall *not* be required . . . shall *not* be construed. . . ." There are no words anywhere in his amendments meaning "under ideal conditions" or "whenever possible" or "at the convenience of the Government." From moment to moment in our long history (the oldest continuous government save for Switzerland's), the several specific provisions of the Bill of Rights can be, thanks to James Madison, only "off" or "on."

To me the First Amendment sounds more like a dream than a statute. The right to say or publish absolutely anything makes me feel insubstantial as a character in somebody else's dream when I defend it, as I often do. It is such a *tragic* freedom since there is no limit to the vileness some people are proud to express in public if allowed to do so with impunity. So again and again in debates with representatives of the Moral Majority and the like, and some of the angrier Women Against Pornography, I find myself charged with being an encourager of violence against women and kiddie porn.

When I was new at such discussions I insouciantly asked a fundamentalist Christian opponent ("Oh, come on now, Reverend") if he knew of anyone who had been ruined by a book. (Mark Twain claimed to have been ruined by salacious parts of the Bible.)

The Reverend was glad I asked. He said that a man out in Oregon had read a pornographic book and then raped a teenage maiden on her way home from the grocery store, and then mutilated her with a broken Coke bottle. (I am sure it really happened.) We were there to discuss the efforts of some parents to get certain books eliminated from school libraries and curricula on the grounds that they were offensive or morally harmful—quite mild and honorable books in any case. But my dumb question gave the Reverend the opportunity to link the books in question to the most hideous sexual crimes.

The books he and his supporters wanted out of the schools, one of mine among them, were not pornographic, although he would have liked our audience to think so. (There *is* the word "motherfucker" one time in my *Slaughterhouse-Five,* as in "get out of the road, you dumb motherfucker." Ever since that word was published, way back in 1969, children have been attempting to have intercourse with their mothers. When it will stop no one knows.) The fault of *Slaughterhouse-Five,* James Dickey's *Deliverance,* J.D. Salinger's *Catcher in the Rye,* several books by Judy Blume, and so on, as far as the Reverend was concerned, was that neither their authors nor their characters exemplified his notion of ideal Christian behavior and attitudes.

The Reverend (as was his right) was making an undisguised attack not only on America's demi-God-given right to consider every sort of idea (including his), but also on the Constitution's insistence that the Government (including the public schools) not declare one religion superior to any other and behave accordingly with the force of law.

So the Reverend was not a hypocrite. He was perfectly willing to say in so many words that there was nothing sacred about the First Amendment, and that many images and ideas other than pornography should be taken out of circulation by the police, and that the official religion of the whole country should be his sort of Christianity. He was sincere in believing that my *Slaughterhouse-Five* might somehow cause a person to wind up in a furnace for all eternity (see the mass promulgated by Pope St. Pius V), which would be even worse (if you consider its duration) than being raped, murdered, and then mutilated by a man maddened by dirty pictures.

He in fact won my sympathy (easy to do). He was not a television evangelist (so easily and justly caricatured), although he probably preached on radio from time to time. (They all do.) He was a profoundly sincere Christian and family man, doing a pretty good job no doubt of imitating the life of Christ as he understood it, sexually clean, and not pathologically fond of the goods of this Earth and so on. He was trying to hold together an extended family, a support system far more dependable than anything the Government could put together, in sickness as in health, for richer or for poorer, whose bond was commonly held beliefs and attitudes. (I had studied anthropology, after all, and so knew in my bones that human beings can't like life very much if they don't belong to a clan associated with a specific piece of real estate.)

The Attorney General's Commission on Pornography, a traveling show about dirty books and pictures put on the road during the administration of Ronald Reagan, was something else again. At least a couple of the panel members would later be revealed as having been in the muck of financial or sexual atrocities. There was a clan feeling, to be sure, but the family property in this case was the White House, and an amiable, sleepy, absentminded old movie actor was its totem pole. And the crazy quilt of ideas all its members had to profess put the Council of Trent to shame for mean-spirited, objectively batty fantasias: that it was good that civilians could buy assault rifles; that the contras in Nicaragua were a lot like Thomas Jefferson and James Madison; that Palestinians were to be called "terrorists" at every opportunity; that the contents of wombs were Government property; that the American Civil Liberties Union was a subversive organization; that anything that sounded like the Sermon on the Mount was socialist or communist, and therefore anti-American; that people with AIDS, except for those who got it from mousetrapped blood transfusions, had asked for it; that a billion-dollar airplane was well worth the price; and on and on.

The Attorney General's Commission on Pornography was blatantly show business, a way for the White House to draw attention to its piety by means of headlines about sex, and to imply yet again that those in favor of freedom of speech were enthusiasts for sexual exploitation of children and rape and so on. (While other Reagan supporters were making private the funds for public housing and cleaning out the savings banks.)

So I asked to appear before the Commission when it came to New York, but my offer was declined. I wanted to say, "I have read much of the heartrending testimony about the damage words and pictures can do which has been heard by your committee. The scales have fallen from my eyes. I now understand that our Government must have the power to suppress words and images which are causes of sexually motivated insanity and crimes. As John the Apostle says, 'In the beginning was the word.'

"I make my living with words, and I am ashamed. In view of the damage freely circulated ideas can do to a society, and particularly to children, I beg my Government to delete from all my works all thoughts which might be dangerous. Save me from myself. I beg for the help of our elected leaders in bringing my thoughts into harmony with their own and those of the people who elected them. That is democracy.

"Attempting to make amends at this late date, I call the attention of the committee, and God bless the righteous Edwin Meese, to the fundamental piece of obscenity from which all others spring, the taproot of the tree whose fruit is so poisonous. I will read it aloud, so audience members under the age of twenty-one should leave the room. Those over twenty-one who have heart trouble or are prone to commit rape at the drop of a hat might like to go with them. Don't say I haven't warned you.

"You Commission members have no choice but to stay, no matter what sort of filth is turned loose by witnesses. That can't be easy. You must be very brave. I like to think of you as sort of sewer astronauts.

"All right? Stick your fingers in your ears and close your eyes, because here we go:

"'Congress shall make no law respecting an establishment of religion, or prohibiting the free exercise thereof; or abridging the freedom of speech, or of the press; or the right of the people peaceably to assemble, and to petition the Government for a redress of grievances.'"

End of joke.

• *Kurt Vonnegut, an American original and social satirist, has published numerous novels, including* Slaughterhouse-Five, *which was burned in the school furnace in Drake, North Dakota.*

The Bill of Rights
by Haynes Johnson

They are not divinely carved on stone like the Ten Commandments and handed down from a mountaintop to the multitudes, nor inscribed on lasting parchment like the Magna Carta and signed with a flourish by royalty, but for Americans the Bill of Rights is the indispensable guarantor of freedom for ordinary people.

Today, on the 200th anniversary of their addition to the Constitution, those first ten constitutional amendments are as serviceable—and as controversial—as ever. They are also as relevant as the latest headlines about a sensational rape trial or the divisive debates over such issues as abortion, school prayer, gun control, pornography, flag burning, and the extension—or restriction—of civil rights, women's rights, gay rights, criminal rights, press rights.

2

Censorship in the Renaissance
A Paradigm for Today?

by Michael R. Collings

Either actively or passively, censorship in one form or another seems endemic in human societies. Certainly for most of the recorded history of human culture, authoritarian control over political expression and artistic endeavor has been the norm rather than the exception. One study of censorship in America, for example, finds the "Beginnings of Censorship" in China in 213 B.C. when the Emperor Shi Hwang-ti burned "the *Analects* of Confucius—and nearly all the other books in China—in order to wipe out old ideas and old loyalties." In China, it seems, the authorities remained steadfastly dedicated to the principles of censorship, taking control of printing in the ninth century, and burning books wholesale as late as 1776, establishing over a millennium and a half of recorded government interference. In Greece, the pattern of censorship extends back as far as the Spartan ban on poetry and the official denunciation of works by Aeschylus, Aristophanes, and Protagoras. Nor was Rome much different. The poet Ovid (later to become one of the most influential sources for ideas, images, and philosophies in Renaissance literature) was exiled from Rome during the first decade A.D. because his *Ars Amatoria* had affronted the moral sensibilities of Augustus Caesar.

In fact, it requires only a cursory glance at most historical periods to understand that as long as artists depend on patronage from a central core of political, religious, or social power, art in all of its forms will generally be subservient to the needs and aims of that power. In a society such as that existing during the Middle Ages in western Europe, for instance, in which virtually all artistic expression was supported directly by patronage from kings, nobles, or the church, artists would in turn and perforce respond overtly or covertly to the wishes of those patrons.

At the risk of oversimplifying what would have been at times a complex matter of balancing allegiances and judging loyalties, it would seem that under such circumstances, most censorship would remain virtually invisible. Writers who implicitly or explicitly supported the existing power structure would be paid for their endeavors; copies of poems or treatises would be authorized, and— with a modicum of luck—the work might survive. Writers attacking that power structure would simply not find willing patrons. Before the sixteenth century in Europe, there were few if any alternative modes of publication other than direct patronage; certainly until the introduction of the printing press in England in 1476, virtually all literary production would have depended on patronage.*

This sense is enhanced by the simple fact that for most of Western history, there has been no independent publishing industry as such. The eighteenth-century poet Alexander Pope—who was tacitly censored by his society for his Catholicism—found one outlet for his creativity by publishing what amounted to bestselling translations of Homer and Virgil. The result was that he became in essence the first English poet to make a living as a poet, largely unaffected by the ups and downs of official patronage; with the fortune made from his translations, he could afford to write about anyone and anything. But before the seventeenth century, literature remained essentially an avocation dependent upon the purses of wealthy individuals or institutions—and as such was more than a little subject to the vicissitudes of political, religious, and social pressures.

The English Renaissance—especially the late sixteenth and early seventeenth centuries—is a most interesting period in this context. According to T.S. Eliot and other early twentieth-century enthusiasts, the psychological pressures felt during the early seventeenth century closely resemble many of those we feel today. An earlier, apparently more stable worldview was crumbling, with cracks appearing almost daily in the facade of a once universally accepted authoritarianism. Morals—and the assumed values that supported them—were changing rapidly. The relationship of religion to daily life was altering radically. Social institutions that once seemed impervious to change were being altered, distorted, even destroyed. Artists were increasingly aware of the discontinuities between their artistic and cultural heritage and their own experiences. Traditional literary forms disappeared, replaced by a restless experimentation with style, structure, content.

And the authorities responded—as have so many in our own time—by repressing the free expression of that restlessness. As early as 1538, the Tudor monarchy established licensing laws as a means of controlling the political content of published material. The laws were provided with a structure to enforce compliance when the Stationers' Company was incorporated in 1557. This guild was chartered to search out and destroy unlicensed presses and printers and, not coincidentally, to destroy "certain seditious and heretical books, rimes and treatises . . . daily published and printed by divers scandalous, malicious, schis-

---

*Geoffrey Robertson makes a case for a certain amount of openness in English literature, particularly in terms of sexual content: "In Britain the *Exeter Book*, one of the earliest surviving examples of Anglo-Saxon literature, contains coarse anatomical riddles, enthusiastically compiled by the cathedral monks, and fourteenth-century Europeans digested without demur the writings of Chaucer and Boccaccio. The *Canturbury Tales* was published by Caxton in unexpurgated form shortly after he commenced printing at Westminster in 1476. . . . In the first dawn of the printed word, little apprehension was felt about the impact of sexual writing upon the few men of the age who might entertain themselves with such a study. Children and workers could not read"; however, he also notes that during these centuries the focus of censorship lay less with obscenity than with the fear of politically subversive literature.

matical and heretical persons." Two years later, Elizabeth I took further steps to ensure that no book could lawfully appear without having been approved by political or religious censors. According to Paul Blanchard, "For a time during Elizabeth's reign every London printing house was searched twice a week by royal agents to see whether it was printing anything improper. A forbidden book was burned by the common hangman, as though a published idea could be killed like a man."

The consequences of Elizabethan licensing acts led to several curious historical episodes. Jasper Ridley outlines one of the most dramatic—if not melodramatic— of these events in the consequences of a particularly inflammatory pamphlet, Stubbs' *The Discovery of a Gaping Gulf whereinto England is like to be swallowed in another French Marriage if the Lord forbid not the banns by letting Her Majesty see the sin and punishment thereof,* an unauthorized publication spurred by Elizabeth's response to the French suggestion that she marry Francis, Duke of Anjou, the brother of King Henry of France. In September of 1579, Anjou came to England to visit Elizabeth. Stubbs and others feared that if the marriage took place, Anjou would attempt to reintroduce Catholicism into England, in which case, England would undoubtedly suffer the equivalent of another Massacre of St. Bartholomew's. In addition, with religious questions momentarily set aside, Stubbs argued that the 46-year-old Elizabeth would probably prove too old to bear a child anyway, and that Anjou would in any event infect her (and any children, however unlikely their births may be) with the syphilis "which he had acquired by his dissolute life."

The pamphlet was illicitly published by William Page in London and circulated through the city. Elizabeth was particularly angered by the book, since it was customary not to publish books criticizing foreign princes, even if diplomatic relations with the princes in question were strained. Elizabeth had, for example, recently asked Philip II to suppress a Catholic book denouncing her as a heretic and a bastard. And she was affronted by the abuse of Anjou, whom she seems to have liked.

Stubbs, the publisher, and the bookseller were arrested, and the government decided that they were to become examples of how the government would deal with recalcitrant Puritans. The three men were prosecuted under the Act Against Seditious Words and Rumours, originally passed to protect Mary and Philip II from "slander, reproach and dishonour of the King and Queen's Majesties"— the punishment for which was to have the right hand cut off. But the Act was now reinterpreted (apparently without historical precedent or warrant) to protect not only the reigning queen but her proposed fiancé, and to make illegal any denunciations of "the Queen's suitor."

Elizabeth pardoned the publisher but ordered the mandatory sentence for Stubbs and the bookseller:

On 3 November they were taken to Palace Yard at Westminster. Before the sentence was carried out, Stubbs spoke to the crowd of onlookers. "I pray you all to pray with me that God will strengthen me to endure and abide the pain that I am to suffer, and grant me his grace, that the loss of my hand do not withdraw any part of my duty and affection toward her Majesty. . . . My masters, if there be any among you that do love me, if your love be not in God and Her Majesty, I utterly deny your love." After the executioner had struck off his hand, Stubbs took off his hat with his left hand, and cried "God save the Queen" before he fainted.

The two men were kept in prison for a year before finally being released.

In the tapestry of Western history, the incident seems little more than a minor curiosity, a footnote in most texts, if it is mentioned at all. But the image of the mutilated Stubbs, bereft of his right hand (which at the time had moral as well as physical overtones, since lefthandedness was considered literally "sinister" and was often seen as emblematic of evil), removing his hat and reasserting his patriotism and his love for the queen who had caused him such suffering remains vivid.

Within a generation, the practice of removing right hands seems to have diminished, but the underlying desire on the part of the government to control literary output remained. Ben Jonson, who became the most influential literary arbiter of early seventeenth-century London and one of the most popular dramatists of the period, at times rivaling even Shakespeare, was imprisoned for writing a play that included politically sensitive references. Even more directly, John Donne—arguably the most important seventeenth-century poet before Milton—was aware of the direct consequences of overt political intrusion. In a scholarly biography of Donne, R.C. Bald defends the poet for his practice of not publishing his early poetry, but rather allowing it to circulate only in manuscript among a close circle of friends, often insisting that no further copies be made.

There has been a tendency to criticize Donne for his reluctance to publish his verses. Yet . . . he was aware that there was a real danger in doing so, not merely to his reputation and his prospects but even to his person. In the previous year the Archbishop and the Bishop of London had been spurred into action, by the scandal caused by the dedication to Essex in Hayward's *History of Henry the Fourth,* to make fresh regulations for the press and, besides ordering "That noe Englishe historyes be printed excepte they bee allowed by some of her maiesties privie Counsell," had forbidden any satires or epigrams to be printed hereafter. As a result of these orders, books had been collected and burned in Stationers' Hall, among them Marston's *Pygmalion's Image,* Davies' *Epigrams,* Marlowe's translation of Ovid's *Elegies,* and Guilpin's *Skialetheia.* Had Donne's satires and elegies been in print they would inevitably have met a similar fate, and his future career would have been jeopardized.

In light of the simultaneous expansion and repression of social and political freedoms during the late sixteenth and early seventeenth centuries, it does not seem entirely illogical that the age that stimulated Shakespeare to create the grandest tragic moments in English literature also systematically limited avenues for public expression. By the time of Shakespeare's death, events were in motion that would ultimately undermine the pretensions to Divine Right of Kings so often argued by James I, and the consequent attempts by those kings (and queens) to control what the people could write and read. Within thirty-five years of Shakespeare's death, the English Parliament met to judge the actions of a reigning monarch, Charles I. Parliament found the king guilty, sentenced him to death, and executed him. In an age when monarchy was assumed to be the norm, when personal control of all aspects of life might rest in the hands of one individual, this extraordinary action was not only revolutionary but virtually unthinkable. That single political act led to the incrementally increased power of Parliament—and finally to the assumption of freedoms that led to the founding of the United States and that are protected by our Constitution and Bill of Rights.

Christopher Hill argues that the radical Protestantism ultimately responsible for the death of Charles I was logically and essentially antithetical to the spirit of censorship. Hill notes specifically that while English Protestantism could be overtly intolerant, in certain important ways it was far more liberal than the competing Continental Catholicism with its Index of forbidden books: "There was no protestant Index like that on which all books advocating the Copernican theory remained until 1757, and on which the works of Descartes stayed still longer. On the contrary: Bodley's first Librarian used to scan the Index carefully so as to know which books and which editions to buy for his Library." Hill goes so far as to note that for a short time during the Commonwealth, from about 1641 through 1660, England enjoyed "complete liberty of the press."

Ironically, however, that same period turned out to be one of the most repressive in terms of censorship. And the loudest voice raised in defense of freedom of the press was led by events to become himself an official censor for the Commonwealth.

John Milton's *Areopagitica* first appeared in November of 1644. It was published in response to a censorship edict of June 1643, designed by a Presbyterian-controlled Parliament to quell political and religious opposition by requiring that all books be submitted to an official censor *before publication,* something not even the Elizabethans had attempted. Milton responded to the act with his typical fervor and genius, writing his pamphlet (as he puts it in the "Second Defense of the English People") to "deliver the press from the restraints with which it was encumbered," and published it without first having it censored, approved, or licensed. Censorship, he argued, has no historical justification, has no redeeming social purpose, and is simply evil: ". . . unless wariness be used, as good almost kill a man as kill a good book: who kills a man kills a reasonable creature, God's image; but he who destroys a good book, kills reason itself, kills the image of God, as it were, in the eye." Throughout the text, Milton denounced censorship with arguments that continue to ring true today. Over three hundred years later, this pamphlet is still considered by many as the clearest articulation of the principles of freedom of press and publication, additionally bolstered by Milton's reputation as the greatest non-dramatic poet in English literary history.

Even in this instance, however, the complexities of the issue rapidly surface. Less than five years after the unlicensed, unregistered appearance of *Areopagitica,* its author had become Secretary for Foreign Tongues to the Council of State (1649)—an official of the "establishment," as it were. As such, he was actively involved with defending and supporting the Commonwealth government. Although Milton was not a voting member of the council, he was influential enough for the council to request on several occasions that he become the official spokesman for that body, and by extension for the government of England. Thus it becomes ironic to note that not only was the censorship law of 1643 (which occasioned the *Areopagitica*) not repealed while Milton was part of the governing body, but that an additional act—Bradshaw's Press Act—was passed by Parliament on September 20, 1649, that broadened the powers of the government to control the press. The earlier law had stipulated that certain materials had to be licensed and registered by government appointees; the new law stipulated censorship of *all* newspapers. Milton seems to have justified his involvement in censorship—and acknowledged that at least part of his vision in the *Areopagitica* had been fulfilled—by noting in a letter to a friend that

> There are no licensers appointed by the last Act, so that everybody may enter his book without licence, provided the printer's or author's name be entered, that they may be forthcoming if required.

In a note to this quotation, however, Milton's biographer, William Riley Parker, identifies a further level of irony: ". . . perhaps *because* he had won part of his argument," Milton agreed to become an official censor himself.

Within months of his appointment to the Council of State, the author of the *Areopagitica* found himself filling a double role as government propagandist/ apologist and censor. In May and June of 1649, he was requested by the Council of State to examine the papers of publishers accused of violating the licensing act, become a tacit if not actual censor. Beginning as early as January 1651, he assumed the post of licenser of the government-sponsored newsletter *Mercurius Politicus.* As Don M. Wolfe argues,

> Like all his comrades in the Council . . . Milton found that as a government official he could hold to his theories of freedom, if at all, only in adulterated form. He took upon himself the duties of censorship no doubt as the one best

qualified among his colleagues to know when to censor; for once in England's history a man with no inferior mind held the power Milton had so dreaded in *Areopagitica*.

"I cannot praise a fugitive and cloistered virtue, unexercised and unbreathed, that never sallies out and sees her adversary, but slinks out of the race where that immortal garland is to be run for, not without dust and heat," Milton writes in the *Areopagitica*. Ideas cannot be restricted by laws; the freedom of each individual to know and with that knowledge to choose must be preserved. Again and again in this treatise and in works like *Paradise Lost*, Milton argues for the freedom of choice . . . and implicitly for the freedom of expression.

Yet even so, he discovered that there are limits. Milton's spirited defense of unlicensed publication remained a mainstay of arguments against censorship when the restored Stuart monarchy again attempted to enforce government licensing; but the writer himself acknowledged the necessity to oversee certain kinds of documents and acted on that knowledge. Milton had noted in the *Areopagitica* that one of the most difficult problems concerning censorship has to do with choosing *who* decides: "It cannot be denied that he who is made judge to sit upon the birth or death of books, whether they may be wafted into this world or not, had need to be a man above the common measure, both studious, learned, and judicious." Milton was all three.

o   o   o

In some senses, this foray into a moment in history leaves us roughly where we began. Censorship has existed throughout most of recorded history—it will, in all probability, continue to exist in one form or another. At times, political regulations have been clearly (from our perspectives, at least) excessive and extreme; at other times, even the staunchest advocates of human choice and responsibility felt the need to exercise caution in what was published and what was not. Milton's case is perhaps unusual only insofar as he himself was unusual—gifted beyond the powers normally allotted to individuals. He was capable of writing a stirring challenge to the existing government, one that continues to echo in our own ears; yet he could not transform that intellectual challenge into practice without compromise.

That may be the challenge we face as well. Like our forebears in the Renaissance, we live in a time when traditional values, roles, relationships, institutions, and even interpretations of history are under constant attack. Some activists attempt to forestall further inroads by eliminating all opposing voices—and we are faced with the prospect of the twentieth-century analogues to the lefthanded Stubbs, mutilated for the "crime" of trying to protect the queen he supported. Others come from the opposite direction, urging the total freedom of expression—but all too often ignore the equally important consideration of *responsibility* in expression. Today's advocates for freedom just as often may become tomorrow's censors, comfortable in their newly gained freedoms and eager to enforce them upon others who do not share the underlying values and moral assumptions.

And so we are left, not with the answer, but with the question. Milton described his vision of England in vivid terms:

> Methinks I see in my mind a noble and puissant nation rousing herself like a strong man after sleep, and shaking her invincible locks. Methinks I see her as an eagle muing her mighty youth and kindling her undazzled eyes at the full midday beam; purging and unscaling her long-abused sight at the foundation itself of heavenly radiance; while the whole noise of timorous and flocking birds, with those also that love the twilight, flutter around, amazing at what she means. . . .

Methinks I see in my mind similar possibilities for us—contingent not only upon access to free expression, but upon our wise and responsible consideration of how that freedom is used.

• *Dr. Michael R. Collings is a professor of English in the Humanities Division at Pepperdine University in Malibu, California.*

3

"On Banned Books"

by Morris L. Ernest

> Where there is an open mind, there will always be a frontier.
>
> —CHARLES F. KETTERING

Excerpted from Banned Books, *"On Banned Books" highlights the fact that censorship has always been part of the human experience . . . and always will. Morris L. Ernest, who successfully defended in court James Joyce's* Ulysses *in 1933 and Radclyffe Hall's* The Well of Loneliness *in 1939, originally wrote this essay for the second edition of* Banned Books *by Anne Lyon Haight.*

. . . **A**nyone who looks over the list of banned books, even casually, must, in the first instance, ask what could have frightened man to suppress books such as *Gulliver's Travels,* in Ireland considered obscene and detrimental to both government and morals; Hans Christian Andersen's *Wonder Stories,* banned by Nicholas I of Russia, who also suppressed *Uncle Tom's Cabin* and *The Scarlet Letter;* or Jack London's *The Call of the Wild,* banned as radical in Italy and Yugoslavia in 1929. In a world where practically everyone has the answers, I am sure that this is one time when the right questions are more important than the answers. Mrs. Haight's volume must, in the minds of people of good will, raise fundamental queries: Have man's fears ever been valid? Why should we trust a government or a church to control our literary diet after we have seen the validity of the former fears of those in power? Are we not better off trusting the people of our nation to accept or reject books in the market place of thought? Have we not staked our all on a gamble, not yet empirically provable, and hence calling for an act of faith, that truth has a better chance of winning out in an open market place of thought rather than by controls placed in the hands of rulers whether ecclesiastical or secular?

We scarcely need additional exhortations such as Milton's *Areopagitica* on the theory of freedom of thought in view of the evidence presented in this volume. Aside from the scientific inquiries undertaken in recent years to discover what effect the printed word has on the people of our nation, the matrix of Mrs. Haight's work proves that any guess as to the danger of ideas at any moment of history looks silly and vapid in the next decades. Even though truth crushed to earth will rise again, the crushing process is unbecoming for free people and may well delay that wholesome march of man toward the development of his potential joys and powers, potentials of the future scarcely discernible at any single moment of history.

We know little about man's ultimate potentials. But one of the brakes preventing man's realization of his potentials may be the failure to explore the roots of man's fear of ideas. Happily, science is now directing its attention in that area. I have always believed that the pen has more might than the sword because throughout man's history the sword has been used to kill even the wielders of the pen; but the words and ideas have the capacity of secret survival or rebirth. For centuries man was most afraid, and hence tried to suppress criticism of the church or its dogma—called blasphemy. Marc Connelly's innocuous and charming play *Green Pastures* was banned in England and Norway because it showed God on the stage. The first edition of Lena Towsley's *Peter and Peggy* was stopped here because the children were not shown saying their prayers. And Dante's *Divine Comedy* was burned in France in 1318, and fell under the Inquisition in Lisbon in 1581. The Spanish Inquisition banned Francis Bacon's *Advancement of Learning*.

The church, maintaining power over masses of illiterate folk, gave evidence of its inner insecurity by endeavoring to maintain power by the suppression of criticism or even diversity of religious opinion. As the power of the church was diminished through the developing sovereignty of the state the insecurity, the fear and hence the censorship shifted from blasphemy into the area of sedition, and then after the democratic process had taken root as opposed to a royal sovereignty the power of the state over man's minds dwindled. And still men and women had to fill their censorious requirements and did so by creating the next big shift, that is, from criticism of the state to references to sex, or in legal terms, from sedition to obscenity.

Literary obscenity is the newest toy of the frightened, and obviously varies among cultures depending upon the sexual folkways. Few sophisticated cultures are free of this fear. In sophisticated cultures the official standards for sexual behavior are as a rule far more rigid and more prudish than the actual practices of the people. No doubt there were a few Greeks who disapproved of homosexuality, lesbianism and infanticide which were all practiced openly; just as among the Jews some may have rejected the world of Solomon and his many wives. I mention these two cultures since our folkway seems to me to have incorporated antithetical features of each. In any event the gap between standards and practices reveals the censorious sexual anxieties of a country.

In 16th Century England, Sir Thomas Malory's *The Birth, Life and Acts of King Arthur* was denounced as "bold adultery and wilful murder." The first printed book to be banned in England was the Tyndale Bible, not for blasphemy but because of Henry VIII's sensitiveness on the subject of divorce. Louis XVI considered Beaumarchais' *Le Mariage de Figaro* immoral; and Boston withdrew from publication Whitman's *Leaves of Grass*.

With the advent of Mussolini, Hitler and Stalin, a combination of fears—

obscenity and sedition—crept into the national patterns. Dictators fear and hence create fears. In Spain under Franco, the twin fears seem to be blasphemy and obscenity. In our own Republic at this time we find two fears, one known as McCarthyism and the other an apparent spurt in the drive against sexual material in books. . . .[1]

Since 1900, two important ideas have taken place that touch on man's fear of ideas. From the days of vellum and quill through Gutenberg and up to the turn of the 20th Century, ideas could reach the minds of people only through speech, writing or printing. During the past fifty years new media have developed—radio, movies and television. Each new medium created new fears. Nevertheless, the persistent pattern continued; the censors who read for sedition, blasphemy or obscenity never felt that they themselves would be corrupted. They were only worried for the souls of others. . . .

Despite random comment of loose-tongued, frightened people, there is as yet little reason to believe that the written word has a provable causal relation to behavior. However, I suspect that the effect, if any, is more often in the direction of acts of omission than commission. . . . Despite the new media there is substantial and increasing agreement that books are the prime enduring source of man's continuing culture. Material flowing over the ether or appearing in the daily newspapers is ephemeral and particularly in our folkway people are apt to say, implying a deviation from fact, "it is only a newspaper story."[2]

Any subject that deals with man's fears or even with his potential hopes should be placed in its historical background. In the main, this volume is concerned not with the open adverse public criticism in the market place of thought as to any particular volume, but with the exercise of sovereignty, whether by church or state, to suppress ideas. In this connection, much of the trouble in our Republic derives from the inaccurate education of our people as to our proud and expanding Bill of Rights. We have adopted the myth that the Founding Fathers were against censorship and that the First Amendment to the Constitution guaranteed freedom of thought. Nothing can be further from the truth. When the Twelve Colonies (Rhode Island failed to appear) banded together in the Convention of Philadelphia in 1787, not a word was mentioned, during those great four months, on the subject of freedom of the press. Our Constitution is silent on the subject. The First Amendment, which is probably the greatest contribution of our nation to the history of government, was inserted only because the States wanted to make sure that the new Federal Government would keep its hands off the censorship business and would leave the entire control over the minds of the people in the hands of the state

---

1. Editor's note: Joseph McCarthy is not with us, but his philosophies are.
2. Editor's note: Times *have* changed. Woodward and Bernstein's reportage of Watergate toppled a president.

governments. Such was the pattern of our nation until around 1920 when the Supreme Court of the United States for the first time held that even the states could no longer abridge freedom of the press. While the daily newspapers early attained a status free from persistent governmental interference, the movies supinely begged for government pre-censorship. Radio and television, as well as movies, fended off governmental controls by horizontal industrial agreements which vitally and, in my opinion, illegally restrict the market place of thought and the intellectual diet of our people.

An odd footnote on one of our present areas of fear. For eighty years, that is up to 1870, there was practically no legislation banning that indefinable subject known as obscenity. After debate of a few minutes in each house of Congress, a frightened neurotic by the name of Anthony Comstock, playing on the sex hypocrisy of our folkways, pushed through our first obscenity laws, promptly to be copied in most of the states of the Union. From 1870 to 1915, the practice of book publishers was to submit manuscripts to the Comstock society. This period, known as the "dark age of books," ended when a few publishers believed that freedom and profits were not antithetical, and during the two decades after 1915 cases were brought to court narrowing to a substantial extent suppressible obscenity.[3] It has been my privilege and joy to participate in many of these cases. Since the great decision of Judge Woolsey in the *Ulysses* case, it has been increasingly clear that no book openly published, openly distributed and publicly reviewed would be denied distribution to our people if the publisher and author did battle with the censors in stout and brave terms. . . .

This book will help all who read it to dig their heels in the ground, having read the historical evidence of man's prior invalid fears of his most precious commodity—ideas.

• *Morris L. Ernst co-authored* Privacy: The Right to Be Left Alone *and* Censorship: The Search for the Obscene. *According to* The Macmillan Company, *publishers of* Censorship, *"Mr. Ernst achieved an international reputation as defense counsel in the historic* Ulysses *case."*

---

3. Editor's note: Years later, in 1973 in *Miller* v. *California,* the Supreme Court legally defined obscenity.

4

"Are There Limits to Free Speech?"

by James A. Michener

> We're developing a very able cadre of American Ayatollahs who are going to do this country in the way the Ayatollah Khomeini is doing Iran in, if we're not very careful. There is a place for those people; they obviously serve a need by taking religion, through television, into the homes of people who don't have it. But when they branch out from that and become monitors of public health and public morals, I find it terrifying.
>
> —JAMES MICHENER, when asked about problems that disturbed him most, from a *Playboy* interview, September 1981

I am a passionate defender of free speech for two reasons. First, I am a writer and exist as such only because as a U.S. citizen I am pretty much free to say and write what I think. The mighty First Amendment of the Bill of Rights ensures me that freedom. Second, in World War II, I helped to defend our nation and learned then to appreciate how precious all freedoms are.

But freedom of speech poses special problems. It can be difficult to define and quite often difficult to exercise. During my writing life, I have wrestled with such matters constantly. A few examples will illustrate how complicated the right to speak freely can be.

When I moved to Alaska in 1985 to write about that immense land, I was visited by the committees of three different groups. One group was Eskimo, one Athabascan Indian and one Metis (half-native, half-Caucasian). But all three delivered the same message. "You're free to write whatever you wish about Alaska, except for two forbidden subjects," they warned me. "We do not need anyone from the lower 48 to come up here and preach to us about either alcoholism or suicide. They are the scourge of our people, and we'll handle them without instructions from you."

One group wanted me to submit anything I wrote for its approval—and threatened me with serious consequences if I didn't. This posed a clear-cut problem: Either I wrote what I saw, or I submitted to censorship. Since I had no plans to write about the two forbidden subjects, I told the groups, "I suppose I'll be able to respect your wishes."

But when I reached farthest north and visited one Eskimo family after another who had lost a member to suicide, and I lived in Wainwright, a remote village where four high school students died in one day from drinking contaminated alcohol, I said: "All bets are off." Then I wrote into my novel the tragic story of an Eskimo girl I called Amy Ekseavik, who is a bright student expected to qualify early for college. The suicide of Amy's father, however, forces the girl to leave school to help out at home. Six months later, word trickles in to Desolation (my fictional name for a town much like Wainwright) that 15-year-old Amy has taken her father's gun, stepped outside her family's sod hut and committed suicide. These were stories about societal ills that had to be told, and to have surrendered to censorship—even of a benevolent kind—would have been wrong.

I am, of course, constantly mindful that freedom of speech has limits. Justice Oliver Wendell Holmes Jr. phrased one neatly: "The most stringent protection of free speech would not protect a man in falsely shouting fire in a theater and causing a panic." Nor is libel against a fellow citizen permitted. Nor lying under oath. These are sensible limits to free speech, and I accept them.

The more difficult questions about the right vs. the responsibility of free speech arise in matters like the suicides of real-life Amy Ekseaviks. When does withholding such information from the public become suppression of free speech? And when does it take the form of common sense for the common good?

I remember the shock I received in the 1932 Presidential election when Franklin D. Roosevelt made a whistle stop in our little town in Colorado and allowed us to see something which had never appeared in a newspaper photograph or a newsreel: "Look! He can barely walk with braces on his legs." Those days of self-censorship are over, and I believe we are better off without them, although some of my friends in the media argue, "It was better in the old days. We didn't chew up our leaders so fast."

Now, to discuss some tough cases which perplex the nation today because they deal with the nitty-gritty of free speech:

Some years ago, I was asked to sign a document protesting government censorship of pornography. At first, I had no trouble signing it, for I agreed with the U.S. Supreme Court, which had refused to outlaw pornography generally but did allow censorship if the material had no redeeming social value. I do not like pornography. I have never patronized shops that sold it and certainly never wrote it myself—but I would not censor it, for I felt that infringing on the First Amendment could do the nation more serious harms than the circulation of a few lascivious picture books.

But as I was about to sign, a man more knowledgeable in this field than I showed me a display of obscene materials he though ought to be censored. I wanted no part of them, but neither did I think they ought to be outlawed. Then he showed me others that presented a score of ways in which men could brutalize, even murder, women. These were hurtful to an orderly society, the products of sick minds and an invitation to abuse women. But should they be censored? I withheld judgment.

Finally, he showed me scenes of gross child pornography, and I was so revolted by this abuse of children—before they reached the age at which they could form, inherit or consciously elect their patterns of sexual behavior—that I cried: "This filth should be outlawed, and the people who purvey it should be in jail!"

I still defend those three opinions. General pornography is distasteful but not censorable. Sadistic materials denigrating women disturb me and probably ought not to be circulated, but I do not know my own mind as to their censorship. Child pornography should be outlawed, as it now is, and its perpetrators jailed.

One of the most perplexing censorship cases in recent memory involved photographs by the late Robert Mapplethorpe on display in a Cincinnati museum last spring. The exhibit contained more than a few shots of explicit homoerotic behavior, and whereas those photos had been viewed in other cities—Philadelphia posted a warning, then set them apart from the other photos—elected officials in Cincinnati found the show to be offensive by local moral standards. Arrests were made; indictments followed. (On Oct. 5, a jury acquitted the museum and its director of obscenity charges.)

How would I have handled this matter? I would not censor the show. I would allow it to circulate and would even encourage interested patrons to judge it on its merits. But if I were a curator in a city where I knew local sensibilities might be offended—and where I might find myself in jail—I probably would not exhibit Mapplethorpe's photographs. Were I in a more liberal community (with job security), I'm sure I would exhibit them—copying the Philadelphia tactic of keeping off to one side shots which should not be shown to schoolchildren.

Increasingly, the battles we are waging today over the freedom of speech have to do with freedom of expression. One case involves a "rap band," 2 Live Crew, which specializes in staccato dialogue heavy with the grossest sexual emphasis. The band cut an album, *As Nasty As They Wanna Be,* which ridicules women as bitches and whores. It advocates that young men abuse their dates in appalling ways that cannot be specified in a family magazine.

A U.S. district judge in Fort Lauderdale ruled the album obscene. As a result, a record-store owner was convicted of obscenity for selling it. And when 2 Live Crew performed in Hollywood, Florida, its sheriff decided that the judge's ruling empowered him to arrest Luther Campbell, leader of the band, for parading obscenity in public. His arrest, trial and recent acquittal resurrect the complex debate over artistic freedom vs. a community's right to restrict sexual material.

How does a noncensorship man like me react? In my reverence for the First Amendment, I would not censor the album. But I might be tempted to try a citizen's arrest—not on grounds of censorship, but because the lyrics are an incitement to the physical abuse and degradation of women.

The latest innovation in the suppression of free speech is called SLAPP (for Strategic Lawsuit Against Public Participation). It works like this: Suppose that I am an aggressive land-developer who wants to convert your public park into condominiums. You, the concerned citizen, are opposed. So you write to the editor of your newspaper, opposing the park's conversion into high-rises. You have not defamed me or abused me. All you have done is exercise your right to free speech during a controversy.

But I am outraged at your intrusion into my plans and slap you with a lawsuit charging libel, defamation, conspiracy, nuisance and other infractions of civil law. I also claim $250,000 in damages—and you find yourself with huge lawyers' fees staring you in the face.

There is little chance that my lawsuit against you could win in court. In many such suits across the country, judges throw the cases out, for they are patently spurious. Yet when other public-minded citizens learn of the cost to you in worry and cash outlay, they are scared away from exercising their constitutional right to join in a public debate.

There is a strong movement to outlaw frivolous SLAPPs, and the courts are beginning to side with aggrieved citizens who have been abused or terrified by such suits. SLAPPs should be halted.

My last case is the most wrenching, for it involves deep-seated visceral feelings: "Should the public burning of the American flag be outlawed?" This act is so repugnant to many loyal Americans that it produces outrage, and when the Supreme Court says that it should be seen merely as one more example of citizens exercising their freedom to express their views, allowed by the First Amendment, those offended cry, "Pass a constitutional amendment outlawing it!" To do so would impair that part of the First Amendment which protects our freedom, and I must oppose it. As a defender of the remarkable pattern of government our nation has evolved, I deplore abuses which defame our flag, but I do not want to see it protected by tampering with our basic law. We can urge members of Congress to pass ordinary acts to achieve that purpose, and I hope they do. But leave the Bill of Rights alone.

I defend freedom of speech so vigorously because of personal experiences. Three of my books have been banned by the nations about which I have written: South Africa, Spain and Poland. My novel *Hawaii* was so poorly received there, because I spoke openly of discrimination, that newspaper editorials advised me to leave the islands and never come back. And the chief of police in Jakarta, Indonesia, announced that he would publicly thrash me if I ever returned to his city. Heavy censorship has been part of my life, but I have lived to see opinion change. In all three nations where my books were banned, I have been invited back as an honored guest. As one critic said to me in Poland: "We still don't like parts of your book, but so many visitors tell us they visited Poland because of it, we have to redefine you as a friend."

More important is the fact that for the past twenty years I have served on one U.S. government board or another, fighting communism and striving to bring the freedom of speech to countries behind the Iron Curtain. This has kept me informed as to the terrible things that can happen in a nation like Romania, for example, when free speech is stifled. In one country after another—first in

Czechoslovakia, then Hungary—when tyrants were finally overthrown, the people turned for democratic leadership to the writers, editors and poets who had fought to keep freedom of speech alive in their countries.

I suppose it always has been that way. Who, after all, were those free-speaking prophets of the Old Testament who ranted against the evils of their rulers but the editors and columnists of their day?

• *This essay, written at the request of* Parade *magazine, was James A. Michener's response to its question why "freedom of speech is so vital to Americans today."*

A recipient of the U.S. Medal of Freedom, Michener has published more than forty books. His most recent: Mexico.

Not surprisingly, he has seen some of his works banned, including Iberia *(by the Spanish government),* The Covenant *(by the South African government), and* Poland *(by the Polish government).*

5

Book Banning Blues
A New Chorus

by John F. Baker

> "How fragile civilization is," Rushdie reflected.
> "How easily, how merrily a book burns!"
>
> —Quoted by W.J. Weatherby from *Salman Rushdie: Sentenced to Death*
> (Carroll & Graf Publishers, New York, 1990)

Every year Americans are treated to a salutary reminder of something we wish they didn't have to be reminded of: the fact that we are a nation where far too many people are trying to prescribe, or often proscribe, our reading. Banned Books Week, sponsored by the American Booksellers Association and the American Library Association, among others, is now in its tenth year, and shows no sign of dying for lack of available candidates. Loyal booksellers fill their windows with examples of books that have been removed from libraries, thrown out of classrooms, challenged by various special-interest groups; they usually get a lot of local press for their efforts, there is a certain amount of editorial tut-tutting, then people tend to forget all about it until next year. And the bannings or attempted bannings go right on.

One of the particularly troubling things about Banned Books Week [in 1990] was that it was taking place in a time when issues of obscenity in the arts were once again on the country's political agenda. The National Endowment for the Arts, battered for months by congressional critics led by Senator Jesse Helms, finally struggled through to new funding for three years and a vaguely worded but still troubling restriction on grant recipients. Joseph Papp of the New York Shakespeare Festival refused a large NEA grant under such conditions, as he has before, and took out provocative ads for his new season in which every production, including Shakespeare's *Henry IV*, was described in such a way that it could be seen as a threat to "right-thinking" viewers.

And that is, of course, one of the key points that has to be made, again and again, about attempts to ban or otherwise censor the arts, including literature. Materials that view human life critically, quizzically or satirically are bound to give offense to someone; and in no time you have an organized group saying that you're trying to destroy the family or endorse sin. Yes, such anxieties can extend even to the contents of the Bible or the dictionary, with the Comstocks particularly alert when it comes to children's books. Someone in Michigan, who must have used a microscope, claimed to have found "dirty things" going on in the busy, cluttered pages of the popular *Where's Waldo?*

How representative of the American public are such groups? They are often so noisy, so adept at letter-writing campaigns and the intimidation of congressional representatives, even sponsors of TV programs, that it sometimes seems they must represent what President Nixon used to call "the silent majority." But in fact the outcomes of two recent jury trials seem to suggest that such people speak only for their narrow selves, and for those adept at stirring them up.

In Cincinnati, a city long noted for civic rectitude, a jury acquitted the director of a local art gallery who had the temerity to exhibit the Robert Mapplethorpe photographs that helped set off the whole NEA uproar. And in Florida, the rap group 2 Live Crew was acquitted by a straight-arrow jury that certainly seemed unfamiliar with rap and its conventions, but found the whole affair, and the performance for which the band was prosecuted, more funny than reprehensible. As one juror commented, in a remark we would like to think represents the feelings of a *real* majority of Americans: "You take away one freedom, and pretty soon they're all gone."

So it's good to remember that when it comes to the courthouse, average Americans are reluctant to fine or jail anyone who local prosecutors, police or vigilante groups think may have transgressed the bounds of decency. They may grumble, but they are not about to be stampeded into action that takes away anyone's liberty or livelihood. "Community standards" have always been an important part of the language in any attempt to define obscenity; it should be encouraging for publishers, librarians and booksellers to note that in two communities specially chosen for their supposedly rigid standards, they proved more relaxed than expected.

There's a last point that those who would ban books never seem to learn: not only does it seldom work for long, but it is often violently counterproductive. Israel's Mossad learned that a few weeks ago when it tried to suppress a book, *By Way of Deception,* by former agent Victor Ostrovsky. The book, which might have been expected to sell mildly, shot straight to the top of the bestseller list, where it has remained ever since; hardly the desired result, as far as Mossad was concerned.

Lesson to be learned as we head into a second decade of Banned Books Week: censors are generally paper tigers—though they can certainly throw a scare into you.

• *John F. Baker is the editorial director for* Publishers Weekly, *the international news magazine of book publishing.*

On Banned Books Week
September 26 to October 3

Endorsed by the Library of Congress's Center for the Book, sponsored by the American Booksellers Association, the American Library Association, the American Society of Journalists and Authors, and the National Association of College Stores, Banned Books Week—in its eleventh year—celebrates the freedom to read.

The theme for 1992 was "Censorship: Old Sins in New Worlds," using Columbus's journey to America as a metaphor for escaping the censorial past.

Bookstores, schools, and libraries nationwide sponsor "exhibits, lectures, discussions, plays and films demonstrating the harms of censorship."

To help the effort, the American Library Association publishes annually a source book and promotion guide, which is updated annually. The 1992 edition includes

an annotated historical list of books that have been banned or have been the object of controversy from 387 B.C. to the present; an annotated list of books challenged or banned this year; a collection of First Amendment quotes; camera-ready art for ads and bookmarks; posters; display ideas; significant First Amendment court cases; and sample news releases.

6

The Political and Religious Control of Books

by Anne Lyon Haight

In the history of censorship, the oldest and most frequently recurring controls have been those designed to prevent unorthodox and unpopular expressions of political or religious opinions. A notable example of the latter was the Roman Catholic *Index Liborum Prohibitorum,* which, at the time it was abrogated, restrained the reading of nearly a sixth of the world's population.

The church's regulation of books can be traced back to Apostolic times, when the Ephesian converts of St. Paul made a bonfire of hundreds of volumes catering to superstition. Most of the early lists and decrees, however, were concerned with establishing which books were to be accepted as part of the Bible, which were recommended reading, and which were heretical.

In 1515 the Lateran Council established the principle of ecclesiastical licensing, a procedure which was formalized and given potency by the Council of Trent in 1546, with the forbidding of the sale or possession of anonymous religious books. It was Pope Paul IV who authorized the first list of banned books in 1557. For nearly four hundred years, the list was issued in numerous editions, with occasional additions and deletions. The last edition was published in 1948, with a list of more than four thousand titles, including some of the masterworks of the Western world. Publication of the *Index* ceased in 1966. Without rescinding the previous decisions, the church's action effectively ended official censorship and control over what Roman Catholics might be permitted to read.

In this century political censorship has consistently taken more dramatic forms and received far greater notoriety than religious bannings. However, recent episodes of suppression, though numerous, are quite limited in scope when compared to the era of Nazi Germany and the communist purge that followed. The first large-scale demonstration occurred on May 10, 1933, when students gathered twenty-five thousand volumes by Jewish authors and burned them in the square in front of the University of Berlin. The bonfire was watched by forty thousand unenthusiastic people in a drizzling rain. Joseph Goebbels, the minister of public enlightenment, delivered an address on "the symbolic significance of the gesture." Similar demonstrations were held at many other German universities. In Munich five thousand schoolchildren, who had formerly seen Marxist literature publicly burned, were enjoined: "As you watch the fire burn these un-German books, let it also burn into your hearts love of the Fatherland." Students entered the bookstores and took without renumeration the books they considered eligible for the bonfire, and had to be prevented from confiscating books from the university library.

The following list consists of some of the most important authors whose works were sacrificed at the fires.

Sholom Asch, Lion Feuchtwanger, Maxim Gorky, Stefan Zweig, Karl Marx, Sigmund Freud, Helen Keller, Jack London, Ernest Hemingway, John Dos Passos, Jakob Wassermann, Emil Ludwig, Arthur Schnitzler, Leon Trotsky, V.I. Lenin, Josef Stalin, Grigori Zinoviev, Alfred Adler, Gotthold Lessing, Franz Werfel, Hugo Munsterberg, Thomas Mann, Heinrich Mann, Erich Maria Remarque, Albert Einstein, Henrich Heine, Felix Mendelssohn, Maximilian Harden, Kurt Eisner, Henri Barbusse, Rosa Luxemburg, Upton Sinclair, Judge Ben Lindsay, Arnold Zweig.

This great destruction of books by the Nazis continued until World War II. In 1938 they made a cultural purge of Austria. Booksellers were forced to clear their shelves of proscribed works, and either to conceal or to destroy them. When word of the purge reached the United States, many offers to buy the books were sent to Vienna by universities and individuals. Some eventually did reach this country.

In Salzburg fifteen thousand people watched a "purification bonfire" of one copy each of two thousand volumes, including Jewish and Catholic books. The ceremony was started by a schoolboy who threw a copy of Kurt von Schuschnigg's *Three Times Austria* on the gasoline-soaked pyre. Meanwhile the crowd sang "Deutschland Über Alles" in the gaily lighted square. The proceedings were under the auspices of the National Socialist (Nazi) Teachers' Association, which had appealed to the public to give up all "objectionable literature," and it was said that the destruction of thirty thousand more volumes would follow.

In Leipzig many of the same books that were burned in the Nazi bonfire on 1933 were suppressed, and in Czechoslovakia the Education Ministry ordered all public libraries to remove and destroy all unpatriotic books, particularly by patriots including ex-President Benes.

In 1944 the great "book city" of Leipzig suffered the loss of many valuable books by the Allied bombings, and in 1946 the Coordinating Council of the American Military Government in Germany ordered Nazi memorials to be destroyed. The object was to eliminate the "spirit of German militarism and Nazism as far as possible." This order to cleanse the German mentality was issued just as the eleventh anniversary of the Nazi "Burning of the Books" was being observed by the free world, and it caused much sharp comment. Included were the works of Hitler, Goebbels, Mussolini, and Marx. The books were placed on the restricted lists in libraries, or in some instances pulped, but no burnings were known to have taken place. At the same time the Communists in East Germany were doing the same thing from their own point of view.

In 1953, in East Germany, the Communist cultural advisers removed from the libraries, schools, and bookshops at least five million volumes by German, Nazi, and foreign authors. Even Marx and Engels did not escape and were expurgated, or rewritten "with historically important additions." It is said that books written before the war about the "good old days" were especially feared.

In 1953–54 it was reported by the refugees from East Berlin that all printed matter including picture papers and crossword puzzles sent to East Germany were confiscated at the border. And in 1969, East German guards at Rudolphstein refused passage to West Berlin of Konrad Adenauer's memoirs and of road maps showing Germany's boundaries before World War II.

• *Anne Lyon Haight is the author of* Banned Books: Informal Notes on Some Books Banned for Various Reasons at Various Times and in Various Places, *from which this excerpt is taken.*

Celebrate Freedom
Read a Banned Book Sweatshirt and T-shirt

Rivertown Trading Company (1-800-669-9999) offers a banned books sweatshirt and T-shirt in the standard adult sizes from medium to extra, extra large. In bold red letters, the first line simply reads, "Celebrate Freedom." In bold purple letters, the last line says, "Read a Banned Book." Centered between those two lines are well-known works of fiction that have been banned:

1984 by George Orwell

A Farewell to Arms by Ernest Hemingway

The Catcher in the Rye by J.D. Salinger

The Color Purple by Alice Walker

Flowers for Algernon by Daniel Keyes

Gone with the Wind by Margaret Mitchell

Of Mice and Men by John Steinbeck

One Flew over the Cuckoo's Nest by Ken Kesey

Ordinary People by Judith Guest

The Adventures of Huckleberry Finn by Mark Twain

The Diary of Anne Frank by Anne Frank

The Great Gatsby by F. Scott Fitzgerald

The Martian Chronicles by Ray Bradbury

To Kill a Mockingbird by Harper Lee

Uncle Tom's Cabin by Harriet Beecher Stowe

7

Stephen King on Censorship*

> I'm very proud. . . . I'm in the company of greats.
>
> —STEPHEN KING on his books being banned

An author whose books have frequently been targeted by censors, Stephen King has spoken out on numerous occasions against censorship, in print and in public. (A few years ago, he fought censorship in his home state when the Maine Christian League unsuccessfully attempted to pass an obscenity referendum.)

As far as censorship goes, with my books or with anyone else's books, I think that censorship is always a power trip. What censorship is at bottom is about who's on top. The issue behind censorship is always somebody saying, "My point of view is more valid than your point of view." If the censorship initiative succeeds, then the answer is "Yes, my views *are* more valid than your views; my views *are* more moral than your views." As far as censorship in public institutions and libraries, censorship has no place. If a book has been banned, I would urge people to immediately go and march and get it put in, or withdraw their support. Stay away.

When it comes to where the action has been for me, which is mostly high school libraries and junior high libraries, where all my books have been banned at one time or another, schools are *in loco parentis;* therefore, they are dealing with minors, and it becomes a more difficult decision.

I think that schools have the right at parental initiative to take books out of the library. But my advice to kids would be: "Whatever it is that your parents and teachers don't want you to read is probably the thing that you need the most to find out." So I would find out what's been censored, what's been pulled from the shelves of your school library, and I would *run* to the nearest public library or to a bookstore and pick it up, whether it's *Cujo, Lord of the Flies,* or *Lady Chatterley's Lover.* Go get it and find out what they don't want you to know because that's what you need to know.

---

*From a videotaped interview conducted by New American Library for its sales force, 1989.

8

Stephen King's Scary Idea

by George Beahm

> Please remember that book-banning is censorship,
> and that censorship in a free society is always a serious matter. . . .
>
> —STEPHEN KING, guest column for *Bangor Daily News*, March 29, 1992

As a bestselling author whose popularity with teenage readers continues unabated, Stephen King's books are frequently the target of well-intentioned but misguided parents. Such was the case at the middle schools in Duval County, Florida, where two novels (*The Dead Zone* and *The Tommyknockers*) were banned after a parent had filed a written complaint. A *USA Today* piece of March 11, 1992, said, "This whole book [*The Tommyknockers*] and others of Stephen King I *skimmed through* [italics mine] are full of filthy language."

"King had no comment," according to the article.

A week later, King did comment, at length, in a guest column—prefaced by an editorial—that was published in his hometown newspaper, the *Bangor Daily News*.

To the kids concerned about book banning, he exhorted them—as he did in a public address in Virginia Beach in 1986—to discover on their own what the fuss is about by going to the source.

To the parents, King correctly pointed out that book banning is "a kind of intellectual autocracy."

And to other citizens in town concerned about book banning, King pointed out that censors have tunnel vision; they want others to see their world *their* way, regardless.

o   o   o

When I began work on this book project, I mentioned its title to a family member—a born-again Christian—who immediately said, "As you know, I'm *for* censorship."

She meant, of course, that she was *for* censoring material that didn't meet her approval. Had I suggested the Bible be censored, she would undoubtedly have responded with a look of horror. "But that's censorship!" she would likely cry.

As King reminds us in his guest column, "Book-banners, after all, insist that the entire community should see things their way, and only their way."

As King—best known for his horror fiction—pointed out, that is "a scary idea."

9

The Freedom to Read

by Anthony Schulte

> The system was simple. Everyone understood it. Books were for
> burning . . . along with the houses in which they were hidden.
>
> —RAY BRADBURY, *Fahrenheit 451*

In her introduction to The Meese Commission Exposed, *Leanne Katz (executive director of the National Coalition Against Censorship) observed that that hearing's "overall tone" left a lot to desired: ". . . a parade of what the commission calls 'victims,' by prosecutors who specialize in pornography, and by police from vice and morals squads. The 'victims' testify anonymously from behind screens to sad personal experience—allegedly caused, pure and simple, by pornography. The cops testify as specialists in child molestation and the harmful effects of pornography.*

"All in all, it's a tawdry picture," she concluded.

Surprisingly, as Katz noted, the commission made no effort to solicit testimony from artists or writers. To draw attention to this situation, the National Coalition Against Censorship organized a public information briefing at which notables from the arts and letters communities spoke out against censorship.

"We are deeply concerned at the direction the commission is taking. Censorship, with all its dangers, seems inevitable," observed Katz.

Anthony Schulte, from the book community, spoke at the briefing. His comments follow.

I and many other publishers are extremely concerned with the increasing prevalence of a mentality that favors legislating, at every level—local, state, and federal—against the freedom of expression that is essential not only for literature and reading, but for the very essence of the American pluralistic society itself.

I am speaking not only of the climate in which the government would restrict the public's access to information on its workings under the rubric of national security classification; in which a government leaker can be prosecuted and convicted of espionage; in which juries are awarding immense libel verdicts against the media, including book publishers, seemingly for carrying a message offensive to the tastes or values of some part of the public. Rather, I am specifically talking about a climate in which John Gardner's *Grendel* can be removed from a twelfth grade high school curriculum in the state of California unless all of the parents of all the senior students have given their permission for it to be taught; in which Judy Blume's widely praised children's book *Deenie* can be removed from elementary school libraries in an upper-middle-class suburban county in Georgia because of isolated parental protests; in which J.D. Landis's novel *The Sisters Impossible* can be withdrawn by the school board from the school library in a town in Oklahoma where one of the town's "leading citizens" objected to the words "hell" and "fart" and its promulgation of "negative values." I'm speaking of the climate in which a prominent and respected New York book publisher had to withdraw from distribution a seriously intended sex education photographic-and-text book for children and parents called *Show Me,* which had been declared not obscene in several court tests; in which some school publishers have found it necessary to publish expurgated versions of *Romeo and Juliet* for classroom teaching purposes; and in which even *Huckleberry Finn* could be removed from the curriculum at certain schools in Virginia as being offensive or racist.

In this climate, a broad range of nonobscene books for adults and for teenagers can be attacked with the support of segments of the community under so-called minors access and display laws. Though such laws have repeatedly been held to be unconstitutional in such states as Colorado, Georgia, and most recently Virginia, they keep coming back in other states, always refashioned. They always encourage local authorities or private individuals to put formal or informal pressure on bookstores to remove or to withhold from display and sale the works of writers ranging from Judy Blume to John Updike, and from Jean Auel to John Steinbeck. In an Orwellian example of the impact of these statutes, the leading department store in Atlanta actually stopped ordering *all* new titles from *all* publishers for a period of several months until the Georgia statute was tested, and of course found wanting, in court. Even Atlanta's best-established purveyor of books could not run the risk of deciding which titles might run afoul of this law.

Who is to decide which shall be considered obscene or pornographic or beyond the protection of the First Amendment: the government—local, state, or federal—a commission, or the market place in which authors, publishers, book reviewers, and readers come together?

In 1970 another federally appointed commission on obscenity and pornography proposed a model statute that the Association of American Publishers and its Freedom to Read Committee considered very carefully and found acceptable. It would place no restrictions, state or federal, on the sale of sexually explicit material that consenting adults choose to read. As publishers, we had no difficulty accepting the proposition that there should be some limitation on the sale or availability of sexually explicit materials to minors so long as these restrictions did not interfere with the rights of adult buyers and readers. We accepted further the notion that unwilling passers-by, as well as minors, should not have displays or promotion for such material thrust upon them in an unavoidable fashion.

These principles seem just as valid for today's America as they did fifteen years ago.

• *Anthony Schulte, formerly the executive vice president of Random House, is a member and recent past chairman of the Freedom to Read Committee of the Association of American Publishers.*

10

Dirty Books

by Art Buchwald

> The dirtiest book of all is the expurgated book.
>
> —WALT WHITMAN, quoted in *Writers on Writing*

Linda Peeples was giving the dinner. When dessert was finished she said, "I have some exciting news for all of you."

"So tell us already," someone said.

"My son George just read his first book."

We all raised our wine glasses to toast the occasion.

"How old is George?" Reilly asked.

"He'll be 18 next month," Linda said.

"That's fantastic," Rowan said. "My son is 21 and he hasn't read a book yet."

"George has always been a bright student," Linda bragged.

"What book did he read?" Frannie Huff wanted to know.

"J.D. Salinger's *Catcher in the Rye.*"

There was an embarrassed silence at the table.

"What's wrong?" Linda wanted to know.

"*Catcher in the Rye* is a dirty book," I said. "Where did he get his hands on such filthy literature?"

"He found it in the school library," Linda said.

Exstrom was outraged. "You ought to report the librarian to the school board. They probably don't even know it's there."

"But George seemed to enjoy it," Linda said defensively.

"Sure he enjoyed it," Reilly said. "It's full of sex and bad words. But it doesn't belong in a high school library. The next thing you know, George will be reading *Huckleberry Finn* and Kurt Vonnegut's *Slaughterhouse-Five.*"

"Or Studs Terkel's *Working,*" I said.

"Not to mention Somerset Maugham's *Of Human Bondage.*"

"Are they all bad books?" Linda asked.

"The worst. They've ruined kids for life," I said.

"But we've been trying to get George to read a book since he was 12 years old. *Catcher in the Rye* was a breakthrough, and it would break his heart if we told him he couldn't read any more like it."

"There are books and there are books," Exstrom said. "My daughter came home from her English class with William Faulkner's *Sanctuary,* and I told her if she ever brought anything like that in the house again I'd throw it in the furnace. I also reported her teacher to the principal."

I said, "If more parents took an interest in what their kids were reading we wouldn't have such a rotten society."

"Well, it's too late now," Linda said. "George has already read *Catcher in the Rye.* What do I do?"

"Watch him closely," Frannie Huff said. "Search his room. If you find a book by John Steinbeck or James Baldwin under his bed, then you know he's in real trouble and I would take his library card away from him."

"I wish I had kept a closer eye on my son. I let him read Hemingway's *The Sun Also Rises* when he was 15 years old, and the next thing I knew he checked out Malamud's *The Fixer,*" Exstrom said.

"There are organizations all over the country that will supply you with lists," I said. "We get our guidance from a couple who censors books in Texas."

"What's George reading now?" Reilly asked.

Linda said, "Voltaire's *Candide.*"

"I hate to tell you this," said Frannie Huff, "but you have a sick kid on your hands."

• *Humorist Art Buchwald's column is syndicated nationally. He has also published several books, though no dirty ones.*

Fahrenheit 451

11

On *Fahrenheit 451*
A Cautionary Tale

by George Beahm

> For while Senator McCarthy has been long dead, the Red Guard in China comes alive and idols are smashed, and books, all over again, are thrown to the furnace. So it will go, one generation printing, another generation burning, yet another remembering what is good to remember so as to print again.
>
> —RAY BRADBURY, Introduction, *Fahrenheit 451*

As Ray Bradbury tells us in his afterword to the Del Rey paperback edition of *Fahrenheit 451,* the 1953 novel that went on to sell over four million copies had humble origins. Although Bradbury had explored the theme of censorship in two short stories (obliquely in "Bonfire," directly in "Bright Phoenix"), his pivotal exploration would be at novella length, in "The Fireman," written in the spring of 1950, under conditions that most writers would have found maddening: feeding dimes into a rented typewriter in the library basement at the University of California at Los Angeles.

"Time was indeed money," Bradbury wrote in the afterword. "I finished the first draft in roughly nine days. At 25,000 words, it was half the novel it would eventually become."

"The Fireman" was published in 1950 by *Galaxy Science Fiction,* a pulp digest that was judged by its gaudy cover, and not by its contents. While there was much ephemera in the pulps—written by hungry writers being paid per word, and literary immortality be damned—there were also diamonds in with the coals: among others, Ray Bradbury.

Expanded into a short novel of approximately 50,000 words, "The Fireman" became *Fahrenheit 451,* a title the stumped Bradbury had arrived at after asking a fire chief at what temperature paper burns.

Bradbury, by asking the right question, had got the perfect title for his book, which went on to become a classic.

A book with longevity, *Fahrenheit 451* burned brightly, going through over seventy printings, including one collector's edition bound, appropriately, in asbestos.

Fahrenheit 451 was also a critical success. As David Pringle wrote in *The Ultimate Guide to Science Fiction,* "Bradbury's only SF novel is short, lyrical and a bit simplistic, but it is generally regarded as a classic."

The story of fireman Guy Montag who burns not houses but books, the novel begins:

> It was a pleasure to burn.
>
> It was a special pleasure to see things eaten, to see things blackened and *changed.* With the brass nozzle in his fists, with this great python spitting its venomous kerosene upon the world, the blood pounded in his head, and his hands were the hands of some amazing conductor playing all the symphonies of blazing and burning to bring down the tatters and charcoal ruins of history.

As the publisher has prophetically noted on the cover to the paperback edition, *Fahrenheit 451* is "the classic bestseller about censorship—more important now than ever before."

12

"Coda" to *Fahrenheit 451*

by Ray Bradbury

In George Orwell's Nineteen Eighty-Four, *Winston Smith, who works at the Ministry of Truth, literally rewrites history. "This process of continuous alteration was applied not only to newspapers, but to books, periodicals, pamphlets, posters, leaflets, films, sound tracks, cartoons, photographs—to every kind of literature or documentation which might conceivably hold any political or ideological significance. Day by day and almost minute by minute the past was brought up to date. . . . All history was a palimpsest, scraped clean and reinscribed exactly as often as was necessary."*

That, in essence, is what some modern readers want with what they read—not the work as it was written, reflecting a certain time and place, but the work as they would want it written; not literature but, instead, revisionist writing.

Orwell, in 1949, had indeed peered into the future. Back then, the phrase "politically correct" didn't exist; today, however, it's seen for what it is: a form of self-censorship.

About two years ago, a letter arrived from a solemn young Vassar lady telling me how much she enjoyed reading my experiment in space mythology, *The Martian Chronicles.*

But, she added, wouldn't it be a good idea, this late in time, to rewrite the book inserting more women's characters and roles?

A few years before that I got a certain amount of mail concerning the same Martian book complaining that the blacks in the book were Uncle Toms and why didn't I "do them over"?

Along about then came a note from a Southern white suggesting that I was prejudiced in favor of the blacks and the entire story should be dropped.

Two weeks ago my mountain of mail delivered forth a pipsqueak mouse of a letter from a well-known publishing house that wanted to reprint my story "The Fog Horn" in a high school reader.

In my story, I had described a lighthouse as having, late at night, an illumination coming from it that was a "God-Light." Looking up at it from the viewpoint of any sea-creature one would have felt that one was in "the Presence."

The editors had deleted "God-Light" and "in the Presence."

Some five years back, the editors of yet another anthology for school readers put together a volume with some 400 (count 'em) short stories in it. How do you cram 400 short stories by Twain, Irving, Poe, Maupassant and Bierce into one book?

Simplicity itself. Skin, debone, demarrow, scarify, melt, render down and destroy. Every adjective that counted, every verb that moved, every metaphor that weighed more than a mosquito—out! Every simile that would have made a submoron's mouth twitch—gone! Any aside that explained the two-bit philosophy of a first-rate writer—lost!

Every story, slenderized, starved, bluepenciled, leeched and bled white, resembled every other story. Twain read like Poe read like Shakespeare read like Dostoevsky read like—in the finale—Edgar Guest. Every word of more than three syllables had been razored. Every image that demanded so much as one instant's attention—shot dead.

Do you begin to get the damned and incredible picture?

How did I react to all of the above?

By "firing" the whole lot.

By sending rejection slips to each and every one.

By ticketing the assembly of idiots to the far reaches of hell.

The point is obvious. There is more than one way to burn a book. And the world is full of people running about with lit matches. Every minority, be it Baptist/Unitarian, Irish/Italian/Octogenarian/Zen Buddhist, Zionist/Seventh-day Adventist, Women's Lib/Republican, Mattachine/FourSquare-Gospel feels it has the will, the right, the duty to douse the kerosene, light the fuse. Every dimwit editor who sees himself as the source of all dreary blanc-mange plain porridge unleavened literature, licks his guillotine and eyes the neck of any author who dares to speak above a whisper or write about a nursery rhyme.

Fire-Captain Beatty, in my novel *Fahrenheit 451,* described how the books were burned first by minorities, each ripping a page or a paragraph from this book, then that, until the day came when the books were empty and the minds shut and the libraries closed forever.

"Shut the door, they're coming through the window, shut the window, they're coming through the door," are the words to an old song. They fit my lifestyle with newly arriving butcher/censors every month. Only six weeks ago, I discovered that, over the years, some cubby-hole editors at Ballantine Books, fearful of contaminating the young, had, bit by bit, censored some 75 separate sections from the novel. Students, reading the novel which, after all, deals with censorship and book-burning in the future, wrote to tell me of this exquisite irony. Judy-Lynn Del Rey, one of the new Ballantine editors, is having the entire book reset and republished this summer with all the damns and hells back in place.

A final test for old Job II here: I sent a play, *Leviathan 99,* off to a university theater a month ago. My play is based on the "Moby Dick" mythology, dedicated to Melville, and concerns a rocket crew and a blind space captain who venture forth to encounter a Great White Comet and destroy the destroyer. My drama premieres as an opera in Paris this autumn. But for now, the university wrote back that they hardly dared do my play—it had no women in it! And the ERA ladies on campus would descend with ballbats if the drama department even tried!

Grinding my bicuspids into powder, I suggested that would mean, from now on, no more productions of *Boys in the Band* (no women), or *The Women* (no men). Or, counting heads, male and female, a good lot of Shakespeare that would never be seen again, especially if you count lines and find that all the good stuff went to the males!

I wrote back maybe they should do my play one week, and *The Women* the next. They probably thought I was joking, and I'm not sure I wasn't.

For it is a mad world and it will get madder if we allow the minorities, be they dwarf or giant, orangutan or dolphin, nuclear-head or water-conservationist, pro-computerologist or Neo-Luddite, simpleton or sage, to interfere with aesthetics. The real world is the playing ground for each and every group, to make or unmake laws. But the tip of the nose of my book or stories or poems is where their rights end and my territorial imperatives begin, run and rule. If Mormons do not like my plays, let them write their own. If the Irish hate my Dublin stories, let them rent typewriters. If teachers and grammar school editors find my jawbreaker sentences shatter their mushmilk teeth, let them eat stale cake dunked in weak tea of their own ungodly manufacture. If the Chicano intellectuals wish to re-cut my "Wonderful Ice Cream Suite" so it shapes "Zoot," may the belt unravel and the pants fall.

For, let's face it, digression is the soul of wit. Take philosophic asides away from Dante, Milton or Hamlet's father's ghost and what stays is dry bones. Laurence Sterne said it once: Digressions, incontestably, are the sunshine, the life, the soul of reading! Take them out and one cold eternal winter would reign in every page. Restore them to the writer—he steps forth like a bridegroom, bids them all-hail, brings in variety and forbids the appetite to fail.

In sum, do not insult me with the beheadings, finger-choppings or the lung-deflations you plan for my works. I need my head to shake or nod, my hand to wave or make into a fist, my lungs to shout or whisper with. I will not go gently onto a shelf, degutted, to become a non-book.

All you umpires, back to the bleachers. Referees, hit the showers. It's my game. I pitch, I hit, I catch. I run the bases. At sunset I've won or lost. At sunrise, I'm out again, giving it the old try.

And no one can help me. Not even you.

• *Ray Bradbury is a dark fantasist who has written novels, and a score of short stories, poetry, and plays. His most popular work is perhaps* The Martian Chronicles, *a poetic exploration of Mars.*

13

American Psycho
Censorship or Editorial Judgment?

by George Beahm

American Psycho by Bret Easton Ellis is a how-to novel on the torture and dismemberment of women. Arguments about its value as social commentary are absurd. Its graphic, gratuitous depiction of the slaughter of women lacks any literary merit. The portrayals of women being tortured, skinned alive, dismembered, and a chapter in which the protagonist attempts to make meat loaf out of one of his victims become another threat in a fabric of misogyny—hatred of women—that permeates our culture and costs women their lives.

—TAMMY BRUCE, president, Los Angeles chapter of National Organization
for Women (from "Fight Violence Against Women with a Boycott,"
USA Today, December 27, 1990)

In the *Washington Post* (November 15, 1990) book columnist David Streitfeld wrote:

Simon and Schuster yesterday abruptly canceled Bret Easton Ellis's controversial new novel, *American Psycho.* The book, which contains vivid descriptions of violence against women, was to be shipped to stores next month. A decision to back off this late in the publication process is extremely unusual, especially for a work of fiction.

The eleventh-hour decision to cancel the book came from chairman Martin Davis of Paramount Communications, Inc., which owns Simon and Schuster. Streitfeld quotes Davis, who explained, "Through the press, I became aware of the book, and then aware of its contents, and it was I who decided we should not put our name on this book. It's a matter of taste."

Apparently it was a matter of taste for others too: "Female staffers at Simon & Schuster were outraged," reported *Entertainment Weekly*, which also noted that "George Corsillo, who designed the jackets for Ellis's previous novels, turned down *Psycho*, citing creative differences."

Predictably, the controversy surrounding *Psycho* made it an attractive publishing commodity, and Random House president Sonny Mehta bought the book, but not as a trade hardback, as Simon and Schuster had intended: "It seems to me appropriate, given the immense coverage and curiosity about Mr. Ellis' new book, that we bring out *American Psycho* in original trade paperback edition, to swiftly reach the widest possible readership."

Ironically, an attempt by the Los Angeles chapter of the National Organization for Women to boycott *American Psycho* had the same effect as the Ayatollah's death sentence on Rushdie had on *The Satanic Verses:* It publicized a book that, otherwise, would likely have had modest sales.

In the nation's bookstores the prevailing opinion was that the customer—not the bookseller—should make the final decision by buying the book or not buying. As Sally Ann Stewart wrote in *USA Today*:

> Mitchell Kaplan, co-owner of Books & Books, Coral Gables, Fla., has already had a woman tell him "I hope you will not display that book." But, he says, "an independent bookstore has the right to carry whatever that bookstore wants. It's a personal matter."

In March 1991 *American Psycho* was published as an original trade paperback under the Vintage Contemporaries imprint from Vintage Books, a division of Random House, Inc.

In its wake *The Writer* queried well-known writers—citing the controversy surrounding the book, with allegations of censorship—and the consensus was that editorial judgment, not censorship, prevailed. As novelist John Jakes explained, "I loathe censorship, but this isn't it. I expected the book to be rushed out by someone else after S & S dropped it. A writer should be free to write anything; a publisher should be equally free to print it, or not."

To which I'd add: booksellers should be free to sell it, or not; and readers should be equally free to buy it.

14

Book Review, *American Psycho*

by Douglas E. Winter

American Psycho is a disturbing book. It's disturbing because it's very difficult for me to separate my feelings of revulsion about what's going on in the book, and the violence that's not just directed toward women—the violence is directed toward the homeless, toward men, toward animals, across an entire spectrum. It's hard for me to separate that from my pervasive feeling that something is really going on in that book, that Bret Easton Ellis is trying very hard to express an entire attitude of an alienated culture.

—STEPHEN KING

As anyone familiar with the horror field—especially its films—knows, Bret Easton Ellis tapped into a familiar vein with American Psycho.

Tammy Bruce, president of the Los Angeles chapter of the National Organization for Women, saw what she wanted to see: a novel attacking women. (I am not certain that she read the book before attacking it.) As anyone who has read the novel knows, Ellis's book does not discriminate—everyone suffers violence at the hands of the novel's protagonist, Patrick Bateman, whose name perhaps intentionally suggests the Bates motel of Psycho *fame.*

In sharp distinction from the reviews (or in some cases, previews) of American Psycho, *Winter's review dissects the novel on the grounds that it is properly a horror story.*

Tammy Bruce, outraged about the novel, said that "we need to show these gatekeepers of American culture that there's no . . . market for fiction about the torturing and skinning of women. . . ."

Tammy Bruce's intentions are good, but her market assessment is dead wrong. Thomas Harris's novel, The Silence of the Lambs, *went on to become a bestselling novel after the release of the blockbuster film version, which won four Oscars, with Anthony Hopkins as Hannibal (the cannibal) Lector and Jodie Foster as the novice FBI agent.*

for Colin Walters

This is, it would seem, the book your parents warned you about.

Bret Easton Ellis's *American Psycho* has managed to obtain more adverse publicity than any [other] novel in publishing history. First Simon and Schuster cancelled the book on the eve of publication for reasons of taste and the extremity of its depictions of violence against women. Then the *New York Times Book Review* offered an unprecedented "sneak preview" of a purloined manuscript, which termed the novel "loathsome." Norman Mailer vented his moral outrage in *Vanity Fair,* while the *Washington Post* called the novel "a contemptible piece of pornography." Although Vintage Books, which earlier published Mr. Ellis's first novel, *Less Than Zero,* has now issued *American Psycho,* it's difficult to find a copy in local bookstores, many of which have declined to display it or have made it available only through special order (and, presumably, in a plain brown wrapper). Ellis-bashing is *de rigueur* among all right-thinking persons, and has become something of a feminist cause.

I respectfully dissent.

"This is no time for the innocent." If the reader endures to reach these words in the closing pages of *American Psycho*—something equivalent to taking a holiday in Beirut—this fact has become brutally obvious. Opening these pages creates the feeling that a medical student must have upon first opening the body of a terminal patient: Wonder, disgust, despair, defeat.

Patrick Bateman, the title character (and indeed, the novel's only true character) is a twentysomething yuppie scum—wealthy, world-weary, and frighteningly fungible. He is forever mistaken for his fellow Wall Street clones, aloft in the Eighties upper caste, equipped with digital and cellular sidearms in their neverending quest for money to be made, and women and drugs and beggars to abuse. Their world is watched over by posters for *Les Misérables* (what else?) and set to a soundtrack of Broadway musicals and vapid rock-and-roll.

As his name suggests, Bateman is the new Norman Bates, no longer a shy mama's boy hidden in a backwoods motel, but a GQ zombie at large on the streets of Manhattan. He is filled with a nameless dread; like the inhabitants of Mr. Ellis's earlier novels, his cup runneth over with blood: A child of plenty, he walks this world in desperate need . . . but for what? There are no new drugs, new possessions or emotions, at least not for long. He is not simply a serial killer; his entire existence is serial, an obsessive, episodic regimen of workouts, taxi rides, phone calls, dinners, clubs, more taxi rides—and, most important, the renting and returning of videos: his story is a tape loop, complete with fast forwards and rewinds. Nothing has dimension: "Surface, surface, surface was all that anyone found meaning in. . . ." Bateman's confession is a lame archaeological dig in which brand names are the paramount detail, by which each trendy meal, each shopping spree, each murder is reported in a deadpan, flood-of-consciousness style meant to numb the reader into submission. The medium is indeed the message: in Bateman's mantralike repetition of designer labels, people are defined not by the color of their hair or eyes or their personalities—for they have none—but by their suits and ties and shirts and shoes: walking manikins, less than zombies.

Despite the hype, Bateman is an equal-opportunity killer. Most of his victims are random, the targets of convenience—small animals, children, delivery boys, the homeless, prostitutes, taxi drivers. When it comes to the opposite sex, however, Bateman is wholly predatory, incapable of relating to women save through their sexuality, interested in nothing but total objectification. Violence becomes his only means of expression: "This is my reality. Everything outside of this is like some movie I once saw." Not surprisingly, he insistently tries to create a new kind of movie, enacting ferociously ultraviolet setpieces.

The violence of *American Psycho* is indescribable out of context; one may as well suggest the reading of autopsy reports for entertainment. This book is vile, it is tasteless, it is not politically correct: It is, in other words, a horror novel of the highest order. That is not to say that *American Psycho* is a good book; but no one has ever suggested that, say, *The Texas Chainsaw Massacre* is a "good" movie, in the sense that film critics or even suburban moviegoers choose to apply that term. What each (dare I say?) entertainment shares is the temerity to offend and the cupidity to seek an audience that will understand.

This is the Literature of Assault, a kind of literary terrorism that has raged for the past several years in horror fiction, virtually unnoticed by the mainstream, under the sobriquet of "Splatterpunk." Where more civilized fiction strives toward a lilting wake-up call to the conscience, "Splatterpunk" is pure and simple slap to the side of the head. It is the Show Me State of fiction, an effort to shock a society so violence-jaded that it may be unshockable, to understand and use the violence of our times as a means of communication. Thus in its better incarnations these writers are trying, albeit desperately, to reinvent the dialogue between reader and writer, to breathe life into the dying art of the printed word.

Certainly Mr. Ellis has succeeded in creating the most talked-about book of the season; whether *American Psycho* is a literary tar baby is another question entirely. What is so troubling to his critics is that Mr. Ellis (unlike, say, Stephen King) cannot be discounted as a purveyor of pulp fiction and yet cannot be credited for indulging in its excesses. Forgotten in this equation is the fact that Mr. Ellis is only twenty-six, still young, still maturing, and entitled to err.

The issue confronting each conscientious writer of horror is whether to terrify or terrorize. For Mr. Ellis, as for most Splatterpunks, the choice is the latter. What is missing from *American Psycho* is a sense of connectedness, of sympathy, of understanding how and why this book should have meaning to most readers. Thus Bateman admits: "There is no reason for me to tell you any of this." This is of course Mr. Ellis's conceit, and his novel both succeeds and fails in its ultimate sense of futility, its implacably controlled absence of reassurance.

This is not the way in which to win friends or influence people. Reading is an act of complicity, and most readers prefer to be treated as something other than puppies whose faces are thrust into their own excrement. It is thus not surprising that Mr. Ellis should find his audience so reluctant to indulge him.

Those readers who are not put off by the intensity of the imagery will, I suspect, find *American Psycho* tedious; others will no doubt search it through for the naughty bits as surely as a fifties teenager scanning *National Geographic.* But there are no cheap thrills here: in this abattoir could no sane person find a hint of prurience.

Those willing to read carefully and with an open mind will find *American Psycho* hypnotic, discomforting, amusing, apocalyptic, annoying, infuriating: an atrocity exhibition of American artifacts as we slouch toward the coming Millennium. For all of its virtues, all of its faults, it reminds us that when we write about horror, normative terms—good, bad, art, trash—are increasingly irrelevant. If fiction is to continue to hold meaning beyond mere entertainment, then it must not simply transcend our daily lives, but on occasion descend into the darkness within and without us. There is thus no reason, and there is every reason, for this story.

When all is said and done, there is but a single certainty: Only those who have read this book deserve to say anything at all about it.

• *Douglas E. Winter, a Washington, D.C., attorney by vocation and a writer by avocation, writes most frequently on the parameters of dark fiction and film. A critic, anthologist, and novelist, Winter is completing a critical study and biography of Clive Barker.*

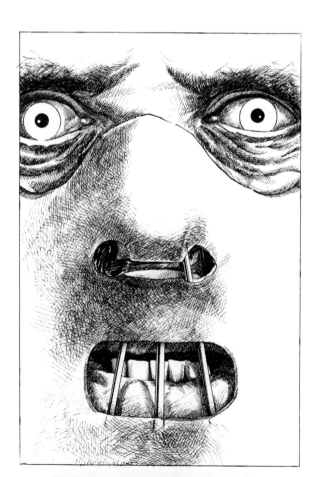

15

Nineteen Eighty-Four
Another Cautionary Tale

by George Beahm

> It was a bright cold day in April, and the clocks were striking thirteen.
>
> —First sentence of *Nineteen Eighty-Four*

Like *Fahrenheit 451,* George Orwell's *Nineteen Eighty-Four* is a cautionary tale. As its current publisher, New American Library, observed, it is "a startlingly original and powerful novel that creates an imaginary world that is completely convincing, from the first sentence to the last four words."

According to Orwell biographer Michael Shelden, *Nineteen Eighty-Four,* originally titled *The Last Man in Europe,* was completed in 1948. Simply inverting the last two digits gave the book its final title, intended by Orwell to place the book at some point in the future.

It as, as Shelden writes, "Orwell's most compelling work," an enduring classic, and a chilling reminder of science fiction at its best, written not to show us the future but, as Ray Bradbury has said, *to prevent it.*

16

Preface to *Nineteen Eighty-Four*

by Walter Cronkite

Cronkite's essay was commissioned especially for the Signet Classic edition of Nineteen Eighty-Four, *published—when else?—in 1984.*

American reporters, given a glimpse of Ayatollah Khomeini's Iran at the end of 1982, were saying it was like *1984*. It's Orwellian, one added.

"Big Brother" has become a common term for ubiquitous or overreaching authority, and "Newspeak" is a word we apply to the dehumanizing babble of bureaucracies and computer programs.

Those coinages have passed into the language with lives of their own. They are familiar to millions who have never read *1984*, who may not even know it as a novel written thirty-five years ago by English socialist Eric Blair, who became famous under the pen name George Orwell.

Seldom has a book provided a greater wealth of symbols for its age and for the generations to follow, and seldom have literary symbols been invested with such power. How is that? Because they were so useful, and because the features of the world he drew, outlandish as they were, also were familiar.

They are familiar today, they were familiar when the book was first published in 1949. We've met Big Brother in Stalin and Hitler and Khomeini. We hear Newspeak in every use of language to manipulate, deceive, to cover harsh realities with the soft snow of euphemism. And every time a political leader expects or demands that we believe the absurd, we experience that mental process Orwell called doublethink. From the show trials of the pre-war Soviet Union to the dungeon courts of post-revolutionary Iran, *1984*'s vision of justice as foregone conclusion is familiar to us all. As soon as we were introduced to such things, we realized we had always known them.

What Orwell had done was not to foresee the future but to see the implications of the present—his present and ours—and he touched a common chord. He had given words and shapes to common but unarticulated fears running deep through all industrial societies.

George Orwell was no prophet, and those who busy themselves keeping score on his predictions and grading his use of the crystal ball miss the point. While here he is a novelist, he is also a sharp political essayist and a satirist with a bite not felt in the English language since the work of Jonathan Swift.

If not prophecy, what was *1984*? It was, as many have noticed, a warning: a warning about the future of human freedom in a world where political organization and technology can manufacture power in dimensions that would have stunned the imaginations of earlier ages.

Orwell drew upon the technology (and perhaps some of the science fiction) of the day in drawing his picture of 1984. But it was not a work of science fiction he was writing. It was a novelistic essay on power, how it is acquired and maintained, how those who seek it or seek to keep it tend to sacrifice anything and everything in its name.

1984 is an anguished lament and a warning that we may not be strong enough nor wise enough nor moral enough to cope with the kind of power we have learned to amass. That warning vibrates powerfully when we allow ourselves to sit still and think carefully about orbiting satellites that can read the license plates in a parking lot and computers that can tap into thousands of telephone calls and telex transmissions at once and other computers that can do our banking and purchasing, can watch the watch and tell a monitoring station what television program we are watching and how many people there are in the room. We think of Orwell when we read of scientists who believe they have *located* in the human brain the seats of behavioral emotions like aggression, or learn more about the vast potential of genetic engineering.

And we hear echoes of that warning chord in the constant demand for greater security and comfort, for less risk in our societies. We recognize, however dimly, that a greater efficiency, ease, and security may come at a substantial price in freedom, that law and order can be a doublethink version of oppression, that individual liberties surrendered for whatever good reason are freedom lost.

Critics and scholars may argue quite legitimately about the particular literary merits of *1984*. But none can deny its power, its hold on the imaginations of whole generations, nor the power of its admonitions . . . a power that seems to grow rather than lessen with the passage of time. It has been said that *1984* fails as a prophecy because it succeeded as a warning—Orwell's terrible vision has been averted. Well, that kind of self-congratulation is, to say the least, premature. 1984 may not arrive on time, but there's always 1985.

Still, the warning has been effective; and every time we use one of those catch phrases . . . recognize Big Brother in someone . . . see a 1984 in our future . . . notice something Orwellian . . . we are listening to that warning again.

• *Walter Cronkite is a former anchorman for the CBS Evening News.*

17

Orwell: The Authorized Biography

An Extract, by Michael Shelden

It is easy to forget that *Nineteen Eighty-Four* is a love story, but the oppressive gloom of the state's control is briefly lifted when Winston and Julia are able to enjoy their secret moments together. For them sex becomes a form of liberation, a way not only of rebelling against the dictates of the Party, but a means by which they can enjoy the sense of freedom in the release of passion. Julia's uninhibited approach to sex is portrayed as a hopeful sign of the ordinary person's determination to be free of outside restrictions, no matter how beneficial they may be in the abstract. The Party is eager to control the sex instinct because it is the one area in each person's life that is so resistant to outside restrictions. If the Party can kill the sex instinct, it can strengthen its control over everyone, but Winston and Julia show that destroying such a powerful urge is impossible and that the mere expression of that urge can be a valid form of protest against Big Brother. It is a reaffirmation of life in the face of Big Brother's attempt to eliminate all signs of a vital existence among his subjects.

After the novel's publication Orwell insisted that he had not tried to be a prophet, that he was trying only to warn the world against the threat of totalitarianism, whether from the Right or the Left. His vision, however, is so realistic and compelling that readers from his day onward have come away from the novel feeling that they have been given a prediction. Big Brother's power is regarded as a force that will rise up at some point in the future and crush humanity. The fact that this vision is so believable is a tribute to Orwell's imaginative use of so many strands of his experience to create a plausible version of an all-powerful state. But it is still an imaginative act, and it was not the work of a man who wanted to overwhelm his readers with pessimism. He wanted to shock them into resisting forces that might someday impose more and more controls over their lives, and if they heeded his warning, the terrors of "1984" could be avoided. . . .

Orwell points out that the great power that is feared one year is often destroyed by its own overreaching ambition within a few years and inevitably loses its aura of invincibility, if not its actual force. He argues there is good reason to believe that this fate will overtake Stalin's Russia just as it overtook Hitler's Germany. "The Russian regime will either democratize itself, or it will perish." He is hopeful that one way or another the regime will die because he thinks that the common man will triumph in the end. Winston Smith may fail, but the Proles have it within their power to destroy Big Brother at any minute if they desire it. The key thing is to bring the restraining force of public opinion into play. As long as public opinion has a chance to make itself heard, the state will have to curb its appetite for power.

18

Notes from Underground

by George Beahm

In addition to guaranteeing Rushdie a worldwide audience and making *The Satanic Verses* "the most famous book of the century," Khomeini assured the novel a unique and enduring place in the history of literature. It became the preeminent symbol of both censorship and freedom of speech, of cultural misunderstanding and shared values. There may never be another work of fiction with such a career.

—DANIEL PIPES, *The Rushdie Affair: The Novel, The Ayatollah, and the West*

When the Ayatollah Ruhollah Khomeini of Iran issued against British author Salman Rushdie a *fatwa*—a religious edict—on grounds of blasphemy for the publication of *The Satanic Verses,* Oscar Wilde's observation came to mind: "Assassination is the most extreme form of censorship."

Despite the protests of the international community, the Iranians have held firm to their conviction that Rushdie's blasphemy cannot be excused, even after he repented publicly in *The Observer* (February 19, 1989):

As author of *The Satanic Verses* I recognize that Moslems in many parts of the world are genuinely distressed by the publication of my novel. I profoundly regret the distress that publication has occasioned the sincere followers of Islam. Living as we do in a world of many faiths this experience has served to remind us that we must all be conscious of the sensibilities of others.

Said the Ayatollah Khomeini: "Even if Salman Rushdie repents and becomes the most pious man of [all] time, it is incumbent on every Muslim to employ everything he's got, his life and wealth, to send him to hell."

The bullet's been fired, and one day it will strike its intended target, Rushdie; nothing can stop the path of the bullet, said an Islamic extremist.

o   o   o

On March 25, 1992, an anonymous American consortium published a $9.95 trade paperback of *The Satanic Verses*. An anonymous spokesman for the consortium told David Streitfeld of the *Washington Post* that "the idea is to publish the book strongly, and demonstrate the strength with which the principles behind the publication are held by everyone in the industry."

The show of solidarity in the publishing community did not, however, translate into sales in the bookstores nationwide. The first printing of 100,000 copies was, in light of public interest, too optimistic. Also, because the media had all but forgotten Rushdie, little attention was paid to its republication. The combination of the two killed book sales—a vivid contrast to the runaway sales of the first hardback edition, when public attention and the media fixed upon Salman Rushdie and his plight.

The world has moved on, but Rushdie cannot. Though he is still writing and publishing, the *fatwa* has taken a toll on him as well as others involved in the book's publication. Rushdie has seen his marriage to American novelist Marianne Wiggins break apart; he has been unable to see his teenage son from his first marriage, and can only talk to him on the phone; and he has lived a life in hiding, moving as necessary to avoid becoming a fixed target—a concern that was underscored when two similar and presumably related incidents occurred: The book's Italian translator, attacked by an unknown assailant, survived the attempt; but the book's Japanese translator did not—he was knifed to death under mysterious circumstances.

In a 1973 address at the PEN Conference in Stockholm, Kurt Vonnegut said:

> It is the feeling in several countries, I know, that fiction can hurt a social order a lot. . . . Writers of such stuff, as Heinrich Böll can tell us, have been jailed, put into lunatic asylums, exiled, or even killed sometimes—for putting certain words in a certain order.

Two decades later, Salman Rushdie—the "reluctant symbol of free expression," as the *Post* characterized him—is living the nightmare Vonnegut described.

A Rushdie Chronology

February 14, 1989: Calling *The Satanic Verses* offensive to Islam, the Ayatollah Khomeini issues the *fatwa*—a religious edict—sentencing the novel's author, Salman Rushdie, to death. Rushdie goes into hiding and Viking Penguin, publisher of the novel, receives several bomb threats.

February 17, 1989: Waldenbooks, B. Dalton, and Barnes & Noble decline to sell *The Satanic Verses.*

February 19, 1989: Rushdie makes a public apology for unintentionally offending Muslims.

February 20, 1989: Writers, publishers, and human rights organizations form a committee called the International Committee for the Defense of Salman Rushdie and His Publishers. Twelve European Community nations recall their diplomats to protest the death threat.

February 22, 1989: Five days after ordering its removal, B. Dalton resumes sales of *The Satanic Verses.*

August 16, 1989: Salman Rushdie and his wife, the novelist Marianne Wiggins, remain in hiding in Britain.

September 4, 1989: A London department store bombing is linked to *The Satanic Verses.*

January 28, 1990: Viking Penguin denies delaying the paperback edition of *The Satanic Verses.*

February 28, 1990: The Authors Guild calls for support of a paperback publication of *The Satanic Verses.*

November 18, 1990: Rushdie publishes *Haroun and the Sea of Stories,* his first book since *The Satanic Verses.*

December 6, 1990: Rushdie surfaces in London to sign his new novel.

December 27, 1990: Iran's spiritual leader says the death threat is irreversible.

January 11, 1991: Rushdie says he now opposes a paperback of *The Satanic Verses;* he embraces Islam.

April 7, 1991: Marianne Wiggins divorces Rushdie.

July 3, 1991: Ettore Capriolo, the Italian translator of *The Satanic Verses,* is stabbed in Milan. He survives.

July 12, 1991: Hitoshi Igarashi, the Japanese translator of *The Satanic Verses,* is stabbed to death in Japan.

December 11, 1991: Rushdie appears in New York City to speak at Columbia University amid tight security.

February 14, 1992: A consortium of writers, publishers, and human rights organizations announce plans to publish a mass-market edition of *The Satanic Verses.*

March 25, 1992: The U.S. consortium, remaining anonymous, publishes a $9.95 trade paperback edition of *The Satanic Verses.*

November 1, 1992: The bounty on Rushdie is increased.

19

Perspectives on
The Satanic Verses

Ayatollah Ruhollah Khomeini: "I inform the proud Moslem people of the world that the author of *The Satanic Verses*, which is against Islam, the Prophet, and the Koran, and all those involved in its publication who were aware of its contents, are sentenced to death. I ask all Moslems to execute them quickly wherever they are found so that no others dare to do such a thing. Whoever is killed doing this will be regarded as a martyr and will go directly to heaven." (From a statement broadcast on Tehran Radio, February 14, 1989.)

Salman Rushdie: ". . . Inside my novel, its characters seek to become fully human by facing up to the great facts of love, death and (with or without God) the life of the soul. Outside it, the forces of inhumanity are on the march. 'Battle lines are being drawn up in India today,' one of my characters remarks. 'Secular versus religious, the light versus the dark. Better you choose which side you are on.' Now that the battle has spread to Britain, I can only hope it will not be lost by default. It is time for us to choose." (From "Choice Between Light and Dark," *The Observer*, January 22, 1989.)

David Devadas: "Calling it 'a deliberate insult to Islam and the holy prophet and an intentional device to outrage religious feelings,' Janata MP Syed Shahabuddin held that it was 'not an act of literary creativity.' He said 'you just have to read it' to know that, but added that he had not." (From "Salman Rushdie: Political Scapegoat," *India Today*, October 31, 1988.)

Jonathan C. Randal quoting Salman Rushdie: "'People in the Islamic world will go to great lengths to prevent free expression and prefer burning books to reading them. But the image of book-burning in Britain in 1988 horrified lots of people who are disturbed by this central iconic image of barbarism. . . . Although the campaign had been going on for several months, this simple image of a burning book finally alerted people in this country to something extremely dangerous and ugly, even people who cannot stand me as a writer.'" (From "Rushdie's Book Burned in Britain," *Washington Post*, January 18, 1989.)

A.G. Mojtabai: "As with Martin Scorsese's film *The Last Temptation of Christ*, much of the outrage has been fueled by hearsay. Some of the noisiest objections have been raised by people who have never read the book and have no intention of ever reading it. This opposition does little to educate a woefully ignorant and prejudiced Western public about the Islamic faith. Banning the book only increases its notoriety: it answers nothing. And there are, I think, real problems in the text that need to be addressed." (From "Magical Mystery Pilgrimage, *New York Times Book Review,* January 29, 1989.)

Michael Hirsley and John Blades: "Frederick Karl, literature professor at New York University, said the Rushdie situation goes beyond history's worst cases of censorship, even threats against writers and bookburnings in Hitler's Germany and Stalinist Russia. 'Nobody ever talked about taking out a contract on an author's life. This is like a mob boss ordering a rubout. . . . This is a new and unbelievable form of insanity.' . . . Noting similarities to American Christian fundamentalists' protests against the portrayal of Jesus Christ in last year's film *The Last Temptation of Christ,* Morsi, of the Islamic Cultural Center of Chicago, said: 'We have some of the same problems with Moslem ministers that you have with Christian ministers. And we also have the same regrettable mixing of politics and religion.'" (From "Moslem Death Threats Turn Novel into City's Best Seller," *Chicago Tribune,* February 17, 1989.)

Jonathan C. Randal: "The Iranian ambassador to the Vatican, meanwhile, defended the ayatollah's death order, citing a story from the Koran about a poet who, in the time of Mohammed, was condemned to death for insulting the Prophet. . . . 'He who offends God must die,' Ambassador Salman Ghaffari told *La Stampa* newspaper." (From "Iran Hints at Death Reprieve if 'Verses' Author Apologizes," *Washington Post,* February 18, 1989.)

Roald Dahl (British author), on Rushdie: "Clearly he has profound knowledge of the Muslim religion and its people, and he must have been totally aware of the deep and violent feelings his book would stir up among devout Muslims. In other words he knew exactly what he was doing and he cannot plead otherwise. This kind of sensationalism does indeed get an indifferent book onto the top of the bestseller list, but to my mind it it is a cheap way of doing it." (Quoted by Craig R. Whitney, "Iran and Britain Move Near Break," *New York Times,* March 1, 1989.)

India Today: "Khomeini's threat has assured Rushdie what his books might not have—a permanent place in literary history. And the threat grows more real and palpable as the fundamentalists retreat into themselves further and harden their position. Rushdie's words in *Midnight's Children* seem chillingly prophetic: 'I had been mysteriously handcuffed in history.'"

20

Interview: Salman Rushdie

Conducted by Karsten Prager

> If you forget me, I will die.
>
> —SALMAN RUSHDIE, quoted in news story, *Newport News Daily Press,*
> August 2, 1992

On a clandestine visit to the U.S., his first since he was sentenced to death by Khomeini for writing The Satanic Verses, *Salman Rushdie pleads not to be forgotten.*

Prager: *For more than 1,000 days, you have been under an all-points death sentence. What's it like to live like that?*

Rushdie: Oddly, I don't that often feel afraid, although the first few days were very scary. But at some point I thought to myself, "If I spend my time being afraid and worried about where the bullet's going to come from, then I'm really going to go crazy." And then I said to myself, "I've got the best protection the British government can offer—it's their job to worry about that. It's not my job." That was a kind of mental trick. What I had to worry about was mentally dealing with the threat and arguing my case and continuing to be what I am.

And that worked most of the time?

Yes. I won't say there aren't moments when the other breaks through, because there obviously are. But by and large, day to day, it works.

How often have you moved?

I haven't kept an exact count. There's a kind of legend around how I get moved every few days. It's never been as bad as that.

But more than a couple of dozen times?

Oh, it's been a lot of places, sometimes for a few days, sometimes for longer periods. I've seen a great deal of Britain I've never seen before. Where there are wide-open spaces, it's possible for me to get out and go for walks.

What I've tried to do is take very slow steps back toward as much of life as I can sensibly have. And that's a matter of instinct and judgment and discussion; the less said about it the better. But from the beginning I have felt the one thing that would be very dangerous to me would be to become an institutionalized prisoner, to give up control of my life to the people whose job it is to look after me. That's why I have constantly pushed against the bars of the cage and tried to make it a bit bigger.

What social life is left?
It's almost entirely telephonic. I call friends.

Do you read?
I read. To an extent, I still lead a writer's life.

So in that sense life has not changed?
All my adult life, if I didn't have several hours a day to sit in a room by myself, I would get antsy and irritable. Now, that particular part of the day has spread to kill the whole day. I used to like the contrast between doing the work and getting out and having a very sociable life. So that's gone. And that's a real, obvious loss.

Who takes care of your daily needs?
I can cook. And I have access to washing machines and dishwashers. Of course, I'm leading my life in premises that also contain armed policemen.

How about your son?
Clearly, I miss him a lot. I wrote a book for him in this time because it was just about the only thing I could do for him. A lot of the normal requirements a child would have of his father I've been unable to discharge. I talk to him every day by telephone. But it's a huge deprivation, not just for me but for him. For the thing that has happened is also an assault on his rights.

You say your marriage is over. Was that caused by your situation?
It didn't help, but it wasn't the critical factor. There were other things that went wrong.

Let's turn to the political side. The Western hostages have been released. Does that help or hurt your cause?
It's a kind of knife edge, as I always thought it would be. Because to an extent I've been a hostage to the hostage situation. Whenever people have tried to make my case very public, to debate it very noisily, it has been suggested that to do so would be to prolong the hostages' plight. Now, since the hostages are out, I am able to speak more freely.

What's the other side of the coin?
The thing I've worried about is that there would be the enormous and quite understandable desire among the public to say, "Thank God, it's all over." Somebody then piping up with "Excuse me, there's one more problem" might generate irritation. "Oh, God, we don't want to deal with that because it's finished, it's over, hurrah, let's have Christmas."
What I'm trying to say is, "It isn't quite the end."

How did you feel when Britain resumed diplomatic relations with Iran last year and your case remained unresolved?

I had very mixed feelings. I would certainly have wished for a clear, overt public statement about the Rushdie case. No such statement was made, apart from a vague statement about how Iran had agreed not to interfere in the internal affairs of Britain. Unfortunately, a few months later there were very vociferous restatements of the threat from Iran, and the bounty money on my head was doubled.

To $3 million?

Well, $2 million—a large amount. And then I heard about my Italian translator being knifed. I heard about my Japanese translator being murdered.

What's your agenda during your U.S. visit?

People need to be reminded constantly that this is not a parochial issue. It's not about one writer of Third World origin in trouble with a Third World power. The publishing of a book is a worldwide event. The attempt to suppress a book is a worldwide event. This is not just about me.

Your problem has to be solved at the political level?

Yes.

But that might involve trade relations, arms deals, whatever? You expect to be part of some political equation?

It's not that I expect to become a part of it, but I am, whether I like it or not. The Iranian government is in breach of international law and at the same time is seeking to get closer to the West. As a citizen of Britain and of Europe, I can at least expect most countries and their allies to say to Iran, "If you wish to put your house in order, show us. . . ."

And Rushdie fits in there?

Yes. Both sides have a genuine interest in getting closer to the other. The West sees Iran as an important force in the gulf. Iran wishes to reconstruct its economy and play a fuller part in the community of nations—and that's legitimate. My part is a tiny part in that equation—it's big for me, but it's a tiny part.

Do you ever feel like giving up?

Certainly. There were very long periods of time when I thought I would never write again. What was the point of it anyway? I'd simply written a novel—a 500-page, complicated, literary novel that insulted even people who hadn't read it. You expect a debate or a dispute, or an argument—that seems to me an entirely legitimate function of art. What you don't expect is an attempt to intimidate the book's publishers and murder the book's author.

Last year you embraced Islam. Why?

I believe there needs to be a secular way of being a Muslim. There are plenty of people in the Muslim world who feel exactly like that—an identity with culture and values—but who are not believers in the theology. That was what I was trying to say, or I would've said it if anybody had listened hard enough. But immediately I was called either a traitor to my cause or a hypocrite.

What if political pressure does not work? Are you living with a life sentence?

I don't want even to contemplate what you suggest because I don't believe the situation is as bleak as that. But the fact is I'm not going to accept it forever.

You've said free speech is life itself. Has it been worth fighting for?

Yes, it has. Yes, it has. Clearly, nobody wants such an incredible distortion of one's daily life; in fact, nothing else will happen in my life of remotely this magnitude.

But at least it's the right plight. At least it's about what I believe most deeply in. And therefore it's possible to fight for it. At least the fight is about the right thing.

• *This inteview was originally published in* Time *(December 23, 1991), under the title, "Free Speech Is Life Itself."*

21

A Folly Repeated

by Norman Mailer

> Mahound shakes his head. "Your blasphemy, Salman, can't be forgiven. Did you think I wouldn't work it out? To set your words against the Words of God."
>
> —SALMAN RUSHDIE, *The Satanic Verses,* quoted in
> *The Macmillan Dictionary of Quotations*

By my limited comprehension of the Muslim religion, martrydom is implicit in the faith. While all faiths sooner or later suggest that a true believer may have to be ready to die for the governing god, it is possible that the Muslims, of all religions, have always been the most dedicated to this stern test. Now it seems as if the spiritual corruption of the twentieth century has entered Islam's ranks as well. Any Muslim who succeeds in assassinating Salman Rushdie will be rewarded with the munificent sum of $5,000,000. This must be the largest hit contract in history. Islam, with all its mighty virtues and vices, equal at the least to the virtues and vices of every other major religion, has now introduced a novel element into the history of theology. It has added the logic of the syndicate. One does not even have to belong to the family to collect. One has only to be the hit man. Of course, the novelist in me insists on thinking how I would hate to be that hit man trying to collect $5,000,000. Now that the deed was done, I might be looked upon as an infidel. "Oh, you see," my Iranian paymaster might say, "we really cannot afford the five million. We lost so many men in the war with Iraq. There are so many widows in need of alms, and we have our orphans, and our veterans who are now missing a limb. Kind killer, we think you might wish to make your charitable contribution."

This is but a novelist's speculation. That is what we are here for—to speculate on human possibilities, to engage in those fantasies, cynicisms, satires, criticisms, and explorations of human vanity, desire, and courage that the blank walls of mighty corporations like to conceal from us. We are scribblers who try to explore what is left to look at in the interstices. Sometimes we make mistakes and injure innnocent victims by our words. Sometimes we get lucky and make people with undue worldly power a bit uncomfortable for a short time. Usually, we spend our days injuring each other. We are, after all, a fragile resource, an endangered species. It is not untypical of the weak and endangered to chew each other up a little on the way down. But now the Ayatollah Khomeini has offered us an opportunity to regain our frail religion, which happens to be faith in the power of words and our willingness to suffer for them. He awakens us to the great rage we feel when our liberty to say what we wish, wise or foolish, kind or cruel, well-advised or ill-advised, is endangered. We discover that, yes, maybe we are willing to suffer for our idea. Maybe we are even willing, ultimately, to die for the idea that serious literature, in a world of dwindling certainties and choked-up ecologies, is the absolute we must defend.

We have had the example of our largest corporate chain of booksellers in America, Waldenbooks, withdrawing *The Satanic Verses* from their bookshelves in order to secure the safety of their employees. Immediately, they were followed by B. Dalton. Both had honest motives, doubtless. What is the use of being upwardly mobile in one's job in a massive corporate chain if security cannot be guaranteed? Get killed selling a book? The end of the world has come. Worse! One could get killed buying a book. Who would ever forgive the corporate chain?

Of course, the option of assessing such danger calmly, and informing employees and customers of the real odds was never engaged—though both chains did eventually change their stance. In Russian roulette, using the classic revolver, there is one chance in six you will kill yourself each time you pull the trigger. I am happy to say I have never played Russian roulette, but if I had, I am certain the odds would have felt much more like even money. I would have needed one part of my brain to explain to the other, over and over, that the odds were really 5 to 1 in my favor.

Waldenbooks has something like a thousand outlets. In one working week from Monday to Saturday, if one terrorist succeeded in making one successful attack on one store, the odds that it would not be the store you worked in would be 6,000 to 1 in your favor. If, as a customer, you spent half an hour in any one of these thousand stores, while it was in the course of being open for eight hours a day for six days, the odds in your favor would increase to 16 times 6,000, or close to 100,000 to 1 on your side. I think such odds, if loudly promulgated, would have brought in as many prospective customers looking for the spice of a very small risk as would have been frightened away; for the employees, a 10 percent increase for temporary combat pay could have been instituted. What are contingency funds for?

No, the answer to why Waldenbooks shut down *The Satanic Verses* is that they sell their product like soup cans. Only the homeless will ever endanger themselves over a can of soup. The largest purveyors of our books do not care about literature, whether serious, half-serious, or failed. The purveyors see books as a commodity that rots into the very spirit of the circulation of money if the books stay too long on the shelf. So, they hire clerks who tend to reflect their own mores. If Saul Bellow were to purchase one of his own novels in a chain where he did not normally shop, and paid for it with his own credit card, the odds that the clerk would recognize his name are about the same as the odds in

Russian roulette—one in six. Saul Bellow could walk in and out of a chain bookstore like a ghost. So could I. So could any other established serious writer who has been around thirty or forty years. Tom Wolfe might be recognized, but then Tom is still the fastest selling can of soup around.

No surprise, therefore, if retail chains of American booksellers seem to have more respect for terrorists than for culture. How, then, can they not help to accelerate the latest mega-farce down the media road?

A serious book which may or may not have been irresponsible in part, as most serious books are—I cannot pretend to define the issue more closely since I, I fear, in company with the people issuing the death threats, have not read it, although I certainly intend to—yes, this serious yet possibly irresponsible contribution to serious literature, if it had been treated like other serious novels which are almost always in part sacrilegious, blasphemous, and secretly against the state, would, if it had encountered no formal outrage, have suffered the fate of other serious books. It would have received good, even hearteningly good, but still modest sales, it would have been discussed, and taken its small place on the shelf of serious works to be picked up again by a few devoted readers. Islam might have been injured by one part in one hundred thousand. Now, Islam is injured vastly more. Oceans of publicity have been given to the sacrilege. I say the act of attracting such attention to a book despised was a willful chosen act by the Muslim leaders. The wise men of Iran know that the Western moral conscience is dulled, and no one in our monotonous Yuppie overlay of skillful surface floating above incalculable horrors such as drug wars and acute poverty is ready to die for any idea, other, conceivably, than receiving a big payoff in cash. So the Ayatollah may have wished to show the great length of the whip he can crack, the whim whose secret name is found in our bottomless pit of terrorism. If we believe in nothing, how can we bear to die? The wise men of Islam know that about us.

One would have to respect the incisiveness of such understanding, if not for the fact that the wise men of Iran are also wholly indifferent to the fate of our literature, and are savagely opposed to those freedoms of expressions we wish to believe we hold dear.

In this period of turmoil, we can now envision a fearful time in the future when fundamentalist groups in America, stealing their page from this episode, will know how to apply the same methods to American writers and bookstores. If they ever succeed, it will be due to the fact that we never found an honest resistance to the terrorization of Salman Rushdie.

I would suggest, therefore, that it is our duty to form ranks behind him, and our duty to state to the world that if he is ever assassinated, it will then become our obligation to stand in his place. If he is ever killed for a folly, we must be killed for the same folly, and we may indeed be, since we will then vow to do our best to open all literary meetings with a reading of the critical pages in *The Satanic Verses*. A folly repeated is no longer a folly but a statement of intent. If what Salman Rushdie wrote was grave folly, then by killing him you will be obliging us to immortalize that same grave folly. For if one writer can be killed on a hit contract, and all concerned get away with it, then we may be better off being hit each of us, one by one, in future contracts, until our chiefs in the Western world may be finally aroused by the shocking spectacle of our willingness, even though we are selfish creative artists, to be nonetheless martyred.

I will not, however, put my name on such a list alone. Like others, I have my family, my projects, my life to see through to its conclusion. Join with me, rather, ten good American authors, male and female, or twenty, or a hundred in such a vow, and we are relatively safe. At least, we are safer to a considerable degree, and can feel honorable to ourselves. We will have struck a real blow for freedom. For the wise men of Iran will know then that we possess our spiritual wisdom, too. Certain acts count for more than others in the defense of freedom and the willingness to embrace an idea at perilous cost to our inner calm may be at the center of what the Western world is all about. If we would ask bookstore clerks to stand and serve, then we must demand more than that of ourselves.

• *Norman Mailer, a leading figure in American letters, is best known for his novel* The Naked and the Dead.

22

The White House's Rushdie Brushoff

by Art Buchwald

> [The novel] is not only offensive but,
> I think most of us would say, in bad taste.
>
> —"[Vice President] DANFORTH QUAYLE on *The Satanic Verses*,
> which he has not read," *People Weekly,* April 3, 1989

When Salman Rushdie, who is under a death sentence by fanatic Iranians, came to Washington last week he was received by members of Congress and the press. But the State Department and the White House refused to speak to him.

Margaret Tutwiler, the State Department spokesman, was quoted as saying that there could be no plans for a meeting "because at this time we felt that such a thing could and possibly might be misinterpreted."

Marlin Fitzwater, who speaks for the White House, said of Rushdie, "I mean, he's an author, he's here, he's doing interviews and book tours and things that authors do. But there's no reason for us to have any special interest in him."

There had to be more than that to the Bush administration's refusal to see Rushdie.

So I called my White House contact, Charlie, at his home late at night.

"Why the freeze on the writer?" I asked him.

"If we let him in to see the president, we risk losing the Hezbollah vote this year."

"I didn't know there was a Hezbollah vote."

"It's not large but they make a lot of noise."

"Is there another angle to this?"

"There is. The White House never takes sides between a writer and those who pass a death sentence on him. Besides, if Mr. Bush saw every artist threatened by the kooks in Tehran he would never get any work done."

"'Fess up, Charlie. When Margaret Tutwiler said that a visit by Rushdie to Bush could be misinterpreted, wasn't she really saying that the United States did not want to do anything to offend Iran?"

"What's wrong with Iran? They have fine citizens who fought Iraq long before we did. The truth is that we have a new agenda for Iran. We don't want to jeopardize it by arranging a photo opportunity between the president and Salman Rushdie, Tehran's greatest enemy."

"But Iran was responsible for the taking of more American hostages than any other country."

"That doesn't compare with someone who writes a satire containing blasphemous statements about a religion. The White House disapproves of people being sentenced for what they write. At the same time, you don't rub a book in a nation's face."

"What's the worst that could happen if the president posed with Salman Rushdie in the Rose Garden?"

"The Iranians might have refused to buy spare parts from us."

"They feel that strongly about it?"

"Americans don't understand other people's cultures. In some countries they kill you for reading a book and in others they kill you for writing one."

"How do you know which is which?"

"That's what we have a State Department for."

"If Rushdie comes again, will the president change his mind about seeing him?"

"I doubt it. It would set a bad precedent if Mr. Bush received every writer who was condemned to death by the Hezbollah. This is not to say that the president is unsympathetic to human rights. We did offer to let Rushdie take a tour of the White House with the other tourists. Not many condemned writers get such an opportunity in a lifetime."

• *In a letter to the editor of the* Washington Post *(April 9, 1992), the president of PEN American Center, Edmund Keeley, commented on the administration's position as explained by Fitzwater: "To do so is to ignore the symbol that Salman Rushdie has become for all those who believe that an author's right to free expression is not only a cultural necessity but an essential quality of any democracy that believes in the freedom of the human spirit. It is both Salman Rushdie's extraordinary predicament and his symbolic role that require all of us to have 'a special interest in him.'"*

23

"A Pen Against the Sword In Good Faith"

An Extract, by Salman Rushdie

The controversy over *The Satanic Verses* needs to be looked at as a political event, not purely a theological one. In India, where the trouble started, the Muslim fundamentalist MP Shahabuddin used my novel as a stick with which to threaten the wobbling Rajiv Gandhi government. The demand for the book's banning was a power-play to demonstrate the strength of the Muslim vote, on which Congress has traditionally relied and which it could ill-afford to lose. (In spite of the ban, Congress lost the Muslims and the election anyway. Put not your trust in Shahabuddins.)

In South Africa, the row over the book served the purposes of the regime by driving a wedge between the Muslim and non-Muslim members of the United Democratic Front. In Pakistan, it was a way for the fundamentalists to try and regain the political initiative after their trouncing in the general election. In Iran, too, the incident could only be properly understood when seen in the context of the country's internal political struggles. And in Britain, where secular and religious leaders had been vying for power in the community for over a decade, the "affair" swung the balance of power back toward the mosques. Small wonder, then, that the various councils of the mosques are reluctant to bring the protest to an end, even though many Muslims up and down the country find it embarrassing, even shameful, to be associated with such illiberalism and violence.

The responsibility for violence lies with those who perpetrate it. In the past twelve months, bookshop workers have been manhandled, spat upon, verbally abused; bookshop premises have been threatened, and, on several occasions, actually firebombed. Publishing staff have had to face a campaign of hate mail, menacing phone calls, death threats and bomb scares. Demonstrations have, on occasion, turned violent, too. During the big march in London last summer, peaceful counter-demonstrators on behalf of humanism and secularism were knocked to the ground by marchers, and a counter-demo by the courageous (and largely Muslim) Women Against Fundamentalism group was also threatened and abused.

There is no conceivable reason why such behavior should be privileged because it is done in the name of an affronted religion. If we are to talk about "insults," "abuse," "offense," then the campaign against *The Satanic Verses* has been, very often, as insulting and abusive and offensive as it's possible to be.

I am not the first writer to be persecuted by Islamic fundamentalism in the modern period; among the greatest names so victimized are the Iranian writer Ahmad Kasravi, assassinated by fanatics, and the Egyptian Nobel laureate Naguib Mahfouz, often threatened but still, happily, with us. I am not the first artist to be accused of blasphemy and apostasy; these are, in fact, probably the most common weapons with which fundamentalism has sought to shackle creativity in the modern age. It is sad, then, that so little attention has been paid to this crucial literary context; and the Western critics like John Berger, who once spoke messianically of the need for new ways of seeing, should now express their willingness to privilege one such way over another, to protect a religion boasting one billion believers from the solitary figure of a single writer brandishing an "unreadable" book.

I would like to say this to the Muslim community: life without God seems to believers to be an idiocy, pointless, beneath contempt. It does not seem so to non-believers. To accept that the world, here, is all there is; to go through it, toward and into death, without the consolations of religion seems, well, at least as courageous and rigorous to us as the espousal of faith seems to you. Secularism and its works deserve your respect, not your contempt.

A great wave of freedom has been washing over the world. Those who resist it—in China, in Rumania—find themselves bathed in blood. I should like to ask Muslims—that great mass of ordinary, decent, fair-minded Muslims to whom I have imagined myself to be speaking for most of this piece—to choose to ride the wave; to renounce blood; not to let Muslim leaders make Muslims seems less tolerant than they are. *The Satanic Verses* is a serious work, written from a non-believer's point of view. Let believers accept that, and let it be.

In the meantime, I am asked, how do I feel?

I feel grateful to the British government for defending me. I hope that such a defence would be made available to any citizen so threatened, but that doesn't lessen my gratitude. I needed it, and it was provided. (I'm still not Tory, but that's democracy.)

I feel grateful, too, to my protectors, who have done such a magnificent job, and who have become my friends.

I feel grateful to everyone who has offered me support. The one real gain for me in this bad time has been the discovery of being cared for by so many people. The only antidote to hatred is love.

Above all, I feel great gratitude toward, solidarity with and pride in all the publishing people and bookstore workers around the world who have held the line against intimidation, and who will, I am sure, continue to do so as long as it remains necessary.

I feel as if I have been plunged, like Alice, into the world beyond the looking glass, where nonsense is the only available sense. And I wonder if I'll ever be able to climb back through the mirror.

Do I feel regret? Of course I do: regret that such offense has been taken against my work when it was not intended—when dispute was intended, and dissent, and even, at times, satire, and criticism of intolerance, and the like, but not the thing of which I'm most often accused, not "filth," not "insult," not "abuse." I regret that so many people who might have taken pleasure in finding their reality given pride of place in a novel will now not read it because of what they believe it to be, or will come to it with their minds already made up.

And I feel sad to be so grievously separated from my community, from India, from everyday life, from the world.

Please understand, however: I make no complaint. I am a writer. I do not accept my condition; I will strive to change it; but I inhabit it, I am trying to learn from it.

Our lives teach us who we are.

• *Originally published in* Newsweek, *this extract is roughly the second half of the essay as published; the first half, a discussion of the novel per se, though outside the scope of this book, is recommending reading for those who have read the novel in question.*

Part 2
Art and the NEA

> **"I am deeply offended by some of the filth
> that I see and to which federal money has gone,
> and some of the sacrilegeous, blasphemous
> depictions that are portrayed by some
> to be art . . . (which) has no business of
> getting one cent of taxpayers' money."**
>
> —President GEORGE BUSH, quoted in *USA Today*, March 27, 1990

24

Artistic Freedom

An ACLU Briefing Paper

> If art is to nourish the roots of our culture, society must set the artist free
> to follow his vision wherever it takes him.
>
> —JOHN F. KENNEDY

Today, across the cultural spectrum, artistic freedom is under assault. Free expression in popular music, photography, painting, cinema and other arts is threatened by pressure from lawmakers, prosecutors and self-appointed guardians of morality and taste. Succumbing to that pressure, more and more music stores, museums, schools, theaters, television stations, bookstores and video shops are restricting the display or availability of images and words deemed to be offensive to one group of citizens or another.

The roots of contemporary efforts to curb free expression in the arts reach back to the early 1980s, when a backlash arose against the cultural freedom of the previous decades. Religious fundamentalists and others, with overt support from the administration of President Ronald Reagan, began to advocate censorship of books, films and television in an effort to enforce cultural conformism. Today, we are reaping the harvest of that backlash as rap singers and museum directors are prosecuted for "obscenity," performance artists are denied government grants and Congress passes new censorship laws.

Artistic expression has come under attack in other periods of our country's history. In 1873, Congress passed a law that prohibited the mailing, shipping or importation of "obscene" and "immoral" matter. The law was used to ban the works of James Joyce, D.H. Lawrence, Voltaire and other great authors, as well as printed information about sexuality and contraception. The American Civil Liberties Union, founded in 1920, first confronted arts censorship in 1926 when the city of Boston banned 65 books, including Theodore Dreiser's *An American Tragedy,* Sinclair Lewis' *Elmer Gantry* and Ernest Hemingway's *The Sun Also Rises.* The ACLU countered the city's action, which popularized the phrase "banned in Boston," with a campaign to repeal Massachusetts' Blasphemy Act and end the censorship of plays and books.

Defending artistic expression, which is one of our most basic freedoms, remains among the ACLU's highest priorities. Here are the ACLU's answers to questions often asked by the public about artistic freedom.

What protects the work of artists from government censorship?

Artistic creations, whatever their medium or message, and even if their content is unpopular or of poor quality, are protected by the First and Fourteenth Amendments to the United States Constitution. The First Amendment declares that "Congress shall make no law . . . abridging the freedom of speech, or of the press," and the Fourteenth Amendment extends that prohibition to state and local governments. The government is forbidden to suppress the creation or distribution of any music, play, painting, sculpture, photograph, film, or even comic book. Some legal scholars have argued that the First Amendment is only applicable to written or spoken *political* expression, but the U.S. Supreme Court has long rejected that interpretation. "We reject the suggestion that the constitutional protection for free speech applies only to the exposition of ideas. The line between the informing and the entertaining is too elusive. . . ."

When and how did the threat to artistic freedom emerge in this country?

Supreme Court Justice William O. Douglas once observed that the First Amendment was "the product of a robust, not a prudish, age." For example, many of the Constitution's framers probably read and enjoyed John Cleland's 1748 bestseller, *Memoirs of a Woman of Pleasure,* better known as *Fanny Hill.* However, the Victorian Age brought extremely rigid and repressive moral standards into vogue in the English-speaking world, prompting both the British and American governments to begin applying sanctions to sexually explicit art and literature.

In 1821, thirty years after adoption of the Bill of Rights, *Fanny Hill* was banned in Massachusetts. In 1842, Congress amended the Customs law to prohibit the "importation of all indecent and obscene prints, paintings, lithographs, engravings and transparencies." In 1868, a ruling by England's highest court established a "bad tendency" test that was appropriated and used by U.S. state and federal courts until the 1930s: The government could ban any material if "the tendency of the matter charged as obscenity is to deprave and corrupt those whose minds are open to such immoral influences and into whose hands a publication of this sort may fall." In 1873, Congress passed the Comstock law, named for Anthony Comstock, who led the Society for the Suppression of Vice. In its first year of existence, that law, which punished first offenders with a $5,000 fine and five years imprisonment, authorized the destruction of 194,000 "questionable" pictures and 134,000 pounds of books "of improper character."

By 1900, criminal obscenity statutes were on the books in thirty states, and censorship of "immoral and indecent" works had become entrenched.

How has the Supreme Court dealt with sexually explicit expression?

In 1957, the Supreme Court announced, in the case of *Roth* v. *United States,* that obscenity is not constitutionally protected because it is "utterly without redeeming social value." In the same decision, the Court replaced the "bad tendency" test with a narrower one that declared a work of art obscene if "to the average person, applying contemporary community standards, the dominant theme taken as a whole appeals to the prurient interest." For the next sixteen years, the Court refined this definition while reversing many state obscenity convictions.

In 1973, a Court grown weary of reviewing and reversing tried to formulate clearer guidelines for evaluating sexually explicit material. In the case of *Miller v. California,* a 5–4 majority declared a work is obscene if, first, "the average person, applying contemporary community standards," would find that "the work, taken as a whole, appeals to the prurient interest . . ." ; second, "the work depicts or describes, in a patently offensive way, sexual conduct specifically defined by the applicable state law"; and third, "the work, taken as a whole, lacks serious literary, artistic, political or scientific value." The *Miller* standard remains in effect today, but no one knows exactly what it means.

Why does the ACLU object to the obscenity exception to the First Amendment?

The perception of obscenity in art is highly subjective. As Justice Douglas wrote, in his dissent in *Miller,* "what may be trash to me may be prized by others." By authorizing our courts to decide what is morally acceptable, we turn them into censorship boards that impose the personal viewpoints and tastes of judges and juries on the rest of society.

Furthermore, formulating a precise definition of obscenity has proven to be impossible. Justice Potter Stewart summed up the problem with his famous one-liner: "I know it when I see it." That assurance is of small comfort to artists, writers, publishers and distributors, who must navigate the murky waters of obscenity law trying to predict what judges will think.

The inherent subjectivity of *any* definition of obscenity has led to the suppression of constitutionally protected expression. Sometimes the suppression is direct and well publicized—for example, the 1990 conviction of a Florida record store owner for selling a certain album of rap music, and the prosecution, in the same year, of an Ohio museum director for exhibiting the works of a celebrated photographer. But even more pervasive is the "chilling effect" that vague standards have on writers and artists, pressuring them to engage in self-censorship to avoid running afoul of a legal definition that means different things to different people.

The First Amendment enshrines the principle that freedom of thought, and expression, are essential to a free society. In practice, the First Amendment's guarantees mean that adults must be free to decide for themselves, without governmental interference, what to read, write, paint, draw, photograph, see and hear.

But don't obscene and pornographic works cause antisocial and even violent behavior?

No direct link between exposure to sexually explicit material and antisocial behavior or sexual violence has ever been scientifically established. In 1967,

President Lyndon B. Johnson appointed a panel of experts to examine this issue. But after three years of extensive research, the National Commission on Obscenity and Pornography found no convincing evidence of a causal connection. Indeed, the commission concluded that the real problem is not sexual imagery but "the inability or reluctance of people in our society to be open and direct in dealing with sexual matters." The commission called for the repeal of existing obscenity statutes, excepting those concerning children, and recommended better sex education, better communication about sexual matters and more research.

In 1985, President Reagan's Attorney General, Edwin Meese, convened another commission, stating that "reexamination of the issue of pornography is long overdue." The Meese Commission, chaired by a zealous anti-pornography federal prosecutor, held public hearings at which a parade of witnesses recounted tales of sexual abuse. The commission then declared that it had established a link between such abuse and pornography and proposed new censorship laws. Soon afterward, several prominent scientists whose studies the commission's report had cited disassociated themselves from the report, charging that their research had been misrepresented.

Social scientists believe that while a troubled upbringing and alcoholism appear to be strongly linked to sexual violence, it is virtually impossible to demonstrate that such violence is caused by pornography. In any case, violent criminals often claim to be inspired by nonpornographic material. Serial killer Theodore Bundy collected cheerleader magazines. John Hinkley stalked President Reagan after seeing the renowned film *Taxi Driver*. And several mass murderers claimed to have been inspired by passages in the Bible. As these examples suggest, blaming books or films for the acts of disturbed individuals is a simplistic approach that could destroy freedom without deterring crime at all.

Even if the government can't suppress art, surely it shouldn't use tax monies to fund art that offends?

The Constitution does not *require* the government to subsidize artists and private art institutions, so a government decision to end all art subsidies would not violate the First Amendment (although that decision would impoverish the nation's cultural life). But as Chief Justice William Rehnquist has said, the Constitution forbids the government, once it has established a subsidy program, to "discriminate invidiously" and "aim at the suppression of dangerous ideas" in its administration of that program. Government funds pay for our sidewalks and streets, but the government cannot decide which ideas and opinions are expressed there. An art subsidy program is like a government-funded street, library, park, or university: a public forum for the expression of diverse ideas.

Art is inherently challenging and often provocative. If the government, fearing controversy, funded only art so bland that it offended no one, creativity would be stifled.

Why does the ACLU object to movie ratings, music labeling, or other voluntary rating systems? Don't they give guidance to consumers, especially parents?

"Voluntary" is a misnomer, given that the movie rating and music labeling systems were established to placate private pressure groups bent on censorship. As one commentator put it, such systems "amount to an elegant form of censorship—elegant because it is censorship made to look like consumer information."

Real information, such as periodicals that actually reviewed books, records and films marketed to young people, could be useful to parents. But rating and labeling systems that are based on vague, simplistic and overly generalized criteria do not really inform. In 1990 and '91, numerous state legislators proposed laws to require the labeling, and banning the sale to minors, of recordings that contain lyrics about sexual activity, drug or alcohol use, murder or suicide. By that standard, a host of operas and literary classics—even the Bible—might be labeled "For Adults Only."

Instead of providing useful information, ratings and labels encourage artists who want to reach the broadest possible audience to censor their own works in advance to avoid restrictive classifications. By promoting this self-censorship, rating and labeling systems act as filters between us and the artist.

But mustn't we protect our children from inappropriate messages and images, especially graphic sex and violence?

Yes, but who should decide which lyrics or movies are not suitable for your children? The government? Self-appointed busybodies? Or should you decide?

Parents differ about what is appropriate for children; therefore, individual parents must be free to make decisions regarding their own children. A majority of the public agrees with that principle: A 1990 Gallup poll showed that 78 percent of Americans believe that parents should do more to protect their children from obscenity, but 75 percent did not want any new laws passed to restrict what the public could see or hear.

Defending artists is fine, but why does the ACLU spend time and money defending pornographers and sleaze merchants?

First of all, the ACLU defends freedom of expression, not the *content* of expression. Second, if we grant the government the power to censor "sleaze," it must also have the power to decide what "sleaze" is. History reveals that the government tends to use such power overbroadly to censor controversial material by calling it "sleaze." Any involvement by the government in deciding which ideas are fit for public consumption robs you of your constitutional right to make that decision for yourself.

Today's climate of intolerance harks back to the "Comstockery" of the late nineteenth century. Once again, a movement is afoot to stifle artistic freedom in the name of stamping out "indecency."

• Book banning in the public schools has targeted John Steinbeck's *The Grapes of Wrath;* Kurt Vonnegut's *Slaughterhouse-5;* J.D. Salinger's *Catcher in the*

Rye; George Orwell's *1984; Tarzan; Little Red Riding Hood;* and the *American Heritage College Dictionary.* J.R.R. Tolkien's *The Hobbit* has been accused of promoting Satanism, and Alice Walker's *The Color Purple* has been charged with undermining family values.

• Nudity is being edited out of films by cable television stations, paintings of nudes are being excluded from art exhibits and theatrical works that include nudity have been banned, or altered, in localities around the country.

• Artists are feeling pressure from government funding agencies to steer clear of art that deals with issues of gender and sexuality.

Censorship is an infectious disease. Permitting restraints on *any* expression sets the stage for attacks on all expression that is artistically and/or politically controversial. The creative spirit must be free. When it is not, society suffers.

"The Boston Massacre"
by Samuel Walker

With thousands of people milling around the Boston Common on April 5, 1926, Arthur Garfield Hays and H.L. Mencken sold copies of Mencken's *American Mercury,* banned that month by the Boston Watch and Ward Society because Herbert Ashbury's article, "Hatrack," made fun of fundamentalists. Hays and Mencken went to Boston, obtained a peddler's license, and provoked an arrest. Hays won an acquittal for Mencken and a court order restraining the Watch and Ward Society. The society, an odd coalition of Protestant Brahmins and puritanical Catholics, retaliated with an even more energetic crusade against indecency. The ensuing "Boston Massacre" popularized the phrase "Banned in Boston" and launched the ACLU's first serious attack on censorship in the arts.

25

"Chairman's Statement"
The National Endowment for the Arts

by John E. Frohnmayer

When most people hear about the NEA, what come to mind are those projects that have created a national uproar; from Senator Jesse Helms to the prominent members of the religious right, the question has been raised: Why not just abolish the NEA?

Throwing the baby out with the bathwater rarely makes sense, and makes no sense in this debate. What its critics don't acknowledge is that the NEA has, for the most part, funded noncontroversial projects.

Among major nations with art programs, the United States—I've been told—has the lowest funding level. As for those who complain about the NEA funding, remember this: in its entire twenty-five-year history, only $\frac{3}{10,000}$ of the grants have been controversial. Now, what other federal program can you think of that has spent its budget so effectively and so well?

John Frohnmayer's "Chairman's Statement," published in the 1990 Annual Report, sets forth the philosophy that has guided the NEA. Put simply, the NEA considers the arts to be a national treasure. (Those in the entertainment industry would agree: American popular culture is a major leading export.)

Over the past year, a conundrum has crossed my mind time and again: what can we do to help the arts play a more meaningful part in our citizens' daily lives, and how can the National Endowment for the Arts better make available quality arts to the citizens of this country? Americans, as a whole, value the richness that art, in its multiple forms, brings to their lives and those of their children. As this report shows, our twofold mission is to support artistic excellence and to provide access to that excellence for all citizens.

The NEA is in the business of promoting creativity. Our grants to artists and arts organizations go to projects that have a positive impact in communities in all parts of our nation. Over the twenty-five-year history of this agency, we have been successful in this mission, yet with the passing of each year, we realize that we have more to do and greater challenges ahead.

An understanding of our culture is fundamental to superior human performance in all endeavors and to the maintenance of our democratic institutions. As Leonard Garment, a lawyer and former cultural adviser to President Nixon, recently said: "[A] child who has not been moved early in life by a poem or a story is not likely to be deeply affected later on by the burning of books. . . ."

Arts Education

The ultimate goal of the Endowment's art education efforts is a citizenry that:

- Recognizes and appreciates the life-enhancing value of all art forms;
- Understands that arts education, with its ability to teach creativity, is fundamental to superior human performance in all endeavors;
- Feels free to give expression to its own innate creativity and humanity through participation in the arts; and
- Provides active support for the arts in both the private and public realms.

For this stewardship of our nation's culture, all Americans—young and old—deserve a quality education which emphasizes the fundamental value of the arts in our lives. The Endowment will expand existing programs which help bring artists-in-residence to schools and other settings and help state arts agencies cooperate with state and local education leaders to develop curricula and joint programs in arts education.

Nurturing our imaginative life is fundamental to our growth as a society. The arts have the power to stimulate students—to inspire them to dream and to dare. Exposure to the arts helps build a well-rounded person with the mental acuity to see and think creatively and critically.

Arts teaches an appreciation of proportion, order, wit and genius. Granted, not everyone can perform or write, sculpt or paint, but all should be given an opportunity to know about visual and spacial composition, harmony, design and structure so that they might better understand our world.

This Administration has declared, and all Americans can agree, that an educated populace should be a first order of priority. A significant part of that education is to sights and sounds, to relationships and proportion, to poetry and plays. In short, it is education to those truths that tell us who we are and allow us to exercise discipline, intelligence, tolerance, compassion and intuition.

Access to the Arts

We will develop more cultural activities for people in rural areas, inner cities, and other areas underserved by the arts. We must ensure adequate facilities for these activities, encourage the use of new distribution channels and promote new techniques, and new venues: community centers, libraries, schools, halls. Every person in every state should have access to the arts. And we must recognize that there is no one *right* way to do or provide art—we are limited only by our imaginations.

Twenty-five years ago there was no National Endowment for the Arts, only a handful of state art agencies, and few active local arts councils. Twenty-five years ago most quality arts organizations were clustered in New York City and a few other metropolitan areas. Twenty-five years ago acceptance, understanding and appreciation of the diversity of American culture were not the prevailing mood. Today quality arts programs can be found in virtually every major city, as well as many small towns, bringing excellent visual arts to Kansas City, music to Pittsburgh, dance to Houston, and so on through the breadth of this country. The National Endowment for the Arts has a catalytic part in helping to make communities places where art can flourish. But we still have far to go—particularly in areas as yet unreached by some of the major arts disciplines.

Our rural program is designed to help citizens in small and isolated communities realize their aspirations in the arts. A thorough study of existing categories, initiatives and programs which have an impact on rural areas is under way to determine which of these efforts might be improved or expanded. Additionally, as mandated by Congress in our reauthorization legislation, five percent of program funds are being transferred to the state arts agencies for rural and inner city initiatives.

Cultural Diversity

We are committed to supporting organizations which reflect the cultural diversity in America. Our Expansion Arts Program was formed to reach organizations "deeply rooted in and reflective of culturally diverse, inner city, rural or tribal communities." Approximately 300 such organizations are funded each year, and Expansion Arts has nurtured many of the celebrated minority arts organizations in America—from the Alvin Ailey Dance Company to El Teatro Campesino to the Japanese-American Cultural & Community Center in Los Angeles. Many more examples can be found under the Expansion Arts heading of this report and throughout all of the disciplines funded by the Endowment.

The people of the United States descend from at least 170 discrete cultural backgrounds, and from each of these backgrounds come art forms—traditional and contemporary—that are aesthetically distinctive, and essential to America's cultural wealth. The Endowment's goal is to assist all elements of America's culture in the maintenance and development of its diverse parts and to promote access to artistic resources and opportunities for all groups. The latter includes enhancing the ability of all Americans to understand forms of artistic expression other than their own. To that end, the Endowment will celebrate the cultural diversity of American art through programmatic and administrative initiatives that extend beyond the Expansion Arts Program and cut across all of the agency's discipline programs.

International Exchange

The arts in every culture represent those deeply embedded cultural values which constitute a glue that holds the society together. The cultural values of our country include energy, innovation, idealism, breadth of thinking, youth and freshness, adaptability and passion. Certainly these aren't all of them, but these are reflected in an art which is uniquely American and about which we hardly need be apologetic. We are eager to share these cultural achievements of our country with the rest of the world, and we expect to learn from the values expressed in the culture of other nations.

At present, we offer modest support to international activities, yet within our limited resources, we've pursued the programs mentioned in the pages of this report. We would like to do more in the international sphere. The plans for the future as twofold:

Reciprocity: we wish to increase two-way exchanges, not only as a service to American art and American audiences, but also to reach out to other artists, institutions and audiences in the community of nations—through more residency programs, institutional linkages, support of "suitcase funds" to enable artists to travel and learn from different cultures, and support of special events such as historical commemorations or the upcoming 500th anniversary of Columbus' voyage to America.

We will also explore *collaborative efforts* with the *states and the private sector,* such as Sister Cities cultural programs, international exhibitions and performing arts tours, and more. For instance, we helped support the Goodwill Arts Festival—which sold a greater percentage of its tickets that the Goodwill Games—in Seattle last summer. Through this festival, American audiences had the chance to watch the Bolshoi Ballet perform or see the Moscow Theater present Chekhov's plays.

Art is a search for truth and understanding, a spirit we have in our international affairs. We must use our idealism and creativity to reach out to other nations and to help find the just solution to international problems. This new age will depend on our willingness to listen, to share ideas and know-how, to see that our strength does not depend only on power, but also on leadership.

The future has never been more in our hands. And together, we can make the next decade the most exciting our world has ever seen.

Support of Cultural Institutions and Artists

Support of the nation's exemplary cultural institutions and American artists continues to be a priority. In times of budget constraints it is possible to lose sight of the repositories of our nation's creativity—these cultural institutions, both large and small, and artists throughout the land that are among our national treasures. These groups, sometimes with large budgets and rich histories, are no less deserving of federal support because of their success. By maintaining America's shared cultural traditions, they play a critical role in preserving the past and exploring the future. That future cannot be mortgaged by assuming that these institutions, which have served Americans so well for so long, can exist without the continued support of the federal government. Cultural policy should safeguard the "cultural treasures" of our society, not only through preservation and conservation efforts, but through a forum to acknowledge and showcase them.

Our cultural institutions include not only the venerated organizations like the Museum of Modern Art, the Lyric Opera of Chicago, or the Philadelphia Symphony Orchestra, but those places, large and small, which help give a sense of identity to community. Institutions like the St. Paul Chamber Orchestra, or the Nelson-Atkins Museum in Kansas City; the Guadalupe Cultural Arts Center in San Antonio, or the Artists of Indian America in New Mexico. . . .

The difficulties and successes of the past year have strengthened our resolve to pursue our mission. We build for the future on the basis of these fundamental findings:

• It is in our national interest to promote the cultural advancement of our society, just as we support progress in scientific and medical research. Art is central to our society, not separate, remote or expendable. Art edifies and enriches our minds and souls. The arts help give us an identity, and support for creativity is a signal of a government's commitment to the growth and well-being of its people.

• Arts activities are a catalyst for economic growth, adding billions to our national economy each year. The arts provide jobs, attract and retain businesses to our communities, and stimulate tourism.

• Art increases the cultural literacy of our citizenry, helping them retain knowledge, making our citizens more thoughtful, productive, and competitive in today's world.

• Federal support shows our commitment to the general welfare of our citizens, particularly in their pursuit of happiness, and support on the national level is a sign to the rest of the world of the value our country places on our culture and civilization.

• Endowment support provides opportunities for artists and arts organizations to grow, and for audiences across the country to experience quality art. The Arts Endowment provides vital national leadership in the arts. Federal support for the arts is a catalyst for the state, local, and regional public support network and for the private sector—foundations, corporations and individuals—none of which have the resources to make funding recommendations from a national perspective.

• Our national arts agency helps preserve the traditions of our diverse cultural heritage and broadens the audience for the arts so that not just the wealthy and elite, but every citizen wishing to participate in our country's cultural activities can do so.

Taken as a whole, the [4,475] grants described in this report represent our commitment to these ideals. The past year was one of change for the National Endowment for the Arts, yet, paradoxically, these changes renew our vigor for our mission and remind us of our commitment to the tenets upon which this agency was founded. Emerson wrote that, "Beauty [in art] will not come at the call of a legislature . . . It will come, as always, unannounced, and spring up between the feet of brave and earnest men." The National Endowment for the Arts will never call great art into being. Indeed, our enabling legislation makes this very point. We are charged with the mission of helping to sustain a climate for creativity, where artists may pursue their vision, and where all citizens may enjoy, acknowledge and learn from excellent art when it chances to appear. With the support of our public and private partners, who enthusiastically value and support the arts, we hope to open doors for every culture and to help the arts in America to flourish.

• *John E. Frohnmayer served as the chairman of the NEA during the most controversial period in its history. Since being forced to leave because of election-year politics from the White House in the wake of conservative Patrick Buchanan's attack on the NEA, Frohnmayer has become an impassioned advocate of freedom of the arts and a frequent public speaker on the subject.* Leaving Town Alive: Confessions of An Arts Warrior *by Frohnmayer is "the story of how a First Amendment moderate went to Washington, D.C., and left a First Amendment radical," according to Houghton Mifflin editor John Sterling.*

The NEA: The White House Perspective
by Shirley M. Green

One month before Frohnmayer addressed the American Society of Newspaper Editors in Washington, D.C., at which he prefaced his remarks by saying, "The views I am about to express are mine. I am not speaking on behalf of the Administration . . .," I wrote to President Bush and asked for his opinion on whether controversial art should be funded at all.

Shirley M. Green, special assistant to the president for presidential messages and correspondence, replied in a letter, dated March 11, 1992.

On behalf of President Bush, thank you for your message about grant-making policies of the National Endowment for the Arts. I am pleased to provide the following information.

The National Endowment for the Arts holds the view that while grant applications should be judged on the basis of artistic excellence and merit, it is in the public interest for the Endowment to fund diversity of expression. All grant applications are reviewed and recommended by a review panel, by the National Council on the Arts, and by the Chairman of the NEA.

President Bush strongly believes that the Endowment must be a conscientious steward of taxpayer funds. The Administration has worked with Congress to legislatively structure NEA's grant-making procedures in order to prevent Federal funds from being used for activities that clearly do not warrant taxpayer financing. As a result, the 1990 reauthorization legislation, the Arts, Humanities, and Museum Amendments, mandates that ". . . the Chairperson shall ensure that artistic excellence and artistic merit are the criteria by which applications are judged, taking into consideration general standards of decency and respect for the diverse beliefs and values of the American public."

Upon enactment of the reauthorization legislation, the Arts Endowment began the careful process of developing policies and procedures to implement all of the provisions of law, including the provision just cited.

Furthermore, once a grant has been awarded and the project that was funded has been completed, there is another mechanism by which the Endowment can verify that all terms and conditions of the grant were met in compliance with the law. All grantees are required to submit a Final Report to the Endowment at the conclusion of the grant period. As with all Endowment grants, if the project did not comply with the terms of the grant, the Endowment has the authority to seek recoupment of Federal funds from the grantee. The same is true if a court were to deem the project, once complete, obscene. Proper oversight of all grants will be exercised by the Endowment to ensure compliance with its authorizing statute, Public Law 101–152, and with all other applicable Federal laws.

NEA recognizes that assertions about a number of its funded projects have been widely disseminated and that these assertions have created concern. You may wish to communicate directly with the Endowment concerning particular grants.

26

The Art Your Tax Money Buys

by John E. Frohnmayer

> As for that famous argument that "I don't want my tax dollars going to pay for . . ." whatever, the answer is clear. I don't want my tax dollars going to soldiers who kill their comrades with "friendly fire" or to cops who punch out a manacled suspect—but I don't therefore favor abolishing the police force or shutting down the Pentagon. . . . Bureaucracies make mistakes. The NEA has made fewer than most. But a nation that cannot afford to finance its arts—even the occasionally tasteless or offensive variety—is a nation that has lost its perspective, its self-confidence and probably its soul.
>
> —DAVID S. BRODER, "Bullying the Arts," *Washington Post,* March 16–22, 1992

As NEA supporters have pointed out, the U.S. spends less on federal support of the arts than any other nation in the world. In fact, it's under a dollar per citizen, as Frohnmayer points out, for art that predominantly has been decidedly non-controversial.

It's your 68 cents, so let's talk about it. That's what each citizen pays in taxes— on average—for everything the National Endowment for the Arts does. You are entitled to know what it buys, who chooses; what we who administer it stand for (that is, unless you're tired of reading and hearing about arts wars, for which I wouldn't blame you).

During the twenty-five years of its existence, the endowment has made 90,000 grants. Of these, about thirty have been controversial. Still, I would guess those thirty—or maybe just a couple of them—are all most of you know about the endowment. Consider the following:

What it buys:

During the past twenty-five years, your tax money that went to the endowment has helped bring into being 70 new choruses and 120 new symphony orchestras. Some of the music that they have made and you have enjoyed is sacred, some secular.

It has helped pay for 364 new theaters at which you have seen plays, both good and bad, depicting love and hate and joy and envy and success and failure— just like our lives.

Your 68 cents has helped created 2,940 local art agencies that produce your strawberry festival, bluegrass competition, flatfoot clogging contests and community sings. Countless of you have, in addition, given your time, dollars and sweat to make these things happen.

And you have spent 68 cents to bring artists to more than 11,000 of your kids' schools—each year reaching 4.5 million children who will know that there is at least one living poet in this country and that those actors on stage and television are real people who probably were kids once too.

A sense of self-worth, of the ability to communicate—that's what the arts teach with your 68 cents—and it is fundamental to all learning, from calculus to drawing.

Who chooses?

A bunch of bureaucrats in D.C.? No, actually you do. More than 1,200 citizens will sit on endowment panels this year to recommend, on a competitive basis, which applications should be funded. Most of you are visual artists, or architects, or dancers or folk arts lovers, but you may also be a pharmacist from Muncie, Ind., or a minister from Louisville, Ky., because at least one knowledgeable lay person sits on every panel. Citizens on the panels are of all races, from all parts of the country and represent diverse viewpoints.

Your panel recommendations, fought over, debated and usually resolved by the consensus of the panel, are forwarded to the National Council on the Arts, 26 distinguished Americans who review these recommendations in public sessions and affirm or reject them. You know some of these council members, because you have been thrilled by Arthur Mitchell's Dance Theatre of Harlem (or his dancing if you were lucky enough to see him); you have been moved by the pathos of an August Wilson play that Lloyd Richards produced; or you have been transported by the beauty of Phyllis Curtin's voice. But you know the others on the council as well, because they are your friends, neighbors, colleagues—good and decent people who care about our society.

Finally, the National Council recommendations for funding come to me, and I can say yes or no. I decided on the basis of our twofold mission: to support quality arts and to make those arts accessible to the American people.

What do we stand for?

I came to the government sharing a common cynicism about government workers. My experience hasn't confirmed it. The government workers here at the endowment are smart, compassionate, incredibly hard-working and in spite of the past two years of arts wars, amazingly good-humored.

I'm chairman of the National Endowment for the Arts—and I'm sure these people serve it so well—because of a belief that people become more human through the arts. Dance, music, drama and design interpret our world in carrying forth its wisdom from generation to generation.

As our enabling legislation says: ". . . while no government can call a great artist or scholar into existence, it is necessary and appropriate for the federal government to help create and sustain not only a climate encouraging freedom of thought, imagination and inquiry but also the material conditions facilitating the release of this creative talent."

But let's return to those few controversial grants, because even though they are only a minuscule percentage of what we have funded, some ask: "How does the endowment serve the public interest by making controversial grants?" First, while the endowment is for everybody, not everything we do is for everyone. With tax dollars you support schools, although not all of you have children. Your taxes build bridges in North Dakota and Arizona over which you may never drive. You may not agree with the agricultural, health, labor or environmental programs your taxes support. It's the compromise we recognize as the social contract.

Second, society grows through living illustrations. Some controversies we resolve; some stay with us, but few are resolved by ignoring them. Sometimes art provides a vehicle—a forum—for that public debate. "Driving Miss Daisy" (the original play was funded by the endowment) prods our conscience gently. Other works prod debate more confrontationally.

Finally, our society is diverse, which is a source of strength as well as a challenge. The endowment's mandate from Congress is not to dictate content, but to seek ". . . artistic excellence and artistic merit . . . taking into consideration general standards of decency and respect for the diverse beliefs and values of the American public." That is exactly what we intend to do. No blacklists, no ideological preconceptions.

We will continue to use your 68 cents—wisely I hope—so that we can leave for our children and their children, a sense of who we are as human beings, what we share as a nation and what we have achieved as a civilization.

NEA Publications

• *Guide to the National Endowment for the Arts: 1992–1993* (96 pages). This publication, wrote Frohnmayer, "is for the general public, so that anyone interested in the work of the National Endowment for the Arts might have an idea of the breadth of our programs and the commitment to excellence. Secondly, it is for those artists and arts organizations seeking support for their work from the Endowment. Finally, the *Guide* is for those individuals who are interested in serving on our panels. We invite those who work in or are knowledgeable about the arts and the work of the Endowment to submit a resume to our Office of Council and Panel Operations."

Part I is an overview of the NEA (its goals, how the NEA works, what the NEA funds, how to apply for a grant, and the application review process). Part II discusses the wide variety of programs it funds (Dance, Design Arts, Expansion Arts, Folk Arts, Inter-Arts, Literature, Media Arts, Museums, Music, Opera, Musical Theater, Theater, Visual Arts, Challenge/Advancement, and International); Parts III–V provide information on its office for public partnership, its arts administration fellows program, and its office of policy, planning, and research.

A useful, thorough document, the *Guide to the NEA* is required reading for anyone who mistakenly thinks the NEA funds "filth" at the expense of everything else.

• *1990 Annual Report* (340 pages, April 1991). Provides details on all programs funded. A typical example: "Lincoln Symphony Orchestra Association, Lincoln, NE, $6,000. To support the series of Young People's Concerts."

Both publications are available at no cost from: National Endowment for the Arts, Nancy Hanks Center, 1100 Pennsylvania Avenue, N.W., Washington, D.C. 20506.

27

Raising Hell

by John E. Frohnmayer

Frohnmayer's remarks were made at the American Society of Newspaper Editors Conference, April 10, 1992, in Washington, D.C.

The views I am about to express are mine. I am not speaking on behalf of the Administration—that's my standard disclaimer for the next few weeks.

I was pleased to be invited to speak to the American Society of Newspaper Editors, for in some ways, being chairman of the Arts Endowment parallels running a newspaper. We both rely on experts to find out the truth (you have writers, I have panelists); we both make decisions—you on what goes in your paper, I, on what applications are funded; we both get barraged by angry people claiming bias. And, I hope, we both believe in the principles of freedom of speech and freedom of expression.

Democracy is constantly in a process of becoming. It is never fixed, never secure, never comfortable. To protect, renew and maintain our democracy, we have the First Amendment:

> Congress shall make no law respecting an establishment of religion, or pro-
> hibiting the free exercise thereof; or abridging the freedom of speech, or of
> the press; or the right of the people peaceably to assemble, and to petition the
> Government for a redress of grievances.

Because of three tensions in our societal fabric, our generation is having more difficulty embracing and re-enfranchising the First Amendment than most.

The first is the tension between the First Amendment and a pervasive strain of anti-intellectualism in American life. The premise of the First Amendment is that we solve our problems through the vigorous clash of ideas. Anti-intellectualism is the unwillingness to use thought, facts and critical discourse to solve problems. We once had a political party in the U.S. that proudly called itself the "Know-Nothings" whose agenda was against "Negroes, foreigners and Catholics." Abraham Lincoln said that if the Know-Nothings ever gained control, he would prefer "emigrating to some country where they make no pretense of loving liberty . . . where despotism can be taken pure, and without the base alloy of hypocrisy." The sound bite, which has become so pervasive in our political fisticuffs, is to the First Amendment as bumper stickers are to philosophy.

Recently, the utter unimportance of facts in the attacks on the Endowment has been astonishing—particularly coming from alleged religious leaders. Certain groups, claiming to speak for all families or all Christians, have hammered away at the Endowment. In a way, they remind me of Swift's maxim, "We have just enough religion to make us hate, but not enough to make us love one another." As Hubert Humphrey said, "The right to be heard doesn't automatically include the right to be taken seriously." But many of these untruths or half-truths have been repeated so often and so unwillingly that they are widely accepted. Example: corn for porn.

The second tension is between the clause prohibiting establishment of a religion and a sense of "chosenness" in American political discourse. Our money says: "In God We Trust." The Pledge of Allegiance to our country acknowledges that we are a nation "under God." Political leaders feel comfortable in telling God to bless us. There is a sense that one must exercise religion (in Ike's words, no matter what it is) to succeed in politics. Couple political use of religious trappings with the theological reductionism that underlies both fundamentalism and anti-intellectualism and we can see why people are calling for laws against blasphemy. (Of course, we have no laws against blasphemy because both the establishment and free exercise clauses of the First Amendment prohibit them.)

The third tension is between the right of assembly and the electronic isolation that our technology has brought us. T.S. Eliot said: "[Television] is a medium of entertainment which permits millions of people to listen to the same joke at the same time, and yet remain lonesome."

With the exception of an occasional school board meeting, we have precious few town meetings or other opportunities for real public debate and discourse. Hence the lobbing of electronic bombs by print or airwaves seldom allows an issue to be squarely confronted, let alone debated.

Thomas Mann said: "Speech is civilization itself. The word, even the most contradictious word, preserves contact—it is silence which isolates." In front of our television sets we are both silent and isolated.

So how do we, in this generation, re-enfranchise the First Amendment and deal with the tensions just described? It will take, in my view, a commitment to build a new social understanding; a vigorous and honest debate to redefine what truths and values define us. We hear lots of talk about "family values," but precious little definition of what that term means. Truths are not self-evident these days and unless we take advantage of the permission the First Amendment gives us to duke it out intellectually, our diverse society will become increasingly brittle until it breaks apart.

We must address calmly and honestly at least: racial and ethnic differences, tolerance, equality of economic opportunity, education, and individual responsibility.

The answer to none of these issues is clear, so we must be prepared to live with ambiguity, frustration, failure and false starts. To do so will require a generosity of spirit that can be born only of a commitment not to let our noble experiment in democracy fail.

I do have some suggestions on how this discourse might be promoted, and not surprisingly, they involve both the arts and newspaper editors.

First, we must have meaningful arts education in every school in the land. The arts are fundamental to the democratic system because they demand involvement. Every child who has honestly written a poem or performed a song or dance has been forever changed. That child has made a covenant of honesty and risk—of communication and commitment to a community. That child has laid vulnerable a part of the self and has placed faith in the community to respond. That child has become a *citizen*.

Second, if we are to be sound emotionally and intellectually, we must also be prosperous economically. Our second most positive balance of trade item is the export of copyrightable materials: movies, television, literature, software. The National Endowment for the Arts has been the farm club for this industry for twenty-seven years—for the insignificant sum of 68 cents per person. It is part of an incredible economic engine, the demolition of which, on purely economic analysis, would be foolhardy.

Newspapers play a vital role in getting out the facts and encouraging the debate. It's no coincidence that the Pulitzer Prizes are awarded not only for journalism, but for fiction, poetry, music and drama as well. Journalism is a kissing cousin to the arts, and so I don't feel reluctant to suggest that you get some different voices in the arts debate. Typically, articles on the Endowment controversy feature the same speakers on the same sides, and the media tend to confer a status on them that may or may not be deserved. There are a number of articulate and knowledgeable people who can speak to this issue, particularly in business, labor, community services, mainline religion, and education. They should be encouraged to do so.

Now let me make a few unscheduled and perhaps impertinent comments about the role of newspapers in promoting the debate that will allow us to redefine the social contract.

First Impertinence

It is my view that political party platforms are meaningless exercises, full of sound and fury, and signifying nothing. They need not be. What if you, as opinion leaders, were to suggest that presidential primaries in your state be totally on issues. The issues would be on the ballot, not the names of the candidates. Those who would be presidents would campaign for concepts and all delegates would be committed only to concepts. Some benefits:

1. It would elevate substance over personality and peccadillos.
2. It would make for some very interesting conventions.
3. It would result in a candidate chosen by the party to carry out its platform rather than vice versa.
4. And, most importantly, it would give the people a real voice in policy—a chance to thrash out, every four years, some clauses in the social contract.

Would it work? Who knows? But it's hard to think it would be worse than we presently have.

Second Impertinence

An accountability scorecard. We all know how short is the memory of the American voter. Compounding the problem is the fuzziness in the system that diffuses responsibility. So the Savings & Loan scandal is an orphan, and the White House and Congress hurl accusations back and forth to sully both of their houses. You could ask each candidate, shortly before the election, what he or she wanted to be judged on—substantively. You could then reprint that scorecard every six months, with updates. I'm not suggesting positions can't or shouldn't change—only that they should not be position de jour—changing to fit the crowd or prevailing breeze.

Third Impertinence

A demand for leadership. Members of Congress and the Executive Branch have full-time jobs and full-time staffs precisely so they can research, analyze, and articulate solutions to the problems that vex us. They are difficult problems, without easy solutions and sometimes with no apparent hope of solution. Leadership requires courage and a willingness to educate constituents. It carries with it a risk that the voters won't like the message and will throw the leader out. It is, as a famous track coach said, simply that you can't do the long jump without getting sand in your shorts.

If we let our leaders rely only on public opinion polls to determine positions on issues, then why have leaders at all? Just have an 800 number so everyone can vote on every issue. Leaders articulate vision—in the neighborhood, at the editor's desk, on Capitol Hill and Pennsylvania Avenue.

Our common goal should be to reinvigorate the First Amendment—its protection of and from religion; the sanctity of ideas in the individual and the press, and our right to come together and decide what we value. In that context, this National Endowment for the Arts, about which I care so deeply, can be easily and gratefully saved from its critics. We must reaffirm our desire, as a country, to be a leader in the realm of ideas and of the spirit. To kill the

Endowment because of a few disturbing lines or images poses a far greater threat to this nation than anything that has ever been funded. It would be a craven admission that we are not strong enough to let all voices be heard.

Newspaper readers don't have to believe every word of the *Washington Times* or the *Washington Post*. And you or I don't have to like everything the Endowment supports, because your government is not the sponsor of those ideas; it is merely an enabler. The ideas belong to our diverse and sometimes brilliant artists—patriots who are bold enough to tell the truth as they see it.

The motto of the old *Chicago Times* was, "It's a newspaper's duty to print the news and raise hell." Sometimes, it's the artist's duty to tell the truth and raise hell, too. We need to face that truth more now than ever.

28

USA Today Interviews

"Let Clash of Ideas Determine the Truth"
with John E. Frohnmayer

USA Today: The National Endowment for the Arts repeatedly has been accused of funding obscene works. What's your response?

John Frohnmayer: That issue, I hope, has been resolved. Congress took $45,000 out of our budget last year and passed language regarding obscenity. I hope we don't have to continue to fight that issue over and over again.

An ad in the Washington Times *and* USA Today, *by the American Family Association, objects to several NEA grants. Are those legitimate concerns?*

The ad is categorically false in a number of particulars:

• It accuses us of honoring Andres Serrano and Robert Mapplethorpe. The word "honoring" I certainly take issue with.

• The ad accuses us of funding Annie Sprinkle, an allegedly pornographic show. We did not fund that show.

• The ad accuses us of something else in New York which we can't even identify. It accuses us of funding two groups which we have not funded in at least six years.

• Finally, it accuses us of funding shows by homosexuals. And I plead guilty, because we do not consider sexual orientation as a criterion for judging grants. Nor do we assume that because of a person's sexual orientation, that person will automatically disobey our law.

You've said, "I am personally and unequivocally opposed to government funding of obscenities. . . . It degrades humanity and it sickens me." If you weren't being accused of funding obscenity, would you have issued such a statement?

Yes, I think I would. The definition of obscenity is that it appeals to prurient interest, that it contravenes community standards and that it's without artistic significance. Anything that comes through our panels is deemed to have artistic significance by the people who look at it. So I think I have a sensitivity to this field and would have been sensitive to it without the critics.

Would you define some of the more extreme examples of Robert Mapplethorpe's and Andres Serrano's work as obscene?

I am not prepared to comment on that because that's not an issue that I was asked to deal with, and I'm not going to second-guess my predecessor.

What would happen if Serrano applied for a grant today?

It would go through the same process that it's gone through before. It would go before the panel, the panel would determine whether it was artistically significant, the national council would give its opinion and, ultimately, I would be asked to respond.

Would the panel consider the previous Serrano exhibit?

The way the legislation is set up, and I think it makes sense, is that the panel can, and in my view should, consider what the past record is.

And, eventually, it would wind up on your desk?

That's right. And I ultimately would have to make the decision based upon what was there. But what you're doing to me, and what I think is grossly unfair, is to say: there's something out there, we don't know what it is or what it looks like, what are you going to do about it? And this is the same thing that the people who are upset about Serrano and Mapplethorpe often are doing. They haven't seen the whole exhibition. They don't know what Serrano intended with his Christ piece.

But they're still offended.

They are offended. And one of the things that art requires is that you confront it. In other words, to try to understand what the artist is doing. If you don't do that, then art hasn't had a chance to convey its message or work its power. Now you might still be offended after you've seen it. You might think it is the worst trash you've ever seen, and I would respect that viewpoint.

The question was, do you consider obscene some of the more extreme pieces by Mapplethorpe and Serrano?

There were 120 photographs in the Mapplethorpe show. If you were to take four or five of those and say, "Are these obscene?" the answer is probably yes. If you take the whole show, which I have not seen, then the answer is probably no. Because the Supreme Court requires that the item be taken as a whole.

What about Serrano?

I have not seen that and I cannot comment on that.

Isn't this similar to what has happened throughout history—some of what we consider classics caused great outrage when they were introduced?

Of course—Goya, the ceiling of the Sistine Chapel, Michelangelo, a lot of the El Greco stuff—the list goes on and on. Same issue, same arguments, same struggle. What we're talking about is the expression of the deepest human emotions and reactions. And my plea is simply, let the clash of ideas determine truth because that's what we have always done in the United States, as opposed to trying to put blinders on.

You've said the media hasn't helped get the story out. In what way?

For the last year almost, the front-page stories have always been Mapplethorpe and Serrano. But the positive stuff doesn't make the news. We've given about 85,000 grants, and maybe 25 or 30 have been severely questioned. Over the last 24 years, we probably funded a million images, separate photos or paintings or sculptures, and we spend all this ink on 15 of them. And then people want to abolish the endowment or want to censure it because of that. Where is the perspective?

You say that the attacks are almost totally without merit. How does that make you feel?

I believe we will be judged not just by what happens today or what Congress does, but ultimately by history. I believe that the truth ultimately emerges from our system which allows people to say, essentially, whatever they want. In terms of me personally, it goes with the job. I'm getting very used to being attacked. I don't like it, but I can certainly live with it.

"Don't Give Tax Money for Obscene Art"
with Phyllis Schlafly
Conducted by Barbara Reynolds

Phyllis Schlafly of the Eagle Forum provided a rebuttal to Frohnmayer's arguments.

USA Today: *What are your objections to the endowment?*

Phyllis Schlafly: America should not have a ministry of culture where a government bureau gives taxpayers' money to selected artists while denying it to others. Every one of those payments is a judgment call of what these bureaucrats think should be funded. And the people who get funded are the pals of those giving out the money.

Who is playing favorites?

The people in the National Endowment for the Arts. The way all of these grants proceed in government is that these people get on commissions and reviewing boards and they recommend each other.

If funds were stopped, art programs for latchkey kids, poetry clubs and fine arts exhibits would be cut. What do you have against those projects?

Whether these are worthy projects is a matter of somebody's opinion. Why didn't they give a grant to have a statue of Rocky on the steps of the museum in Philadelphia? Why don't they give grants to other people who, in my opinion, are worthy? It's a judgment call as to whether they're worthy or not.

Whose judgment?

That's beside the point. I don't think that we should have a federal bureau deciding which art is worthy of funding and which is not. That's the way they do it in communist countries.

How should those decisions about art funding be made?

In the free market. Nobody was giving William Shakespeare a government grant. He went out and sold his plays in the free market, and people liked to go to them. The American people have been extremely generous to the arts. They gave $6.4 billion of private donations to art in 1987. Those artists who can't sell their works in the free market should not come back and say they have a right to spend the taxpayers' money.

Isn't it possible, though, that artists with great potential might never get the training or the backing to develop successfully?

That is simply not true. There are art museums in all cities, usually available free to the poor. The great art of the world has survived and existed without government funding. This NEA only came into existence as part of Lyndon Johnson's spending program. And it has mushroomed since then. We certainly had plenty of fine art available to everybody before 1966.

You have criticized the work of Robert Mapplethorpe, among other artists, as obscene. Isn't that really the reason you oppose NEA funding?

Some of the art that has been funded by the NEA is obscene. Some of it involved child pornography, which is illegal. These things simply prove that the NEA is irresponsible in spending the taxpayers' money.

If the NEA stopped funding sexually or religiously controversial work, would you feel any differently?

When they were doing innocuous things like giving money to symphony orchestras, nobody was making a fuss. But now that they have proven their irresponsibility, they ought to be cut off. It was a bad idea in the first place.

You've mentioned communist countries which impose censorship. What makes your proposals any different from what they are doing?

There's no issue of censorship here. Mapplethorpe can go out and sell his art to the people who like his work. Nobody's locking him up, and nobody is saying that he cannot take pictures or sell them. The issue is whether he can force the taxpayers to pay for it.

You've accused the NEA of funding Mapplethorpe when, in fact, it gave a matching grant for an exhibition in which his work was a small part. Why are you overstating the case?

All that means is that the NEA funded a middleman who turned around and put up the money for Mapplethorpe. That doesn't excuse the NEA from responsibility. If the NEA is so irresponsible that it gives money to obscene art, it ought to be called to account. I don't see how government money can be given out without some type of standards.

Should government set the standards?

If we don't like the government setting standards for art, then the answer is that the government shouldn't be putting money into art at all.

Has this controversy been a boon to groups such as yours by galvanizing people who are offended by sacrilegious or sexually explicit art?

I don't know anybody who has raised money on it, but people have a right to give their money for anything they want. The religious right is not asking for taxpayer funding. It's these obscene artists who are demanding taxpayer funding.

29

Art, the First Amendment, and the NEA Controversy

by Jesse Helms

The most controversial political figure in the NEA controversy, Senator Helms has been vilified by some in the arts community, and praised by the religious right for his efforts to restrict NEA funding for controversial art.

America has been caught up in a struggle between those who support values rooted in Judeo-Christian morality and those who would discard those values in favor of a radical moral "relativism." As Congressman Henry Hyde has said, "the relativism in question is as absolutist and as condescendingly self-righteous as any sixteenth-century [Spanish] inquisitor."

For my part, I have focused on the federal government's role in supporting the moral relativists to the detriment of the religious community. I confess that I was shocked and outraged last year when I learned that the federal government had funded an "artist" who had put a crucifix in a bottle of his urine, photographed it, and gave it the mocking title "Piss Christ." Obviously, he went out of his way to insult the Christian community, which was compounded by the fact that Christian taxpayers had been forced to pay for it.

As one distinguished federal judge wrote in a personal letter to me, when a federally-funded artist creates an anti-Christian piece of so-called art, it is a violation of an important part of the First Amendment which guarantees the right of all religious faiths to be free from governmentally-sanctioned criticism. When the National Endowment for the Arts [NEA] contributes money to an artist for him to use to dip a crucifix in his own urine for public display, it is no different [in terms of church and state entanglement] from a municipality's spending taxpayers' money for putting a crucifix on the top of city hall.

The controversy over Andres Serrano's so-called art had hardly begun when it was disclosed that the NEA also had paid a Pennsylvania gallery to assemble an exhibition of Robert Mapplethorpe photographs which included photos of men engaged in sexual or excretory acts. The exhibit also included photos of nude children. A concerned Borough President in New York City sent me a copy of an NEA-supported publication in New York, *Nueva Luz*, which featured photos of nude children in various poses with nude adults, men with young girls, and young boys with adult women.

All of those "works of art" were offensive to the majority of Americans who are decent, moral people. Moreover, as any student of history knows, such gratuitous insults to the religious and moral sensibilities of fellow citizens lead to an erosion of civil comity and democratic tolerance within a society. Therefore, funding such insults with tax dollars surely is anathema to any pluralistic society.

This was the basis of my offering an amendment to the Interior Appropriations bill to prohibit the NEA from using tax dollars to subsidize or reward "art" which is blasphemous or obscene. Congress unwisely enacted only a severely weakened version of the amendment that does not even prohibit funding for such works as those by Mapplethorpe and Serrano—which created the controversy. Even so, this weakened amendment has been the target of unfounded and often absurd criticisms.

Opponents of the legislation often make the following unfounded and misleading allegations:

1. Restrictions on federal funding for the arts constitutes direct censorship. This is a deliberate attempt to confuse censorship with sponsorship. Such deliberate misrepresentations are intellectually dishonest.

The Constitution gave Congress the responsibility and duty to oversee the expenditure of all federal funds—including funding for the arts. The amendment originally proposed, as well as the one passed, was intended to forbid the federal government from taking money from citizens by force and then using it to subsidize or reward obscene or blasphemous art. The amendment clearly limits the issue to the question of whether the government should use tax funds in the role of a patron (sponsor) for such "art." The legislation in no way "censors" artists; it does not prevent artists from producing, creating, or displaying blasphemous or obscene "art" at their own expense in the private sector.

Therefore, sanctions comparisons between the amendment and communist dictatorships in Eastern Europe fall on their face. In communist countries everything is paid for by the government; therefore, if not approved by the government, it is not produced. Western democracies, on the other hand, rely on the private sector where ideas are left free to compete with minimal or no governmental participation.

Thus, it should be obvious to all that, despite the amendment, American artists who choose to shock and offend the public can still do so—but at their own expense, not the taxpayers'. Censorship is not involved when the government refuses to subsidize such "artists." People who want to scrawl dirty words on the men's-room wall should furnish their own walls and their own crayons. It is tyranny, as Jefferson said in another context, to force taxpayers to support private activities which are by intent abhorrent and repulsive.

The enormous response I have received from throughout the country indicates that the vast majority of Americans support my amendment because they were aghast to learn that their tax money has been used to reward artists who had elected to depict sadomasochism, perverted homoerotic sex acts, and sexual exploitation of children.

2. Subsidizing some art forms but not others (obscene art) constitutes indirect censorship. If this is true—and it isn't—the NEA has been in the censorship business for twenty-five years, which means that the only way to get the government completely out of the "censorship business" is to dismantle the NEA.

By its very nature, the NEA has the duty to establish criteria for funding some art while not funding others. So, those who are crying "censorship" in this regard are ignoring the defect of their own logic (or lack thereof). Do they not see that, following their logic, every applicant denied federal funding can protest that he has been "censored" by the subjective value judgments of the NEA's artistic panels?

3. Is there such a thing as obscene art? The vast majority of taxpayers would first ask themselves whether something is obscene—and if it is, then it's not art. However, some verbose art experts—and the NEA—do just the opposite. Anything they regard as "art" cannot be obscene no matter how revolting, decadent, or repulsive. As NEA's Chairman John Frohnmayer told a California newspaper, "If an [NEA art] panel finds there is serious artistic intent and quality in a particular piece of work, then by definition that is not going to be obscene."

4. Federal funding restrictions must use the obscenity definition outlined by the Supreme Court in Miller v. California. It is important to remember that the Supreme Court has never established an obscenity definition for the purposes of restricting government funding. But Chairman Frohnmayer and the "arts community" erroneously assert that the Constitution requires that the definition in *Miller* v. *California* be used in both restricting federal funding and banning obscenity. However, refusing to subsidize something does not "ban" it. In order to ban obscenity, *Miller* v. *California* requires that government prove that materials (1) appeal to a prurient interest; (2) depict in a patently offensive manner sexual or excretory activities or organs; and (3) lack serious artistic or scientific value.

Numerous cases show that the Court does not apply the same standards to government's refusal to fund First Amendment activities as it does to the government's effort to ban such activities.

For example, in *Maher* v. *Roe,* the Court stated that merely because one has a Constitutional right to engage in an activity, he or she does not have a Constitutional right to Federal funding of that activity. As long ago as 1942, in *Wickard* v. *Filburn,* the Court stated that, "It is hardly lack of due process for the Government to regulate that which it subsidizes." And recently as 1983, in *Regan* v. *Taxation with Representation,* a unanimous Court reiterated a litany of cases holding that restriction on the use of taxpayers' funds, in the area of expressive speech, does not violate the First Amendment and need not meet the same strict standards of scrutiny.

Thus, it is unlikely that the Supreme Court would require Congress to use [the] *Miller* test in its entirety in order to prohibit the NEA from funding obscenity. In fact, I believe the Court would uphold a Congressional prohibition on funding for any patently offensive depictions or descriptions of sexual or excretory activities or organs regardless of the presence or absence of artistic merit.

It would be interesting if Congress should decide to adopt the *Miller* standard in its entirety because *Miller* allowed a jury of ordinary citizens to decide if something is or is not obscene. The 1989 amendment approved by Congress on the other hand, effectively grants the NEA and its elitist arts panels sole authority to decide what is or is not obscene for purposes of government funding.

Thus, the legal effect of the current law is to prohibit nothing. The NEA can cloak even the most patently offensive depictions of sexual or excretory conduct with "artistic merit" simply by deciding to fund the work, thereby making it legally non-obscene. This was precisely what the current amendment's drafters intended since they wanted to deceive the public into assuming that federal funding for obscenity had been prohibited—when, as a legal matter, it has not. Since last fall, Chairman Frohnmayer has asserted that he would and could fund the Mapplethorpe exhibit under the language passed by Congress.

5. The original Helms amendment is not enforceable. This is nonsense, and those who say that know that it's nonsense. There was nothing vague about it—and the Federal Communications Commission is having no problem making the determination that various broadcasts are indecent and/or obscene. The Postal Service is able to do the same thing concerning obscene or indecent mail. The Justice Department's National Obscenity Task Force has been able to determine what is obscene under the federal criminal statutes.

If the FCC, the Postal Service, and the National Obscenity Task Force can handle their responsibilities in this regard, why cannot the NEA do likewise?

6. The amendment chills artistic expression. The "arts community" is fond of asserting that prohibiting NEA funding of obscene art will either "destroy art in America" or, at best, "lead to art which is bland." On the other hand, they also argue that the NEA has funded only about twenty controversial works out of 85,000 grants over the last twenty-five years. (This, by the way, is statistical manipulation, but that's an argument for another day.)

The point is this: The "arts community" cannot have it both ways. Either the NEA is funding so many controversial works that eliminating such funding will devastate the arts community—or the NEA has funded so few (twenty in twenty-five years) that an obscenity restriction could have no more than a negligible impact.

My response to the first argument is that if art in America is so dependent on obscenity in order to be creative and different, then Congress has a duty to the taxpayers to shut the NEA down completely, thereby slowing America's slide into the sewer. My answer to the second argument is that if so few offensive works have indeed been subsidized by the NEA, why all the fuss from the "arts community"?

In summary, the National Endowment for the Arts has always had the responsibility and the duty to decide what is and is not suitable for federal funding of the arts—and that has been precisely the problem. The NEA has defaulted upon that responsibility. It has been insulated from mainstream American values so long that it has become captive to a morally decadent minority which delights in ridiculing the values and beliefs of decent, moral taxpayers.

It should therefore be evident that as long as the NEA is given the sole authority to decide what is artistic—and thus not obscene—the agency intends to continue to fund obscenity under the pretense that it is "art"—even when the taxpayers disagree. Congress, as a minimum, should use the entire *Miller* test by allowing a panel of lay citizens—and not the self-appointed elitists at the NEA—to decide whether patently offensive works merit taxpayer funding.

Or Congress could just adopt my original amendment, and let the "arts community" continue to howl.

Perspectives

"We can de-fund the poisoners of culture, the polluters of art; we can sweep the debris that passes for modern [art] outside so many public buildings; we can discredit self-anointed critics who have forfeited our trust. . . . This is all-important: Not simply to cut out the rot, but to seek out, to find, to celebrate the good, the true, the beautiful. But, first, tell Jesse to hold the fort; help is on the way." Patrick Buchanan (*Washington Times,* August 2, 1989)

"In our free country, artists have a right to produce whatever works they wish. They have no right to produce it at the taxpayers' expense." James J. Kilpatrick (Universal Press Syndicate, *Charlotte Observer,* August 2, 1989)

"If a democratic society cannot find a way to protect a taxpaying Christian heterosexual from finding that he is engaged in subsidizing blasphemous acts of homoeroticism, then democracy simply isn't working. Senator Helms is doing the wholesome thing, weighed in political as well as aesthetic terms." William F. Buckley, Jr. (Universal Press Syndicate, *Greensboro Daily News & Record,* August 2, 1989)

30

To the Congress of the United States

from Pat Robertson

In the June 20, 1990, issue of the Washington Post, *Pat Robertson, as president of the Christian Coalition, published a full-page ad, a public letter, explaining his position on the NEA controversy.*

Ladies and Gentlemen:

You are being asked to appropriate funds taken from the American taxpayers in order to continue the National Endowment for the Arts.

In recent years the NEA has used funds provided by you to pay for exhibitions of paintings and photographs depicting:

- Two naked men engaged in anal intercourse
- Little children with exposed genitals
- One man urinating in the mouth of another
- Jesus Christ immersed in a jar of urine
- The Roman Catholic Pontiff immersed in a vat of urine
- Jesus Christ shooting heroin into his arm

This November you will face an electorate:

- Furious at being forced by you to pay for the greed of savings and loan manipulators
- Disgusted with your handling of your pay raise
- Shocked at the revelation that you have been looting the Social Security Trust Fund for years
- Discouraged at your inability to balance the federal budget

Do you also want to face the voters with the charge that you are wasting their hard-earned money to promote sodomy, child pornography, and attacks on Jesus Christ?

You could choose to fund the NEA while refusing public funding for obscenity and attacks on religion. But the radical left wants you to give legitimacy to pornography and homosexuality. So you are being asked to vote like sheep for $175,000,000 with no strings attached.

Of course, when you vote, you may not have any risk.

We may not be able to give out 100,000 copies of the Mapplethorpe and Serrano "art" to registered voters in your district.

There may be more homosexuals and pedophiles in your district than there are Roman Catholics and Baptists. You may find that the working folks in your district want you to use their money to teach their sons how to sodomize one another. You may find that the Roman Catholics in your district want their money spent on pictures of the Pope soaked in urine.

But maybe not.

There is one way to find out.

Vote for the NEA appropriation just like Pat Williams, John Frohnmayer, and the gay and lesbian task force want.

And make my day.

Sincerely,

/signed/ Pat Robertson
President, Christian Coalition

Resolution No. 4

On Government Support of Obscene and Offensive Art*

Whereas, God has ordained government to do good work; and

Whereas, Southern Baptists have historically supported the constitutional rights of free speech and have opposed undue censorship; and

Whereas, Regulation of government funding of art, or certain types of expression claimed to be art, is not censorship of the arts; and

Whereas, The Supreme Court recently stated in *Rust* v. *Sullivan* that government may regulate expressive activity to conform to public policy as a condition for obtaining public funding; and

Whereas, The National Endowment for the Arts (NEA) has, increasingly in recent years, demonstrated a pattern of support for obscene, offensive, morally repugnant, and sacrilegeous "art"; and

Whereas, The Chairman of the NEA [Frohnmayer], who is appointed by the President, has demonstrated a clear lack of sensitivity to the concerns of evangelical Christians and others regarding the funding abuses of the NEA; and

Whereas, Last year, despite pleas from evangelical Christians and others, Congress and the President failed to support legislation which would have placed meaningful restrictions on what the NEA is permitted to fund but instead adopted an ineffectual standard calling for "general standards of decency"; and

Whereas, Since last year's ineffectual action by Congress, additional homoerotic, pornographic, and sacrilegeous "art" has been funded by the NEA with the explicit approval of its Chairman; and

Whereas, Some members of Congress and the President continue to oppose content restrictions on NEA funding.

Therefore be it Resolved, That we the messengers to the Southern Baptist Convention meeting in Atlanta, Georgia, June 4–6, 1991, recognizing the influence which the NEA has on our culture, deplore the lack of initiative by the President and Congress in addressing the continuing abuses of the NEA; and

Be it further Resolved, That we urge the President to act immediately to remove the current Chairman of the NEA and replace him with an individual who will stop funding obscene, offensive, morally repugnant, and sacriligious "art"; and

Be it finally Resolved, That we call on Congress and the President to set standards which will prevent the funding of obscene, offensive, morally repugnant, and sacriligious "art," or, if that is not done, to cease funding the National Endowment for the Arts.

*From *Christian Life Commission,* October 31, 1991, reprinted in *Congressional Record* (vol. 137, no. 159, October 31, 1991).

31

An Open Letter to Congress
from Emergency Committee for the Arts

We, the undersigned, believe very strongly and very positively in the National Endowment for the Arts.

We are Americans from many walks of life, from across the broad political spectrum, from across our nation.

What brings us together is that we share, with millions of our fellow citizens, an appreciation for the important role of the arts in American life.

Children's dance workshops; local, regional and nationally-acclaimed painters and sculptors; community theaters; ballet troupes; musicians ranging from the folk to the symphonic—all contribute something very special.

Over the past quarter century, the National Endowment for the Arts has been the catalyst that has put art within the reach of so many Americans. It has provided all manner of artists with small amounts of seed money, in most cases, that have been enhanced by the contributions of state and local governments and, most important, by the private sector, corporations as well as individuals.

For over twenty-five years and 80,000 separate projects, the National Endowment for the Arts has flourished. And it is unfortunate that, recently, the NEA has become a subject of political controversy. Misrepresentation and misunderstanding threaten its integrity, perhaps even its survival.

At a time when countries around the world are moving toward greater political and cultural freedom—and when playwrights, poets and painters, musicians and dancers are assuming positions of greater status in their societies—Americans should dedicate themselves to even greater support for our artists and for those institutions, both public and private, that encourage artistic expression.

As the National Endowment for the Arts celebrates its twenty-fifth anniversary, we urge the Congress to safeguard what has evolved from a national resource to a national treasure.

H. Brewster Atwater, Jr.	Michael D. Eisner
Winton Blount	Lawrence A. Fleischman
Derek C. Bok	Betty Ford
John Bryan	Stanley M. Freehling
Anne Cox Chambers	Dr. Hanna Holborn Gray
William T. Coleman, Jr.	Vartan Gregorian
Walter Cronkite	Andrew Heiskell
C. Douglas Dillon	Rev. Theodore Hesburgh

Vernon E. Jordan
Arthur Levitt, Jr.
John L. Loeb
Kenneth A. Macke
Robert H. Malott
V. Rev. Val A. McInnes
Paul Mellon
Dominique de Menil
J. Irwin Miller
Raymond D. Nasher
Frederick M. Nicholas
Michael Ovitz

William S. Paley
Joseph Pulitzer, Jr.
S. Dillon Ripley
David Rockefeller
Leonard L. Silverstein
Dr. Frank Stanton
S. Frederick Starr
Saul Steinberg
Robert S. Strauss
Arthur Ochs Sulzberger
Phillip Von Blon
John Young

Here's What Some U.S. Presidents Had to Say During Their Terms of Office

George Bush: "I don't know of anybody in the Government or any Government agency that should be set up to censor what you write or what you paint or how you express yourselves."

Ronald Reagan: "Artists stretch the limits of understanding. They expand ideas that are sometimes unpopular. In an atmosphere of liberty, artists and patrons are free to think the unthinkable and create the audacious. They are free to make both horrendous mistakes and generous celebrations. Where there's liberty, art succeeds. In societies that are not free, art dies."

Jimmy Carter: "More effectively than weapons, more effectively than diplomacy, the arts can communicate, people to people, the spirit of America, the spirit of a diverse and proud people."

Gerald Ford: "I firmly believe that, in order to inspire the people's pride in the Government, we must provide them with manifest evidence of its vitality, creativity and efficiency by setting the highest standards in architectural design, environmental planning and visual communication."

Richard Nixon: "The highest expression of the quality of a nation is found in the development of its arts and refinement of its humanistic concerns. For this development to reach its full potential, it must be the expression of a whole people, and it must be available for the enjoyment of the whole world."

Lyndon B. Johnson: "We can maintain and strengthen an atmosphere to permit the arts to flourish, and those who have talent to use it, and we can seek to enlarge the access of all our people to artistic creation."

32

At Issue
Should Congress Restrict
the Types of Art That
Can Be Funded by the NEA?

> None of the funds authorized to be appropriated pursuant to this Act may be used to promote, disseminate or produce (1) obscene or indecent materials including, but not limited to, depictions of sadomasochism, homoeroticism, the exploitation of children, or individuals engaged in sex acts; or (2) material which denigrates the objects or beliefs of the adherents of a particular religion or non-religion; or (3) material which denigrates, debases or reviles a person, group or class of citizens on the basis of race, creed, sex, handicap, age or national origin.
>
> —Helms amendment for NEA funding

YES says Sen. Jesse Helms, R–N.C. (speech on the floor of the Senate, July 26, 1989):

I have fundamental questions about why the federal government is involved in supporting artists the taxpayers have refused to support in the marketplace. My concern in this regard is heightened when I hear the arts community and the media saying that any restriction at all on federal funding would amount to censorship. What they seem to be saying is that we in Congress must choose between: First, absolutely no federal presence in the arts; or second, granting artists the absolute freedom to use tax dollars as they wish, regardless of how vulgar, blasphemous, or despicable their works may be.

If we indeed must make this choice, then the federal government should get out of the arts. However, I do not believe we are limited to those two choices and my amendment [restricting funding for some types of art] attempts to make a compromise between them. It simply provides for some common sense restrictions on what is and is not an appropriate use of federal funding for the arts. It does not prevent the production or creation of vulgar works, it merely prevents the use of federal funds to support them. . . .

There is a fundamental difference between government censorship—the preemption of publication or production—and governmental refusal to pay for such publication and production. Artists have a right, it is said, to express their feelings as they wish: only a Philistine would suggest otherwise. Fair enough, but no artist has a preemptive claim on the tax dollars of the American people; time for them, as President Reagan used to say, "to go out and test the magic of the marketplace." . . .

At a minimum, we need to prohibit the Endowment from using federal funds to fund filthy works like Mr. [Andres] Serrano's and Mr. [Robert] Mapplethorpe's [photographs]. If it does not violate criminal statutes and the private sector is willing to pay for it, fine! However, if federal funds are used, then Congress needs to ensure the sensitivities of all groups—regardless of race, creed, sex, national origin, handicap, or age—are respected.

Federal funding for sadomasochism, homoeroticism, and child pornography is an insult to taxpayers. Americans for the most part are moral, decent people and they have a right not be be denigrated, offended, or mocked with their own tax dollars.

o   o   o

NO says Wayne Lawson, executive director of the Ohio Arts Council (testimony before the House Education and Labor Subcommittee on Postsecondary Education, March 21, 1990):

Congress in 1965 understood that federal control of artistic content would stifle the arts and defeat the purposes for which the Arts Endowment was established. What was understood then is also true today.

The fact is that the National Endowment for the Arts and its grantees—among which we count the nation's great art institutions—fund art on the basis of quality. Each grant application submitted to the Endowment is put to the test of review by a panel of citizens from all over the country. When grants are matched at the local level with private dollars, citizens are again involved in the process of bringing that artistic expression to their community.

If the Arts Endowment finds itself forced to restrain from entertaining applications to support the broadest possible artistic expression, and artists restrain themselves from proposing work that is risky or provocative, public support for the arts would become no more than a source of dollars available only to the most broadly acceptable.

The only federal grantees would be an establishment of official artists and official arts organizations. What is truly American in our system of support for the arts would thereby be destroyed with a resulting centralized governmental ministry of culture replacing our essentially democratic citizen-driven system. . . . Only safe art will be funded, and stimulating, challenging work will be left out.

It is a problem that when art offers us the full range of views of the world— the world in all its diversity and the world as it can be imagined—we sometimes condemn those views we don't already like, rather than explore and learn from those views different from ours. The test of democracy is not that the majority gets its way, but that the minority's free access to the full choice of ideas is protected along with its ability to express those ideas. The government's role should be to support all voices, controversial or not. . . .

By supporting the risk-takers as well as the generally popular, the NEA provides to the American people the opportunity to choose in ways that reflect our needs, concerns, and vision as a nation, and fulfills government's responsibility to all its people, majority and minority alike.

33

Newsweek Interview
John Frohnmayer on Tough Times at NEA

Conducted by Daniel Glick

Under attack from the religious right, Frohnmayer found himself a political pawn sacrificed when the pressure became too great for the Bush administration to endure. During a nonelection year, Frohnmayer may have served out his term, albeit under a cloud of continued controversy; however, 1992 being an election year, Frohnmayer had no chance and few friends in the administration, and was told to turn in his resignation.

Newsweek: Were you in fact fired?

John Frohnmayer: In essence, I was. I had indicated a desire to leave, but they handed me my hat before I could. I told the president in October that I had a desire to return to private life. In January, I told him I had delayed that somewhat. I got called in on Feb. 20 and was told I needed to announce my resignation the next day.

How do you feel now? Betrayed?

One of my primary feelings was relief, because this job has been unrelentingly difficult.

Both sides of the fence have criticized your management style as inconsistent. From the left, the so-called loyalty oath was an issue. From the right, your defending of Poison [a film about homosexual life] was considered indefensible.

I said from the beginning that I believed the Helms amendment of 1989 [which forbade the use of NEA grants to make "obscene" art] was unconstitutional. My conscious decision was to hang a light on it, to put it in the conditions [of a grant]. I got battered for the "loyalty oath," as Joe Papp called it, but the result was that it was declared unconstitutional and we were done with it. And I defended *Poison* because it was a quality work of art. I don't think I have ever been in a position where I did not defend a quality work of art.

The NEA enabling legislation says that it should not be subject to political pressures. Have the arts finally become too politicized?

[What] has gone wrong [are] the politicians who demand that the only art that be funded is that which will not offend a mainstream person. That perspective turns our whole system upside down. The First Amendment protects the speaker, not the listener. It protects the right to articulate an idea which may be offensive to some. And if we are going to fund the arts, we've got to be able to deal with ideas that are not mainstream. Otherwise, the funding of art is going to be elevator music, Pablum™. So for those who claim it's not a First Amendment issue—it goes to the very soul of what this country is, being able to accommodate differences and live with them.

The government doesn't sponsor the ideas of any of the artists that we fund; it is merely the enabler that allows these things to happen. The analogy is that the government is the provider of the Hyde Park soapbox, and the artist is the provider of the ideas. The ideas can be in the whole spectrum of beliefs and values that are encompassed in the American people. But to hear some of our critics, you'd think there is a unified American value that somehow everybody can sign on to. That's not the case.

How much "guidance" did the White House give you at the NEA? Did you get "We've got to stop these kinds of grants"?

I think that the White House's impression of how you deal with the arts endowment is "Just make it noncontroversial." That doesn't have a whole lot of relation to reality, because the arts deal with controversy. Bizet was booed out of the opera house; the impressionists were thought to be wild animals in late-nineteenth-century France. To suggest the arts should be noncontroversial is to fundamentally misunderstand the nature of the beast.

What do you feel were your major mistakes?

Well, I made one right out of the box. I suspended a grant for Artist's Space, but I corrected that and reversed myself. We didn't broaden the base of support for the arts [quickly enough]. What ultimately got us reauthorization [in 1990] was not just the arts world but the AFL-CIO, the American Conference of Mayors, education people, chambers of commerce. We [also] just got drubbed by the fundamentalist religious community in their persuading lots of good, thinking people that what was going on was blasphemy. They pointed to Serrano's "Piss Christ," and David Wojnarowicz's image of Christ with a crown of thorns and a needle in his arm. Mainline theologians didn't say, "Wait a minute. Both images could be consistent with Christian theology," namely, taking on the sins of the world by Christ and the terrible degradation to the son of God that mankind did. Yet mainline religion hasn't come into the debate in any significant way. What fundamentalists call blasphemy may have been the artist's intent to make a statement on faith, or at least of faith in doubt.

There will be calls to restrict—or even abolish—the NEA. Do you fear the NEA is doomed?

It could happen. But my belief is that it is a very small minority of our populace that is making this noise about being offended . . . Unless [good] people will say they won't be intimidated by this kind of cultural terrorism, then I think the endowment is threatened. There is [also] a responsibility on the part of the artist to articulate to the public what the artist is trying to do.

What are your plans?

I would like very much to run a private foundation which deals with the arts. I hope to continue to speak about the importance of arts for education, for the good of the country. I really wouldn't have traded my time here. It was not fun, but for being at the vortex of an issue I care deeply about, I couldn't have found any place like it.

Let's Stop Playing Politics with Support of the Arts
USA Today Editorial (extract)*

. . . Any arts chairman has to skate between extremes—a blue-nose fringe that objects to any sexually explicit art and a libertine wing that sees censorship in any consideration of public taste.

Tilt one way, and the most daring artists are squelched. Tilt the other way and public anger kills art funding entirely.

The endowment shouldn't be allowed to fall into hands that would strangle its most vital mission—bringing to the public works of artistic merit that might not otherwise be widely seen. Some of those are bound to be controversial.

They should be. Inspiring debate is part of art's function. Nothing can be set off-limits for funding simply because some consider the subject matter or the artist's lifestyle offensive. . . . The new NEA chairman shouldn't shrink from funding exhibits just because they're troubling. For artistic vision to grow, popular taste needs to be challenged.

*February 24, 1992.

34

Dark Days
"Artists as Enemies, Ideas as Demons"

by George Beahm

> I leave with the belief that this eclipse of the soul will soon pass and with it
> the lunacy that sees artists as enemies and ideas as demons.
>
> JOHN FROHNMAYER, parting comments to his staff,
> *Washington Post,* February 22, 1992

On May 6, 1992, the *Washington Post* ran a front-page story headlined "Acting Arts Chief to Steer Cautious Course: Endowment's Anne-Imelda Radice Seen Reversing Frohnmayer." The story by Kim Masters, who has been covering the NEA controversy since its inception, made it clear that Radice would be the "decency czar" that Frohnmayer was not. As Radice told the *Post:*

> If we find a proposal that does not have the widest audience . . . even though it may have been done very sincerely and with the highest intentions, we just can't afford to fund that. . . . The concerns of the taxpayers, the concerns of the Congress . . . have as much weight [as artistic merit].

Racide's disinclination to fund controversial works like Mapplethorpe's homoerotic photographs and "Wild Thing" (a poem published in a literary journal, *Queer City*), was a radical shift from her predecessor's position and outraged some in the arts community. The *Post* quoted Charlotte Murphy of the National Association of Artists Organizations: "Clearly, she is sacrificing challenging work, the First Amendment and the future of the arts to supposedly save the endowment."

Although Radice's position regarding controversial art aligns the NEA with the expressed interests of the administration, it is not reflected in the NEA's budget; in fact, as Elizabeth Kastor of the *Washington Post* points out, the proposed budget for 1993 will remain fixed at its 1991–92 level of $177 million. Meanwhile, other federal art-related agencies will see their budgets expanded by up to 10 percent.

The *Post* quoted Melanne Verveer, executive vice president of People for the American Way:

This comes at a time when the arts are really facing severe constraints in serving the public. There are museums closing early. There are dark days. The administration should be sending a clear signal that it recognizes the importance of the arts both in serving the nation's spirit and in serving the economy.

NEA detractors—especially Rev. Donald Wildmon's American Family Association—would simply prefer to see the NEA shut down permanently. As Wildmon's son Tim elaborated: "We don't have a National Endowment for the Rodeo or a National Endowment for Scuba Divers. We think artists can make it fine on their own."

Others, however, feel the NEA has on the whole been a responsible steward of federal funds while promoting the arts in general, as *Newsweek's* Peter Plagens pointed out:

. . . [T]he censors are wrong to regard the NEA's minuscule budget (less than that for the country's military bands) as a gravy train for undeserving bohemians. If Americans could choose where their tax money went, the endowment would probably be a lot richer than it is.

As far as the arts community at large was concerned, the clock had struck thirteen o'clock—it was Orwell time, it opined.

Subsequent events underscored the arts community's concerns. Predictably (and sadly), Radice vetoed funding for several controversial exhibits, which generated a storm of controversy from the arts community. To protest Radice's rubber-stamping of the administration's art views, some NEA-funded organizations refused to accept their funding; others sued; and some members of the NEA's arts panels, tasked to recommend projects for approval, resigned in protest.

The message was clear: If it offends, it's not what the NEA will fund.

Or as Alice in *Alice's Adventures in Wonderland* observed: " 'Curiouser and curiouser!' "

President Clinton, succeeding President Bush, is expected to name Anne-Imelda Radice's successor in the spring of 1993. Just as Radice was a controversial figure in the arts community, her successor is likely to be just as controversial—this time, among conservatives, especially the religious right.

Put simply: the pendulum has swung the other way.

35

Robert Mapplethorpe: Persona Obscura

by George Beahm

I ask you: Which portrait of Robert Mapplethorpe was the *real* man behind the work? The angelic, admittedly feminine portrait published in the *Current Biography Yearbook 1989*, or the cheeky photo—a self-portrait—of a man with a bullwhip handle inserted up his rectum?

Both, it seems, were Mapplethorpe, comfortable in his duality. "My work is about seeing—seeing things like they haven't been seen before," he told an interviewer in 1986. To Mapplethorpe this meant showing the world in all its beauty—stylized portraits, figure studies, and photographs of flowers—and its darker side: homoerotic lifestyles with their sadomasochistic culture, which most people tend to ignore or condemn outright. As he told Dominick Dunne, "For me S & M means sex and magic, not sadomasochism."

The portraits, the figure studies, and still-life studies of flowers were what the arts community expected; the stylized portraits of the S & M subculture and its ties to homoeroticism were not. As *Current Biography Yearbook 1989* explained:

> When his graphic photographs of the homosexual S & M scene first appeared publicly in 1977 at the art gallery the Kitchen, they turned the art world upside down, destroying previous notions of what subject matter was considered permissible in photography and redefining the traditional concept of beauty.

Mapplethorpe, who died of AIDS-related complications on March 9, 1989, was by no means a persona obscura. The world at large beheld Mapplethorpe burst onto the scene with the retrospective exhibit "Robert Mapplethorpe: The Perfect Moment"; however, within the arts community, Mapplethorpe was well-known, as *Current Biography Yearbook 1989* points out:

> Mapplethorpe's photographs have appeared in one-person exhibitions at, among other institutions, the Corcoran Gallery of Art in Washington, D.C. (1978), the Musee National d'Art Moderne, Paris (1983), the Stedelijk Museum,

Amsterdam (1988), and the National Portrait Gallery, London (1988). His work is included in the permanent collections of the Museum of Fine Arts, Houston; the Hara Museum of Fine Arts, Houston; the Hara Museum of Contemporary Art, Tokyo; the Corcoran Gallery in Washington, D.C.; the Boston Museum of Fine Arts; the Stedelijk Museum, Amsterdam; the Victoria and Albert Museum, London; and the Australian National Gallery, Canberra.

According to Mapplethorpe Foundation President Michael Stout, quoted by the *Washington Post,* Mapplethorpe's photographs are highly collectible. "Some of Robert's pictures sell for sixty, eighty, one hundred thousand dollars. But basically the bulk of his work was black-and-white silver gelatin prints, which are certainly in the twelve- to twenty-five-thousand-dollar range. And people do buy Mapplethorpe."

A philanthropist, Mapplethorpe established a year before his untimely death a foundation in his name with the purpose of "establishing, improving or expanding museums that exhibit photographic art, as well as funding efforts to end the AIDS epidemic," according to *Washington Post*'s Todd Allan Yasui.

Ironically, Mapplethorpe never lived to see "Robert Mapplethorpe: The Perfect Moment"—a major retrospective of 175 pieces—exhibited nationwide without major incident in such cities as Philadelphia, Chicago, Berkeley, Hartford, and Boston. A further irony: the Corcoran Gallery in Washington, D.C., which featured a one-man show of his work in 1978, canceled Mapplethorpe's retrospective exhibit because of concerns that it would affect its federal funding. A harbinger of things to come, the controversy surrounding the Corcoran cancellation of the exhibit was dwarfed by the controversy that surrounded it in Cincinnati, when the Contemporary Arts Center and its director Dennis Barrie were indicted on obscenity charges.

On September 28, 1990, the trial opened and prosecutor Frank Prouty explained, "The pictures are the state's case." Central to the case was the question, "Is it art?"

On October 5, 1990, after a mere two hours of deliberation, the jury acquitted a vindicated Barrie. As juror James Jones told the *Cincinnati Inquirer,* "The pictures were not pretty. No doubt about it. But as it was brought up in the trial, to be art it doesn't have to be pretty."

Dennis Barrie, curator of the museum, visibly relieved at the verdict, concluded that "Robert Mapplethorpe was a great artist. It was a tremendous show. We should have never been here in court. . . . But I'm glad the system does work."

The Reverend Donald Wildmon, founder of the American Family Association, felt differently and told the Associated Press, "This is not a landmark, Pearl Harbor decision. This was just another obscenity trial."

Wildmon simply didn't get it. Far from being just another obscenity trial, as he summarily dismissed the landmark case, Barrie's stand in Cincinnati was proof positive that its citizenry understood the dangers of censorship.

When the show later exhibited in Boston in August 1990, the *Washington Post* reported that "a lone protester was surrounded and drowned out by hundreds of supporters asserting free speech and denouncing censorship." As Ed Boyce of Boston told the *Washington Post,* "Those who would like to shut the exhibit down are homophobes and bigots. If they can stop a piece of art, there's no limit to what can be suppressed."

Bound to Please: *Mapplethorpe*

An offering as one of its "Beautiful Books & Unusual Gifts: The Best of 1992," Book-of-the-Month Club is offering *Mapplethorpe:* "A startling retrospective of the controversial photographer's work, ranging from breathtaking photographs of flowers and dynamic portraits to the provocative sadomasochistic and nude images that have made Robert Mapplethorpe a *cause célèbre.*"

An edition comprising 280 duotone photos, *Mapplethorpe* is, as BOMC suggests, bound to please.

36

Cincinnati: City Under Siege

by Marcia Pally

Museums have long been considered cultural treasures, celebrating the diversity of art—sacred or profane. In Cincinnati the limits of art became a burning issue in 1990 when the Contemporary Arts Center museum director Dennis Barrie was indicted on obscenity charges for exhibiting photographer Robert Mapplethorpe's exhibit, "The Perfect Moment."

Dennis Barrie, museum director and specialist in American art, was invited this past spring to lead a cultural delegation to Kharkov in the Ukraine, U.S.S.R. He was asked to arrange cultural exchanges between the United States and the Soviet Union, and to speak on the development and function of the arts in a free society. But as the former Iron Curtain countries were turning toward freedom, Barrie had to cancel his trip because he was facing a prison term for a museum exhibit in Cincinnati.

At 2:30 P.M., April 7, the police closed the doors of Cincinnati's Contemporary Arts Center, charging the museum and Barrie, its director, with pandering obscenity and the misuse of a minor in photography. The offending works were seven photographs by Robert Mapplethorpe included in a 175-piece retrospective of the artist's work, titled *Robert Mapplethorpe: The Perfect Moment*. If convicted, Barrie faces fines and a stay in jail. H. Louis Sirkin, Barrie's lawyer, can't remember another instance when the cops have busted a museum: "It's a protected place, like libraries and universities, for research or artistic purposes."

Two of the contested photographs are portraits of children, one of a boy in the nude and the other a girl with her skirt askew (each taken with the permission of the child's parents). The now 19-year-old boy, Jesse McBride, says his mother "was friends with Robert . . . I would run around naked a lot at that age. I'd stop and he'd snap a shot. . . . It never occurred to me that it would be a big deal." *New York Times* columnist Andy Grundberg called the girl's photo "guileless and charming." Five other photos, from Mapplethorpe's *X Portfolio*, depict explicit, consensual, adult homosexual acts, more clinical than erotic.

The remainder of the exhibit—on an otherwise uneventful tour from Philadelphia, Hartford, Chicago, and Berkeley, California, and on its way to Boston—is comprised of adult portraits and, one of Mapplethorpe's favorite subjects, flowers.

Throwing more than 400 visitors out of the Contemporary Arts Center (C.A.C.), the police spent the next hour videotaping the exhibit as evidence for the prosecution. Some 1,500 people gathered outside to protest. Among them were Donald and Carol Balleison of Louisville, Kentucky, who had come to Cincinnati to celebrate their 30th wedding anniversary. The city seemed a natural choice, with its impressive orchestra and ballet, conservatory and museums. The Balleisons planned to eat at the city's five-star restaurant and take in a few exhibits.

Instead they came across the police raid, which Carolyn said, reminded her of "Germany 1932." Apparently, several of the protesters shared Mrs. Balleison's observation. Pressed against the C.A.C. door, the crowd shouted continuously for nearly two hours, making the Nazi salute to emphasize the analogy and chanting, "Not the church, not the state, we decide what art is great" and, more cynically, "Let's go burn the library," "Maybe Khomeini should come to Cincinnati," and finally, "CincinNazi."

A man standing next to Mrs. Balleison told her that the Ku Klux Klan had marched in nearby Oxford, Ohio, that morning, and wondered what the police were doing here. When the C.A.C. doors reopened at 4:10 P.M., the crowd broke into the national anthem.

"At least they didn't padlock the museum or confiscate the pictures," said Barrie. "We knew a grand jury had been through in the morning when the exhibit opened, and we knew vice was coming. We knew when they left the courthouse, when they stopped for lunch. We had no idea what they would do and all we could do is wait.

"Let me tell you, no matter what anyone says, the thought of going to jail is terribly frightening when it's you who's actually going." Barrie is a steady, soft-spoken man with elegantly clipped white hair and beard. Baronial in his well-cut suits and fashionable suspenders, he does not go in for roughhousing. "I'm a museum curator," he said. "I did not want to be taken out in handcuffs." A skirmish erupted briefly when the police tried to prevent a radio reporter from moving through the crowd. No one was hurt.

While more than 80,000 people visited *The Perfect Moment* during its seven-week run and museum membership is up 80 percent, the C.A.C. stands to lose considerable sums over the Mapplethorpe show. No public moneys were used to sponsor the exhibit, and last March the C.A.C. withdrew from Cincinnati's annual Fine Arts Fund, which raises money for more than half a dozen local cultural institutions. Barrie feared that the inclusion of the suddenly controversial C.A.C. would hamper the fund's ability to raise support for other beneficiaries.

A native of Cleveland, Barrie considers himself an "informed liberal person, not in the radical class by any means," whose greatest moment of controversy prior to the Mapplethorpe exhibit was the installation of a bicentennial sculpture featuring four pigs—in honor of Cincinnati's past as the meat-packing capital of America—that offended a few citizens who wanted a "classier image,"

Barrie said. Barrie holds a doctorate in American cultural history from Wayne State University in Michigan and a master's degree from Ohio's Oberlin College. Before his position at the C.A.C., he worked with the Archives of American Art for the Smithsonian Institution, first in Washington, D.C., and then as Midwest area director in Detroit, where he met his wife Diane. They have two sons, Ian, eleven, and Kevin, eight.

Barrie booked *The Perfect Moment* in late 1988, before the Corcoran Gallery in Washington, D.C., canceled its Mapplethorpe exhibition, fearing loss of its National Endowment for the Arts grant. And before Senator Jesse Helms tried to ban N.E.A. funding for any work that offends "the adherents of a particular religion or nonreligion," as the Helms bill specified.

"As soon as the Helms uproar started," Barrie said, "I knew we'd have a rocky ride in Cincinnati—letters to the editor and the like. But I didn't expect a coordinated onslaught against the institution. And I never thought I'd end up in a court of law."

Never a boomtown, Cincinnati made its money in the last century with salt-of-the-earth industries—food processing, machine tools, rails—and grew steadily, attracting conservative spenders of German stock to its current population of 1.4 million. Unlike many American cities, it has no single large ghetto. Working-class neighborhoods make their way between quaint middle-class clapboards and the impressive mansions of the corporate elite. Cincinnati's top businesses today include General Electric and Procter & Gamble. Executives of the latter, and of Peat Marwick Corporation, remained on the C.A.C. board during the Mapplethorpe fracas, but "it's understood," said Barrie, "that other companies should no longer be approached."

Cincinnati was also home to Charles Keating, who 30 years ago began his campaign against "indecency." After successfully prosecuting a candy-store owner for selling adult magazines, Keating founded Citizens for Decent Literature, which later became Citizens for Decency Through Law. Keating is now under investigation for the billions of taxpayers' dollars required to bail out his Lincoln Savings and Loan depositors. It appears that while Keating was crusading against what he termed indecency, he was quietly making millions of dollars in S & L investments.

Keating is not Cincinnati's only crusader. This March, before the Mapplethorpe exhibit had even hit town, a newer local group called Citizens for Community Values (C.C.V.) began agitating against his work.

C.C.V. was founded in 1983 by Dr. Jerry Kirk, director of the National Coalition Against Pornography, also headquartered in Cincinnati. National Right to Life President John Willke also makes his home in Cincinnati, as do the organizations People United Against Pornography, STOP (Stand Together Opposing Pornography), and the National Coalition on Pornography, which received training from Donald Wildmon's American Family Association. C.C.V. is currently headed by Monty Lobb, Jr., a graduate of Olivet Nazarene University and the

University of Dayton Law School. It was Lobb's father who had approached Kirk about combating "the growing evil of pornography" in Cincinnati.

A March 1990 C.C.V. internal memo recommends applying "peer and financial pressure" to keep Mapplethorpe's photos out of Cincinnati. The group launched a massive letter-writing campaign, sponsored full-page newspaper ads, and urged county prosecutors to close the exhibit by police action.

Opposition to the exhibit escalated, with threats to cut support for the arts—especially from a proposed arts center in the downtown area—and for the Contemporary Arts Center in particular. Special pressure was levied against the Central Trust Company, where C.A.C. Board Chairman Chad Wick was employed, including a disinformation campaign claiming that Central Trust financially backed the Mapplethorpe show. In one of their more inventive moments, opposition groups urged their constituencies to send in Central Trust bank cards cut in two. In mid-March, Wick resigned from the C.A.C. board to take the pressure off Central Trust, though no Central Trust money was used for the Mapplethorpe exhibit.

A recent issue of C.C.V.'s newsletter lists its accomplishments in 1989, among them: persuading Rite Aid Drugs to remove adult magazines such as *Playboy* and *Penthouse* from its 1,400 stores nationwide, developing chapters in eight counties that survey local video stores for adult material, attempting to persuade video-store owners to remove adult tapes voluntarily, assisting in the prosecutions of 20 video-store owners in three states, preventing cable programs with adult programming from entering the Cincinnati area, and initiating a boycott against Bonded and Speedway gas marts for their sale of *Playboy* and *Penthouse*.

The *Cincinnati Post* reported on March 24 that members of the Contemporary Arts Center board who agreed to talk to the press about the opposition's tactics asked to remain anonymous "for fear of economic intimidation against their employers and businesses."

Perhaps unexpectedly, museum directors and art critics across the country have supported the C.A.C. and the Mapplethorpe show. The comment by Martin Friedman, director of Minneapolis's Walker Art Center, that nothing in today's art world "has ever compared to this" is typical. But the response to the controversy by local residents is more telling: In a *Cincinnati Post* poll of Hamilton County, 59 percent of the respondents said that the exhibit should have its day in town. Karen Widder told the *Cincinnati Enquirer*, "This is my hometown; I was born and raised here . . . I don't see what the big deal is." Dayton Merrit of Covington, Kentucky, told the *Cincinnati Post* that he found some of the photos "too personal for public exhibit. But they have a right to be shown. Freedom is what this [exhibit] is all about, and that's what *this* was all about," pointing to his "Vietnam Vet" baseball cap. "That's what I fought for?" Mark Phillips and Richard Rubin of Columbus waited for three hours to see the exhibit and called the photos "great." Estelle Fischer of Pleasant Ridge especially liked the male nudes. Marla Steiner of Dayton called the police action, not the photos, "a personal affront."

Garda Mann, a native of Cincinnati and mother of two, explained that she had always thought society limited personal freedom and that the line should be drawn between porn and art. "But they," she said, "were trying to draw the line. Who are they to make that decision for me, for any of us? Closed minds produce mediocre ideas. This Mapplethorpe business makes you think of *1984*, and you wonder if Cincinnati isn't some test case to see how much people can be controlled."

Cathy Marucci of the Mt. Adams neighborhood in Cincinnati told the *Cincinnati Post* that "people have been taking photos of nude women for years. Now people are finally taking pictures of men, and everyone's getting upset."

David Ross, director of the Institute of Contemporary Art in Boston, which is currently exhibiting *The Perfect Moment,* believes that homophobia is a bottom line in the fray. "There have been dozens of artists who have photographed naked children," he said. "But they have never been photographed by someone who has been identified as an overtly homosexual male. So because he [Mapplethorpe] was gay and photographed a naked child, ipso facto he becomes somehow involved in pandering, pederasty, or child pornography. It if was by a heterosexual, it would be just 'charming.' "

Considering the motives of his opponents, Barrie said, "There would have been some right-wing outcry had the photos been of women, or of a man and a woman, but not as grand an outcry. Men still call most of the shots in our society and most men are threatened by homosexuality. AIDS is just the latest excuse.

"Men are always in some race with other men about penis size," Barrie continued. "They're threatened by the genitalia in the photos, and they're so afraid of being thought homosexual they go to any lengths to prove they aren't. So they end up repressing anything that brings homosexuality into the open. The ones who are the most afraid scream the loudest.

"The other reason," said Barrie, "that the right wing finds Mapplethorpe so upsetting is race. His pictures portray black men with dignity and power, and that's hard for many whites to take. Remember Jesse Helms screaming on the floor of Congress last summer about the photo of a black and white man embracing. We've had a higher percentage of black visitors to the Mapplethorpe exhibit than to any other, including shows of black artists."

The state of Ohio no longer has sodomy laws against homosexual acts, and Terry Flanigan, of the local chapter of ACT UP (an AIDS activist group), believes gay life is tolerated in Cincinnati as much as it is in Columbus or Indianapolis. Gay news and culture magazines can be purchased at a few downtown newsstands. Gay sexual material is as restricted as heterosexual fare. In the Cincinnati area, no adult videos of any sort can be sold or rented. The city has no adult bookstores or X-rated cable entertainment, even if one chooses it for private viewing in one's home and is willing to pay for it. In his column in the *St.*

Paul Pioneer Press, James Lileks called Cincinnati the place "where you can be arrested for thinking of a banana and a doughnut in the same thought." No magazines featuring hard-core material are permitted, and those soft-core magazines that can be sold are available on a few downtown news racks but not in convenience, grocery, or drug stores. Gothic romances such as *Terms of Surrender, The Pistoleer,* and *Mrs. Ward's Refusal* are more widely found, with their many antebellum-gowned, open-throated, and swooning ladies on the covers. The periodicals *True Detective, Front Page Detective,* and *Inside Detective* are also casually available, sporting stories of mayhem and photos of corpses on the newsprint inside.

Local newspapers covering the Mapplethorpe fracas preceded their articles with "explicit language" warnings. In order to keep sexually related phone services out of town, Cincinnati Bell canceled all 976 exchanges, including chess and "gab" lines. The Cincinnati Public Library segregates material into its adult-book room, where library cardholders under the age of 18 may not go without written parental permission and a specially stamped card. (The national American Library Association discourages labeling by age in the belief that librarians should not decide for an entire community which books will be banished to the X-rated room. "Should it be sex or sexism?" asked the head of the A.L.A.'s Office of Intellectual Freedom.)

"We don't have censorship," said the library's director of public relations. "In 1971 the library board adopted a policy that very carefully governs all acquisitions. We haven't had trouble because we make sure to follow it."

Though the recently X-rated art film *The Cook, the Thief, His Wife & Her Lover* played Cincinnati in an art theater near the university, the city's newspapers would not carry the ad for it. In late April, County Sheriff Simon Leis, Jr., threatened to prosecute anyone selling the new 2 Live Crew album.

So for adult entertainment, Cincinnatians . . . drive. Until a few years ago, it was possible to buy magazines and videos in neighboring Newport, Kentucky, but local "decency" sweeps have flattened what used to be Cincinnati's playground to a sandbox. Only a few clubs remain—where women dance in G-strings and tassels—crowded, club managers say, with guys driving cars with Ohio license plates. "We see all kinds," said one dancer, "lawyers, judges, stockbrokers, car dealers, insurance salesmen. . . . Those Cincinnati men support us well."

About the Newport strip, C.C.V. spokesman Phil Burress said, "[There are] still parts that aren't clean. We want to get all eight counties surrounding Cincinnati clean of sexually oriented businesses. What we're trying to do is get it as far away from here as possible."

Adult videos and magazines are available to Cincinnatians in outlying Butler and Clermont counties, or in Dayton, Lexington, Columbus, and Indianapolis, respectively 47, 75, 100, and 110 miles away.

The history of Cincinnati's obscenity prosecutions goes back over 30 years—

almost as long as sexually explicit material has been popularly available—beginning with Mr. Keating's candy-store victory in 1956. In the early seventies, Simon Leis, Jr. (then county prosecutor and later county sheriff) shut massage parlors with "nuisance abatements" and the help of Keating's Citizens for Decency Through Law. The state of Ohio passed an organized-crime bill that converted obscenity sales from a misdemeanor to a felony, carrying a 25-year prison sentence. The law was declared unconstitutional. In 1973 Leis and Keating went after the plays *Hair* and *Oh! Calcutta!* and the film *Last Tango in Paris.*

In 1983 a grand jury indicted Warner Amex Cable Communications on four obscenity counts for showing two sexually explicit films on the Playboy Channel. (The charges were later withdrawn.) With the eighties video boom, stores in Hamilton, Clermont, and Warren counties were indicted for pandering obscenity, with the intended chilling effect that keeps adult videos illegal or hard to come by. In 1988 the city of Cincinnati threatened to prosecute the Beastie Boys rock group. Martin Scorsese's *The Last Temptation of Christ* never ran in a Cincinnati theater and many video stores there refuse to stock it. In 1988 the vice squad reviewed a production of *Equus* before Playhouse in the Park, a local theater company, opened it to the public.

On April 9, 1990, the *Cincinnati Post* questioned whether Cincinnatians are more conservative than the rest of the nation, or if the city's reputation might be based more on "a handful of politicians and conservative leaders . . . [who] have forged political careers championing anti-pornography causes." City council member Guy Guckenberger called obscenity prosecutions the traditional way for county prosecutors to attain "high visibility."

With somewhat less restraint, Kymberly Henson, head of the newly formed Voice Against Censorship, called Cincinnati a "boss town—always was and still is. At the turn of the century, we had Boss Cox, and today we have the county prosecutor and the sheriff's boys. The city council has very little power and the mayor isn't even full-time." Several city council members told the press that they were uncomfortable with the charges against the C.A.C., but were "reluctant to interfere," as was Mayor Luken.

Mark Mezibov, counsel for the local chapter of the A.C.L.U., and in his private practice also an attorney for the C.A.C., put it this way: "If the city, the prosecutors, and the judges were interested in defining obscenity in Cincinnati, they could've done it in the hearing we asked for before the show opened. We invited them to see the exhibition and Arthur Ney, the prosecutor, wouldn't even show up. Then the judge threw our request out of court.

"Obscenity trials work for reelection in this town, and everyone goes along with them. If there's no vocal opposition to them, why should politicians change their approach? In Cincinnati, the way to get along is to go along."

The Mapplethorpe excitement may have benefitted the prosecution also by deflecting attention from scandals that had been tainting law enforcement and city government. Earlier this year, then Hamilton County auditor, Joe DeCourcy, was investigated in connection with charges that he gave tax breaks to friends. His nephew, County Commissioner Joe M. DeCourcy, was recently indicted for assault, wanton endangerment, and drunken driving after getting into a head-on collision late at night in a state vehicle. Four years ago, Hamilton County's ability to administer funds and facilities was called into question when several workers at a county children's shelter were accused of child sexual abuse and an aide at a city hospital killed more than two dozen patients.

Penthouse attempted to contact those involved with the C.A.C. prosecution. County Sheriff Leis told his secretary to say that he wasn't interested in being interviewed by *Penthouse.* C.C.V. Director Monty Lobb told his secretary to say "It's a conflict of interest for an anti-pornography group to be talking to a pornographer." Jerry Kirk, director of the National Coalition Against Pornography, did not take or return *Penthouse*'s calls.

Charles Gerhardt, press liaison for County Prosecutor Ney, agreed to speak with *Penthouse,* saying, "We're just upholding Ohio law against disseminating obscene material and we can't selectively prosecute." When asked why Ney's office did not prosecute local bookstores or libraries that held copies of Mapplethorpe's photographs or other books that contain photos of unclothed children, such as *The Family of Children,* Gerhardt said, "We got complaints about this museum exhibit and we'll decide what to do about those other places when we get a verdict."

"I couldn't give in to them," Barrie said. "It comes from my family. They were average Americans from Cleveland who believed in the Constitution and in America as a tolerant society. My father called me when the Mapplethorpe issue broke and said, 'Goddamn it. They cannot tell you what to see!' He's almost 70 years old.

"What Cincinnati offers," Barrie went on, "is the old hypocrisy of cleaning up your home turf so you don't have to admit sexual passions by day, and reserving some forbidden place for night desires. I can just picture the sheriff and county prosecutors passing around copies of the Mapplethorpe photos: 'Hey, let me see that really horrible one again.'"

To Sirkin, Cincinnati's "offer" is more ominous: "Cincinnati is a one-party, ol'-boys'-club town. . . . The C.C.V. are so limited in their concern for 'community values' that when I asked [C.C.V. spokesman] Tom Grossman what he thought about the K.K.K. marching 35 miles away, he said, 'It's not our problem.'"

"We've been too complacent," Barrie said, "especially in the art world, where we think we're immune from harm. I was anguished when the Corcoran bent to political intimidation. I went to my board and asked them to back me. I know it sounds hokey, but it's about freedom of choice."

"There was no question about supporting Dennis [Barrie] because it's basic to America," said C.A.C. Board President Roger Ach. "Our system allows us to speak our minds and learn about a wide variety of things, including what's in those photographs. The radical Right and the radical Left meet somewhere on the dark side. The religious Right is no different from Stalinists who sought to limit people through political control."

Attorney Mark Mezibov is more cynical. "The C.A.C. was an easy issue. It became a fashionable way to stand up for a principle and look like a good person. I doubt those people who supported the C.A.C. would march for adult-video sales."

"Maybe not march," said Kymberly Henson of Voice Against Censorship, "but maybe now, after the C.A.C. raid, they'd make a phone call. A lot of people are asking how the C.A.C. bust could happen and the answer is *Last Tango, Oh! Calcutta!, The Last Temptation of Christ,* and before that, adult videos and magazines. It's always easier to say nothing. You have to protest when the cost of protesting isn't too high for the average guy."

Roger Ach, a five-generation Cincinnatian, believes, "Most Cincinnatians would agree, if the issue was presented in a thoughtful way. That's not what the C.C.V. did and not what our local government did. It's supposed to be the function of government to consider issues thoughtfully, to put a buffer between emotions and public policy. Are we in danger of losing our freedoms? Every day, since 1776. The day you stop protecting them is the day you start to lose them."

The Perfect Moment closed in Cincinnati on May 26. Since the fracas began, the city has seen a run on Mapplethorpe mementos—catalogs, T-shirts, buttons, posters, and the like. The C.A.C. sold $20,000 in paraphernalia between April 7 and 12; the local B. Dalton and Waldenbooks ran out of Mapplethorpe stock within days of the exhibit's opening.

Michael Stout, executor of the Mapplethorpe estate, reports that several of the artist's photographs have tripled in price over the last year. Three black-and-white self-portraits auctioned at Sotheby's brought between $35,750 and $38,500 each. A suite of three floral still lifes brought in $60,500. According to Stout, the controversy has made Mapplethorpe a good investment, "even for the Japanese."

Dennis Barrie was subsequently acquitted of obscenity charges.

• *Marcia Pally is a social researcher and the author of* Sense and Censorship: The Vanity of Bonfires.

37

USA Today
Interview with Dennis Barrie

Conducted by Barbara Reynolds

USA Today: One photograph at issue in your obscenity trial showed a man urinating into the mouth of a man kneeling before him. How can you defend that as art?

Dennis Barrie: It can be art when the intent is a serious intent. The five photographs, which deal with sadomasochistic acts, while you have to see them in the context of why and what they were supposed to do, in essence were Mapplethorpe's statement on that aspect of homosexual life. It's a political and an artistic commentary on a lifestyle that he, in essence, was portraying.

And a toddler with her dress raised, exposing her genitals, is art?

The issue with the pictures of the children was never obscenity. And that should be clearly stated. Because those photographs are innocent. The state claimed there wasn't parental permission for the showing of those photographs. Indeed, there was parental permission. Because they were not obscene or even thought to be obscene by anybody. And those are quite beautiful photographs.

Both you and 2 Live Crew have been acquitted on obscenity charges. But isn't the public—by bringing these cases to trial in the first place—trying to suggest you're starting to go too far?

The public said the other thing. Two very public juries rejected what law enforcement has said. In both cases, law enforcement took the action and, in both cases, law enforcement is obviously out of step with the public. Those juries—and the jury comes out of the community, whether it's in Florida or in Ohio—rejected how law enforcement is trying to restrict what the society can see or hear. Both trials were affirmations of the fundamental belief that this society has in protecting First Amendment rights.

But Cincinnati, as a community, has set its own standards. It doesn't want adult bookstores, X-rated theaters, peep shows or nude dancing. Doesn't this ruling go against what the community appears to want?

The purposes of a museum are far different from the purposes of a peep show and an X-rated bookstore. The museum is showing work that may have sexual content or very difficult content for far different reasons than one of those establishments. And what they were saying [with the verdict] was yes, while we may have our community standards, they are perfectly fitting within our standards.

Do you think people on a jury can decide what's obscene and what's not when even the Supreme Court seems to have difficulty?

The Supreme Court has a three-prong test to prove whether something is obscene or not. A jury can decide that because they have a very clear-cut way of deciding whether something is obscene or not. And the most important aspect of that test is whether the work before them, whether it's a novel or a movie or a photograph, has any political, social, artistic or educational value. And if it does, I'm sorry, it's not obscene. And that's what the Supreme Court has said over and over and over again.

Should the federal government be in the business of financing art?

When you get into the whole issue of federal money, what has been spent in terms of federal money that has been "offensive" has been far and few between. I mean, [Sen. Jesse] Helms and others have made an issue out of that that simply has blown it out of proportion. The National Endowment for the Arts has such a brilliant record of funding things that have real value that the argument that it's funding lewd and horrible things so often has no basis in reality.

On Thursday, you will receive the Hugh M. Hefner First Amendment Award for your successful fight to protect artistic freedom. As a result of that verdict, do you think artists now will find more freedom?

No, I don't think that. They're going to find less freedom. Because this is a period in which enough political clout has been activated to really try to crush creativity in this country. And that's going to have the effect of self-censorship, which has already started to occur all across the nation.

How so?

In other words, don't do risky or challenging work, don't present challenging plays, or don't present challenging dance or controversial exhibitions. Artists and the arts institutions for the next few years, because of the impact of Helms and others, are going to do less controversial work.

But this issue deals with obscenity.

The issue goes far beyond the issue of sexuality and art. The people who oppose federal involvement in the arts and propose censorship don't stop at sexual issues; let's be real. They have a political, social agenda. They would just as soon curtail political expression, social expression, expression dealing with minorities as they would works dealing with sexual content.

By having a major museum such as yours displaying his art, were you legitimizing the artistic value of Mapplethorpe's work?

Mapplethorpe was an artist who was seen all over the world. His intent was not pornographic. His intent was to deal seriously with an aspect of society that, believe me, is difficult. There are lots of things shown that have serious value that are also horrible and repulsive.

For example?

The photographer who took photographs of the death camps in Germany. There is a serious reason for showing those things in the context of a museum. Whatever value or lesson you want to get out of it, there are real reasons for looking at that work. That doesn't mean you advocate mass murder. It doesn't mean you advocate genocide. You're trying to draw attention or focus upon these things to make a statement.

Who really won in this case?

I actually think "the people" won. I think, quite honestly, it was a real statement that Americans don't want censorship. And I think these people basically said in this decision that we, as adults, will decide if it has a serious purpose and we will decide whether we should see it or not see it. And a government agency is not going to tell us whether we can or not.

• *In 1992 Dennis Barrie, citing personal reasons, stepped down as the museum director of the Contemporary Arts Center.*

38

What Do Artists Want from Us?

by Irving Kristol

Once upon a time, when the idea of a National Endowment for the Arts was under consideration, I had some lively arguments with my conservative friends. I supported the idea, they opposed it. Their opposition was based on the simple and straightforward principle that the state had no business involving itself in this area, which should be left to private philanthropy. I argued that it would be good for our democracy if it showed an official interest in educating the tastes and refining the aesthetic sensibilities of its citizenry.

I won the argument and now wish I hadn't. They were more right than, at the time, they could know.

In retrospect, I can see that my error derived from the fact that I really had only a superficial understanding of what was happening in the arts world and no understanding of what this portended for the future evolution of what we now call "the arts community." I was raised in a generation that was taught to appreciate the virtues of modern art, from Renoir to Picasso and even Jackson Pollock and "abstract expressionism," though I had to admit that this last stage had no appeal to me. "Pop art" and "minimalist art" I tended to dismiss as trendy fads.

But what I was utterly unprepared for was the emergence of what is now called "post-modern art," which is politically charged art that is utterly contemptuous of the notion of educating the tastes and refining the aesthetic sensibilities of the citizenry. Its goal, instead, is deliberately to outrage those tastes and to trash the very idea of an "aesthetic sensibility."

It is very difficult to convey to people who do not follow the weird goings-on in our culture an appreciation of the animating agenda of the "arts community" today. An ordinary American reads about a woman "performing artist" who smears chocolate on her bare breasts, and though he may lament the waste of chocolate or nudity, it does not occur to him that she is "making a statement," one that the "arts community" takes seriously indeed.

Even museum trustees in Washington, D.C., or Cincinnati—an elite, educated and affluent group of art philanthropists—had no idea what Mapplethorpe was up to in his photograph of a bullwhip handle inserted into his rectum. All they knew is that Mapplethorpe was a very talented photographer (which he was), that no such talent could ever create obscene work (which is false) and that any discriminating judgment on their part was a form of censorship that verged on the sacrilegious. Those trustees are there to raise money and watch the museum's balance sheet. They may or may not know what they like, but they would never presume to assert what is, or is not, "art." To qualify to become a museum trustee these days one must first suffer aesthetic castration.

To reach our current condition, it took a century of "permanent revolution" in the arts, made possible, ironically, by a capitalist economy that created affluent art collectors and entrepreneurial art dealers. "Patrons" of the arts were replaced by "consumers" of the arts, giving the artists an intoxicating freedom.

It was the artist, now, who told us what was and was not "art"—not the patron, or the philosopher, or the public. The function of the spectator was to welcome revolutions in taste by permitting himself to be intimidated and indoctrinated by the "arts community," consisting of artists themselves but also and especially (since artists are not usually articulate) art critics, art professors, art dealers, museum directors, etc. The most important spectators who were so intimidated and indoctrinated were the media, which now automatically approach anything declared to be "art" by the "arts community" with the kind of deference, even pseudo-piety, once reserved for the sphere of religion.

As with most revolutions, some impressive creative energies were released, some enduring accomplishments were achieved. But, again as with most revolutions, the longer it lasted the more the destructive impulse began to dominate over the creative. Yesteryear's creative contributions were, after all, what the latest revolutionary phase had to subvert and overthrow.

After World War II, it became even more difficult to distinguish artists from publicity-hungry, pseudo-artists, from people "making statements" of one kind or another, such "statements" being the essence of pop art, minimalist art, environmental art, and now post-modern art. That practically all of this activity was infused by an anti-bourgeois ethos was unsurprising, since it was simply mirroring the literary and academic culture in this respect. The bourgeois way of coping with this situation was to purchase and "consume" this art as a commodity, to inventory it and then at some point to expel it from its system into an underground sump, usually located in the basement of museums. Co-optation, not censorship, was the strategy.

But this strategy does not work with the last and, one suspects, final phase of the revolution we are now witnessing. Today, the destructive element has almost completely overwhelmed the creative. What the "arts community" is engaged in is a politics of radical nihilism; it has little interest in, and will openly express contempt for, "art" in any traditional sense of the term. It is no exaggeration to say that the self-destruction of "art" is a key point in its agenda, accompanied by the "deconstruction," not only of bourgeois society, but of Western civilization itself.

"Deconstruction" is an intellectual-ideological movement that is enormously popular in the humanities departments of our universities, which seek to free themselves from the "hegemony" of Dead White Males (DWMs is the common reference) such as Shakespeare or Dante so as to justify offering a university course on, say, the TV program "The Simpsons." There are no standards of excellence other than those we improvise for ourselves, which is why members of the "arts community" can solemnly believe and assert that whatever they do is "art." The public has the right—nay, the obligation—to support it, but not to question it.

What they do, in fact, is powerfully shaped by certain radical ideological currents: radical feminism, homosexual and lesbian self-celebration and black racism are among them. This explains why, though it is *de rigueur* to insult public figures, no one in the "arts community" would ever dare insult Rev. Louis Farrakhan. Any such painting would promptly be vandalized, to the applause of an "arts community" opposed to censorship. It also explains why there is so little pornography, in the traditional sense, in post-modern art. Such pornography evokes lust for heterosexual engagement, which post-modern art disapproves of since it is thought to debase women. Only homosexual and lesbian sex is allowed to be celebrated.

Where will it all end? One does have the sense that we are witnessing either a final convulsion in the history of modern art (and of modern culture) or, perhaps, a final convulsion of Western civilization itself. Most of us would credit the first alternative. But where does that leave the National Endowment for the Arts, founded in a different time and on quite different assumptions about the role of the arts in American life?

The most obvious response would be to abolish the NEA, perhaps over a period of a few years to mitigate the financial shock. This is not going to happen, however. After all, many major institutions—symphony orchestras, for instance, and large museums—have inevitably become dependent on NEA grants. The trustees of these institutions have considerable influence with members of Congress, who are much happier opening funding spigots than closing them. And the media, it goes without saying, would be horrified at such an effort at "censorship," now redefined to include absence of government funding.

A more limited response would be to move the NEA away from involvement with the most active and turbulent sectors of the "arts community" by requiring that it make only grants of $50,000 or $100,000. The institutions receiving this money would be held responsible for any regrants they make.

Most of the controversial grants one hears of are small-to-modest. But they do serve an important role in legitimating the activity that is being funded. With $10,000 from the NEA, an "experimental workshop in the arts" can approach foundations and corporations with a plausible claim to respectability. That is precisely why they will fight tooth and nail for the continuation of the small-grants program—grants made by other members of the "arts community," their "peer groups," to their friends and allies. Just how Congress will respond to such a reform, now being bruited, remains to be seen.

But one interesting and important fact has already become clear: Our politics today are so spiritually empty, so morally incoherent, that—except for a few brave souls—liberals have been quick to dismiss as "yahoos" anyone who dares to confront this assault on the foundations of liberalism and conservatism alike. A great many conservatives, for their part, having long ago been ideologically disarmed, are more embarrassed than interested at having to cope with this issue at all. Something is definitely rotten in the vital areas of our body politic.

• *Irving Kristol is coeditor of* Public Interest *and the publisher of* National Interest.

39

In Praise of Censure

by Garry Wills

> Even freedom of speech has to be regulated.
>
> —TOTTIE ELLIS, vice president of Eagle Forum (from *USA Today*)

Originally published in Time *(July 31, 1989), this essay, an opinion piece, was reprinted in* Citizen *(November 1990), a publication of Focus on the Family, a conservative family organization. As* Time *pointed out: "We would like to take this opportunity to clarify something. When Focus on the Family requested permission to reprint the essay, they did not tell us that it would be edited, and that ellipses would not be used to indicate cuts made in the text. Nor had we known that an editorial comment would accompany it. Had we known, they would not have received reprint permission."*

Rarely have the denouncers of censorship been so eager to start practicing it. When a sense of moral disorientation overcomes a society, people from the least expected quarters begin to ask, "Is nothing sacred?" Feminists join reactionaries to denounce pornography as demeaning to women. Rock musician Frank Zappa declares that when Tipper Gore, the wife of Senator Albert Gore from Tennessee, asked music companies to label sexually explicit material, she launched an illegal "conspiracy to extort." A *Penthouse* editorialist says that housewife Terry Rakolta, who asked sponsors to withdraw support from a sitcom called *Married . . . With Children*, is "yelling fire in a crowded theater," a formula that says her speech is not protected by the First Amendment.

But the most interesting movement to limit speech is directed at defamatory utterances against blacks, homosexuals, Jews, women or other stigmatizable groups. It took no Terry Rakolta of the left to bring about the instant firing of Jimmy the Greek and Al Campanis from sports jobs when they made racially denigrating comments. Social pressure worked far more quickly on them than on *Married . . . With Children*, which is still on the air.

The rules being considered on college campuses to punish students for making racist and other defamatory remarks go beyond social and commercial pressure to actual legal muzzling. The right-wing *Dartmouth Review* and its imitators have understandably infuriated liberals, who are beginning to take action against them and the racist expressions they have encouraged. The American Civil Liberties Union considered this movement important enough to make it the principal topic at its [1989] biennial meeting . . . in Madison, Wis. Ironically, the regents of the University of Wisconsin had passed their own rules against defamation just before the ACLU members convened on the university's campus. Nadine Strossen, of New York University School of Law, who was defending the ACLU's traditional position on free speech, said of Wisconsin's new rules, "You can tell how bad they are by the fact that the regents had to make an amendment at the last minute exempting classroom discussion! What is surprising is that Donna Shalala [chancellor of the university] went along with it." So did constitutional lawyers on the faculty.

If a similar code were drawn up with right-wing imperatives in mind—one banning unpatriotic, irreligious or sexually explicit expressions on campus—the people framing Wisconsin-type rules would revert to their libertarian pasts. In this competition to suppress, is regard for freedom of expression just a matter of whose ox is getting gored at the moment? Does the left just get nervous about the Christian cross when Klansmen burn it, while the right will react only when Madonna flirts with crucifixes between her thighs?

The cries of "un-American" are as genuine and as frequent on either side. Everyone is protecting the country. Zappa accuses Gore of undermining the moral fiber of America with the "sexual neuroses of those vigilant ladies." He argues that she threatens our freedoms with "connubial insider trading" because her husband is a Senator. Apparently her marital status should deprive her of speaking privileges in public—an argument Westbrook Pegler used to make against Eleanor Roosevelt. *Penthouse* says Rakolta is taking us down the path toward fascism. It attacks her for living in a rich suburb—the old "radical chic" argument that rich people cannot support moral causes.

There is a basic distinction that cuts through this free-for-all over freedom. It is the distinction, too often neglected, between censorship and censure (the free expression of moral disapproval). What the campuses are trying to do (at least those with state money) is use the force of government to contain freedom of speech. What Donald Wildmon, the free-lance moralist from Tupelo, Miss., does when he gets Pepsi to cancel its Madonna ad is censure the ad by calling for a boycott. Advocating boycotts is a form of speech protected by the First Amendment. As Nat Hentoff, journalistic custodian of the First Amendment, says, "I would hate to see boycotts outlawed. Think what that would do to Cesar Chavez." Or, for that matter, to Ralph Nader. If one disapproves of a social practice, whether it is racist speech or unjust hiring in lettuce fields, one is free to denounce that and to call on others to express their disapproval. Otherwise there would be no form of persuasive speech except passing a law. This would make the law coterminous with morality.

Equating morality with legality is in effect what people do when they claim that anything tolerated by law must, in the name of freedom, be approved by citizens in all their dealings with one another. As Zappa says, "Masturbation is not illegal. If it is not illegal to do it, why should it be illegal to sing about it?" He thinks this proves that Gore, who is not trying to make raunch in rock illegal, cannot even ask distributors to label it. Anything goes, as long as it's legal. The odd consequence of this argument would be a drastic narrowing of the freedom of speech. One could not call into question anything that was not against the law—including, for instance, racist speech.

A false idea of tolerance has not only outlawed censorship but discouraged censoriousness (another word for censure). Most civilizations have expressed their moral values by mobilization of social opprobrium. That, rather than specific legislation, is what changed the treatment of minorities in films and TV over recent years. One can now draw opprobrious attention by gay bashing, as the Beastie Boys rock group found when their distributor told them to cut out remarks about "fags" for business reasons. Or by anti-Semitism, as the just disbanded rap group Public Enemy has discovered.

It is said that only the narrow-minded are intolerant or opprobrious. Most of those who limited the distribution of Martin Scorsese's movie *The Last Temptation of Christ* had not even seen the movie. So do we guarantee freedom of speech only for the broad-minded or the better educated? Can one speak only after studying whatever one has reason, from one's beliefs, to denounce? Then most of us would be doing a great deal less speaking than we do. If one has never seen any snuff movies, is that a bar to criticizing them?

Others argue that asking people not to buy lettuce is different from asking them not to buy a rocker's artistic expression. Ideas (carefully disguised) lurk somewhere in the lyrics. All the more reason to keep criticism of them free. If ideas are too important to suppress, they are also too important to ignore. The whole point of free speech is not to make ideas exempt from criticism but to expose them to it.

One of the great mistakes of liberals in recent decades has been the ceding of moral concern to right-wingers. Just because one opposes censorship, one need not be seen as agreeing with pornographers. Why should liberals, of all people, oppose Gore when she asks that labels be put on products meant for the young, to inform those entrusted by law with the care of the young? Liberals were the first to promote "healthy" television shows like *Sesame Street* and *The Electric Company.* In the 1950s and 1960s they were the leading critics of television, of its mindless violence, of the way it ravaged the attention span needed for reading. Who was keeping kids away from TV sets then? How did promoters of Big Bird let themselves be cast as champions of the Beastie Boys—not just of their *right* to perform but of their performance itself? Why should it be left to Gore to express moral disapproval of a group calling itself Dead Kennedys (sample lyric: "I kill children, I love to see them die")?

For that matter, who has been more insistent that parents should "interfere" in what their children are doing, Tipper Gore or Jesse Jackson? All through the

1970s, Jackson was traveling the high schools, telling parents to turn off TVs, make the kids finish their homework, check with teachers on their performance, get to know what the children are doing. This kind of "interference" used to be called education.

Belief in the First Amendment does not pre-empt other beliefs, making one a eunuch to the interplay of opinions. It is a distortion to turn "You can express any views" into the proposition "I don't care what views you express." If liberals keep equating equality with approval, they will be repeatedly forced into weak positions.

A case in point is the Cocoran Gallery's sudden cancellation of an exhibit of Robert Mapplethorpe's photographs. The whole matter was needlessly confused when the director, Christina Owr-Chall, claimed she was canceling the show to *protect* it from censorship. She meant that there might be pressure to remove certain pictures—the sadomasochistic ones or those verging on kiddie porn—if the show had gone on. But she had in mind, as well, the hope of future grants from the National Endowment for the Arts, which is under criticism for the Mapplethorpe show and for another show that contained Andres Serrano's *Piss Christ,* the photograph of a crucifix in what the title says is urine. Owr-Chall is said to be yielding to censorship, when she is clearly yielding to political and financial pressure, as Pepsi yielded to commercial pressure over the Madonna ad.

What is at issue here is not government suppression but government subsidy. Mapplethorpe's work is not banned, but showing it might have endangered federal grants to needy artists. The idea that what the government does not support it represses is nonsensical, as one can see by reversing the statement to read: "No one is allowed to create anything without the government's subvention." What pussycats our supposedly radical artists are. They not only want the government's permission to create their artifacts, they want federal authorities to supply the materials as well. Otherwise they feel "gagged." If they are not given government approval (and money), they want to remain an avantgarde while being bankrolled by the Old Guard.

What is easily forgotten in this argument is the right of citizen taxpayers. They send representatives to Washington who are answerable for the expenditure of funds exacted from them. In general these voters want to favor their own values if government is going to get into the culture-subsidizing area at all (a proposition many find objectionable in itself). Politicians, insofar as they support the arts, will tend to favor conventional art (certainly not masochistic art). Anybody who doubts that has no understanding of a politician's legitimate concern for his or her constituents' approval. Besides, it is quaint for those familiar with the politics of the art world to discover, with a shock, that there is politics in politics.

Luckily, cancellation of the Mapplethorpe show forced some artists back to the flair and cheekiness of unsubsidized art. Other results of pressure do not turn out as well. Unfortunately, people in certain regions were deprived of the chance to see *The Last Temptation of Christ* in the theater. Some, no doubt, considered it a loss that they could not buy lettuce or grapes during a Chavez boycott. Perhaps there was even a buyer perverse enough to miss driving the unsafe cars Nader helped pressure off the market. On the other hand, we do not get sports analysis made by racists. These mobilizations of social opprobrium are not examples of repression but of freedom of expression by committed people who censured without censoring, who expressed the kinds of beliefs the First Amendment guarantees. I do not, as a result, get whatever I approve of subsidized, either by Pepsi or the government. But neither does the law come in to silence Tipper Gore or Frank Zappa or even that filthy rag, the *Dartmouth Review.*

• *Because Albert Gore is no longer a senator but the Vice President, his wife Tipper— at the forefront of the debate regarding music labeling—has disassociated herself, at least officially, from the PMRC.*

40

The Naked Truth

by Dave Barry

Obscenity. Pornography. Naked people thrusting their loins. Should these things be legal? What is obscenity? What is art? What exactly are "loins"? How come nobody ever calls the office and says: "I can't come to work today because I have a loinache?" These are some of the serious questions that we must ask ourselves, as Americans, if we are going to get away with writing columns about sex.

These issues are relevant right now because of the raging national debate over the National Endowment for the Arts, which was established to spend taxpayers' money on art, the theory being that if the taxpayers were allowed to keep their money, they'd just waste it on things they actually wanted. Because, frankly, the average taxpayer is not a big voluntary supporter of the arts. The only art that the average taxpayer buys voluntarily either has a picture of Bart Simpson on it or little suction cups on its feet so you can stick it onto a car window.

So if you left it up to the public, there would hardly be any art. Certainly there would be no big art, such as the modernistic sculptures that infest many public parks. You almost never hear members of the public saying, "Hey! Let's all voluntarily chip in and pay a sculptor $100,000 to fill this park space with what appear to be the rusted remains of a helicopter crash!" It takes concerted government action to erect one of those babies.

The taxpayers also cannot be relied upon to support performing arts such as opera. As a taxpayer, I am forced to admit that I would rather undergo vasectomy via Weed Whacker than attend an opera. The one time I did sit through one, it lasted approximately as long as fourth grade and featured large men singing for forty-five minutes in a foreign language merely to observe that the sun had risen.

My point is that the government supports the arts for the same reason that it purchases $400,000 fax machines and keeps dead radioactive beagles in freezers: Nobody else is willing to do it. The question is, should we carry this concept further? Should the government require taxpayers not only to pay for art, but also to go and physically admire it? This program could be linked with the federal court system:

Judge: Mr. Johnson, you have been convicted of tax evasion, and I hereby sentence you to admire four hours of federally subsidized modern dance.

Defendant: NO! NOT MODERN DANCE!

Judge: One more outburst like that and I'm going to order you to also watch the performance artist who protests apartheid using a bathtub full of rigatoni.

So federal art is good. But now we must grope with the troubling question: Should the government support smut? And how do we define "smut"? You can't just say it's naked people, because many famous works of art, such as the late Michelangelo's statue of David getting ready to fight Goliath, are not wearing a stitch of clothing. Which raises the question: Why would anybody go off to fight in the nude? Was it a tactic? Perhaps this explains why Goliath just stood there like a bozo and let himself get hit by a rock.

"Hey!" he was probably thinking. "This guy is naked as a jaybird! What's he trying to AWWRRK."

Some people argue that a work is not pornographic as long as it has redeeming social value. But you can find people who will testify in court that almost anything has redeeming social value:

Prosecutor: So, Professor Weemer, you're saying that this video depicts an ecology theme?

Witness: Yes. The woman displays a LOT of affection for the zucchini.

On the other end of the spectrum, some people think just about everything is evil. For example, the Rev. Donald Wildmon, a leading anti-pornography crusader, once mounted a crusade against a Mighty Mouse cartoon. I swear I am not making this up. In this cartoon, Mighty Mouse took a whiff of something; the cartoon makers said it was clearly flower petals, but the Rev. Wildmon was certain Mighty Mouse was snorting cocaine.

Of course, it's difficult to believe that Mighty Mouse, even if he is a cocaine user, would be stupid enough to snort it on camera. But, as parents, we have to ask ourselves: What if the Rev. Wildmon is right? And speaking of cartoon characters with apparent drug problems, how come Donald Duck has been going around for fifty years wearing a shirt but no pants? Flashing his loins! Right in front of Huey, Dewey and Louie, his so-called "nephews," if you get my drift! And consider this: If you call up the Walt Disney public relations department, they'll tell you that Mickey and Minnie Mouse are not married, despite having the same last name. Come to think of it, they also have "nephews."

My point is that the obscenity/art issue involves many complex questions, and we owe it to ourselves, as Americans, to give them some serious thought. You go first.

• *Humorist Dave Barry is a syndicated columnist and author.*

Child Safe Art

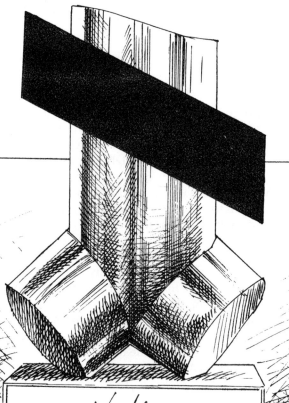

Nude
after Brancusi

Part 3
In the Schools

**We are not going to be intimidated.
Ever since there have been books, there have
been people who wanted to censor them
and sometimes burn them.**

—THOMAS WILLIAMSON, of Harcourt Brace Jovanovich,
publisher of "Impressions"

41

Battle over the Books
Grave Impressions

by Jeff Meade

According to People for the American Way, school censorship incidents are on the rise dramatically. In the 1990-91 school year, there were 264 incidents; in the 1991–92, it jumped to 376.

The problem, of course, is that concerned parents want their children to learn the values they espouse, and thus wish school textbooks and school library books to reflect their thinking. If, as it often is, a parent holds deeply held religious values, conflicts will inevitably result. The question, then: Does the view of one parent (or a minority of parents) take precedence over the views of the parents who have no objections?

Often, one hears of censorship efforts, but only in the abstract—just numbers. In this piece, however, the abstract becomes real as Jeff Meade tells the story of school censorship at the Ridgeview Elementary School in Yucaipa, California. At the heart of the issue: a controversial seventeen-book series called "Impressions."

For all the celebrated cases in the media—especially those of popular culture figures like Madonna, rapper Ice-T, 2 Live Crew, and artists like Andres Serrano and photographers like Robert Mapplethorpe—the real war is being fought in schools across the country. A war of words that can erupt in physical confrontations, intimidation, and harassment, this is a cultural battle in which the values of evangelical Christians are irreconcilable with secular thinking and humanism.

"**M**y family just moved into a new home, but our neighbors won't say hello to us. They kept their children away from our daughter. We've had our windows egged, and broken glass thrown in front of our house."

Michele Peters' eyes fill with tears and her voice sounds far away when she talks about it. A first grade teacher at the Ridgeview Elementary School in Yucaipa, Calif., she is not usually given to dark moods. Her smile reflects the generous, patient nature of a woman who spends her days among small children, alternately dishing out bits of wisdom and wads of Kleenex. But now, Peters sits in a stiff-backed chair in the principal's office, her face a mask of sadness.

Peters is not alone. Suzy Smith says she found a nail driven into one of the tires of her car. Like Peters, her colleague at Ridgeview, Smith is usually easy-going. But in this case, the gloves come off. She says, "I don't know how you can be a teacher and not take it personally."

Peters and Smith have lived for years in and around Yucaipa, a dusty, sun-baked little town in the foothills of the San Bernardino Mountains, Peters for 16 years and Smith for 22. Both are experienced teachers who have made their careers in the Yucaipa Joint Unified School District. This is their town, a place where people have always tried to get along. That is, until last year, when the school district adopted a controversial 17-book, elementary-level reading series called "Impressions." Peters and Smith helped select the series, and they taught from it. And for exercising their professional judgment, they believe, they have been singled out for rough treatment.

Depending on your point of view, "Impressions" is either a treasure-trove of children's literature or a passport to perdition. Published by Harcourt Brace Jovanovich Inc., "Impressions" is a popular whole-language-based anthology of short stories, classic fairy tales, and nursery rhymes, drawing on the work of writers as diverse as Laura Ingalls Wilder and C.S. Lewis, Beverly Cleary and T.S. Eliot, Arnold Lobel and A.A. Milne. Schools in California, Idaho, Oregon, and Washington now use the series, and it is under consideration in Georgia and New Mexico.

Teachers consider "Impressions" a lavishly illustrated blend of sophistication and wholesomeness—challenging, yes, but as innocent as Dick and Jane. And yet, throughout California and in a few towns and cities in Washington, Oregon, and Idaho, "Impressions" has aroused the righteous indignation of some parents who see in its pages a challenge to traditional family values. Within its fairy stories and nonsense rhymes—"Beauty and the Beast," "In a Dark, Dark Wood," "Shut the Windows, Bolt the Doors"—they detect a not-so-subtle emphasis on violence, death, and the occult. Not a few believe they see the hand of Satan himself. One way or another, they want the series out of the schools.

Teachers cry censorship and charge that the parents are attempting to alter the curriculum to reflect fundamentalist Christian beliefs. But parents say that they are merely trying to protect their children by exercising their right to influence schoolbook selection to reflect local values.

"This was never a book-banning issue," says parent Bob Isenberg, one of the founders of the Parent/Citizen Association of Yucaipa/Calimesa, which sprang up practically overnight in response to the introduction of "Impressions." "We're exercising our rights, rights that we've always had, and teachers don't like that. But this is America."

Bowing to pressure from parents like Isenberg, as well as from several conservative Christian groups, five school districts in Idaho and California have removed "Impressions" from the curriculum. But in Yucaipa, the dispute has bubbled over into a recall election, with parents attempting to oust two school trustees who voted first to approve the series and later to retain it. The emotional, often ugly feud has put teachers on the defensive. Some say they have received harassing telephone calls and, in some cases, physical threats. Not surprisingly, the debate has disrupted the learning environment in Yucaipa schools.

Says Peters: "Teachers go to school each day not knowing what to expect. One morning, there were 40 parents picketing in front of the school. They wanted to come inside and see what we were doing, whether what we were doing was right."

"It's almost like someone is sitting on your shoulder, just waiting for you to make a mistake," adds Smith, an authentic apple-cheeked, curly-haired schoolmarm, whose two grown sons attended district schools. "Classrooms are being torn apart."

The tragedy, both teachers say, is that in the Yucaipa public schools, harmony has always been the byword. Now, everyone wonders whether the schools—or Yucaipa itself—can ever be the same.

o   o   o

On the surface, Yucaipa seems as unchanging as the San Bernardino Mountains that loom to the east and west, cradling the town like cupped hands. It is a starkly beautiful landscape of rocks, sand, and prickly pear. Yucaipa is close to the Southern California smog belt—Los Angeles is a 90-minute drive west on the San Bernardino Freeway—but in some ways, Yucaipa might as well be as far away as the moon.

A few thousand feet below the chiseled peaks, in the shops and businesses that line Yucaipa Boulevard, life goes on much as it always has. At the Bit of Country restaurant, blue-shirted school-bus drivers swap gossip over warm apple pie. Old friends sip coffee at Mr. Crum's Donut House, scanning the obits in the *Yucaipa News-Mirror,* looking for names of people they know. Impulsive couples, defying the gloomy statistics and promising to forsake all others, opt for the fast-food approach to matrimony at the Yucaipa Wedding Chapel ("Open 24 Hours").

It is a town of contrasts, of old, rusting pickup trucks and new executive haciendas, social statements in sand-colored stucco. Young families, refugees from the smog, have moved in; the population soared from 24,000 to 34,000 between 1984 and 1988. Retirees have arrived, as well, to live in one of the town's numerous mobile-home parks—featureless, tightly packed places with oddly Elysian names like "Yucaipa Land Yacht Harbor" and "Rancho del Sol."

Above all, Yucaipa remains a deeply religious town. On countless front lawns, God-fearing Yucaipans have erected monuments to their faith, swinging metal placards at curbside, like scriptural Burma Shave signs: "The Righteous Shall Be Glad in the Lord" and "Prepare to Meet Thy God." In the window of the old Holsinger's Furniture Store on Yucaipa Boulevard hangs a sign announcing "The New Home of Abundant Life Fellowship, Where God Reigns and Miracles Happen."

Altogether, Yucaipa supports more than 40 houses of worship: Seventh-Day

Adventist, Baptist, Church of Christ, Mormon, Catholic, and more. The Parent/Citizen Association of Yucaipa/Calimesa, the organization dedicated to removing "Impressions" from the schools, meets in one of these, the Green Valley Foursquare Church.

Despite the chosen meeting place and the acknowledged traditional religious beliefs of most of its members, PCAYC leader Dennis Riley denies that the group follows a conservative, religious agenda.

Riley defines the issue as the parents' right to have a say in textbook selection. He voices serious reservations about what he sees as the relentlessly dark and supernatural content of the series, stories and poems with no overlying theme of redemption, no happy endings. He sees children being encouraged to write about their innermost thoughts and fears, which, he believes, could constitute an invasion of family privacy. And he tells stories of local children with recurring nightmares being sent to see psychologists to allay the fears stirred up by the sometimes gloomy themes.

" 'Impressions' presents an abstract caricature of the human form," explains Riley, a wooly-bearded man who owns an apple orchard on the outskirts of Yucaipa and who also edits PCAYC's newsletter, *The Sentry.*

"It takes stories like *Anne of Green Gables* and grafts gratuitous violence into them. It also contains contemporary fiction of the minimalist genre, like *Harriet the Spy* and *The Green Gilly Hopkins,* which offer degrading detail and don't redeem the characters. They're silly and vulgar and crass."

Relatively few of the stories, Riley says, offer a moral conclusion. And far too many of the series' offerings, he adds, dwell on what he calls "the dark side." Three out of five selections, he claims, concern death and dying. Take a look, he says, at the James Stephens poem, "The Wind," in one of the second grade texts: *The wind stood up, and gave a shout;/He whistled on his fingers, and/Kicked the withered leaves about,/And thumped the branches with his hand,/And said he'll kill, and kill, and kill;/And so he will! And so he will!*

Even if "Impressions" did encourage children to read, write, and speak more expressively—which Riley frankly doubts—the means would not justify the end. "You don't sacrifice character on the altar of literacy," he says.

Paul Jessup, the Yucaipa district's soft-spoken curriculum coordinator, has read most of the stories in the books. He says it's too soon to show concrete performance results, but teachers report that the district is on the right track. "We feel it is already being successful," says Jessup, a button-down, self-described political ultraconservative and Bible reader. "Our teachers are pleased with the results they're seeing."

Jessup has also heard Riley's views and those of other parents, but he simply does not see what they see. He flips open one of the texts to a story by Frank Modell, called "One Zillion Valentines." At the end of the story, one little boy gives another little boy a valentine card. Then, on the next page, there is an old traditional rhyme, called "Lavender's Blue." One of the lines reads: *And we shall be gay, dilly dilly, and we shall both dance . . .*

Some of the parents, Jessup says, put the two together and come up with what amounts to a classroom endorsement of male homosexuality. "They say the juxtaposition has to be more than circumstantial," Jessup says.

(One parent, according to the *Los Angeles Times,* even attempted to make the case that one could see the face of the Devil in an illustration that had been photocopied and turned upside down.)

Nevertheless, Jessup says he respects parents' demands to take part in text-book selection. In fact, he says, parents were invited to inspect the series.

"Impressions" first came to Yucaipa in the spring of 1989. Teachers in all the district's elementary schools tested three different book series in the hope of selecting one for use in the 1989-90 school year and the following six years, as a transition from basal readers to true whole language—real literature, but without the safety net of textbooks and ready-made lesson plans.

"Our goal is a completely literature-based curriculum," says Jessup. "Before 'Impressions,' we were in a skills-based mode. Literature was secondary to the skills being learned in any subject. We're turning that around, with literature as the hub."

The district displayed all three book series under consideration in the schools and the town library. No one stepped forward to say good or ill about any of them, Jessup says, and when it came time to select the one series, 80 percent of the teachers chose "Impressions." Both the school administration and the school board of trustees concurred with the teachers' choice.

In September 1989, "Impressions" reached the Yucaipa elementary schools. As the school year began, teachers sent notes home to all parents, explaining the change. Still, no complaints. But the honeymoon ended quickly. In October, news reports of parental challenges to the "Impressions" series in other California districts—Hacienda la Puente, East Whittier, and Dixon—began circulating in Yucaipa. Soon, the complaints started pouring into Jessup's office.

"We had about a hundred complaints within the first 90 days," Jessup says. "And then in November, 150 parents came to our school board meeting." About that time, PCAYC came into being.

In reponse to requests from those parents, the school board ordered a review of the series, to be conducted by a principal, teacher, librarian, and a parent from each elementary school. At the next meeting, the one attended by 1,000 to 1,200 Yucaipa citizens, the review committee gave the "Impressions" series a clean bill of health. At that time, the board offered parents an alternative—separate classes for their children, drawing exclusively from books on the core literature list.

Even though both Riley and Isenberg claim that most parents share their views, more than 80 percent of the elementary school students in Yucaipa remained in "Impressions" classrooms. "Since we have alternatives at every site," says Jessup, "I would take that as an indication of parents' satisfaction with the series."

A few parents did accept the alternative. Between 5 percent and 20 percent of the district's children switched to the "core curriculum" classes, depending on the school. Still, many parents considered the compromise a slap in the face. "Their objection," explains Jessup, "was that the alternative was not a textbook. It's not a hardback, and so it would not really be equal."

To Isenberg, the alternative was tantamount to a declaration of war. Isenberg, a heavyset man with a direct, penetrating gaze, helped organized PCAYC. He's an executive recruiter who drives a long white LTD Crown Victoria, with vanity tags that pose the whimsical question: "8 LIFE EZ."

At the moment, he says, it ain't so easy. "The alternative was not offered to us," he complains. "It was dictated to us."

Isenberg claims district administrators had told him earlier that there weren't enough sets of books on the core list to go around, and that there were no lesson plans for the books the district did have. Even if there were enough books and lesson plans, Isenberg says he would refuse to accept separate-but-equal status for his daughter and son. For the moment, he has placed them in a private school. "The alternative is out and out segregation," he says between drags on a Benson & Hedges menthol.

No matter what the alternative, Isenberg adds, PCAYC will fight as long as "Impressions" is offered to any child. "My concern is quality material for the classroom," he says. "Literature for literature's sake is fine in the public realm. But books in school have more impact. There are overtones and undertones to this series that could give a child a wrong message." When asked for a specific example, Isenberg responds: "You can't look at a single story. It's not just one story. The issue is the series."

In light of the school board's response to PCAYC's concerns, the parents' group initiated a recall campaign against school board president Jan Mishodek and trustee Stephen Miller, eventually gathering 5,603 signatures on a recall petition. Of these, the California courts recently ruled 4,400 valid. To get on the ballot, the group needed only 4,000 names, so Mishodek and Miller will have to face the voters—and four PCAYC-backed candidates—on Nov. 6.

In response to the recall effort, a citizen's group banded together to resist PCAYC. The Committee Opposed to the Recall Election consists mostly of parents, Jessup says, though it is led by a former school trustee, Normal Miller, and a retired teacher and administrator, Nulah Carmer. CORE also enjoys the support, both moral and financial, of the district's teachers. The group argues that the school board must represent all the district's taxpayers—not just the vocal minority.

Although members of the school board have been targeted, on the theory that they are ultimately responsible for policy, other members of the school community believe more may be at stake than the future of two politicians. The real aim, some say, is control over what teachers teach. And to get that control, winning PCAYC candidates might clean house. "Riley wants us out," says Jessup. "He's been asking to see administrators' contracts."

Even though teachers in the district have responded as if they, and not the school board, were under attack, Isenberg denies that PCAYC has targeted teachers. In fact, he sees them as instruments of the board's will, pawns in Yucaipa's passion play.

"This is not a teacher issue," he says. "Those teachers will teach whether you give them a book or a rock. Teachers are hired to teach. And who establishes what teachers teach? The school board!"

Despite Isenberg's reassurances, Jan Murphy, a third grade teacher at Yucaipa Elementary School, can't help but wonder: Should teachers feel threatened?

Toward the end of the spring semester last year, Murphy was teaching a two-week unit on Cinderella, taking the children first through an Indian version of the old folk tale featured in "Impressions," following up with references to the Disney cartoon, and reading similar stories from other cultures, including French, Egyptian, and Chinese.

"I ended with Grimm's 'Aschenputtel,'" she says, "and that's a little bloody. But you're talking about a book my folks bought me the year I was born, in 1950."

On the day Murphy read the Grimm Brothers' treatment of the hapless Cinderella, a parent happened to be sitting in, listening to how the teacher wrapped it all up. "She heard me tell the children how, at different times, thoughts are expressed by different cultures, by people from different ethnic backgrounds," she recalls. "The next thing I know, a school board member was calling with a complaint."

For Murphy, this Cinderella story had a happy ending. At the school board member's request, the principal dropped by to take a look at Murphy's curriculum materials. "I brought it all out, and she said, 'This is wonderful!'" Since then, Murphy has been asked to show other teachers how she uses the stories. "It came full circle. It worked in my favor."

But things don't always work out that way, says Ann Milne, a second grade teacher at the district's Dunlap Elementary School. Overall, she says, the effect of the anti-"Impressions" campaign has been chilling.

She also refutes Isenberg's calm disclaimers. "Teachers have been told that they aren't good Christians, that they're Satanists," she says. "Well, I've been telling ghost stories for 24 years. I hate to tell you how long I've been using 'In a Dark, Dark Wood.' It also makes me angry as a parent. They're trying to deprive my children of a good series."

Forrest Turpen says he understands why teachers react so vociferously. "It happens all the time," says the executive director of the Christian Educators Association International, a California-based national political group. "They get defensive," says Turpen, himself a former teacher and administrator. "Whether we like it or not, that element of humanness gets in the way of what we should really be looking at, which is, what's best for boys and girls?"

CEA is one of several religious groups involved in the effort to remove "Impressions" from schools, wherever and whenever it turns up. Others include national political groups such as the Citizens for Excellence in Education and the Traditional Values Coalition. What's happening in Yucaipa can be seen as part of a broad-based national campaign, though Turpen denies it. CEA, he says, hasn't offered the Yucaipa parents group much more than information on how to make their voices heard.

Turpen, for one, doesn't understand the Yucaipa school administration's resistance. In California, he says, school districts can choose from among 17 approved reading series.

"Some would say the series presents values that are not consistent with traditional American values," says Turpen. "One committee of parents in Stockton, Calif., reviewed the whole series and found 52 percent of the stories lent themselves to witchcraft."

Aside from the possible moral concerns, Turpen says the "Impressions" series is also flawed from an academic viewpoint. For one thing, he says, many of the books have never been screened. Only the texts used in grades 1, 2, and 3 have been approved by the state board of education, he says, a point confirmed by a spokesman for the state. No "content check" was done on the texts used in kindergarten and the older grades to determine whether they were appropriate for children in those age groups. These books are approved for use, Turpen says, only if local schools petition the state for permission.

In other states where the series is approved or being considered, almost no one shares the view that the series is flawed. If anything, it earns rave reviews.

Take, for example, these comments from a textbook review committee composed of teachers, citizens, and school administrators in Broward County, Fla., hardly a hotbed of liberalism: "[T]he selections are of high interest and stimulating . . . the illustrations are varied and beautiful." And this review from Florida's Dade County: [A]n excellent program. Moreover, the manuals are comprehensive and instruct teachers in current methods. Our only regret is that the program includes only K-3 and not 4-7." (Only the K-3 books were submitted in Florida.)

What CEA and others would like to see in place of "Impressions" is a reading series with greater emphasis on traditional Judeo-Christian values, stories of personal courage and individual ability. "Impressions," Turpen says, offers a more pessimistic approach, emphasizing despair, gloom, and hopelessness. "If you believe what the psychologists are telling us, for those children who have already been traumatized by separation and divorce, there is a good chance that over time this series will add to the confusion in their life."

To Paul Hauck, a clinical child psychologist in Davis, Calif., more confusion stems from not teaching children to think critically about the issues that will confront them in life.

"These parents don't have the view that you teach children to think independently," says Hauck, who reviewed the series out of professional curiosity when the controversy came to nearby Dixon. "They want a teacher who will sit down with the children and tell them what to think." Unfortunately, he says, children who grow up with this rigid, black-and-white view of the world often discard those ideals when they learn that life is often more complicated.

Hauck also disagrees with allegations that the series is likely to frighten children. "Frequently, those concerns come out of parents looking at these materials, first, through the eyes of an adult, and, second, looking at them with a biased point of view," he says. "Children take a cue from their parents. If parents say, 'This is bad or this is dangerous,' children will look at it and respond in the same way. Parents who are most upset about this tend to have children who also react to it in ways that are upsetting."

In any case, Hauck suggests, "Impressions" probably isn't the issue. Parents in Yucaipa and other communities, he says, are really using the controversy to advance a traditional, authoritarian point of view.

Donna Fowler, issues director for People for the American Way, concurs. The nonpartisan constitutional liberties organization has defended "Impressions" at every turn.

"I think what you see in California is real opportunism on the part of a couple of far-right groups trying to promote their own agenda in the schools," Fowler says. "They are straightforwardly pushing a Christian agenda. You've got somebody there who's on a witch hunt, and you can bet they'll find a witch."

What's happening in Yucaipa is not unusual, Fowler says, and in this case "Impressions" is only a means to an end. At another time, in another place, the target might be science books that don't give equal treatment to creationism. It isn't simply, she says, a quarrel over local values.

"I'm always a little skeptical about this business of prevailing local values," she says. "Public schools are remarkably alike across this country. There are shared values. In 18 school districts in California, 14 went through a careful review process and voted to retain the series with the support of a lot of other parents in the community. Prevailing local values do not support removal of the 'Impressions' series."

"What we've tried to do," she says, "is to put this issue in the larger context of what we see as a culture war going on in the country. It's part and parcel of other efforts to attack freedom of expression."

According to a recent study conducted by the watchdog organization, attacks on textbooks, plays, and supplemental reading rose during the last school year to an all-time high of 244 incidents in 39 states. The study, titled *Attacks on Freedom to Learn,* noted that the assault on "Impressions" is one of the most vigorous since the so-called "Scopes II" controversy in Tennessee in 1985. In that case, far-right censorship groups took court action to ban a reading series that they said offended their religious sensibilities. They won the first judicial round but lost on appeal.

In every instance, Fowler charges, far-right religious groups prey on the fears of community members, typically asking them to sign petitions to support the removal of books that most have never seen.

But their main thrust, she says, is to get their members elected to local school boards. In this, Fowler concludes, "they have not been very successful."

Dennis Riley, who does not see himself as a religious extremist—he says he doesn't even attend church on a regular basis—would no doubt like to make People for the American Way eat its words come election day.

And he resents being cast in the role of intruder in the affairs of the schools. Riley, whose three children have attended Yucaipa schools, says public education is his business.

"On a local level, people have a right to exercise their own sensibilities when it comes to education," Riley says. "We don't want supernatural concepts in the guise of folklore and cultural diversity. Would you rather resist now, when it's still manageable, or wait until it's no longer possible? I'd rather do it now."

Finally, Riley wants teachers to know that he is not the enemy—even though they have treated him like one. "They want to talk about hate mail," he says, laughing. "Come talk to us. We've had insult heaped upon insult; we've been called dangerous radicals and fanatics. It's going to be a long time before that goes away. But we've only attacked the textbooks. We haven't attacked the people."

Ann Milne, not surprisingly, disagrees. And she reacts viscerally to the suggestion that teachers would blithely continue to use a textbook that hurts children on the orders of the school board. "Do they really think I would pick a book that would be harmful to a child?" she asks. "I would never harm a child."

And after seeing the school board's attempts at appeasement rejected, she is beginning to doubt that the Parent/Citizen Association of Yucaipa/Calimesa can ever be fully satisfied. "If we roll over for this," she asks, "what are we going to roll over for next?"

42

"Don't Let Zealots Censor Kids' Books"

USA Today Editorial*

Some parents in Yucapia, Calif., see the face of Satan in their children's schoolbooks.

These parents say that if you turn the picture of a field of lavender upside down, you can see the devil.

The picture, accompanying the song *Lavender's Blue,* comes from a page in one of a series of textbooks—for grades kindergarten through sixth—called "Impressions."

Now in use across the USA, "Impressions" is an anthology of classic short stories, poems and folk tales intended to stimulate children's interest in reading. It has won plaudits from school administrators and teachers for doing just that.

Yet, five school districts have rejected or removed the series and two others are reviewing it because of some parents' complaints the pages are filled with Satanism, violence, immorality and disrespect for authority.

The Yucaipa board looked at the picture—upside down—and didn't see what the parents saw. Board members also reviewed the other complaints and, like 13 other districts, voted to keep the books.

People sometimes see what they want to see—not what's really there. People sometimes want others to see things only one way—their way.

Unfortunately, that's why "Impressions" isn't the only book controversy, just the latest.

More and more, parents—often motivated by members of conservative or religious fundamentalist groups—are challenging textbooks.

Over the years, studies by People for the American Way . . . and the American Library Association have shown increasing censorship of reading matter in the nation's schools.

• The school district of Culver City, Calif., removed an adaptation of *Little Red Riding Hood* from its reading list because it describes Grandma as having a glass of wine.

• Parents in Vancouver, Wash., demanded Judy Blume's *Forever* be removed because it was too sexually explicit. After review, the school district voted to retain the book.

*August 28, 1990.

• A library in Saginaw, Mich., removed *Garfield: His Nine Lives* from the children's section because some parents said it contained themes too mature for children.

Similar fights are going on from New York to Florida.

That's why we must be aware of their actions and wary of their motives. That's why we mustn't let local school boards become the battleground for religious views. How threatening can Little Red Riding Hood and Garfield be to our First Amendment rights of free speech and thought?

Parents, and teachers, do have a right to participate in the review process when districts are considering selections. But final decisions must rest with the school boards.

Parents do have a right to teach their children their beliefs and values—but at home, not in public schools.

And parents do have a right, when all other options fail, to request an alternative recommended reading list.

But parents do not have the right to censor what the majority of other children can read.

The impressions we give our children through books should not be a world of narrow minds and limited vision, but of diverse experiences and limitless possibilities.

43

Local Pro-Censorship Group Formation

by Washington Coalition Against Censorship

School Censorship: An Emergency Response Manual, though published for those in the Washington State school systems, "provides information for parents and other concerned citizens to help protect students' rights to use books and other media. Freedom of expression includes the right to read what one chooses, the right of access to a wide variety of materials presenting many points of view, and the freedom to make one's own decisions and choices about all these matters."

When a book comes under attack from a group, the Washington Coalition Against Censorship offers a strategy to combat it.

Call the Coalition at (206) 784-6418 to order its manual (Washington Coalition Against Censorship, 5503 Seventeenth N.W., #640, Seattle, WA 98107).

You become aware of the formation of a group to promote censorship of school materials or curriculum or teaching methods.

1. Contact this group and get their information (this may require help from someone unknown to them, if you are known). Record the name of the group, the name of your contact person, and the date contact was made.

2. Learn about their membership.

3. Get on the group's regular mailing list. Subscribe to any existing newsletters/publications of this group.

4. Collect newspaper clippings about this group.

5. Find out if this group has national affiliations and/or is affiliated with any national school censorship groups.

6. Ask for information about this group from: (1) your school administration, noting dates, phone numbers, names of contacts, and their responses. (2) your school board (noting the same information as above). (3) your local teacher's association (the name can be found in the local phone directory or from school administration). Note same information as above. (4) Librarian's associations (these contacts may be obtained from your school librarian, the school administration, or the phone directory; note same information as above).

7. Share your information with all of the above.

8. Begin to set up a support group. Form a coalition of local parents, citizens and groups concerned about the issue. Keep all names, dates, phone numbers and other basic information: what you did, how, and when.

9. Involve your group in studying the issue.

10. Consider holding a public information meeting. Your most valuable tools in the fight against censorship are open discussions and dissemination of the facts. You must make other parents, teachers, board members, and citizens aware of the situation.

11. Contact the media.

44

The Religious Right Must Guard American Values

by Jerry Falwell

> Censorship has become a necessity because perverted educators have felt that presenting life in the raw produced a better product than the tried and proven methods of a few generations ago . . . with their emphasis on morality, integrity and striving for perfection."
>
> —ROBERT BILLINGS, quoted in *Censorship News,* March 1982

In his inaugural address on March 4, 1797, John Adams, our second President, stated that one means of preserving our Constitution was to "patronize every rational effort to encourage schools, colleges, universities, academies, and every institution for propagating knowledge, virtue, and religion among all classes of people." He spoke of the high destiny of this country and of his own duties toward it, having been "founded on a knowledge of the moral principles and intellectual improvements of the people deeply engraved on my mind in early life." When John Adams graduated from Harvard, its handbook for "rules and precepts" stated: "Let every student be plainly instructed and earnestly pressed to consider well [that] the main end of this life and studies is to know God, and Jesus Christ, which is eternal life. And therefore to lay Christ in the bottom as the only foundation of all sound knowledge and learning."

Our Founding Fathers knew the importance of education. They consider it a privilege of free men to be educated and to perpetuate their freedom by teaching the religious principles upon which our republic was built. When John Adams was President he said, "So great is my veneration for the Bible that the earlier my children begin to read it, the more confident will be my hope that they will prove useful citizens of their country and respectable members of society."

Education Passes on Society's Values

D. Bruce Lockerbie says in his recently published book *Who Educates Your Child?* "Education is a framework like the forms that hold molten lead or liquid concrete, helping to mold character. Education is a mirror to reflect the development of that character. In other words, education is the instrument for carrying out society's philosophical goals."

In the past, parents did not have to worry about the education on their children because the schools—the public schools—were without question the best in the history of the world. I remember when I attended Mountain View Elementary School in Lynchburg, Virginia. I enrolled there in 1940 and spent six years there. Every week we attended chapel. Someone would read the Bible to all of the students and we would have prayer and sing hymns. We were taught to reverence God, the Bible, and prayer. Although, at that time, I was not a Christian and I did not know the Bible or have any religious knowledge, I gained a respect for God, the Bible, the church, and for things that were holy. I learned all those principles in a public school.

Until about thirty years ago, the public schools in America were providing the necessary support for our boys and girls. Christian education and the precepts of the Bible still permeated the curriculum of public schools. The Bible was read and prayer was offered in each and every school across our nation. But our public schools no longer teach Christian ethics, which educate children and young people intellectually, physically, emotionally, and spiritually. The Bible states, "The fear of the LORD is the beginning of knowledge" (Prov. 1:7). I believe that the decay in our public school system suffered an enormous acceleration when prayer and Bible reading were taken out of the classroom by the U.S. Supreme Court. Our public school system is now permeated with humanism. The human mind has been deceived, and the end result is that our schools are in serious trouble. . . .

Amoral Humanism

Humanism claims a "life adjustment" philosophy. The emphasis is placed on a person's social and psychological growth instead of on factual knowledge. "Socialization" has become the main purpose of education. Students are told that there are no absolutes and that they are to develop their own value systems. The humanist creed is documented in two humanist manifestos, signed in 1933 and 1973. Humanists believe that man is his own god and that moral values are relative, that ethics are situational. Humanists say that the Ten Commandments and other moral and ethical laws are "outmoded" and hindrances to human progress.

Humanism places man at the center of the universe. The philosophy of naturalism projects man as an animal concerned only with fulfilling the desires of the moment. It teaches that man is not a unique and specific creation of God. Man is merely the ultimate product of the evolutionary process who has gained a sense of intelligence that prevents him from acting like an animal.

Naturalism looks on man as a kind of biological machine. In that philosophy of life, sexual immorality is just another bodily function like eating or drinking. Man lives a meaningless existence in which the only important thing is for him to make himself happy in the here and now. It is a philosophy of "do your own thing." Its slogan is "If it feels good, do it." Neither philosophy offers moral absolutes, a right and a wrong. Not only are these philosophies destroying our educational system, but they are destroying the basis and the foundation of the Christian family as well.

Negating Basic Values

Basic values such as morality, individualism, respect for our nation's heritage, and the benefits of the free-enterprise system have, for the most part, been censored from today's public-classroom textbooks. From kindergarten right through the total school system, it almost seems as if classroom textbooks are designed to negate what philosophies previously had been taught. Under the guise of sex education or value clarification, many textbooks are actually perverting the minds of literally millions of students. Let me lay out a brief summary of quotes that I have taken from textbooks I have in hand. These textbooks are actually being used in the classrooms of our American schools. I have found quotes such as these: "To truly induce completely creative thinking we should teach children to question the Ten Commandments, patriotism, the two-party system, monogamy, and laws against incest."

Here is another: "It's tactless if not actually wrong not to lie under certain circumstances."

Another: "To be a better citizen a person needs to learn how to apply for welfare and how to burn the American flag."

"There are exceptions to almost all moral laws depending on the situation."

"Honesty is not something you either have or don't have."

"American society is ugly, trashy, cheap, and commercial, it is dehumanizing, its middle-class values are seen as arbitrary, materialistic, narrow, and hypocritical."

"To be successful in our culture one must learn to dream of failure."

"Only by remaining absurd can one feel free from fear."

A textbook entitled *Human Sexuality: A Course for Young Adults* was approved by the California State Board of Education. Recommended to the board by the State Commission on Curriculum, the book is intended for children aged twelve to fourteen, in the seventh and eighth grades. Sex is described explicitly in words and pictures. The book advises children that because parents are old-fashioned and narrow-minded about moral values, the home is the worst place to learn about sex. It presents the view that perversion is in the eyes of the beholder, saying that unusual sexual behavior should not be considered a perversion simply because it is out of the ordinary. Students are informed that strong disapproval of premarital sexual activity is not shared by the majority of the world's cultures. Infidelity is condoned. The book spoke about subjects such as homosexuality, incest, masochism, masturbation, sadism, and nymphomania.

Many parents would be appalled and shocked if they examined the textbooks from which their children are being taught in America's schools today. Books are very significant factors in society. The textbook business for elementary and secondary schools is an $823-million-a-year business.

When you find an advanced society such as ours, you will find that books have played an important part in the development of that society. The Book of all books has been and always will be the Word of God, the Bible. The foundation for our government, our laws, our statutes, our civilization, the structures of our home, our states, and our churches has come from the Word of God. America's past greatness has come because she has honored the Bible. The attitude America's people take toward the Bible is in direct proportion to the stability of America as a nation. . . .

Anti-Value MACOS

Mel and Norma Gabler head a group called Educational Research Analysts. The Gablers have been known all across America for their efforts to improve the textbooks of America's schools. . . .

Mel Gabler points out in a pamphlet entitled *Have You Read Your Children's School Textbooks?* that the federal government has funded a particular series of studies called "MACOS," which stands for "Man: A Course of Study." Designed for fifth-grade children, this course was hailed by liberals when it came out in 1972 as one of the greatest programs ever developed. Supposedly, MACOS teaches why man is more human than other animals and so on. But as the Gablers have pointed out, the study includes wife-swapping, men practicing cannibalism, the killing of baby girls, and eleven-year-old students role-playing leaving their grandmothers to die. The thirty MACOS booklets are filled with more examples of such cruelty, violence, and death.

MACOS was produced by the National Science Foundation and was the brainchild of Jerome Bruner, a Harvard psychologist specializing in experimental behavior. MACOS was intended to teach the universal bond among all men through a series of discovery lessons on a variety of cultures. The aim was to have children step outside of their own cultures to question values that they may have already learned. The required training for teachers forbids any new questions or clarifications to be inserted. The teacher is helpless. All questions come from manuals that have to be followed exactly, and the students are not allowed to look for answers in extracurricular source material of their own or their parents. All answers must be obtained from the course books, the simulated games, and the films. MACOS is a perfect example of a closed system of government indoctrination for neutralizing the values taught by church and home.

Children who take this course are not to take their booklets home. When parents try to examine these booklets, they find it is very difficult. Parents should be prepared for such pacifying statements as, "The books teach realism; students should learn about other cultures." Students are faced with values that are anti-American, that equate man with the animals, and that display harsh attitudes toward a home and family. Children are taught that there are no absolute rights or absolute wrongs and that the traditional home is one alternative. Homosexuality is another. Decency is relative.

Inquiries in Sociology notes, "there are exceptions to almost all moral laws depending on the situation." But if God, or the integrity of the Bible, or creationism is included uncritically in a textbook, that book is immediately labeled as biased.

Indoctrinating Children

Hitler knew exactly how to indoctrinate people. He went right to the children and in their schoolrooms. Fascism was taught until at one point in time the children became his slaves. Children were ready and willing to turn their parents in to the state for disloyal statements. Prayer and Bible reading were taken out of the schools because they might "offend" some child who did not believe in God. The other 99 percent of the children had to listen to evolution and secularism, humanism, and vulgarity.

The textbook *Many Peoples, One Nation* (1973) contains this statement: "No nation on earth is guilty of practices more shocking and bloody than in the United States at this very hour." The National Education Association (NEA) is urging that a film, *The Unknown War,* put together by Soviet film makers, be shown to school children. The film is nothing less than Soviet propaganda.

In the book *Are Textbooks Harming Your Children?* author James Hefley points out that the Gablers were disturbed by a report from an NEA affiliate, the National Council for the Social Studies. The report, "The Study and Teaching of American History," helped to explain the changes in recent history texts. The report said: "Our principle for selecting what is basic in . . . history involves a reference to its predicted outcome. Our 'emphasis' will be determined by what we find going on in the present. . . . Most of us have pledged our allegiance to an organized world community. . . . The teacher who adopts this principle of selection is as intellectually honest as the teacher who relies upon the textbook author—and far more creative. . . ." We find that public education has become materialistic, humanistic, atheistic, and socialistic. This is a far cry from what our Founding Fathers intended education to be. It is a far cry from the motto of the United States of America, "In God We Trust."

• *Rev. Jerry Falwell is the founder of Moral Majority, Inc.*

45

Diversity in Collection Development
An Interpretation of the
Library Bill of Rights

from American Library Association

The cornerstone of the ALA is its Library Bill of Rights, clarified through published interpretations. Diversity in Collection Development affirms the importance of intellectual freedom, "the essence of equitable library services."

Throughout history, the focus of censorship has fluctuated from generation to generation. Books and other materials have not been selected or have been removed from library collections for many reasons, among which are prejudicial language and ideas, political content, economic theory, social philosophies, religious beliefs, sexual forms of expression, and other topics of a potentially controversial nature.

Some examples of censorship may include removing or not selecting materials because they are considered by some as racist or sexist; not purchasing conservative religious materials; not selecting materials about or by minorities because it is thought these groups or interests are not represented in a community; or not providing information on or materials from non-mainstream political entities.

Librarians may seek to increase user awareness of materials on various social concerns by many means, including, but not limited to, issuing bibliographies and presenting exhibits and programs.

Librarians have a professional responsibility to be inclusive, not exclusive, in collection development and in the provision of interlibrary loan. Access to all materials legally obtainable should be assured to the user, and policies should not unjustly exclude materials even if they are offensive to the librarian or the user. Collection development should reflect the philosophy inherent in Article II of the *Library Bill of Rights.* . . . A balanced collection reflects a diversity of materials, not an equality of numbers. Collection development responsibilities include selecting materials in the languages in common use in the community which the library serves. Collection development and the selection of materials should be done according to professional standards and established selection and review procedures.

There are many complex facets to any issue, and variations of context in which issues may be expressed, discussed, or interpreted. Librarians have a professional responsibility to be fair, just, and equitable and to give all library users equal protection in guarding against violation of the library patron's right to read, view, or listen to materials and resources protected by the First Amendment, no matter what the viewpoint of the author, creator, or selector. Librarians have an obligation to protect library collections from removal of materials based on personal bias or prejudice, and to select and support the access to materials on all subjects that meet, as closely as possible, the needs and interests of all persons in the community which the library serves. This includes materials that reflect political, economic, religious, social, minority, and sexual issues.

Intellectual freedom, the essence of equitable library services, provides for free access to all expressions of ideas through which any and all sides of a question, cause, or movement may be explored. Toleration is meaningless without tolerance for what some may consider detestable. Librarians cannot justly permit their own preferences to limit their degree of tolerance in collection development, because freedom is indivisible.

• *Adopted July 14, 1982. Amended January 10, 1990, by the ALA Council.*

Library Bill of Rights

The American Library Association affirms that all libraries are forums for information and ideas, and that the following basic policies should guide their services.

1. Books and other library resources should be provided for the interest, information, and enlightenment of all people of the community the library serves. Materials should not be excluded because of the origin, background, or views of those contributing to their creation.

2. Libraries should provide materials and information presenting all points of views on current and historical issues. Materials should not be proscribed or removed because of partisan or doctrinal disapproval.

3. Libraries should challenge censorship in the fulfillment of their responsibility to provide information and enlightenment.

4. Libraries should cooperate with all persons and groups concerned with resisting abridgment of free expression and free access to ideas.

5. A person's right to use a library should not be denied or abridged because of origin, age, background, or views.

6. Libraries which make exhibit spaces and meeting rooms available to the public they serve should make such facilities available on an equitable basis, regardless of the beliefs or affiliations of individuals or groups requesting their use.

Adopted June 18, 1948. Amended February 2, 1961, June 27, 1967, and January 23, 1980, by the ALA Council.

46

How Conflicting Values Result in Challenges

by Nancy Motomatsu and Jean Wieman

Motomatsu and Wieman's comments were excerpted from a presentation delivered at the "Intellectual Freedom: The First Amendment and the Right to Know" Institute, at Honolulu, Hawaii, on June 14–18, 1982.

One view: The purpose of education is to transmit the traditions of our culture and to reinforce the value of the family. **Another view:** The purpose of education is to teach students to question, to explore, to grow in understanding and thus change their view of the world.

One view: It is the role of the schools to teach the basic skills—reading, writing, and arithmetic. **Another view:** Citizens in a democracy need more than the basic skills; they must be able to make informed decisions, critical judgments, and to think for themselves.

One view: My children don't need schools to emphasize the sordid aspects of life. **Another view:** Students need to be able to deal with the real world as it is, which often is not the world we would like.

o   o   o

Exaggerated only somewhat, the diverse perceptions above are manifestations of divergent individual and societal values, expectations, and desires. These differing, often conflicting views, are usually deeply rooted in family and moral values, rules, and roles. Before children enter first grade, they will have participated in over 20,000 hours of verbal reinforcement of the family values structure and specific behavioral expectations.

In a pluralistic society, the wide range of family values and resultant differing educational expectations must be considered carefully as we plan educational programs to meet the needs of all students.

For many adults, childhood is perceived as a time of questioning and openness to new and unfamiliar learning experiences—experiences which extend to those available within the sometimes limited environment of the family structure. Sometimes parents may purposefully arrange these experiences in order to expose their children to other "real worlds" which they may encounter as they grow in independence. Other parents may feel the need for surrounding their children with the old, the tried and true, and familiar. Reinforcement of the established family values (minimizing the exploration of ideas and experiences which do not conform to their set of rules and values) provides a measure of security and continuity in an upsetting world which does not conform to "traditional" roles.

The broad purposes and traditions of American education have evolved over many decades. These principles have been defined, refined, tested, and approved by not only the educational establishment, but by parents and society in general and in particular, the broad middle class spectrum of society.

Generally, statements of educational goals or principles include phrases such as: "develop the skills necessary for critical thinking and effective decision-making," "accept and appreciate the cultural diversity of our community and the world," "understand and appreciate the values and traditions of our American democratic world." . . .

It is inconceivable to us as educators that the above fundamental purposes of education might be open to challenge. In fact, at this stage of generality, they seldom are questioned. However, as these principles are translated into actual educational practices, the potential for conflicts relating to common educational values and, therefore, the ideas presented in many instructional materials, become explosively apparent.

If we say we believe that our school should present information on all sides of an issue and guide students to responsible decision-making . . . *How should we respond to the family whose basic fundamental values will not allow consideration of more than one view . . . the "right" one?*

If we say we believe that our students should know how other people around us act, feel, and believe . . . *How can we respond to the family which believes that schools should select only literature which enforces the ethical or moral teachings of their own family?*

If we say we believe that the prime purpose of education is to encourage students to think for themselves, broaden their outlook, and see the world differently as a result . . . *How do we reassure those parents who fear children thinking for themselves and thus making different value judgments than the parent?*

o   o   o

Many of our strongly held educational values—teaching children to be critical thinkers, preparing students to live in a global and pluralistic society, helping children make wise decisions about their own lives—in fact, any educational goal outside of teaching basic skills and facts may be perceived as dangerous to certain personal or religious values.

Manifestations of Challenges

To those of us in library media positions in the schools, the conflicts may manifest themselves in challenges as to what books should or should not be housed in our libraries; what magazine subscriptions should be purchased; what constitutes "appropriate" reading for a seventh grader (but not for a sixth grader). In the broader concept, however, the conflicts are based on different perceptions regarding the purposes of education.

For some adults, freedom of thought and the need for children to question and to think critically for themselves are rational and desired outcomes of education; for others, they represent a threat to their own moral view of right or wrong. For these adults, the world today is perceived as two separate camps: moral and immoral, right and wrong. In the views of adults who regard much of what they see in the world "outside" of their own value structure as strange or unacceptable, even exposure to books and ideas which run counter to their own beliefs and values is dangerous to the immature minds of their children.

Adults' sincere fears of such "contamination" from exposure to alien books and ideas result in protests against curriculum content, teaching methods, "lack of standards," and instructional materials.

o o o

Challenges to instructional materials seem to focus on four major areas:

1. *Disrespect for traditional and orthodox conceptions of God and the Bible.*
   - From a parent (Kanawha County, West Virginia): "The textbooks from the first to sixth grade teach God to be a myth. The Bible teaches children to obey their parents. . . . We stand to lose the respect of our children and suffer the loss of the parent-child relationship."
   - From Phyllis Schlafly (of the Eagle Forum): "Parents have the right to expect schools to permit voluntary prayer and teach the 'fourth R' (right and wrong to the precepts of the Ten Commandments)."
   - From Rev. Jerry Falwell: "Textbooks have become absolutely obscene and vulgar. Many of them are openly attacking the Bible."

2. *Use of profanity, vulgar language, and sexual explicity.* From a parent [no address]: "The book is filled with drawings of men and women making love in sexually explicit positions. It's filled with gutter language. I don't send my child to school to learn garbage! Is this 'literature' my tax dollars are paying for?"

3. *Disrespect for authority.* From Norma Gabler [of Educational Research Analysts]: "For years we taught the academic skills. The important thing was to teach the child to read and write. We had good, wholesome stories. We taught the good, the true, and beautiful. Now it is a steady stream of

violence and disrespectful attacks on the home, our government, our American heritage."

4. *Advocacy of moral relativism.* From Norma Gabler: "The schools no longer aim to teach facts, skills, and knowledge . . . right or wrong. The aim is to change the thinking and values of children. . . . It's an insidious attempt to replace our periods with their question marks. It's wrong to steal. When a teacher asks my child, 'Is it ever right to steal?' my child will begin thinking there's *no* right or wrong. [Stealing's] *always* wrong."

47

Some Specific Objections by Pro-Censorship Groups to Educational Materials

by Washington Coalition Against Censorship

Pro-censorship reactions arise most often in the U.S. when citizens are faced with a downturn in the economy, a perceived threat to national security, or great social changes which threaten traditional social and religious values. During the early 1980s, Americans have experienced all three of these developments.

Unfortunately, these pro-censorship organizations have been very successful in focusing popular fears and frustration on the public schools. Schools, being the most accessible arm of the government, have been held responsible for lower SAT scores, more student drug use, greater violence, higher crime rates, declines in morality, teenage pregnancy, and a host of other social ills.

Ultra-conservative organizations have expended much effort in identifying specific types of courses, teaching methods, and educational materials that they feel are particularly responsible for the many problems of society. They have made this information available to concerned parents on the local level and have encouraged them to work for the cancellation of targeted courses, the elimination of certain teaching methods, and the alteration or removal of targeted educational material like books, films, etc.

Edward B. Jenkinson, a professor of English Education at Indiana University, compiled a list of subjects, courses, and materials which ultra-conservative pro-censorship groups find objectionable. The following are taken from his list:

1. sex education
2. drug education
3. values clarification
4. the study of psychology and the use of psychological principles in teaching
5. sociology
6. anthropology
7. the humanities
8. ecology
9. world geography (if there is mention of "one-worldism")
10. world history (if there is mention of the United Nations)
11. ethnic studies
12. literature by black authors

13. profanity
14. violence
15. books that do not champion the work ethic
16. books that do not promote patriotism
17. books that do not promote the family unit as the basis of American life
18. mythology and stories about pagan cultures and lifestyles
19. books and stories that "defame" historical figures by revealing their weaknesses
20. "trash" (e.g., *The Catcher in the Rye, Go Ask Alice, Black Boy, Flowers for Algernon,* etc.)
21. works by "questionable" writers, including Langston Hughes, Dick Gregory, Ogden Nash, Richard Wright, Joan Baez, Malcolm X, and others
22. phase-elective English programs
23. books that contain any print that is not horizontal and reads from left to right
24. the use of role-playing as a teaching tool
25. sensitivity training
26. behavior modification
27. assignments that lead to self-awareness and self-understanding
28. situation ethics
29. assignments that help students make value judgments
30. human development programs
31. stories about the supernatural

In the Eyes of the Beholder

If one were to eliminate all the subjects and materials objected to by these pro-censorship groups, there would be little left to teach students in the public schools. Professor Jenkinson also includes additional categories in his list:

• Suggestive titles . . . A woman campaigned for the removal of the book *Belly Button Defense*—a book for basketball coaches—because of the title.

• *Making It with Mademoiselle* was attacked because of the title and was only allowed back into the school library when it was discovered that it was a pattern book for dressmaking.

• Literature written by homosexuals. "*Save Our Children* wishes to thank those members of our community who, with their contributions, helped sweep us to victory in Florida. The battle has only begun, however, and soon we will carry our campaign all over the nation. . . . For years homosexuals have been hogging the news with their demands for equal rights, and it is time we pushed back. It is time that, along with thieves and murderers, they be branded for the sinners they are and removed from society. . . . You can fight to eliminate homosexual literature from our schools and libraries. This includes works by such homosexuals as: Emily Dickinson, Willa Cather, Tennessee Williams, Oscar Wilde, Walt Whitman, Hans Christian Andersen, Horatio Alger, Jr., Rod McKuen."

• Materials that contain negative statements about parents. . . . Textbook guidelines distributed at a meeting of "concerned citizens" in Minnesota noted that classroom "materials, textbooks, audio and/or visual aids must not portray parents as unloving, stupid, hypocritical, old-fashioned, possessive, nor in any other negative way." Similar statements have been made by censorship groups elsewhere in the U.S.

• Magazines that report the harsh realities of life. . . . Censors have objected to *Time, Newsweek,* and *U.S. News & World Report* because they publish stories about war, crime, death, violence, and sex; censors have attempted to have them banned not only from classroom use but also from school libraries.

• Nudity. . . . Textbook critics have objected to: reproductions of Michelangelo's "The Creation" from the Sistine Chapel; a drawing of a nude boy in Maurice Sendak's *In the Night Kitchen;* and pictures of models in bathing suits in *Sports Illustrated.*

"Freedom to Read"

Taking a page—so to speak—from *In the Night Kitchen,* the controversial nude boy reappeared in a new piece of art by Maurice Sendak, "Freedom to Read." The color illustration, commissioned especially for the 1991 American Booksellers Association convention held in New York City, shows the nude boy reading a book; behind him is a carnival of food, appropriately fashioned with book titles (a loaf of rye bread bears the title of J.D. Salinger's controversial *Catcher in the Rye*).

The Sendak image was available to conventioneers on T-shirts and book bags from the American Booksellers Association; also, the image was available from Every Picture Tells a Story (836 North LaBrea, Los Angeles, CA, 90038) as a full-color lithograph, signed and numbered by Sendak, in two versions: a 24 x 31 inch print, an edition of 275 ($500); and, for $800, in an edition of only 90, the same print (with a smaller image size) signed by dozens of "the greatest authors, children's book illustrators, and performing artists of our time, including: Jeffery Archer, Neil Simon, Gloria Steinem, Chris Van Allsburg, Whoopi Goldberg, Alan Dershowitz, John Sayles, Garry Trudeau, Betty Henley, Harrison Ford, Lane Smith, Harlan Ellison, Mary Higgins Clark, Leo Buscaglia, Dan Rather, Barry Moser, William Warfield, Robin Williams . . . and many, many more." (Others were asked but declined, citing time constraints; among them, Stephen King.)

The proceeds from the sales of both lithographs go to benefit the American Booksellers Association Foundation for Free Expression and Sendak's nonprofit national children's theater, Night Kitchen.

48

Common Questions and Answers

by Washington Coalition Against Censorship

The following points are frequently raised by parents or concerned groups in discussions of school censorship.

Why should my tax dollars be spent on vulgar stories? Why should books in a school library contain words you can't report on TV or print in the newspaper?

The concept and definition of "vulgarity" is subjective and differs from person to person. A book can't be eliminated because it is offensive to *some* people. When used in books and literature, especially fiction, vulgarity or obscenity reflects an expression of character. It's dishonest for authors to portray characters with language which is artificial for that character.

Furthermore, obscenity exists in daily life and daily conversation. Studs Terkel's book, *Working,* which has been banned in several school libraries, is an oral history of conversations with ordinary workers. Terkel recently defended his work before a Pennsylvania school system, and said he used the profanity because "people talk as people talk. Sometimes they use street language. . . ." He read aloud from a passage, and substituted dashes for the profane words. "What do you remember most? The words I dashed, or the thought (the firefighter) said? I leave it to you."

Why must stories and books be negative and represent ugly situations?

Authors don't create the world, they just reflect it. To deny that problems exist is to deny the possibility of dealing with these problems and solving these problems. Parents frequently argue that if a library purchases and shelves an offensive book, then it condones what the book contains. This reflects a misunderstanding of the function of a school library: to provide a comprehensive and balanced collection of information for students. A library will stock books on both Hitler and Jesus in a biography section. This selection, which does not indicate support or approval of either individual, simply [acknowledges] that both are important to world culture and history. In striving for balance, most school libraries will provide materials on both creation and evolution, for instance. That availability in a library is not the same as the actual teaching of "creation science" in a science classroom, however. The function of a library differs from that of a classroom.

Which individual librarian ordered this book—name, political affiliation, and religion? (Posed by individuals in an audience.)

Naturally, this information is not provided; the individual librarian follows library policy in ordering appropriate materials, in keeping with professional standards.

My daughter is too young for this book—I'm protecting her from this stuff.

While parents can keep their own children from reading certain selections, they cannot ban those materials so that no other children may read them. The obligation of a library is to provide a wide range of materials for all students who have access to that library.

One does not provide protection by refusing to deal with or discuss thorny issues. The increase in teenage pregnancy statistics can be seen as evidence as to what happens when children are not provided with adequate information and knowledge about issues such as developing sexuality.

Children are formulating many more questions and interests, at an earlier age, than ever before, because of better communications, media, and technology. It's best that they receive adequate answers and guidance within the home; it is naive to assume that, on their own, children won't question and find out what they want to learn if their questions are discouraged in the home setting.

If movie theaters are forced to rate films, and if bookstores have to keep their smut behind counters, why can libraries have all their materials out in the open, and not be subjected to a rating or labeling system?

Movie industry distributors and exhibitors developed their rating system in response to inevitable legislation which would require such a system. Labeling, or rating, prejudices viewers or readers. Ratings are arbitrary, artificial, and invalid as a determinant of the quality or composition of a film or book.

In a library system or bookstore, the presence of a book does not indicate endorsement. The American Library Association position on labeling states, "No one person should take the responsibility of labeling publications. No sizable group of persons would be likely to agree either on the types of material which should be labeled or the sources of information which should be regarded with suspicion."

Why can't school librarians just put offensive books on a restricted access shelf?

Restricted access to materials (i.e., closed or locked shelves, labeled as "adults only" in public libraries, or restricted to certain ages in school libraries) is censorship, albeit more subtle than direct removal. In school libraries, professional librarians are responsible for selecting materials suitable for the curriculum, interests, and educational levels of students who use the facility. Restricted shelves are inappropriate because they reflect the imposition of one standard (i.e., an irate parent or particular group) upon all students who use the library.

I'm afraid of the impact of certain books upon my child's behavior. I read about a high school senior committing suicide after reading Richard Bach's Illusions.

There is no way to determine the impact of any book on any individual. Each person brings his or her own history, biases, interpretations, and upbringing into everything that is seen or read. There have been studies and research conducted for decades trying to measure impact; it has simply been impossible. Susan Madden, Young Adult Librarian for King County Libraries, worked for several years in the Juvenile Justice system. She frequently states that she never saw a kid in the probation system because he *read* a book, but rather because they couldn't or wouldn't read books.

Perspectives: School Censorship

In the August 28, 1990, issue of *USA Today,* the topic for the editorial page was textbook censorship. The paper took the position that while parents have the right to restrict what *their* child can read, they don't have the right to restrict what *other* children should read. Guest columnist Julianne Malveaux echoed the paper's comments, noting that "reading *is* fundamental. It opens doors we may choose to walk through. . . . Censorship limits those options and slams the doors."

Of the six people the paper chose randomly, four of them believed that, given a choice between textbook censorship or not, they opted for the freedom to read.

The opposing view, tendered by Robert L. Simmons (founder and president of Citizens for Excellence in Education and the National Association of Christian Educators), held that "left-wing ideologists such as People for the American Way, Planned Parenthood and the National Education Association are making millions of their own public-school publications and subverting the minds of 44 million U.S. children."

49

How Parents Can Refute
the "Censor" Label

by Greg R. Jesson

One word that strikes fear in the hearts of most Americans is "censorship." The word evokes images of Nazi terror, KGB tyranny and book-burning bonfires. We imagine one of our deepest, most revered rights going up in smoke, as those with power rob us of our opportunity to freely think.

But in recent years, "censor" has been applied by liberals to anyone who disagrees with them. If you don't want your tax dollars to subsidize profane art, you are a "censor." If a publisher doesn't want to publish a violent novel, he is a "censor." If a local cable system refuses to carry MTV, it is a "censor."

As the word "censorship" has come to be applied to almost anything, it has come to mean nothing.

The most outrageous use of the word is its application to parents of school-age children. If a parent expresses concern over a child's third-grade reader, for example, the parent is a "censor," according to People for the American Way, the National Education Association and other like-minded groups.

Supportive parents are seen by many educators as those who don't ask questions, and concerned parents are often seen as meddling in the school system. This leads to the rather paradoxical conclusion that the less involved the parents are with their child's education, the more supportive they are presumed to be.

How do parents refute the charge that they are "censors"?

Point out this unexpected consequence: "If my attempting to restrict what you teach my children constitutes censorship, then your attempting to restrict what I can disagree with does, too. If my disagreeing with you is censorship, then your disagreeing with me is also [censorship]. You can't have it both ways; if one is censorship, then they both are."

The censorship that was so powerfully described in Orwell's *1984*, or in Bradbury's *Fahrenheit 451*, has nothing to do with parents, or even a community, protecting their children. Censorship is government suppression of any form of expression prior to its production. But many writers who should know better define the word far more broadly.

For example, William Noble writes in "What Every Writer Should Know About Censorship" about parents of a fourth-grade student objecting to a certain book because of its "profane language." Noble then asks, "If censors and book-banners can shape and define what we write, where does that leave free expression?" The answer, of course, is that free expression is left right where it has been since the First Amendment was written. If parents don't want their children reading profane literature in the fourth grade, Mr. Noble is still perfectly free to write whatever he wishes (libel, national security, and obscenity, etc., excepted by the Supreme Court). The point is that parents, in seeking to protect their children from harmful literature, are not preventing anyone from producing such literature—and therefore are not censors.

If finding certain material unsuitable for the education of children is censorship, then People for the American Way itself is guilty of it. PAW asked in 1990 that Alabama ban the supplementary science book *Of Pandas and People* from Alabama schools. PAW argued that the book violated separation of church and state, but *Of Pandas and People* is not a religious work and does not use the words "God" or "church." It does call into question the evidence for evolution.

PAW's inability, or unwillingness, to see themselves also as censors is a glaring example of intellectual dishonesty. As syndicated columnist Cal Thomas remarked, "It was precisely for such two-faced positions that the word hypocrisy was invented."

How much censorship itself has been turned upside down was expressed by George Will when he said:

> It is . . . a scandal beyond irony that thanks to the energetic litigation of 'civil liberties' fanatics, pornographers express expansive First Amendment protection while first graders in a Nativity play are said to violate First Amendment values.

• *Greg R. Jesson is the research manager for Focus on the Family's public policy department.*

50

Who Are the Real Censors?

by Phyllis Schlafly

As Terry O'Neill (editor of Censorship: Opposing Viewpoints) *characterized Phyllis Schlafly: She is "a highly energetic, conservative political activist . . . best known for her campaign against the Equal Rights Amendment. She is a strong defender of traditional family and religious values." Schlafly, of Eagle Forum, publishes* The Phyllis Schlafly Report, *from which this piece was excerpted.*

"Censorship" has been a trendy media subject ever since People for the American Way (PAW), colloquially known as People for Norman Lear's Way, started issuing annual press releases on the subject about eight years ago.

The word "censorship" is completely misused by PAW. As the dictionary confirms, "censorship" is an act by a government of someone acting in an official capacity. What PAW continually complains about is not government actions but parents, taxpayers and citizens speaking out against something of which they disapprove. Surely they should enjoy a First Amendment right to do that.

The misused and overused word "censorship" reaches its height of silliness when it comes to the question of the selection of books for the public schools. Out of the millions of books available, only a tiny handful can possibly be used in the classroom. When a few score of books are chosen for classroom use, does that mean that the rejected millions are "censored"? The word loses all meaning in that perspective.

We can probably all agree that *Playboy* and *Hustler* should be prohibited for use in the public school classroom. Once we make that admission, it is clear that we are not wrestling with weighty issues of "First Amendment" or "academic freedom," but merely with matters of judgment as to what is wise and appropriate to give to other people's minor children, and at what age.

When parents attempt to protect their children from school materials offensive to their religion or values, PAW labels this "censorship," and asserts the right of the public school to force on children "a broad spectrum of ideas that may challenge comfortable assumptions or inherited wisdom."

But who gave the curriculum dictators the authority to select books that "challenge" the children's religion, values, or parents? How did such books get into the public schools in the first place? Don't the rest of us have any First Amendment rights NOT to be forced to read materials we find offensive?

The notion that school personnel have some kind of "right" or "academic freedom" to force reading or visual materials on an involuntary captive audience of other people's minor children, in contravention of parental wishes, was invited by liberal anti-parent pressure groups such as PAW, the American Civil Liberties Union (ACLU), and the National Education Association (NEA).

According to People for the American Way's 1989 press release called *Attacks on the Freedom to Learn,* parents and taxpayers are winning nearly half their local curriculum battles. That is good news, but PAW reports it as bad news. "The censors," PAW says, "were successful in banning educational materials or restricting their use in nearly half of the challenges to instruction." The "censors," of course, are those exercising their First Amendment right of free speech and their parental rights to protect the faith and morals of their children.

PAW's report consists of a state-by-state survey on parental challenges to classroom instructional materials. According to the PAW survey, the subject area that drew the largest number of complaints during the previous year was witchcraft, satanism and the occult. Here is a sampling of these complaints by parents as reported in the PAW booklet called *Attacks on the Freedom to Learn.*

In Colorado, parents objected to a curriculum containing "elements of hypnosis and self-hypnosis and new-age kinds of things." In Florida, parents objected to *Devils and Demons* because it "might lead children to a life of devil worship."

In two districts in Georgia, parents objected to the excessive number of books in school libraries dealing with the occult and satanism. In Iowa, parents objected to middle-school children being given *Unnatural Talent* because it promotes satanism.

In one Illinois district, parents objected to the classroom use of *The Charming* because its stories of "demonic power and possession" are unsuitable for sixth graders. Other Illinois parents objected to giving seventh graders the guide for the London Dungeon, a museum depicting torture practices.

In one Kansas district, parents objected to *The Headless Cupid* for "teaching witchcraft." In another Kansas district, parents objected to using *The Witch Grows Up* with elementary school pupils because it makes "witchcraft look like a viable lifestyle."

In Maine, parents filed a complaint against *Stars, Spells, Secrets, and Sorcery* because it features "step-by-step instructions to set up an occult group." In New Hampshire, parents objected to the use of "Dungeons and Dragons" in a junior high school course because it promotes satanism.

In New Jersey, parents complained about *Devils and Demons* because its discussions of witchcraft and satanism are inappropriate for elementary school students. Elsewhere in New Jersey, parents objected to *Halloween ABC* because it contains "an offensive, evil, satanic theme which is inappropriate for younger children."

In Nevada, parents objected to second graders being given relaxation tapes that taught New Age and Far Eastern religions and which introduced them to a "white rabbit who is their friend and has the potential to invite a demon into their lives." In Ohio, parents of middle-school children objected to *Curses, Hexes and Spells* and *Servants of the Devil* for containing "satanic material."

In Oregon, parents objected to *The Restless Dead* for being "demonic" and "totally preoccupied with the occult." In another Oregon district, parents objected to *The Magic Grandfather* because of its preoccupation with magic and witches. In a third district, Oregon parents complained about *The Devil's Piper* because it encourages young minds to "pursue the occult," and to *The Prince in Waiting* because it promotes "positive attitudes toward the occult and ridicule toward Christianity."

In Texas, community members objected to the *Invitation to Psychology* text because it "very blatantly teaches transcendental meditation" and promotes "Eastern religion." In Washington, community members objected to DUSO and other programs because they may indoctrinate children in "New Age spiritualism," "Eastern religion," and occultism. In Wisconsin, parents objected to the film *Children of the Corn* because it promotes "the occult and rebellion by children."

Those who object to this type of classroom abuse apparently must endure being called "censors" by PAW. But parents should consider that label a badge of honor; it shows their concern to protect their children from being scared in the classroom.

People for the American Way's 1988 report on alleged "censorship" in U.S. public schools set forth a long series of complaints made by parents about school curricula and classroom materials. Few people realize how really offensive are the materials involved in these incidents of alleged "censorship."

Here are some specific parents' complaints about textbooks and library books, as quoted in PAW's 1988 booklet on "censorship." Each individual phrase below is from a different incident and is a direct quotation from the PAW booklet. For convenience, these quotations are bunched in paragraphs according to subject.

One large category of parents' complaints involved the language used in the school books: "objectionable language . . . foul language . . . profanity and unsuitable language . . . every swear word there is . . . filth and smut . . . offensive language . . . littered with dirty words . . . full of obscenities . . . repulsive language . . . vulgar language . . . dirty, filthy language . . . obscene, trashy gutter language that would gag a maggot."

Another category involved incest: "a 14-year-old girl's experience of incest . . . passages on incest."

Many parents complained about "graphic sexual scenes . . . sexually oriented language and content . . . explicit sexual references . . . overly explicit . . . encouraged promiscuity . . . promote extramarital sex and casual sex . . . rape, prostitution and drugs."

Here is another group of textbook complaints made by parents in various states: "promoting the occult and the worship of Satan . . . witchcraft and the occult . . . demonic . . . mocking God . . . preoccupation with occult practices, violent and aberrrant behavior . . . books on the occult . . . teaching magic and witchcraft . . . overtones of witchcraft, mysticism, and fantasy . . . the religion of the occult . . . advocating satanism, the occult, and witchcraft . . . teaching magic and witchcraft."

Parents objected to school books that promote off-beat behavior: "teaching children how to feel comfortable with pornography and feelings of incest . . . promoting prostitution, promiscuity, homosexuality and bestiality . . . replete with scenes of intrusion, oppression, cannibalism, abduction, transformation, incantations, deceptions, threats."

Another category of parental complaints involved teaching religion in the classroom: "Hinduism, mind control, and brainwashing . . . yoga exercises . . . mind control techniques . . . promoting Far Eastern religion . . . discussing Eastern religions."

Some complaints involved attacks on religion: "teaching values and morals contradictory to Judeo-Christian traditions . . . implying that God is not sovereign . . . secular humanism . . . situation ethics . . . teaching religion and invading students' privacy."

Some parents complained about anti-parent textbooks: "discussions that questioned parental authority . . . anti-family . . . ideas that conflict with family values . . . persistent themes of rebellion against parent and authority figures . . . a negative value system."

Other parents objected to school books that indoctrinated children with concepts of "globalism (one-world government) . . . world peace through nuclear disarmament . . . lack of an American perspective."

Many parents complained that materials were simply inappropriate for school instruction at particular ages: "negative and frightening illustrations . . . too scary for first-graders . . . depressing . . . sarcasm and humor not comprehensible by children . . . filth and garbage . . . violent acts by children."

Every phrase above was a specific complaint about an actual book in use in public schools in 1988, according to the PAW report. This attempt by parents to protect their children from such material is labeled "censorship" by PAW.

Look Who's Censoring Books

John Buchanan, chairman of People for the American Way, appeared before the Alabama State Textbook Committee in January 1990 to urge censoring a 1989 supplementary science book called *Of Pandas and People* by Percival Davis, Dean Kenyon and Charles B. Thaxton.

What made this event so amusing is that PAW, which was founded by Norman Lear, has been carrying on a flamboyant national advertising campaign, with TV ads and direct-mail solicitations, opposing what it calls the "censorship" of books used in public schools or libraries. But when it came to the matter of this supplementary book for tenth-grade Alabama public school students, PAW came down hard on the side of banning it from science classrooms.

Of Pandas and People was offered by Haughton Publishing Company of Dallas for inclusion on the list of state-approved books which may be bought by public schools with state education funds. It was not suggested that the book be required or that it be adopted as the sole or even the primary science textbook.

Thousands of parents had complained to the State Board of Education that all the science textbooks currently used in Alabama public schools exclusively teach evolution as the only acceptable theory of life's origins. *Of Pandas and People* was written to conform to the guidelines in the U.S. Supreme Court's most recent decision about origins, *Edwards* v. *Aguillard,* as well as the Alabama State Board of Education policy that teachers may present "various scientific theories about the origins of life."

At this hearing, Buchanan called *Pandas* a "creationist tract" and said it "would breach the walls of church-state separation and use the public schools as branch offices of their churches." He did not explain how the book could do this, since *Pandas* does not mention God, church, creation, or the supernatural.

Pandas identifies evolution as a theory and analyzes scientific information said to support both the evolution theory and an alternate theory for the origin of life, which *Pandas* calls "intelligent design." This is the theory that organisms started with "a blueprint, a plan, a pattern, devised by an intelligent agent."

The book does not purport to give final answers to the question of biological origins, but is intended to be a balanced and intellectually honest treatment. Using a method of inquiry widely used in the sciences, the book presents students with fact as fact (such as the fossil record), theory as theory, and stimulates them to draw their own conclusions.

It is just this type of non-religious, non-dogmatic approach which the U.S. Supreme Court called for in *Edwards* v. *Aguillard.* The publisher of *Pandas* presented an impressive list of testimonials from scientists from a wide variety of universities, including Brandeis, Oxford, Princeton, Yale, Texas A & M, and the University of Texas.

Before the Textbook Committee voted, the publisher's attorney withdrew the book from consideration so that no action was taken on the book. The attorney, Francis H. Hare Jr., cited two reasons for his action. First, State Superintendent of Education Wayne Teague made several highly prejudicial and hostile remarks to the Committee, 73 percent of whose members were his own appointees. Teague called *Pandas* "another effort to circumvent some Supreme Court rulings that bar religion from public school classrooms."

The second reason cited by Hare was that the Textbook Committee adopted an unfair procedure for the hearing which did not comply with the Alabama Administrative Procedures Act and which denied the publisher due process and the opportunity to respond to its accusers. One member of the Textbook Committee, Norris Anderson of Birmingham, resigned because of what he called the "unfair way" in which the public hearing was conducted. Anderson, who has been a high school teacher and textbook writer, argued that *Pandas* would let schoolchildren think for themselves.

We will be watching People for the American Way's next annual report on censorship to see if *Of Pandas and People* is listed as one of the books censored during 1990.

• *Phyllis Schlafly is the founder and president of the conservative group Eagle Forum.*

51

Using Parents as a Trojan Horse for School Censorship

by Arthur J. Kropp

Because People for the American Way (PAW) was criticized extensively by Schlafly, it seemed appropriate for PAW to respond. PAW President Arthur J. Kropp welcomed the opportunity and provided his perspective.

In communities across America, we're witnessing a widening censorship epidemic in the public schools. The new "activists" leading the charge seem intent on removing or restricting everything from books like *My Friend Flicka* and *Of Mice and Men,* to educational films, to sex education curricula.

The mostly conservative political groups funding and guiding many of these challenges are trying to convince the public that they are motivated solely by parental concern about "values" and what's being taught in our classrooms. In fact, reality tells us that this parental concern is more of a "Trojan horse" for the long-term political agenda of Right-wing lobbying groups seeking to control what our children learn. That's not an outcome to which most parents in this country aspire.

Most parents, along with most citizens, are alarmed by the rapid rise in school censorship incidents. A 1992 People for the American Way report, *Attacks on the Freedom to Learn,* found that such attacks jumped from 264 in the 1990-91 school year, to a new high of 376 in 1991-92. They ranged from challenges to curricular material to organized attempts to pressure the school system to efforts to remove books from libraries. But while those numbers are frightening, they don't tell the whole story.

Even when the censors ultimately lose a battle, their efforts spread fear, drive up costs for already strapped school systems and often divide communities—all in the name of "protecting" children from information and ideas the censors abhor. Listen to Religious Right "education" crusader Robert Simmons, head of a group that calls itself Citizens for Excellence in Education: "And if they call you a censor because you're asking to remove these books, just remember that censorship is society's way of preventing ideas and things happening that can destroy the entire society."

Sadly, Rev. Simmons has little faith in America or its people. As far as I know, the open discussion of ideas can never "destroy" a truly democratic society. In fact, it represents the healthiest of vital signs, and safeguards the freedom to learn for all of our children.

Equally important, and contrary to Religious Right rhetoric, opposition to school censorship campaigns does not connote hostility to parental involvement in the schools. Parents are and should be encouraged to involve themselves in review processes for new curricula, for example. Parents have every right to seek alternative assignments for their children, and toward that end more and more schools are developing policies that can be accommodating.

But there is a big difference between this positive parental involvement and accommodation and the censorship attacks People for the American Way documents in its annual report, *Attacks on the Freedom to Learn.* In the typical censorship incident, an individual or very small group—sometimes parents, sometimes not—attempt to dictate to an entire community what all children can or cannot read or learn. To most observers, that kind of "dictating" crosses the line into censorship. And the results—for the children, the parents and the community—can be very destructive.

Take one example—Woodland, California, where a censorship attack on the elementary school reading series, "Impressions," is still wending its way through the courts. Ostensibly the challenge was launched by two local parents, Doug and Kathleen Brown. But their concerns about "Impressions" were quickly seized and manipulated by a Tupelo, Mississippi-based organization called the American Family Association. AFA, led by the Rev. Don Wildmon, offered to represent the Browns, and sued the school district. As AFA did in similar civil suits, they alleged that the "Impressions" reading series, which contains a lively mix of classic stories and folk tales—including some Halloween stories— promotes "witchcraft" as a religion.

The AFA lawsuit, beyond being frivolous and opportunistic, refused to acknowledge that "Impressions" was chosen after a lengthy review process that included extensive parental input. However, the nuisance factor in their legal challenge did nothing to diminish the very serious financial consequences for the under-financed school district, which now faces a legal bill topping $60,000. Meanwhile, the costs continue to mount even after a federal court rejected the AFA attack. Rev. Wildmon's group is appealing the dismissal.

The no-nonsense stand taken by a group of Woodland parents willing to fight back shows clearly just how hollow the right-wing claims of protecting parents really are. It was parents in Woodland who decided to intervene on the side of the school district because they opposed AFA's attempt to censor the books. As one Woodland parent, Margaret Grissom, put it: "By trying to bully our schools and our parents, the AFA is trying to dictate what can and cannot be taught in Woodland." As in many other communities across America, it is the parents who are among the *first* to stand up for the freedom to learn.

That is an example in which their children can take pride.

• *Arthur J. Kropp is president of People for the American Way, a 300,000-member nonpartisan constitutional liberties organization.*

In the Beginning

Introduction: Creationism v. Evolution

When it comes to textbooks: as go California and Texas, so goes the nation, as People for the American Way explains in a 1992 report:

> The Religious Right's quest to gain control over the public schools in California must be examined in context. For years the textbook market in the United States has been driven by the demands of two states, California and Texas, that share two critical traits: first, they are the most populous states in the nation, and second, they select textbooks at the state level, as opposed to locally. The result has been that textbook publishers tailor texts to meet the specific demands of these two states, and, due to the resulting economies of scale, those books are offered for sale in almost every school district in the nation. In short, California and Texas drive the textbook market.
>
> The Religious Right long ago realized this important economic point and has made the two states the focus of a decade-long battle to force textbooks to reflect their particular sectarian ideology. The chief battleground in this on-going war on public education has been biology texts and, specifically, their treatment of evolution.
>
> Evolution is, of course, the cornerstone of modern biology. But many fundamentalists regard it as heretical to their own religious views, because they find it incompatible with the Biblical account of Genesis. Notably, most Christians are not similarly troubled, finding evolution and the Bible's account of Adam and Eve wholly compatible. Nevertheless, the modern Religious Right has campaigned against evolution since its inception, carrying on the battle that touched off the Scopes Monkey Trial of the 1920s.
>
> In this effort, the Religious Right for many years sought to maintain a stranglehold on biology textbooks nationwide, by controlling the content of books in Texas and California. By any measure, they were successful. In fact, a 1985 review of popular biology books conducted by a team of biology and education experts for People for the American Way found that one-sixth of all biology books surveyed did not even mention the word "evolution," and fully half covered the subject inadequately.
>
> Slowly, the Religious Right's grip on textbooks has loosened in the last few years, but to this day, both states have found it necessary to make meaningful political compromises with the Religious Right in the course of their textbook guideline and adoption proceedings.

In California the state school board made concessions to the Religious Right during the most recent biology "framework" proceedings in 1989. [In 1992], California . . . [adopted] new science texts based on these guidelines, opening up another avenue for Religious Right lobbying on Creationism.

In "Judgment Day Approaches for Vista Schools," published in the *Los Angeles Times* (1992), Carol Masciola reported that "the Christian right captured a majority of seats on the Vista Unified School District's board of trustees, marking the first time in at least a decade that religious conservatives have dominated any school board in San Diego County. . . ."

The two people elected were Joyce Lee, a substitute teacher and pastor's wife, and John Tyndall, accounting director at the Institute for Creation Research. On the issue of creationism v. evolution, the *Los Angeles Times* quoted Lee: "If evolution is a theory and creationism is a theory, and we're teaching our kids to be creative, thinking adults, why do we give them only one theory to think about?" Tyndall added: "I'm obviously sympathetic toward creation science. I think it would be beneficial to have both of those theories in the science classroom, with neither one being presented as the truth."

According to the *Los Angeles Times,* Lee and Tyndall have discounted concerns of bias and bringing a Christian-based agenda to the forefront. The concerns, however, seem to have a basis in reality, as the paper reports:

They're advocating changes such as:

• Reducing access to library books. (Lee favors placing an asterisk on the front of any library book that a parent complains about, and thereafter requiring all students to have signed parental permission to borrow the books.)

• Teaching that the biblical theory of creation has as much scientific merit as the theory of evolution.

52

Evolution as Religion

by Henry M. Morris and Gary E. Parker

It is an amazing thing that the modern establishments in science, education and the news media continually portray creationism as religious and evolutionism as scientific. While the purpose of this book is to discuss only the scientific aspects of the two models, it is important also that readers at least be aware that evolutionism is much more "religious" in essence than creationism. Not only does the creation model explain the scientific data better than the evolution model, but evolution serves as the basic philosophy for many more religions of the world, past and present, than does special creation.

Evolutionary Religions

The following is a partial listing of those religions that are structured around an evolutionary philosophy: Buddhism, Animism, Liberal Judaism, Hinduism, Spiritism, Liberal Islam, Confucianism, Occultism, Liberal Christianity, Unitarianism, Religious Science, Unity, Humanism. Many of the above, of course, could be broken down into various religious sub-groups, all believing in evolution.

I am not claiming that all of these are based on modern Darwinism, for most of them antedate Charles Darwin. Nevertheless, they are all anti-creationist evolutionary religions, and have generally adapted easily to modern "evolution science."

The basic criterion on evolutionism is the rejection of a personal transcendent Creator who supernaturally called the space-time universe into existence out of nothing but His own omnipotence. All of the above religions regard the universe itself as eternal, constituting the only ultimate reality. Processes innate to the eternal space-time cosmos have developed the universe and its inhabitants into their present forms. These natural processes may, in many cases, be personified as various gods and goddesses, but they are really just the natural processes innate to the universe itself. In some cases, the cosmos itself may be regarded as living and intelligent, giving rise not only to animals and people but also to "spirits" who inhabit it. All of these concepts are evolutionary concepts, since none of the components or inhabitants of the universe are accepted as the products of fiat creation by an eternal Creator. The very existence of such a Creator is either denied or incorporated into the cosmos itself.

The religions listed above are all extant religions, but the same discussion could apply to all the ancient pagan religions as well, all of which were essentially various forms of pantheism, and none of which were based on creation. Many of them (Epicurianism, Atomism, Stoicism, Gnosticism, pre-Confucian Chinese religions and many others) had cosmogonies quite similar to modern "scientific" evolutionary cosmogonies. Most of them incorporated astrology, spiritism and idolatry into their systems as well.

Thus, evolution is surely a religion, in every sense of the word. It is a world view, a philosophy of life and meaning, an attempt to explain the origin and development of everything, from elements to galaxies to people, without the necessity of an omnipotent, personal, transcendent Creator. It is the basic philosophy of almost all religions (except the few monotheistic religions), both ancient and modern. It is absurd for evolutionists to insist, as they often do, that evolution is science and creation is religious.

What they really mean is that evolution is *naturalistic,* and they arbitrarily define science as "naturalism," instead of retaining its traditional meaning as "knowledge" or "truth." However, to insist arbitrarily that the origin and development of everything must be explained naturalistically begs the whole question and amounts to nothing but atheism. Not all evolutionists are atheists, of course, but evolutionism itself is atheism, essentially by definition, since it purports to explain *everything* in the universe without God.

Atheism, of course, is also religious in essence. It must be accepted solely on faith, for it would be completely impossible to prove. Isaac Asimov admits as much:

> Emotionally, I am an atheist. I don't have the evidence to prove that God doesn't exist, but I so strongly suspect he doesn't that I don't want to waste my time [Asimov, 1982].

Now Asimov has an enormous knowledge of the scientific data in every field, and is probably the most prolific science writer of all time. If *he* doesn't have the evidence to prove atheism, then no one does! He *believes* it; it is his religion, and the same is true of most of the *leaders* of evolutionary thought today. The American Humanist Association, of which he is the current president, defines humanism as "a nonatheistic religion," and the first two tenets of the famous Humanist Manifesto state that humanism is based on the naturalistic origin of the universe, and of man, respectively.

Not only are the religions of atheism and humanism firmly grounded in evolutionary philosophy, but so also are a host of social, economic and psychological systems which have had profound effect on human moral behavior and thus also are fundamentally religious. This includes such politico-economic systems as Marxism, Fascism and Nazism, and such psychological systems as Freudianism, behaviorism and existentialism. It would include racism, imperialism and laissez-faire capitalism on the one hand, and socialism, communism and anarchism on the other. The list could go on and on, every item illustrating and reinforcing the fact that evolution is basically a religious concept, not a scientific theory. It is "evolution science," not "creation science," that is the oxymoron!

Creationist Religions

There are essentially only three modern creationist religions, in contrast to the dozens of evolutionary religions and religious philosophies. These are the *monotheistic* faiths—orthodox Judaism, orthodox Islam, and orthodox Christianity. These are all founded upon belief in one self-existent eternal Creator, who called the universe itself into existence in the beginning, as well as all its basic laws and systems.

Belief in this primeval special, completed, supernatural creation is consistent with all genuine facts of science, which is sufficient warrant for identifying this belief as "scientific creationism" or "creation science." This is further strengthened by the historical fact that most of the great scientists of the past who founded and developed the key disciplines of science were creationists. Note the following sampling:

Physics (Newton, Faraday, Maxwell, Kelvin)
Chemistry (Boyle, Dalton, Pascal, Ramsay)
Biology (Ray, Linnaeus, Mendel, Pasteur)
Geology (Steno, Woodward, Brewster, Agassiz)
Astronomy (Kepler, Galileo, Herschel, Maunder)

These men, as well as scores of others who could be mentioned, were all creationists, not evolutionists, and their names are practically synonymous with the rise of modern science. To them, the scientific enterprise was a high calling, one dedicated to "thinking God's thoughts after Him," as it were, certainly not something dedicated to destroying creationism.

It is also noteworthy that the various evolutionary religions of the world, discussed in the preceding section, are probably decadent forms of primeval worldwide monotheism. Ethnologists, archaeologists and cultural anthropologists have frequently noted evidence, in the traditions and artifacts of people all over the world, of dim recollections of a "high God," recognized originally as the Creator of all things in the earliest forms of their faith, but long since having deteriorated into an evolutionary pantheism, polytheism and animism. In the modern world, these have still further deteriorated into atheistic materialism, often now mis-labeled "evolution science." See Samuel Zwemer (1945) and Don Richardson (1981) for further discussion of the worldwide primeval belief in creation and an omnipotent Creator.

Still more recently, however, the barren materialism of modern evolutionism is provoking a return to evolutionary pantheism, now being arrayed in the more sophisticated terminology of modern technological scientism.

• *Henry M. Morris and Gary E. Parker are the coauthors of* What Is Creation Science? *Morris is president of the Institute for Creation Research.*

53

Scientific Illiteracy

by Frederick Edwords

> So why do people who call themselves Christians object to Evolution? I suspect that the reason isn't very flattering: it damages their ego—their sense of self-importance. That same impulse made their counterparts, four hundred years ago, refuse to accept the now indisputable facts of astronomy. . . . It also brought Italian science to a full stop for centuries—a chilling reminder of what a victory for Creationism could do to American education.
>
> —ARTHUR C. CLARKE, "The Menace of Creationism"

The world today, and especially the United States, is in the midst of a period of dramatic scientific, technological and social change unparalleled in human history. Numerous new discoveries, developments, and ideas have converged at once on humanity and have begun to alter the way the world thinks and operates.

In many ways, the social changes we are experiencing have been fostered by new technologies which, in turn, have been made possible through recent scientific discoveries. Much has been written about how our lives, values, economic relationships, and sense of our place in the world are being transformed by such things as effective birth control devices, surrogate parenting, robotics, high-tech farming, alternate energy, satellite communication, and computerization. Our children will be even more affected. Each new technology has traceable roots in modern science. For example, the discovery of the DNA molecule made possible gene splicing and the patenting of new life forms. Discoveries in physics made possible television, computers, some forms of alternate energy, and space exploration. Discoveries in biology and chemistry are making possible new foods and energy sources. The list goes on. Clearly, we are living in a world revolutionized by science.

And yet, isn't it ironic that most people living in this world or even in the United States—the most scientifically and technologically advanced nation on the globe—do not understand the scientific method? Even literate people—people who have had thirteen years of formal education in our society, read books, heard lectures, watched television documentaries, and perhaps even attended college—often still do not understand the way science works. Furthermore, they rarely have even a conversational knowledge of some of the most significant scientific discoveries or major theories of our century.

How many people could tell you much, if anything, about charmed quarks, gluons, black holes, quasars, cladistics, punctuated equilibrium, genetic drift, recombination of DNA, or something called Australopithecus afarensis? Yet, these words involve matters that spell the transformation of our knowledge of physics, the universe, the classification of life forms, evolution, chemistry, and the origin of our own species. Why don't most people know about them? Why aren't our children assigned the book Albert Einstein wrote that explains relativity in terms understandable by anyone with a high school education? Why are people, instead, told that Einstein's theory is too esoteric to be grasped by the general population?

Is it that most educated people, particularly Americans, aren't interested in science? Is it that they don't care about theoretical things, new developments, and the frontiers of knowledge?

Nonsense!

They care very much about these things. It is just that for some reason their attention has often been directed away from the exciting realm of real science and toward the fantasy world of pseudoscience.

The same people who couldn't tell you what a gluon is to save their lives could tell you volumes about pyramid power, iridology, biorhythms, kirlian photography, psychokinesis, and flood geology.

Who are these people? *We* are these people. *We* have all suffered through the same education and the same culture, and this is the kind of food for thought we have been served. It is time to recognize that we have not been served well, that we have legitimate grounds for complaint, and that we must act now to ensure that the next generation is not raised on the same paltry fare.

o   o   o

It is inexcusable that, in such an advanced nation as this, it becomes headline news when the California state superintendent of public instruction wants to have evolution adequately covered in science textbooks. Should this still be a controversial issue? Are there really reasons why he shouldn't want to do it? Does it make sense to think that the voters might throw him out if he gets the state to stop using substandard teaching materials?

Yet, it was indeed a controversial issue when Bill Honig launched a program to improve the quality of education in California. There were those who, believing the earth and universe to be a mere ten thousand years old, were offended at the notion of millions and billions of years of change. These same people, believing that almost the entire fossil record was laid down within a single year during a worldwide flood occurring around 4000 BC, were offended at the notion of the geologic column. And it was these people—believing that life forms must have been specially created, yet that all life on the planet today

today is descended from a few "basic kinds" of plants and animals that survived the flood in a big boat—who were offended by the teaching of evolution. These people, the so-called scientific creationists, have had tremendous political clout. Their major legislative effort, the Louisiana creationism law, will now come before the U.S. Supreme Court. They have caused havoc in our public schools from coast to coast and are not about to stop.

In the face of this we must ask, "Whose educational system is it, anyway?" Does it belong to the people, or to the pseudoscientists? Is the job of education to provide state-of-the-art knowledge in each area of study, or should the focus be to avoid conflict with vocal religious minorities who have a very different agenda for our public schools?

You can't answer these questions until you have looked closely at the science textbooks used in the United States and, because Canadian schools buy from American publishers, in Canada as well. It is these textbooks that are responsible in part for today's current widespread scientific illiteracy. And it is this scientific illiteracy that has made possible the growth of pseudoscience.

If you have not read a public school science textbook lately, you are probably in for a shock. Certainly the scientists and educators who challenged the textbooks submitted for adoption in California were taken aback. They could not believe that modern publishers would offer such inaccurate and ill-conceived material under the guise of science education. Let me provide a few examples.

One textbook stated that scientists "believe dinosaurs to have inhabited the earth." This sounds more like a confession of faith than a position based upon evidence firmly established in our body of knowledge since the Renaissance. Yet, when complaint was made about this at a textbook hearing, one defender of the book declared that frequent use of the phrase "some scientists believe" was quite appropriate because *National Geographic* used the phrase in its November 1985 issue and that ought to settle the matter.

This same man boasted that he had succeeded in firming up statements in one textbook. He had changed the sentence, "many scientists think that dinosaurs were the ancestors of modern reptiles" to the more strongly worded, "scientists classify dinosaurs as the ancestors of modern reptiles." What he didn't seem to know was that scientists do *not* classify dinosaurs as the ancestors of modern reptiles. Modern reptiles come from an entirely separate evolutionary line. Dinosaurs are the ancestors of modern birds.

Furthermore, most people seemed to miss the point that timid utterances about subjects related to evolution are not the way to be "scientific." After all, none of the textbooks describe genetics as "the study of beliefs about the possibility of inheritance" or state guardedly that "most astronomers believe that Saturn has rings." Genetics and astronomy are not as "controversial" as evolution (since there are few religious objections to current scientific conclusions in these areas), so statements are allowed to be bolder.

In any event, this is the sort of education our children are receiving. It is also the sort of education that members of boards of education had received. This became painfully obvious during the textbook hearings before the California State Board of Education, when one board member found perplexing the scientific view that the north and south poles have changed places several times in the history of our planet. She wondered why scientists couldn't make up their minds! She also found evolution unconvincing because she could not imagine how asexual life forms could ever evolve into male and female forms. Nonetheless, she said she was in favor of science because it had made possible cosmetics and skin cremes.

o   o   o

In a recent poll commissioned by the National Science Foundation, it was learned how woefully uneducated Americans are. Over 40 percent of those polled believed that "rocket launchings and other space activities have caused changes in our weather" and that "it is likely that some unidentified flying objects that have been reported are really space vehicles from other civilizations." Forty percent agreed that "some numbers are especially lucky for some people." In the same survey, people were asked to rate their own understanding of a few modern technological terms. Eighty-two percent felt they had a general understanding of radiation, which is surprising since only 67 percent felt they understood how a telephone works. A mere 57 percent felt they grasped the workings of computer software, and only 49 percent felt confident talking about the gross national product. These results led organizers of a recent science conference, sponsored jointly by the National Science Foundation, the American Association for the Advancement of Science, the National Science Teachers Association, Pennsylvania State University, and others, to declare boldly:

> Evidence abounds that we are graduating students who are unprepared and unable to grasp even day-to-day issues—the technical content of issues ranging from the safety of contraceptive devices or nutrition to robotics, gene-splicing, or the recent explosion of the space shuttle the *Challenger.*

This has become a major concern in a nation so dependent upon science and technology.

But, as noted before, it is not a lack of interest in science that lies at the root. It is positive belief in pseudoscientific ideas, particularly those that are religiously motivated, and harsh opposition to mainstream science that are the real problem. So long as "scientific" creationists remain persuasive, the public will find it easy to buy into the notion that effective teaching of evolution constitutes "secular humanism." So long as science itself is sometimes viewed as "cold" and "materialistic," people will seek the supposedly "warmer" ideas of mysticism, especially mysticism that they think is made possible through discoveries on the frontier of the "New Physics."

But there is more at stake here than simple public ignorance: there is the issue of the freedom of scientists to carry on their research. Some creationists want to require that for every dollar spent on "evolution research" an equal amount be spent on "creation research." They want national park guides to be required to give the creationist explanation of natural wonders side by side with the evolutionary explanation. And they want museums to carry creation exhibits to match the evolution exhibits.

What would be the effects of such policies? Since creationists hold that the universe is only ten thousand years old, this makes modern astronomy a joke. Since they reject radiometric dating as invalid, they contradict modern nuclear physics. Since they argue that Earth is only ten thousand years old as well, they are at odds with geology. Since they are offended by the human and animal family tree, they must oppose most of modern biochemistry.

Pseudoscience, in its own way, becomes antiscience. And if research grants dry up in these areas, what will happen to the space program, nuclear technology, the search for fossil fuels and alternative energy sources, and the development of new medicines? What will happen to American leadership in these areas and, with it, the American economy?

Fortunately, American creationists, mystics, and other pseudoscientists cannot make scientific knowledge disappear. At best, they can only make it disappear from North America. They can only foster a scientific illiteracy that will hand world leadership to other nations, leaving us in the dust of history. They can only hamstring and retard new developments capable of eventually improving the lot of the world's peoples. They can't stop progress altogether. Humanity will survive and prosper in spite of them, even if none of us alive today lives to see the result.

But, somehow, I'm not consoled by this. The eventual triumph of knowledge over the forces of ignorance and bigotry is not enough. The growth of our body of scientific knowledge should not be retarded. When there is no good reason why advanced societies should offer a second-rate education in science, then action should be taken to remedy the situation. John Dewey said it well: "Nothing but the best, the richest and fullest experience possible, is good enough for man." Let's not cut ourselves, or our world, short. We can insist upon excellence—and, by insisting, be deserving of the same.

• *Frederick Edwords is the national administrator of the American Humanist Association and a member of the board of directors of the National Center for Science Education and the New York Council for Evolution Education.*

54

Interview: Isaac Asimov

Conducted by Bill Moyers

> We are convinced that masses of evidence render the application of the concept of evolution to man and the other primates beyond serious dispute, concluded the Pontifical Academy of Sciences, prompting Arthur C. Clarke to write:
>
> > This should settle the matter, as far as those who call themselves Christians are concerned. For whatever their doctrinal differences, surely even the most fanatical Protestants will admit that the Vatican does speak with a certain authority on matters of faith.

In Beginnings: The Story of Origins—of Mankind, Life, the Earth, the Universe *(Berkeley Books, 1989), the late Dr. Isaac Asimov wrote about the creation of the Earth with a scientific, not biblical, explanation. In an aside to the reader, Dr. Asimov wrote:*

> *God created the Earth, they say, with all the fossils already in place and with all the other evidence of a long age for the Earth as well. This was done either to fool humanity, out of a malicious sense of humor, or to test people's faith in revelation over observation and reason, or for other trivial un-Godlike motivations. Some who are wedded to the literal words of the opening portion of the Bible might accept this sort of argument, but thinking people, even if sincerely religious, do not.*

Dr. Asimov was the most prolific writer popularizing science in our time and was frequently asked in interviews about his views on creationism. Not surprisingly, Dr. Asimov held steadfastly to his convictions to the end of his days.

In the 1989 book of interviews conducted by Bill Moyer, A World of Ideas, *the question was again posed.*

Moyers: *In 1980 you were afraid that the fundamentalists who were coming into power with President Reagan were going to turn this country even further against science, especially with their demands that biblical creationism be given an equal footing in the classroom with science. Have they made those inroads that you feared?*

Asimov: Fortunately, the currents have been against them. But they still put pressure on school boards and parents, and it's become a little more difficult in many parts of the nation to teach evolution.

The fundamentalists see you as the very incarnation of the enemy, the epitome of the secular humanist who opposes God's plan for the universe. . . . Are you an enemy of religion?

No, I'm not. What I'm against is the attempt to place a person's belief system onto the nation or the world generally. We object to the Soviet Union trying to dominate the world, to communize the world. The United States, I hope, is trying to democratize the world. But I certainly would be very much against trying to Christianize the world or to Islamize it or to Judaize it or anything of the sort. My objection to fundamentalism is not that they are fundamentalists but that essentially they want me to be a fundamentalist, too. Now, they may say I believe evolution is true and I want everyone to believe that evolution is true. But I don't want everyone to believe that evolution is true; I want them to study what we say about evolution and to decide for themselves. Fundamentalists say they want to treat creationism on an equal basis. But they can't. It's not a science. You can teach creationism in churches and in courses on religion. They would be horrified if I were to suggest that in the churches they teach secular humanism as an alternate way of looking at the universe or evolution as an alternate way of considering how life may have started. In the church they teach only what they believe, and rightly so, I suppose. But on the other hand, in schools, in science courses, we've got to teach what scientists think is the way the universe works.

But that is what frightens many believers. They see science as uncertain, always tentative, always subject to revisionism. They see science as presenting a complex, chilling, and enormous universe ruled by chance and impersonal laws. They see science as dangerous.

That is really the glory of science—that science is tentative, that it is not certain, that it is subject to change. What is really disgraceful is to have a set of beliefs that you think is absolute and has been so from the start and can't change, when you simply won't listen to evidence. You say, "If the evidence agrees with me, it's not necessary, and if it doesn't agree with me, it's false." This is the legendary remark of Omar when they captured Alexandria and asked him what to do with the library. He said, "If the books agree with the Koran, they are not necessary and may be burned. If they disagree with the Koran, they are pernicious and must be burned." Well, there are still these Omar-like thinkers who think all of knowledge will fit into one book called the Bible, and who refuse to allow it is possible ever to conceive of an error there. To my way of thinking, that is much more dangerous than a system of knowledge that is tentative and uncertain.

• *Bill Moyers is an acclaimed television journalist, widely respected for his work at PBS and CBS News. His "A World of Ideas" series, broadcast in the fall of 1988, put outstanding thinkers on the air every night for ten weeks. His conversations with teacher and mythologist Joseph Campbell were the basis for the best-selling book* The Power of Myth *(from* A World of Ideas *by Bill Moyers).*

Arthur C. Clarke on "The Menace of Creationism"

In a non-fiction collection, 1984: Spring (A Collection of Futures), *Arthur C. Clarke wrote the essay "The Menace of Creationism" in response to a schoolteacher who wrote to ask his opinion about the debate surrounding evolution v. creationism.*

. . . Creationism is not a matter of *opinion*—mine or anyone else's. Evolution is a FACT, period. What *is* a matter of opinion is Darwinism. That is a THEORY—and it's unfortunate that many people (sometimes deliberately, sometimes ignorantly) confuse the two.

Part 4
Seduction of the Innocent

The popularity of Allan Bloom's recent book, *The Closing of the American Mind*, is a barometer of how strongly contemporary Americans fear the destruction of our moral gyroscopes. Bloom argues that indiscriminate freedom is pernicious. The marketplace-of-ideas metaphor in modern freedom-of-speech thinking tends to elevate openmindedness above all other public values. But in a milieu in which the only enemy is the person not open to everything, Bloom asks, how are shared goals, visions of the public good, and meaningful social contact any longer possible? If we are forced by the First Amendment to sublimate the sublime in the name of tolerance, how will we ever take control of our own destinies? From this perspective it is wrong to celebrate freedom of speech for its own sake, for the same reason that it is wrong to celebrate openmindedness for its own sake: Such libertine reveling leads to a moral relativism in which everything is tolerated, even intolerance. Rather than a cohesive nation with a shared sense of promise of American life, we become an atomistic confederation of selfish individuals.

—RODNEY A. SMOLLA, *Jerry Falwell v. Larry Flynt* (pp. 24-25)

55

Interview with Barry Hoffman

Conducted by George Beahm

> The First Amendment was designed to "invite dispute," to induce "a condition of unrest," to "create dissatisfaction with conditions as they are," and even to stir "people to anger." The First Amendment was not fashioned as a vehicle for dispensing tranquilizers to the people. Its prime function was to keep debate open to "offensive" as well as to "staid" people. . . . The materials before us may be garbage. But so is much of what is said in political campaigns, in the daily press, on TV or over the radio. By reason of the First Amendment . . . speakers and publishers have not been threatened or subdued because their thoughts and ideas may be "offensive" to some.
>
> —WILLIAM O. DOUGLAS, *Miller* v. *California*, June 6, 1973 (413 U.S. 15, p. 1453)

Barry Hoffman, publisher of Gauntlet, *is no stranger to censorship. A junior high school teacher in Pennsylvania, Hoffman, in his early forties, has fought a continuing battle with unhappy parents that have criticized the school plays he has written, in addition to attacking the reading curriculum he teaches.*

After "a few" people in the Home at School Association complained about a school play, Scream from the Heart, *that dealt with teenager runaways, on the grounds that it might encourage them to do so, Hoffman found his play carefully scrutinized to screen out anything deemed offensive.*

Though he had, up to then, written and produced one play a year for the school, after Scream from the Heart, *he was not invited to do so. It was, as he put it, the "final form of censorship."*

In his classroom he found himself under attack from concerned parents that, without reading the texts in question, condemned his choices of Robert Bloch, Dean Koontz, Robert McCammon, Richard Matheson, and most especially Stephen King. "Whenever we got to King," he explains, "there would be a parent that, for one reason or another, would say, 'I'm upset about this.' Instead of coming to me and asking if the child could read something else, he'd go to the principal who'd asked me to justify what I was doing and make it uncomfortable for me to use such materials."

"You're reading Stephen King, and he writes things that are dirty—there's cursing, there's profanity," as he had been told by several parents.

Concerned about what he perceived as the growing wave of censorship, not only in school but throughout our society, Hoffman put together Gauntlet *on a bare bones budget; the first issue was published in 1990. Printed on newsprint,* Gauntlet *ran 112 letter-size pages, included contributions largely from the fantasy-horror community: Ray Bradbury, Ramsey Campbell, Ray Garton, Steve Rasnic Tem, Harlan Ellison, Isaac Asimov, Rex Miller, Dan Simmons, Henry Slesar, Douglas E. Winter, William F. Nolan, and many others.*

What sets Gauntlet *apart from other publications is its no-holds-barred approach to its graphics. Visually shocking imagery, though, intended to arrest the reader's attention, has had its downside. Mainstream bookstores, chain stores like Waldenbooks and B. Dalton, and numerous libraries decided* Gauntlet *was not for them.*

In "Frothing from the Mouth," Hoffman's first-issue editorial, publisher/editor Hoffman explained the magazine's philosophy:

> *Why* Gauntlet*? It's not that we really need another magazine to glut the shelves, do we?*
>
> *Yes, we do! Today, in this country of ours, where freedom is valued above all else, there's no mass-appeal, general-interest magazine on censorship and the limits to free expression. No magazine that publishes censored material. No magazine that allows both sides to be heard—that actively encourages those who would limit freedom of expression to hit you with their best shot. No magazine that encourages dialogue to the converted. No magazine that includes original fiction from mainstream to horror dealing with threats to First Amendment rights. . . . Be forewarned, though. You may find* Gauntlet *outrageous, irritating . . . even blasphemous. If you're uncomfortable with some of the material in this magazine—if we touch a nerve—it's by design.* Gauntlet *is not for the squeamish. There's probably something, in fact, to offend everyone. After reading through this issue, even First Amendment purists may ponder if there should, indeed, be limits to free expression.*

Since that first issue, much has happened—and not happened, as it turned out. Although three subsequent issues were published (no. 2 in 1991, no. 3 and no. 4 in 1992), the magazine continues to evolve as it seeks to find its place in a marketplace that, frankly, finds Gauntlet *taboo. Shifting to a 6 × 9 inch trade paperback,* Gauntlet *has changed its packaging but not its contents. Those who were offended by Allen Koszowski's illustrations for Ray Garton's* Crucifax *in issue no. 1 or S. Clay Wilson's taboo-breaking artwork would, in later issues, encounter the blasphemous (photo art by Harry O. Morris), the shocking (art by John Borkowsi, depicting a nude woman masturbating, with blood dripping between her breasts), the horrifying (an art gallery illustrating the works of Stephen King), and (to First Amendment purists) the Unspeakably Obscene (a publicity head shot of Sheriff Navarro of Dade County in Florida).*

A biannual publication, Gauntlet *is available directly from the publisher (Gauntlet, 309 Powell Road, Springfield, PA 19064). Existing largely on subscription revenues, Hoffman offers back issues as well as a T-shirt, depicting the cover art from the first issue. For those of a charitable nature, donations are cheerfully* *accepted. A gift of $20 (or more) will get your name published in Gauntlet as a "Patron of Free Expression."*

Years before Hoffman published his iconoclastic journal, he had been writing about censorship for the official Stephen King newsletter, Castle Rock. *Anyone who read Hoffman's pieces knew his stand against censorship would not end there. When* Castle Rock *ceased publication, Hoffman felt the need to continue writing on censorship matters.* Gauntlet *was the inevitable result.*

This short interview with Hoffman was conducted in January 1992, prior to the publication of Gauntlet #3.

Beahm: *What was the genesis of the magazine?*

Hoffman: After my play *Scream from the Heart* was derailed along with the entire program, I had a lot of time on my hands. After submitting to small presses, I became interested in editing a magazine. I thought that if I could find something to publish on an annual basis, I'd be interested. At that time the theme of censorship intermingled with my interest in editing a magazine, and that was the genesis of *Gauntlet.*

What then?

I knew I wanted *Gauntlet* to be an ongoing publication, but I didn't know exactly what shape or form it would take.

Did your students have any hand in your getting the magazine off the ground?

Yes. Actually, the jumpstart for *Gauntlet* was my kids in class that, over the past few years, had written letters to Ray Bradbury. They would read his stories and compare them to the videos that came out, then write letters critiquing his material; he'd write back with a letter to the whole class.

When I decided to do *Gauntlet,* I wrote and asked him to write a story for it. He wrote back saying he couldn't do anything right now—he was working on "The Ray Bradbury Theater" and also leaving for Europe soon—but that I was free to use "Coda," the afterword to *Fahrenheit 451.*

With Bradbury's name associated with *Gauntlet,* I was able to write to other authors and say, "Bradbury has already committed to taking part." As a result, it lent legitimacy to the enterprise and helped secure a number of authors who otherwise might not have participated.

You're a big fan of Stephen King's, in and outside the classroom. Did you approach him?

Yes, but he was reluctant to take part in the first issue because he wanted to see it first, to see if it would be something of substance. After the first issue was published, I sent it to King, began work on the second issue, and asked to use his essay "The Dreaded X." He immediately said yes. Once he saw what *Gauntlet* was about, he was very interested in taking part.

From the beginning, my conception for *Gauntlet* was to publish for the general public. It would not be aimed at academicians. It would be a general-interest publication incorporating original work, fiction, censored work, and debates.

The first issue didn't have a particular theme; I just went to sources where I could get material, most of it dealing with censorship in the writing community, though there were a few pieces dealing with comics and art censorship.

The whole point of *Gauntlet,* I felt, was to provide the issues that had no easy answers. I wanted to provide a forum for debate, covering both sides of the story, and let the reader decide for himself.

Gauntlet

• Issue #1 (1990; 112 pp., $8.95): A fledging effort, a magazine seeking an identity, this is a potpourri of articles, essays, fiction, opinion pieces, etc. (Looking back, Hoffman commented: "*Gauntlet's* first issue was a primer—a sometimes simplified overview—on free speech." Still, it's a good place to start, especially if you want to get your sensibilities shaken.)

• Issue #2 (1991; 402 pp., $8.95): Promoted as a "Stephen King Special," the second issue matures in format and in contents. A hefty collection, *Gauntlet #2* is organized by topic, giving it a sense of organization that the first issue admittedly lacked. Besides the Stephen King section, topics included: a news section, a piece on the Motion Pictures Association of America (MPAA), the controversy surrounding rap group 2 Live Crew, a section on Ray Bradbury, articles on kiddie porn, censorship in comics, censorship in the visual arts, debates on subjects of current controversy (e.g., should the names of rape victims be published?), along with fiction and opinion pieces. (Looking back, Hoffman commented: "With this issue we more skillfully opened up the Pandora's box to expose the breadth and scope of censorship. We've also tackled issues with no simple answers—like publishing the names of rape victims without their permission—for to oppose censorship doesn't mean there shouldn't be limits to free expression. What those limits are, you have to determine.")

• Issue #3 (1992; 338 pp., $12.95): The format (trade paperback, 6 x 9 inches) has become its standard and, in addition to the usual cross-section of material, Hoffman has decided to theme each issue; this one's on political correctness. "*You* are the final arbiter as to what is political correctness and where you stand. Hell, straddle the fence, if you wish, as there are no easy answers. . . . Navigating the minefield of political correctness is no simple matter, as you shall see," writes Hoffman in his "Editorial Meanderings."

• Issue #4 (1992; 178 pp., a two-issue subscription [November and May] is $20 plus $2 for postage and handling).

Now biannual, *Gauntlet* promises to cover the censorship scene on a more timely basis. This issue's theme is media manipulation and censorship, as publisher/editor Hoffman explains in his "editorial meanderings": "The major free expression issue of 1992, to date, has been the media—both manipulation of and manipulation by the media. While an easy target (especially for politicians), at no time has the media, itself, come under such scrutiny, attack and abuse [as now]. At no time have there been more instances where the media *made* news by its actions, as opposed to reporting or commenting on the news."

56

Seeing Is Not Believing

by Douglas E. Winter

for Alejandro Jodorowsky

Seeing is not believing.

Forget those wellworn platitudes about the reality of things seen: What you see in not always what you get. Whether on a used-car lot or in a court of law, the eyes are weak arbiters of the truth. Investigators of air disasters find that eyewitnesses often provide the least reliable evidence: that most anyone, from airline pilots to air traffic controllers to the proverbial bystander, will swear under oath to the actuality of things that never could, or did, happen . . . because that is what they saw. It is little wonder that psychology professors are fond of treating their classrooms to an unexpected intruder and later asking students for written descriptions of what took place: inevitably the reports are as varied as the blind man's takes on the elephant.

Truth, like beauty, is in the eye of the beholder . . . until we come to the visual arts: film, television, photography, sculpture, painting, illustration. Comics.

Pictures.

When it comes to pictures, an increasing number of people insist that seeing is believing, that images are as literal as a fundamentalist's reading of the Bible. Thus, we are told, certain pictures are taboo . . . so terrible that we must be denied them. We are given codes, ratings, regulations, advisory stickers, warning labels, bans, burnings, boycotts, gag orders, raids, seizures, arrests, indictments, prosecutions.

All for our own protection.

To stop us from seeing.

o   o   o

I make my living by writing. Because the right words are difficult enough to find, I live in constant awe of those with the talent to make pictures appear on paper. When I see the work of visual artists, painters, cartoonists, it seems nothing less than magic. I tried to draw when I was young, illustrating my stories with matchstick men and monsters; what little talent I had then seems to have disappeared completely with the years. Words have proven an easier, perhaps safer, means of trying to tell others what I saw and felt. But for the most part, I still write what I see, and want my readers to see what I write.

Pictures.

It is often said that words are a wounded, if not dying, art; that our interest in comics is simply another sign of rampant illiteracy and cultural decline. Some embrace terms like "graphic novels" to justify their indulgences, buying into the elitist impulse to find "real" art only in the hallowed halls of galleries and museums, to deny that it should (or could) be popular, accessible to all. This notion—that art is not for the people, but for the pleasure and understanding of an initiated few—is at the heart of the problem.

Art, whether in pictures or words or music, is about communication; and it is not just words, but all forms of communication, that are endangered. Sitting mesmerized in the glow of our electronic screens, we no longer interact, have dialogue, communicate. We have become a society of watchers, living out the lives that others portray for us—receivers, rather than assessors and exchangers, of information. For better or worse, text—and, more important, context—increasingly lacks meaning. We have neither the time nor the patience nor the need for it. We are what we see.

Pictures.

Think for a moment of the gravity of that idea. For what is it that we see—or, better put, that we are shown? The entertainment industry's search to satisfy the collective consumer consciousness seeks the lowest of common denominators: The art that can be taken at face value. That no one could possibly misunderstand. That is what it is.

Pictures.

Modern entertainment is obsessed with surface, and only surface. Bestselling novels become exercises in the unexpected, and our most popular writers are packaged and sold like brand name products—with each new King or Collins or Clancy, we embrace a literature less of quality than of quality control. In film, we witness the likes of Paul Verhoeven, flush with Hollywood money, disintegrate from the genius of *Spetters* and *The Fourth Man* into the folly of *Robocop* and *Total Recall,* less movies than overblown Nintendo games. Even music has succumbed to surface, as looks become more crucial than licks or lyrics, spawning classical poseurs like violinist Nigel Kennedy and Grammy Award winners who are nothing more than voice-over impostors.

Pictures.

We should not be surprised. Salvador Dali gave us fair warning more than sixty years ago, writing that "people only see stereotyped images of things, pure shadows empty of any expression, pure phantoms of things, and they find vulgar and normal everything they are in the habit of seeing every day, however marvellous and miraculous it may be. . . ."

What better description of modern television or film or fiction . . . or comics? Today we are assaulted at every turn with stereotyped images, pure and empty shadows; and the marvels and miracles, like those of Christianity, seem distant memories, relics of an irredeemable past.

o   o   o

I remember my first comic books: *Classics Illustrated* adaptations of *The Octopus* and *War of the Worlds.* My brother and I shared copies of *Turok, Son of Stone.* At Graham's Drug Store, across from the dentist's office, I put down my dimes for the first issue of *The Fantastic Four* (which I still own) and the debut of Spiderman in *Amazing Fantasy.* In my youth, comics were the most tangible of my waking dreams, documentary proof that the strange ideas that rattled in my head could exist outside of me. Like paperback novels and B movies, those ten-cent delights were my constant companions, links to the otherworld that kept pushing so desperately into my thoughts and fighting to find expression.

But of all those comics, I remember most two books that I found at age eight or nine, while vacationing with my parents in Boston. There, in a tiny used bookstore, I bought two pre-Comics Code wonders: an issue of *Phantom Lady* and a Korean War extravaganza. *Phantom Lady* was the most overtly sexual document to have come into my young and suddenly trembling hands; its eponymous heroine was like a jump charge to my waking libido. If this comic stole my heart, then the other book was a vicious punch to the gut, a wildly patriotic saga of the atrocities of the godless North Koreans and the righteous violence of G.I. revenge. Here was my first sight of splatter: a bazooka round blasting through the chest of a soldier, sending a plume of flame and blood and guts out of his back. I found that I could not stop looking.

From there it was all downhill; not until the films of Leone, Peckinpah and Argento did pictures again produce such intense emotions in me. Even in the early 1960s, the corporate bigboys, D.C. and Marvel, were the usual (if not only) show in town, and the Comics Code held sway. Heroes were super . . . and square. Still, there were moments—the Charlton *Gorgo* and *Reptisaurus* comics were the next best thing to a new Toho rubber monster movie; and one fine day, a neighborhood friend unearthed a trove of his older brother's E.C. Comics, not to mention a 3-D comic whose images so shocked me that I cannot remember them at all, only the sensation of dread that they produced each time I prepared myself to look.

Although Fredric Wertham would argue to the contrary, these are affectionate memories—and, I think, positive events. Not all children are fortunate enough to greet sex and death so safely. While today, thirty years later, Tipper Gore and Donald Wildmon fret over the lyrics of N.W.A.'s new album or the special effects in the latest *Friday the 13th,* children are being born with AIDS, others gunned down in schoolyards. Like Wertham and so many other witchhunters throughout the centuries, Gore and Wildmon and the other high priests of the latest Inquisition know that images are far more vulnerable than behavior. After all, we are a society far more proficient at regulating pictures than drugs or firearms.

Consider, if you will, obscenity: a depiction that we, as a society, have determined is outside our constitutional right of free speech. The rationale is that words or pictures (or, indeed, as the Supreme Court has recently instructed, dances) are not necessarily "speech" but, under certain circumstances, something else, something so foul that no one should experience them, even voluntarily—this despite the fact that erotica is a multi-billion-dollar industry, which suggests that not a few Americans are interested in whatever it has to offer.

Just why this particular kind of expression should be dishonored has changed over the years, as indeed has its definition. Where once partial nudity or sexual abandon would have fit the bill, our enlightened society now thinks of obscenity in terms of "hard core" sex; yet we often look the other way, allowing XXX material to exist, behind a plain brown wrapper, so long as its participants are over 18 years in age, one of them is female, and the acts depicted seem consensual.

Strange, almost fetishistic, rules guard us from the taint of the obscene: A bare female breast is taboo on broadcast television or in an Indiana strip joint, but is readily available for viewing in health, fashion, geographic and men's magazines (not to mention cable television and even PG-rated movies); videos starring Traci Lords suddenly are pulled from the shelves when we learn that she was younger than she appeared; two consecutive buttock thrusts automatically earn an X or NC-17 rating for a motion picture, regardless of its other content; most major metropolitan newspapers will not print the word "fuck," but will provide photographs of corpses in every imaginable state of mutilation and decay. How does one even begin to explain a society that winces at the thought of naked bodies on television yet cheers the repeated images of rockets and high explosives flaring on the screen throughout the news coverage of the Gulf War?

o   o   o

In recent years, as the Puritan veneer of our morality has begun to fade, the issue surrounding obscenity has become one less of prurience—we seem at last willing to admit that sex is a part of our lives—than one of supposed oppression or exploitation: Thus *Playboy* is guilty less for its photographs of women than for its ideas about them. A "slasher" film is suspect not because it is about murder, but about murdering women. The nudity, the violence, the picture, are not morally correct because they are not politically or socially correct.

One of the more daft and yet dangerous notions confronting art in the 1990s is the growing belief that "correct" goals may justify repression—that wrongs against women or a racial minority or another worthy group may be remedied through . . . well, let's just say what it is: mind control. I was once sent a contract for an anthology that provided that none of the stories would feature violence or cruelty toward children or animals. I refused to write for the book, even though my story involved nothing of the sort. The idea that women or children or African-Americans or Jews or Siamese cats are species protected from the ambit of art is an abhorrent one, for it is through art that their causes are best and most persuasively championed. We allow Nazis to parade through our streets precisely because we will allow *everybody* the freedom to assemble and speak their minds. If we did not, then there might not have been Suffragettes, or a civil rights movement—at least not for long.

Censorship in the name of even the most worthy of causes inevitably results in serious abuses. Child pornography is the best example. Our laws, emboldened by the lofty ideal of protecting the weak, become more sweeping where children are at issue—which sounds like a good idea, until we learn what it means in practice.

In my home town, an artist photographed her children, barely more than babies, in the nude. She wanted to use the photographs, as she had done in the past, as models for her paintings for nymphs and fairies. The processing laboratory summoned the police, and in short order the artist's home was ransacked pursuant to a search warrant and her children taken into custody by the state.

It *can* happen here . . . it happens every day. In this country and in Canada, the rubric of "child pornography" has been used to justify raids on comic stores, under the convenient presumption that comic books are for children.

It is the "helpless" eyes of our children that of course provide the excuse for the emasculation of our television screens, for the labeling of record albums, for the motion picture ratings system, and for the Comics Code. Dr. Wertham would be proud: The seduction of the innocent has become the byword for the sedation of the informed. Yet if the daily news is to be believed, censorship has proved remarkably unsuccessful at policing morality: teenage sex and crime and drug and alcohol abuse have reached an all-time high, which suggests many things that censors would rather not hear—mostly that they have not been particularly good parents or ministers or educators or politicians.

I am forever fascinated that it is the artists who must be held responsible: that the parents who tolerated their child's drug abuse should sue a heavy metal band for his suicide; that anyone would even begin to believe Jimmy Swaggart, let alone Ted Bundy, when they sought to place the blame for their crimes on pornography. But the reason is unnervingly simple: It is the artists whom these people fear. The artists dare to speak; they dare to show us things.

Pictures . . . but pictures that may not be what they seem.

When Goya told us, "I saw it with my own eyes," he spoke profoundly of the horrors of war that he painted—but he showed us not only the literal reality of what he had seen, but the awful truth that we could see these horrors as well.

When we think about taboo—about what others would hide from our sight—we must remember that a picture is not always just a picture. That these illustrations, these representations, are glimpses of that someplace dark and dangerous inside us all . . . worthy reminders of the lesson, taught so long ago by di Cosimo and da Vinci, that an artist's task is to contemplate the cracks in the wall until he sees an alternative world that only art is capable of revealing.

As artists, as writers, as viewers and readers, we must look deeply and fearlessly into those cracks, the shadows, the darkness within and without us, in search of the truths that are waiting to be found.

To look is to invent.

Seeing. But not believing.

• *Douglas E. Winter is a D.C. attorney who writes frequently on popular culture.*

57

Wertham's *Seduction of the Innocent*

by George Beahm

Published by Rinehart & Company in 1953, *Seduction of the Innocent* was Dr. Fredric Wertham's magnum opus. Wertham was convinced that comic books were contributory to juvenile delinquency, and *Seduction of the Innocent*, as Mike Benton wrote in *The Illustrated History of Horror Comics: I, Seduction of the Innocent*, presented, at best, a skewed perspective:

> By juxtaposing quotes from crime and horror comics with clinical accounts of juvenile murders and sex crimes, Wertham managed to damn all comic books by association. Particularly indefensible were the extracted pictures Wertham selected from the crime and horror comics. Presented out of context and in stark black and white in his original book, the comic book images of torture and horror were enough to accomplish the book's purpose of arousing public sentiment against the comics.

As Harlan Ellison pointed out in "It Ain't Toontown," an article for *Playboy,* ". . . comics would rot your brain. And if you didn't believe it, along came the Fifties' own Cotton Mather, the late Dr. Fredric Wertham, who . . . could give you chapter and verse, gore and protuberant nipples on how mind-rotting these evil comics were."

Testifying before a Senate subcommittee on juvenile delinquency, Dr. Wertham—considered a credible witness—soberly told them in no uncertain terms that comic books contributed to children's moral decay.

The subcommittee, according to Benton, concluded: "It was the publishers' responsibility . . . to regulate their comic books to 'standards of decency' before someone else did it for them." As Benton concluded, "It may not have been censorship, but it certainly was intimidation."

After October 1954, comics displayed a stamp, "Approved by the Comics Code Authority," literally a stamp of approval. Comics were never quite the same until years later in the sixties, when independent comic book publishers published without any restrictions—a reaction to the conservatism of mainstream comic book publishing.

Seduction of the Innocent:
Dust Jacket Copy (1953)

This is the most shocking book of recent years. And it should be the most influential.

Seduction of the Innocent is the complete, detailed report of the findings of famed psychiatrist Fredric Wertham on the pernicious influence of comic books on the youth of today. No parent can afford to ignore it.

You think your child is immune? Don't forget—90,000,000 comic books are read each month. You think they are mostly about floppy-eared bunnies, attractive little mice and chipmunks? Go take a look.

On the basis of wide experience and many years' research, Dr. Wertham flatly states that comic books:

- Are an invitation to illiteracy
- Create an atmosphere of cruelty and deceit
- Stimulate unwholesome fantasies
- Suggest criminal or sexually abnormal ideas
- Create a readiness for temptation
- Suggest forms a delinquent impulse may take and supply details of technique

These are only some of the points raised—and documented.

Dr. Wertham also discusses many other deeply disturbing questions. He has found that comic books harm the development of reading from the lowest level of the most elementary hygiene to the highest level of the appreciation of good literature.

He has found an appalling lack of scientific method on the part of professionals who have for years paid no attention to comic books, although they are practically the only reading for many children. He believes that comic-book reading helps children to get rid *not* of their aggressions, as many "experts" state, but of their inhibitions.

It is important to remember that all Dr. Wertham's findings are based on a study of comic *books,* not newspaper comic strips which are required to observe the same standards of good taste as the newspapers in which they are published.

"The most subtle and pervading effect of crime comics on children," Dr. Wertham writes, "can be summarized in a single phrase: moral disarmament. It consists chiefly in a blunting of the finer feelings of conscience, of mercy, of sympathy for other people's suffering and of respect for women as women and not merely as sex objects to be bandied about or as luxury prizes to be fought over. They affect children's taste for the finer influences of education, for art, for literature, and for the decent and constructive relationships between human beings and especially between the sexes."

Dr. Wertham's suggested remedy, a public-health approach to legislation on the subject, must be seriously considered by all who claim to take the slightest interest in the mental health of our children.

58

Comics Code of Comics Magazine Association of America, Inc.

Dr. Fredric Wertham, a psychologist who saw comic books and their effects as a public health issue, was considered a credible witness when he testified before a Senate subcommittee. Not long afterward, the comics book industry opted for self-regulation. The comics code was the result.

Since its inception in the fifties, the code has applied only to mainstream comics. Today, most mainstream comics subscribe to the comics code; on their covers is a small logo, a stamp, the comics code's seal of approval.

Because of the growth of the specialty market—independent comic book stores catering to collectors—the mainstream comic book publishers like Marvel and D.C. took a page from the independent publishers and issued comics without submitting to the comics code review.

Ironically, independent publishers label their comics with mature themes, though they are not signatory to any code.

Code for Editorial Matter: General Standards, Part A

1. Crimes shall never be presented in such a way as to create sympathy for the criminal, to promote distrust of the forces of law and justice, or to inspire others with a desire to imitate criminals.
2. No comics shall explicitly present the unique details and methods of a crime.
3. Policemen, judges, government officials and respected institutions shall never be presented in a way as to create disrespect for established authority.
4. If crime is depicted it shall be as a sordid and unpleasant activity.
5. Criminals shall not be presented so as to be rendered glamorous or to occupy a position which creates a desire for emulation.
6. In every instance good shall triumph over evil and the criminal shall be punished for his misdeeds.
7. Scenes of excessive violence shall be prohibited. Scenes of brutal torture, excessive and unnecessary knife and gun play, physical agony, gory and gruesome crime shall be eliminated.
8. No unique or unusual methods of concealing weapons shall be shown.
9. Instances of law enforcement officials dying as a result of a criminal's activities should be discouraged.
10. The crime of kidnapping shall never be portrayed in any detail, nor shall

any profit accrue to the abductor or kidnapper. The criminal or the kidnapper must be punished in every case.

11. The letters of the word "crime" on a comics magazine cover shall never be appreciably greater in dimension than the other words contained in the title. The word "crime" shall never appear alone on a cover.
12. Restraint in the use of the word "crime" in titles or sub-titles shall be exercised.

General Standards, Part B

1. No comic magazine shall use the word "horror" or "terror" in its title.
2. All scenes of horror, excessive bloodshed, gory or gruesome crimes, depravity, lust, sadism, masochism shall not be permitted.
3. All lurid, unsavory, gruesome illustrations shall be eliminated.
4. Inclusion of stories dealing with evil shall be used or shall be published only where the intent is to illustrate a moral issue and in no case shall evil be presented alluringly nor so as to injure the sensibilities of the reader.
5. Scenes dealing with, or instruments associated with walking dead, torture, vampires and vampirism, ghouls, cannibalism and werewolfism are prohibited.

General Standards, Part C

All elements or techniques not specifically mentioned herein, but which are contrary to the spirit and intent of the Code, and are considered violations of good taste or decency, shall be prohibited.

Dialogue

1. Profanity, obscenity, smut, vulgarity, or words or symbols which have acquired undesirable meanings are forbidden.
2. Special precautions to avoid references to physical afflictions or deformities shall be taken.
3. Although slang and colloquialisms are acceptable, excessive use should be discouraged and wherever possible good grammar shall be employed.

Religion

1. Ridicule or attack on any religious or racial group is never permissible.

Costume

1. Nudity in any form is prohibited, as is indecent or undue exposure.
2. Suggestive and salacious illustration or suggestive posture is unacceptable.
3. All characters shall be depicted in dress reasonably acceptable to society.
4. Females shall be drawn realistically without exaggeration of any physical qualities.

Note: It should be recognized that all prohibitions dealing with costume, dialogue or artwork apply as specifically to the cover of a comic magazine as they do to the contents.

Marriage and Sex

1. Divorce shall not be treated humorously nor represented as desirable.
2. Illicit sex relations are neither to be hinted at or portrayed. Violent love scenes as well as sexual abnormalities are unacceptable.
3. Respect for parents, the moral code, and for honorable behavior shall be fostered. A sympathetic understanding of the problems of love is not a license for morbid distortion.
4. The treatment of love-romance stories shall emphasize the value of the home and the sanctity of marriage.
5. Passion or romantic interest shall never be treated in such a way as to stimulate the lower and base emotions.
6. Seduction and rape shall never be shown or suggested.
7. Sex perversion or any [implication] to same is strictly forbidden.

Code for Advertising Matter

These regulations are applicable to all magazines published by members of the Comics Magazine Association of America, Inc. Good taste shall be the guiding principle in the acceptance of advertising.

1. Liquor and tobacco advertising is not acceptable.
2. Advertisements of sex or sex instruction books are unacceptable.
3. The sale of picture postcards, "pin-ups," "art studies," or any other reproduction of nude or semi-nude figures is prohibited.
4. Advertising for the sale of knives, concealable weapons, or realistic gun facsimiles is prohibited.
5. Advertising for the sale of fireworks is prohibited.
6. Advertising dealing with the sale of gambling equipment or printed matter dealing with gambling shall not be accepted.
7. Nudity with meretricious purpose and salacious postures shall not be permitted in the advertising of any product; clothed figures shall never be presented in such a way as to be offensive or contrary to good taste or morals.
8. To the best of his ability, each publisher shall ascertain that all statements made in advertisements conform to fact and avoid misrepresentation.
9. Advertisement of medical, health, or toiletry products of questionable nature are to be rejected. Advertisements for medical, health or toiletry products endorsed by the American Medical Association, or the American Dental Association, shall be deemed acceptable if they conform with all other conditions of the Advertising Code.

59

All in Color for a Dime

by George Beahm

> Whenever you hear a public discussion of comic books, you will sooner or later hear an advocate of the industry say with a triumphant smile, "Comic books are here to stay." I do not believe it. . . . I am convinced that in some way or other the democratic process will assert itself and crime comic books will go, and with them all that sustains them. But before they can tackle Superman, Dr. Payn, and all their myriad incarnations, people will have to learn that it is a distorted idea to think that democracy means giving good and evil an equal chance at expression. We must learn that freedom is not something that one can have, but is something that one must do.
>
> —FREDRIC WERTHAM, *Seduction of the Innocent* (Rinehart & Co., 1953), p. 395

In the opening segment of Stephen King's movie *Creepshow,* an enraged father snatches a comic book out of his son's hands and throws the book into the trash.

It is a moment that crystallized a horrific moment for young kids everywhere—myself included—as we remembered *our* collections trashed: comic books condemned without a fair reading (or, more accurately, any reading), our protests shunted aside. ("I don't have to *read* trash to *know* it's trash!" shouts the parent.)

It was, perhaps, our first brush with the ugly realities of life, reinforcing the message that parents weren't always right, that prejudice could replace logical thought. *We know what's best for you! We're only trying to protect you!*

o o o

In the wake of Fredric Wertham's well-intentioned but misguided book, *Seduction of the Innocent,* parents in the sixties were led to believe comics polluted kids' minds.

Times have changed, but prejudices against comics have not. As Wertham and his fellow witch hunters from the fifties knew, when you go on a witch hunt, you will almost certainly find plenty of "witches." Ironically, the hunt still continues today, as ultraconservative Christian groups like Focus on the Family find much at fault with today's comic books, making little (or no) distinction between mainstream and alternative comics, comics for children and comics intended for adults.

Taking a page from Wertham's book, Focus on the Family has, on at least two occasions, written against comic books. In *Citizen* (June 1989) "Mean Comics" is a front-page story, subheaded: "Batman is now a sinister psychotic, Superman has sexual fantasies, and comic-book publishers are out of control." In *Parental Guidance* (July 1991) the cover story again focuses on comics, specifically comics with movie tie-ins: "Violent Films: The Comic Book Connection."

Has Focus on the Family got a valid point, or has it simply taken up where Wertham left off, looking for witches to burn at the stake?

Batman, one of the comic books under attack by Focus on the Family, was ironically the subject of controversy this summer, not because of the comic but because of the movie: McDonald's, which had presumably screened the movie, heavily promoted *Batman 2* tie-in products in a nationwide ad campaign. As a result, kids begged their parents to take them to see the movie that, to many concerned parents, was an excessively dark interpretation by director Tim Burton, replete with graphic scenes and sexual innuendoes. (What male can ever forget Catwoman—Michelle Pfeiffer, clad in a skin-tight leather costume—astraddle Batman and licking his face?)

Has *Batman* (or, in fact, other mainstream comics) changed over the years? For Focus on the Family, *Batman*—using the first movie as the yardstick— "symbolizes . . . the dramatic changes taking place in the world of comic books."

"What," asks Focus on the Family, "is happening to this once-innocent form of entertainment for children?"

The simple truth is that, like all other forms of popular culture, comic books have undergone a process of maturation . . . and so has the industry. Mindful of Wertham's legacy, of the prejudice that still surrounds comics today, the industry has opted for self-regulation instead of enforced regulation from the outside. A distinction is made between those books intended for children, and those intended for more mature audiences. Labeled appropriately ("suggested for mature readers"), comics—whether published by mainstream companies like Marvel or D.C., or published by independent publishers that sell only through comic specialty stores catering to serious collectors—offer something for everyone: Disney publishes a full line of comics for kids, as do other publishers; *Archie* comics, *Barbie* comics, and other "kid-lit" clearly appeal to the grade-schoolers. And for those in an older age group, more sophisticated material is available, including superhero books that explore moral ambiguities. And for adults only (eighteen and up), adult comics are available—print equivalents to "R"- and "NC-17"-rated movies.

Here, then, are some commonly asked questions about comics:

1. Aren't comics just for kids?

In a word: no. Comic books are not just for kids, a fact more obvious today than ever before. For those outside the industry, the stereotyped images of "floppy-eared bunnies, attractive little mice and chipmunks" (to quote from the flap copy of *Seduction of the Innocent*) persist. For those working in the industry, comics have evolved into an adult medium, with everything "adult" implies, from X-rated comics (recalling the *Tijuana Bibles* of yesterday) for adults only, to the maturity of Art Spigelman's allegorical *Maus,* the story of the Holocaust told in comic book form, which earned its creator a Pulitzer.

Not only serious in intent but taken seriously as a medium, comics today, like movies, are packaged to appeal to a wide range of readers: preteens, young adults, and adults.

2. I didn't know comics were prescreened prior to publication by the Comics Code Authority. Does it screen all comics?

No, it doesn't. The 1954 code, similar in scope to television's standards and practices, is still enforced, though understandably more liberal in its interpretation. Still, there are mainstream comic book publishers that aren't signatory to the CCA, a situation analogous to movies that are unrated because they aren't submitted to that industry's ratings board, MPAA. To their credit, many publishers label their books on the cover, so you know what you are buying.

That doesn't mean, though, that you should rely entirely on the industry's labeling programs. Read the comic in question for yourself to judge its appropriateness as reading material for your child. To reject the comic out-of-hand without a reading sends the message that prejudice is acceptable behavior.

3. I have a problem with kids reading comics, period. Don't comics pollute their minds?

On the contrary, comics—even at an early age—will likely do something that movies and videogames *can't* do for your children: engage their imagination at an early age and give them a love for reading. Countless writers, artists, and filmmakers point to comics as their entry point into the world of imagination. If you are the kind of parent that is likely to condemn comics of all kinds because your gut feeling is that they "pollute" minds, ask yourself this question: Would you rather have your child *reading* or parked in front of the family television, for hours on end, watching vacuous programming and action-packed, gun-filled movies on videotapes, or playing videogames?

Like others in their generation, popular storytellers Stephen King, Ray Bradbury, and Steven Spielberg grew up on a diet of comic books. Their imaginations in part were fueled by comics; they began reading at an early age; and all three continue to entertain us with amazing stories.

I am reminded of Spielberg, especially, because of the frequent images in his movies of doors opening . . . with the suggestive possibilities of what may be on the *other* side.

How sad that there are those who seek to keep *all* the doors to imagination nailed shut, closed forever. That, I think, is a real obscenity.

o   o   o

Kids *will* find ways to entertain and amuse themselves. Comic books, if chosen properly, can get them hooked on reading at an early age; then, like many others, they will go on to read books (fiction and nonfiction) and magazines for entertainment as well as self-education.

Industry studies show that the average adult reads on the average one book a year, typically a work of popular fiction. What message, one asks, does *that* statistic send to kids?

It is tempting to point out that if today's disapproving parents had read comics as kids, perhaps some of them would read more today. The appetite for words is cultivated early—or, regrettably, not at all.

Fredric Wertham on Censorship
(from *Seduction of the Innocent,* p. 326)

What is censorship? The [comic book] industry has obscured that by claiming that the publisher exercises a censorship over himself. That is not what censorship means. It means control of one agency by another. When Freud speaks of an internal censor in the human mind, he does not mean that instinctive behavior can control itself. He specifically postulates another agency, the superego, which functions as a censor. The social fact is that radio, books, movies, stage plays, translations, do function under a censorship. So do newspaper comic strips, which all have to pass the censorship of the editor, who sometimes—as in the case of the *Newark News*—rejects advance proofs. Comic books for children have no censorship. The contrast between censorship for adults and the lack of it for children leads to such fantastic incongruities as the arrest of a girl in a nightclub for obscenity because she wrestles with a stuffed gorilla, when any six-year-old, for ten cents, can pore for hours or days over jungle books where real gorillas do much more exciting things with half-undressed girls than just wrestling.

60

Interview
Colleen Doran and David Weaver

Conducted by George Beahm

From Dr. Wertham in the fifties to conservative Christian groups and today's comic book critics like Thomas Radecki (a psychiatrist who is the research director for the National Coalition on TV Violence), comics have taken a bad rap.
    Who speaks for the medium?
    Comic book artists and retailers, of course.
    Here, then, are two prominent people in the industry that strikes a blow for—as Superman would say—truth, justice, and the American way!

Colleen Doran *has been drawing comics professionally since she was sixteen. Best known as the creator of* A Distant Soil, *a work in progress that she now publishes as an independent comic book from her own Aria Press, Doran has done a large body of work for D.C., Marvel, Disney* (Beauty & the Beast), *and numerous independent publishers, illustrating the works of Clive Barker and Anne Rice, among others. Voted as a "fan favorite" (twentieth out of several hundred) in a poll conducted by the industry's newspaper,* Comic Buyer's Guide, *Doran resides in Newport News, Virginia.*

Dave Weaver *is a book retailer whose specialty stores cater to comic book enthusiasts. Weaver has operated Benders, located in downtown Hampton, Virginia, for thirteen years; across the Chesapeake Bay in Chesapeake—not far from Pat Robertson's 700 Club and Christian Coalition—Weaver owns Zeno's. Favorite watering holes for local pros, fans, and serious collectors, both of Weaver's stores carry a full range of newsstand product, including (of course) comics.*

George Beahm: *In terms of subject matter, isn't it misleading to lump all comics together?*
    Dave Weaver: Yes. Comics are aimed at several different audiences, including some geared for older audiences.

What do you do to ensure children don't pick up the comics inappropriate for them?
    Weaver: We have a separate section at the back of the shop with signs posted,

"No one under 18." And we keep an eye on it. For mature material, if a kid comes in with his parents, we ask them if they want their child reading it. For instance, last week we had a child buying Eclipse's "True Crime" cards, which depict mass murderers and psychos. The parent said, "He sees it on TV. It's no big deal." So I don't think you see anything in comics that you don't see already on TV.

What is your response to the allegation by Focus on the Family that "today, comic books are surpassing even television, movies and other forms of the popular culture for graphic violence, sexual explicitness, occult themes, profanity and obscenity"?

Weaver: On mainstream comics, it's just wrong. There are comics which are explicit, but they're not for children.

Focus on the Family said, "Clearly, comic book writers, artists and publishers are pushing the limits of the medium today." Colleen, as an artist, writer and publisher, what is your response?

Doran: I'm a storyteller. I'm not interested in offending anyone. My function is to give people entertainment, and comics are entertainment. But no matter what you write, no matter what you draw, no matter what you say, there will always be someone that will object to it, no matter how harmless you think it is. There's absolutely nothing we can do about what people *think* we create.

What is your response to Focus on the Family's allegation that "parents who rightly restrict a child's diet of violent imagery at the theater but allow a youngster to freely explore the world of comic books may unknowingly be opening the door to an obsession with graphic violence"?

Doran: The presumption is that *all* comics are filled with graphic, gratuitous violence—that's not true. Also, it's the *parents'* right and responsibility to raise their child and therefore their absolute right and responsibility to regulate their child's forms of entertainment. I don't have any objection to that.

Their newsletter presumes that all comic books are for children, which is not the case. We do everything we can to differentiate between books that are for children, and those that are not. And if the parents have any question, they should accompany their child to the comic book shop and discuss what is appropriate reading material.

My problem is that they not only object to what people in their own family should read, but also what *other* families should read.

Dave, as a retailer, what do you do to screen the material you buy for your store?

Weaver: The catalogues we get are marked with content notes regarding nudity, sexual material, and extreme violence. Frequently, they enclose flyers that will show the artwork. If we're uncertain about the content, we just won't order it. We don't order things blindly.

Dave, from your perspective as a retailer, how often do you see children buying comics in your store?

Weaver: We have a lot of school-age kids, whom we direct toward the Disney books. Most of our clientele is over eighteen; they are comic book collectors and serious readers. We have an older group that know what they are looking for, can afford to buy books, and want the specialty merchandise that other stores don't carry.

Colleen, comics used to cost pocket change. Now, depending on the book, only the well heeled can afford them. Obviously, they aren't kid-priced anymore. What happened?

Doran: Back in the fifties, when the first witch hunt against comics started, comic books were cheap—a nickel or a dime. Today, we're talking about comic books that start at a dollar and go up to $50 for a limited-edition hardback like *Electra*. You're going to have to dig deep; even the regular edition of *Electra* is $25.

Colleen, where do you see kids buying comics these days?

I see kids clustered around comic book racks in the mall and in convenience stores like 7-Eleven, which generally have the mainstream comics from Marvel and D.C., and occasionally the popular ones from independent publishers, but not often. Even then, stores like Waldenbooks carry graphic novels, which are pretty expensive. At comic book conventions, most people I see are adults.

Would you say that comics have, in a sense, matured?

Doran: I'd say so, but it goes back to one's definition of what is objectionable. We're storytellers—we're not here to provide moral reform.

Besides, most of what you see in comics is no more extreme than what you can get on daytime television, prime time, or afternoon programming.

A Distant Soil

For a sampling of what the alternative publishers are offering, check out *A Distant Soil*. Available in specialty stores nationwide (check your yellow pages under "Comic Books"), Doran's series is available by subscription: issues no. 1 through 4 are $1.75 each; an eight-issue subscription is $12.50.

A comic book with black-and-white interiors and full-color covers, *A Distant Soil*, says Doran, appeals predominantly to female readers in their late teens and midtwenties.

Send orders to: Aria Press, 12638-28 Jefferson Avenue, Suite 173, Newport News, VA 23602-4316.

The Movie Ratings Game

61

The Censorship Game
Hype in Hollywood

by Gary L. Wood

Both sides play this game. It's obvious that MPAA's Classification and Rating Administration, which established and oversees the ratings, recognizes the realities of the marketplace. Why else would there be so few G ratings? Why else would a PG be placed on a movie like *Star Wars*, which featured no profanity, no sex, but a brief glimpse of skeletal remains and a severed alien limb?

—PHIL BERANDELLI, "Rated 'G'—For Gone?" *Washington Post*, August 16, 1992

Long before the MPAA established its rating code, the Production Code held sway over Hollywood's films. "[The only way] to curb the evil influence of evil pictures was to have the pictures made right . . . at the source of production," said Martin Quigley, cocreator of the Production Code, on the code's first purpose, in Melinda Corey and George Ochoa's book of quotes about Hollywood, The Man in Lincoln's Nose.

Making pictures "right" at the source *of production? Whether Quigley would have admitted it or not, that's censorship of the worst kind.*

The movies have come a long way since Clark Gable shocked the nation in the thirties with his line in Gone with the Wind: *"Frankly, my dear, I don't give a damn."*

Some critics today have said the movies have finally gone too far: too much sex, and too much violence. For their troubles, filmmakers "voluntarily" edit frames to get the rating downgraded; an X is the kiss of death, and an NC-17 is the breath of death. Far better is the coveted R, in which youths under seventeen can see it if accompanied by a parent or an adult guardian. (Then, too, with the lax security in most theaters, especially multiplex cinemas, it's all too easy to buy a ticket for a PG-13 film and sneak next door to see the R-rated film.)

Gary Wood, in this piece, discusses the dimensions of censorship in Hollywood. Obviously, the game is rigged, but when it's the only game in town. . . .

What is censorship in Hollywood?

The answer depends on whom you ask. To a struggling screenwriter who feels he has a dynamite, cutting-edge script, censorship is when the studios—caring nothing for "art"—only want to make "formula" films that will make money.

To a producer whose film has just received an NC-17 rating from the Motion Pictures Association of America (MPAA), censorship is when the ratings board applies such a rating to a film, effectively limiting its audience, stifling its commercial potential, and discouraging studios and others from making such films in the future.

During the filming of 1992's *Basic Instinct,* a crowd of gay activists gathered outside of the Tosca Cafe in San Francisco where the film was in production. The crowd was upset about the subject matter of the film: a bisexual woman and a lesbian were both major suspects in a murder case. The activists had demanded changes in the Joe Esterhas script. When their demands were not met, they decided to disrupt filming by screaming and shouting outside of the bar. *Time* magazine quoted one gay leader, who said, "Hollywood has once again decided to sacrifice the lives of gay men and lesbians in order to make money."

Executives at Carolco and Tri-Star Pictures, the film's producers, replied, "Censorship by street action will not be tolerated." The film was completed and became a major hit, despite the first recorded case of attempted street censorship.

Its controversy fueled another debate. "Should WASPs be the only villains? I mean, no Italians, no blacks—if there are no minorities that can have socially deviant behaviors—I don't get it," said actor Michael Douglas of *Basic Instinct.*

In *Premiere,* Peter Biskind wrote:

[Michael] Douglas's reaction is not all that hard to understand, either. [Actors] . . . don't like to be told what to do, particularly by people who aren't waving million-dollar checks. Charges of racial or gender stereotyping are guaranteed to provoke a chorus of wounded howls—"censorship," "artistic freedom"—whereby victimizers are magically transformed into victims.

What is censorship in Hollywood?

All of these "victims" and "censors," whether they know it or not, are merely players in a much larger game. As Joe Baltake for Knight-Ridder Newspapers wrote:

It has become a game, the only game in town, in fact. It's called hype, of course, and with the decline of the star system, the advancement of rival amusements and, especially, the desensitization of moviegoers, it has taken on greater prominence, virtually keeping the film industry afloat. . . . Sometimes the hype is more important than the movie itself.

Amid this game, no organization has played the villain more times than the Motion Picture Association Film Rating; but to understand the game, one must know the rules. MPAA President Jack Valenti explained that his organization merely applies a label to the film for use by parents and theater owners. The system is strictly voluntary, and it is up to the individuals to choose to abide by it or not; the MPAA is merely making a recommendation. A parent may still allow his child to see an NC-17 film, or a theater owner may let a child see an R film without a parent.

As if to further prove the voluntary nature of the system, in 1982, the Dallas, Texas, Ratings Board decided to label Steven Spielberg's *Poltergeist* with an R, even after the MPAA had given it a PG. Spielberg fought—and won.

Valenti said:

> The ratings system has been in effect since November 1, 1968 . . . twenty-four years. I think most people understand that it's voluntary, which is the source of its legal strength. We've won all of the court cases we've been involved in because the judges have determined that *because* it is voluntary, it does not trample on anybody's First Amendment rights because nobody is *forced* to do *anything*.
>
> In speeches and articles, we have tried to emphasize the fact that it is voluntary; but it's very difficult to make sure that everybody knows that.

This may perhaps not be news to those outside the industry, but Valenti says that the insiders already know this and simply manipulate the rating system to their best advantage.

The process begins when a producer submits his film to the ratings board. As Valenti explained, "We will schedule a time for when that film is to be shown. It is screened *only* by the members of the ratings board. The producer is not in there. No outsiders are in there at all.

"After they screen the picture, they discuss it. Sometimes they screen parts of it again. Then at the end of that discussion, they vote on what rating it should have. They pass that provisional rating along to the producer. He either accepts it or, if he doesn't accept it, comes back and says, 'Why did I get this? I don't want an R. I want to get a PG-13.'

"They tell him, essentially, that they don't *edit* films; instead, they'll say, 'There were scenes of sexuality, or violence, or the language, or such and such.' Then it is up to the producer as to whether he and the director want to make excisions; they do the editing. They can bring it back again and maybe it's still an R. He may edit some more, bring it back, and the members of the ratings board say, 'Okay, you got a PG-13.'"

There is no limit to the number of times a film can be submitted, but after two tries it must go back to the "back of the line," allowing for schedules to be maintained and other films to be screened.

"The Appeals Board, the Supreme Court of the Ratings System, is the last word for a film. It consists of representatives of independent film distributors, major distributors, and theater owners," Valenti observed.

"About two-thirds of the time that a film is submitted to the Appeals Board, the ratings board is sustained; about one-third of the time, it's overturned. It's a quasi-judicial setting. The film is screened for the Appeals Board. After the screening, the representative of the ratings board tells them why he thinks that rating is right. The producer or the director of the film then tells why he thinks it is wrong; both answer questions, then leave the room. In a private session the Appeals Board discusses and votes by secret ballot."

In 1983 Brian de Palma's *Scarface* received an X rating for its graphic violence. De Palma recut the film four times, but still received the X. After arguing to the Appeals Board, de Palma received an R rating. In 1992 David Lynch submitted the film version of his television series, *Twin Peaks: Fire Walk with Me,* and received an X rating. After Lynch explained to the MPAA that the material they objected to had already appeared on the television series, his film received an R rating without a cut.

Other films are not so lucky and must go into the marketplace with an NC-17—the adult rating that replaced X. *Henry and June* was the first film ever to be rated NC-17. Others, perhaps in defiance or in hopes of circumventing the system, send their films out with *no* rating rather than branded with an NC-17— a strategy used for *Henry: Portrait of a Serial Killer.* Still, this strategy is ineffective because theater owners apply their own voluntary limitations by announcing that no one under 17 will be admitted, despite the lack of an MPAA rating.

As Valenti elaborated, "There are no precise guidelines to rating a film. The ratings board tries to answer the question, 'Is the rating the one that most parents would feel to be accurate?' Ratings are advance cautionary warnings for parents before they let their children go see it."

The system has come under fire by the general public because the general guidelines for rating a film have, over the years, relaxed. In the thirties, for example, in *Gone with the Wind,* Clark Gable uttered the then controversial line, "Frankly, my dear, I don't give a damn." Today, however, the word "damn" is heard in G-rated films. Valenti responds: "Since the days of Clark Gable, hasn't society changed? Then why would movies remain untouched by change? You've got things on television today that come into your home that you never had in movies years ago."

There is also the general belief that the ratings board is much more lenient on violence and deals more harshly with sexual material. Valenti, however, disagrees. "That's not true. As a matter of fact, we're probably harder on violence than anything. Most of the pictures that get NC-17 get it for violence; then some of the violence is cut out to get an R."

Case in point: *Stephen King's Sleepwalkers,* which, as its director Mick Garris pointed out, "got four NC-17's before we finally got an R."

But the claims that make the biggest headlines are those from the filmmakers that cry economic censorship at the MPAA's NC-17 rating. Since its inception, approximately forty films have got that rating. Only a handful of them went into the marketplace; the rest went directly to video.

Producers of recent films receiving the NC-17 ratings for movies like *Henry and June, The Cook, The Thief, His Wife and Her Lover,* and *Whore*—feel that it severely limits box-office potential.

Valenti, however, remains adamant, despite the claims. "We never rate a movie based on its economic viability. We only rate what's on the screen. If it happens to hurt the movie, [remember] we didn't make the movie. So we don't listen to people who say, 'This film rating is hurting me financially.' Our response is, 'That's the film you made—we didn't make it.'

"I think producers are like gamblers. They want as lenient a rating as they can get because that widens the potential audience, but that's not our concern. The duty of the ratings board is to rate on what we think the parents of America would most likely call the accurate rating for that film."

One of the more interesting controversies in recent years surrounded Ken Russell's *Whore*, which received an NC-17. Because the film dealt realistically with the graphic reality of prostitution, Children of the Night—a social agency in Los Angeles that works with runaway teenagers—got involved and came out in support of the film, but not another film on prostitution, *Pretty Woman*, rated PG-13. They maintained that the MPAA was sending out a mixed message, since "It's okay to run away to California to become a prostitute because your Prince Charming may arrive and save you," the message of *Pretty Woman*. Both Children of the Night and the filmmakers of *Whore* maintained that, given the nature of the two films, teenagers ought to see *Whore* but the NC-17 rating prohibited them from doing so.

Valenti defended the ratings board's decision to give Disney's *Pretty Woman* a PG-13. "*Pretty Woman* has no sex in it *at all*. *None*. It's the *Cinderella* story. The point is that [the character in *Pretty Woman*] left the profession of prostitution. But the people who produced *Whore* used the ratings system as a patsy to go on television and get publicity for the film by bashing it. Miramax did that brilliantly with *The Cook, The Thief, His Wife and Her Lover,* and so did the people who produced *Henry: Portrait of a Serial Killer*. They went on every talk show in America and publicized their film by talking about censorship. I understand and everybody in our business understands that to publicize a film you bash the ratings system."

"As to which film teenagers should see"—*Whore* or *Pretty Woman*—"we leave that decision to parents. If some parents believe that their children should see *Whore,* fine; it's *their* decision, not ours."

The filmmakers maintain, however, that the NC-17 rating and the cooperation of the theater owners will not allow parents to let their children see *Whore*.

Perhaps Bob Keeshan (of *Captain Kangaroo*) put it best: "Parents have to take the basic role of guiding their children in selection of television programs, or records, or motion pictures, or anything else. You really can't turn that responsibility over to anybody else, and it doesn't make any practical sense to turn it over to anybody else. You really have to do it as a parent.

"We would never think of calling the police and saying, 'I'm sending my child out to play. Stop all traffic!' You assume the responsibility of training your child to stay out of the street and out of harm's way. . . ."

• *Gary Wood, who writes frequently on popular culture movies, writes regularly for* Cinefantastique.

62

The Voluntary Movie Rating System *

by Jack Valenti

> The new classification system, which rates all films . . . in terms of suitability of the material for various levels of audiences, has created a scheme in which just about everything is now possible in motion pictures. . . . Jack Valenti, who introduced the system, is a realist, and knows that the system is imperfect, "but you cannot get perfection in this world, my friend."
>
> —JACK VIZZARD, from *See No Evil: Life Inside a Hollywood Censor* (1970)

How It All Began

When I became president of the Motion Picture Association of America (MPAA) in May 1966, the slippage of Hollywood studio authority over the content of films collided with an avalanching revision of American mores and customs.

By summer of 1966, the national scene was marked by insurrection on the campus, riots in the streets, rise in women's liberation, protest of the young, doubts about the institution of marriage, abandonment of old guiding slogans, and the crumbling of social traditions. It would have been foolish to believe that movies, that most creative art form, could have remained unaffected by the change and torment in our society.

A New Kind of American Movie

The result of all this was the emergence of a "new kind" of American movie—frank and open, and made by filmmakers subject to very few self-imposed restraints.

Almost within weeks in my new duties I was confronted with controversy, neither amiable nor fixable. The first issue was the film *Who's Afraid of Virginia Woolf?* in which, for the first time on the screen, the word "screw" and the phrase "hump the hostess" were heard. In company with the MPAA's general counsel, Louis Nizer, I met with Jack Warner, the legendary chieftain of Warner Bros. and his top aide, Ben Kalmenson. We talked for three hours, and the

---

* © 1987, 1991 by the Motion Picture Association of America, Inc.

result was deletion of "screw" and retention of "hump the hostess," but I was uneasy over the meeting.

It seemed wrong that grown men should be sitting around discussing such matters. Moreover, I was uncomfortable with the thought that this was just the beginning of an unsettling new era in film, in which we would lurch from crisis to crisis, without any suitable solution in sight.

The second issue surfaced only a few months later. This time it was Metro-Goldwyn-Mayer, and the Michelangelo Antonioni film *The Blow-Up*. I met with MGM's chief executive officer because this movie also represented a first—the first time a major distributor was marketing a film with nudity in it. The Production Code Administration in California had denied the seal. I backed the decision, whereupon MGM distributed the film through a subsidiary company, thereby flouting the voluntary agreement of MPAA member companies that none would distribute a film without a Code seal.

Finally, in April 1968, the U.S. Supreme Court upheld the constitutional power of states and cities to prevent the exposure of children to books and films which could not be denied to adults.

It was plain that the old system of self-regulation that began with the formation of the MPAA in 1922 had broken down. What few threads there were holding together the structure created by Will Hays, one of my two predecessors, had now snapped. From the very first day of my own succession to the MPAA president's office, I had sniffed the Production Code constructed by the Hays Office. There was about this stern, forbidding catalogue of "Dos and Don'ts" the odious smell of censorship. I determined to junk it at the first opportune moment.

I knew that the mix of new social currents, the irresistible force of creators determined to make "their" films (full of wild candor, groused some social critics), and the possible intrusion of government into the movie arena demanded my immediate action.

Within weeks, discussions of my plan for a movie rating system began with the president of the National Association of Theatre Owners (NATO), and with the governing committee of the International Film Importers & Distributors of America (IFIDA), an assembly of independent producers and distributors.

The Birth of the Ratings

By early fall, I was ready. My colleagues in the National Association of Theatre Owners joined with me in affirming our objective of creating a new and, at the time, revolutionary approach to how we would fulfill our obligation to the parents of America.

My first move was to abolish the old and decaying Hays Production Code. I did that immediately. Then on November 1, 1968, we announced the birth of the new voluntary film rating system of the motion picture industry, with three organizations, NATO, MPAA, and IFIDA, as its monitoring and guiding groups.

The initial design called for four rating categories:

- G for General Audiences, all ages admitted;
- M for mature audiences—parental guidance suggested, but all ages admitted;
- R for Restricted, children under 16 would not be admitted without an accompanying parent or adult guardian;
- X for no one under 17 admitted.

The rating system trademarked all the category symbols, except the X. Under the plan, anyone not submitting his or her film for rating could self-apply the X or any other symbol or description, except those trademarked by the rating program. (The X rating's name has been changed to NC-17, a trademarked symbol—No Children Under 17 Admitted.)

Our original plan had been to use only three rating categories, ending with R. It was my view that parents ought to have the right to accompany their children to any movie the parents chose, without the movie industry or the government or self-appointed groups interfering with their rights. But the theater owners organization (National Association of Theatre Owners) urged the creation of an adults only category, fearful of possible legal redress under state or local law. I acquiesced in NATO's reasoning and the four category system, including the X rating, was installed.

So, the emergence of the voluntary rating system filled the vacuum provided by my dismantling of the Hays Production Code. The movie industry would no longer "approve or disapprove" the content of a film. But we would now see our primary task as giving advance cautionary warnings to parents so that parents could make the decision about the moviegoing of their young children. That decision is solely the responsibility of parents.

Changes in the Rating System

We found early on that the M category (M meaning "Mature") was regarded by most parents as a sterner rating than the R category. To remedy this misconception, we changed the name from M to GP (meaning General audiences, Parental guidance suggested). A year later we revised the name to its current label, "PG: Parental Guidance Suggested."

On July 1, 1984, we made another adjustment. We split the PG category into two groupings, PG and PG-13. PG-13 meant a higher level of intensity than was to be found in a film rated PG. Over the past years, parents have approved of this amplifying revision in the rating system.

On September 27, 1990, we announced two more revisions.

First, we introduced five-to-eight word explanations of why a particular film received its R rating. Since, in the opinion of the Ratings Board, R-rated films contain adult material, we believed it would be useful to parents to know a little more about that film's content before they allowed their children to accompany them. These explanations would be available to parents by calling the local theater playing that picture, or inquiring at the box office.

Second, we changed the name of the X category to NC-17: No CHILDREN UNDER 17 ADMITTED. The X rating over the years appeared to have taken on a surly meaning in the minds of many people, a meaning that was never intended when we created the system. Therefore, we chose to go back to the original intent of the design we installed on November 1, 1968, in which this "adults only" category explicitly describes a movie that most parents would want to have barred to viewing by their children. That was and is our goal, nothing more, nothing less.

We have now trademarked "NC-17: No CHILDREN UNDER 17 ADMITTED" so that this rating symbol and the legend can be used only by those who submit their films for ratings. (Application for trademark registration pending.) Other rating symbols are already federally registered trademarks. Those who do not choose to participate in the rating system can take their film to market using any letters or descriptions they desire, except the trademarked symbols and legends of the rating system.

What the Ratings Mean

G: "General Audiences—All ages admitted."

This is a film which contains nothing in theme, language, nudity and sex, violence, etc. which would, in the view of the Rating Board, be offensive to parents whose younger children view the film. The G rating is *not* a "certificate of approval," nor does it signify a children's film.

Some snippets of language may go beyond polite conversation but they are common every-day expressions. No stronger words are present in G-rated films. The violence is at a minimum. Nudity and sex scenes are not present; nor is there any drug use content.

PG: "Parental Guidance Suggested; some material may not be suitable for children."

This is a film which clearly needs to be examined or inquired about by parents before they let their children attend. The label PG plainly states that parents may consider some material unsuitable for their children, but the parents must make the decision.

Parents are warned against sending their children, unseen without inquiry, to PG-rated movies.

There may be some profanity in these films. There may be violence, but it is not deemed so strong that everyone under 17 need be restricted unless accompanied by a parent. Nor is there cumulative horror or violence that may take a film all the way into the R category. There is no drug use content.

There is no explicit sex in a PG-rated film, although there may be some indication of sensuality. Brief nudity may appear in an unrestricted film, but anything beyond that puts the film into R.

The PG rating, suggesting parental guidance, is thus an alert for special examination of a film by parents before deciding on its viewing by their children.

Obviously the line is difficult to draw. In our pluralistic society it is not easy to make subjective judgments without incurring some disagreement. So long as parents know they must exercise parental responsibility, the rating serves as a meaningful guide and as a warning.

PG-13: "Parents strongly cautioned. Some material may be inappropriate for children under 13."

A PG-13 film is one which, in the view of the Rating Board, leaps beyond the boundaries of the PG rating, but does not quite fit within the restricted R category. Any drug use content will initially require at least a PG-13 rating. In effect, the PG-13 cautions parents with more stringency than usual to give special attention to this film before they allow their 12-year-olds and younger to attend.

If nudity is sexually oriented, the film will generally not be found in the PG-13 category. If violence is rough or persistent, the film goes into the R (restricted) rating. A film's single use of one of the harsher sexually derived words, though only as an expletive, shall require the Rating Board to issue that film at least a PG-13 rating. More than one such expletive must lead the Rating Board to issue a film an R rating, as must even one of these words used in a sexual context. These films can be rated less severely, however, if by a special vote, the Rating Board feels that a lesser rating would more responsibly reflect the opinion of American parents.

PG-13 places larger responsibilities on parents for their children's moviegoing. The voluntary rating system is not a surrogate parent, nor should it be. It cannot, and should not, insert itself in family decisions that only parents can, and should, make. Its purpose is to give prescreening advance informational warnings, so that parents can form their own judgments. PG-13 is designed to make these parental decisions easier for those films between PG and R.

R: "Restricted, under 17 requires accompanying parent or adult guardian." (Age varies in some jurisdictions.)

In the opinion of the Rating Board, this film definitely contains adult material. Parents are strongly urged to find out more about this film before they allow their children to accompany them.

An R-rated film has adult content that may include hard language, or tough violence, or nudity within sensual scenes, or drug abuse or other elements, or a combination of some of the above. That is why parents are counseled, in advance, to take this advisory rating very seriously.

NC-17: "No children under 17 admitted." (Age varies in some jurisdictions.)

This rating declares that the Rating Board believes that this is patently an adult film. No children will be admitted. NC-17 does not necessarily mean "obscene or pornographic" in the oft-accepted meaning of those words. These are legal terms and for courts to decide. The reasons for the application of an NC-17 rating can mean strong violence or sex or aberrational behavior or drug abuse or any other element which, when present, most parents would want to be off-limits for viewing by their children.

The Public Reaction

We count it crucial to make regular soundings to find out how the public perceives the rating program, and to measure the approval and disapproval of what we are doing.

Nationwide scientific polls, conducted each year by the Opinion Research Corporation of Princeton, New Jersey, have consistently given the rating program high marks by parents throughout the land. The latest poll results show that 75 percent of parents with children under 18 found the ratings to be "very useful" to "fairly useful" in helping them make decisions for the moviegoing of their children. This is an all-time high for the rating system.

On the evidence of the polls, the rating system would not have survived if it were not providing a useful service to parents.

The rating system isn't perfect but, in an imperfect world, it seems each year to match the expectations of those whom it is designed to serve—parents of America.

• *Jack Valenti is president of the MPAA, and his comments were excerpted from a booklet published by the MPAA,* The Voluntary Movie Rating System.

"Rated 'G'—For Gone?"*

"It's no secret that the G rating has become a marketing albatross for moviemakers. Ironically, a movie that carries a G today must deal with marketing problems similar to those attached to the X rating—either label elicits a public bias. . . . The numbers tell the tale. Of the 614 movies rated by the Motion Picture Association of America in 1991, only 14 were rated G. Another 87 received a PG. That means MPAA found only 15 percent of American movies last year suitable for children under age 13.

"In contrast, 375 movies—about 60 percent—received an R rating. Of the remainder, 118 were rated PG-13, and 20 received either an X or its replacement, NC-17, established in 1990."

*PHIL BERANDELLI, "Rated 'G'—For Gone?" *Washington Post,* August 16, 1992

63

Statement on Labeling
An Interpretation of
the Library Bill of Rights

from American Library Association

Labeling is the practice of describing or designating materials by affixing a prejudicial label and/or segregating them by a prejudicial system. The American Library Association opposes these means of predisposing people's attitudes toward library materials for the following reasons:

1. Labeling is an attempt to prejudice attitudes and as such, it is a censor's tool.
2. Some find it easy and even proper, according to their ethics, to establish criteria for judging publications as objectionable. However, injustice and ignorance rather than justice and enlightenment result from such practices, and the American Library Association opposes the establishment of such criteria.
3. Libraries do not advocate the ideas found in their collections. The presence of books and other resources in a library does not indicate endorsement of their contents by the library.

A variety of private organizations promulgate rating systems and/or review materials as a means of advising either their members or the general public concerning their opinions of the contents and suitability or appropriate age for use of certain books, films, recordings, or other materials. For the library to adopt or enforce any of these private systems, to attach such ratings to library materials, to include them in bibliographic records, library catalogs, or other finding aids, or otherwise to endorse them would violate the Library Bill of Rights.

While some attempts have been made to adopt these systems into law, the constitutionality of such measures is extremely questionable. If such legislation is passed which applies within a library's jurisdiction, the library should seek competent legal advice concerning its applicability to library operations.

Publishers, industry groups, and distributors sometimes add ratings to material or include them as part of their packaging. Librarians should not endorse such practices. However, removing or obliterating such ratings—if placed there by or with permission of the copyright holder—could constitute expurgation, which is also unacceptable.

The American Library Association opposes efforts which aim at closing any path to knowledge. This statement, however, does not exclude the adoption of organizational schemes designed as directional aids or to facilitate access to materials.

• *Adopted July 31, 1951. Amended June 25, 1971; July 1, 1981; June 26, 1990, by the ALA Council.*

Television

64

The Outer Limits
Network Program Standards

by George Beahm

> Written standards cannot cover the entire universe of situations and must,
> therefore, be worded broadly. These will be applied with flexibility, taking
> into consideration context and character.
>
> —From "Preamble," *Program Standards* (Capital Cities, ABC, Inc.,
> Department of Broadcast Standards and Practice, May 15, 1989)

There is no question that television is the most potent medium of mass communication today. Virtually every home in the U.S. has at least one television, which means that it has become a window to the world for hundreds of millions of Americans.

Acknowledging its power, the three major networks have set limits to the content of television programs. Ironically, these same rules do not apply to advertisers, airing contradictory messages on the same networks, nor do they apply to cable programs.

Whereas once there were three choices—ABC, CBS, and NBC—there is, through cable, a world of choices: CNN, movie channels, and specialized programming. Unlike the three networks with programs reaching the limits of acceptability, cable programming goes beyond what some would consider the outer limits: R-rated movies on movie channels, whereas networks would "edit" for broadcast; sexually oriented shows like "The Playboy Channel," the visual equivalent of *Playboy;* and local channels that, depending on the location, leave little to the imagination.

Because televisions show both network and cable programming, another double standard exists, blurring the picture of what should be broadcast into homes: What's the point in seeing a movie "edited for television" when, on the same television, a cable movie channel will show the movie in its unexpurgated form?

Some would say the networks are simply behind the times, that they should expand the boundaries of network programming. Ironically, there exists even within network programming a double standard: what is not permissible on television programs *is*, in fact, permissible in ads that air throughout the programs.

For instance:

• Alcohol "should be de-emphasized" and "care should be exercised to avoid glamorization or promotion of alcoholic beverages." Beer advertisements, however, sent out a contradictory message. As *Playboy* put it in "The Swedish Bikini Team," sex and brew are a bewitching brew:

> After five years of TV commercials in which men hoisted beers in the great outdoors and swore, "It doesn't get any better than this," Old Milwaukee's ad agency had a brain storm. *Wait! What if it does?* Enter the Swedish Bikini Team, five buxom blondes designed to make men sweatier than the coldest bottle of brew. They appear out of nowhere, preposterously gorgeous proof that Old Milwaukee can make your best day sexier, bubblier, perfect. . . . They are magical creatures, able to find beer drinkers by E.S.P. (Extraordinary Swedish Pulchritude).

• With some exceptions, organizations can't solicit for funds, yet televangelists rely on the medium to reach millions of potential contributors.

• Noting that children watch some adult programs, the network wants producers to take this into account "in the presentation of material. . . ."

These same children, however, can flick through channels and see R-rated films on movie channels, or see MTV's sexually suggestive music videos.

• In its clause on "drug use and abuse," the network notes that "the portrayal of cigarette smoking shall be de-emphasized," yet for many years cigarette ads—now banned—portrayed smoking in a glamorous manner.

• Films are screened "to determine whether they require deletions or are completely unacceptable." The network then provides a "deletion report" as a guideline for editing the film. (Compare, for instance, the network televised version of Eddie Murphy's *Trading Places* with the film version—worlds apart. Similarly, the tone of Stephen King's *Stand by Me* changes as the network deletes the natural dialogue of the young boys.)

• The network allows talk-show guests to discuss their current projects, but only up to a point—"gratuitous plugs" are discouraged.

Flick the channel, though, and tune in to an "infomercial"—a cleverly disguised ad with the appearance of a program, a wolf in sheep's clothing.

• On the subject of "professional advice," the network permits no "medical" advice "except when it conforms with law and recognized ethical and professional standards."

What, then, does one make of the profusion of ads for weight loss, for everything from Thigh Master to liquid diets?

• Under "sexuality," the network states that "in a changing society issues of human sexuality portrayed with sensitivity are appropriate programming fare."

Still, one sees no ads or programming that actively promotes condom use or safe sex in a direct manner, at a time when AIDS has become an international health issue and public scandal.

Let's admit it: the networks do have program standards, but what they really enforce is the double standard, highlighting the uneasy relationship between programming and advertisements.

65

Interview: Madonna

Conducted by Forrest Sawyer

Ma·don·na *n.* **1.** the Virgin Mary (usually prec. by *the*). **2.** a picture or statue representing the Virgin Mary. **3.** (*l.c.*) *Archaic.* an Italian title of formal address to a woman. [1575–85; < It: my lady]
The Random House Dictionary of the English Language (2d ed., unabridged), p. 1154

Ma·don·na *n.* **1.** Metamorphic, ballsy, shock rock artist, entrepreneur, and feminist pushing outer limits; born Madonna Louise Ciccone. **2.** Boy Toy. **3.** (Un)like a Virgin. **4.** Baby Doll [most recent incarnation for cover of *Vanity Fair*, October 1992].

It was too hot for MTV, but it was news, so ABC's "Nightline" ran the full, unedited music video, "Justify My Love" on December 3, 1990. (Not to waste a good marketing opportunity, Madonna later released it as a music video single.)

Following the video, Madonna was interviewed by Forrest Sawyer. Sure to infuriate some, Madonna defends her video and herself—with brio.

Predictably, Madonna's latest project—an oversized book titled, simply, Sex, has created a firestorm of controversy.

Sawyer: It has become virtually a seasonal affair. The weather changes, and there is a new Madonna controversy. This one is a video that MTV, the popular cable music video channel, refused to air. Instantly, a storm of questions arose. Is this a kind of censorship? Has Madonna finally gone too far? We'll look for some answers when I talk with Madonna in just a few minutes, and we will see—in its entirety—the video that has caused all this noise.

But first, the controversy itself, with correspondent Ken Kashiwahara.

Ken Kashiwahara: [voice-over] Nudity, suggestions of bisexuality, sadomasochism, multiple partners. Finally, MTV decided Madonna had gone too far. Her latest video, "Justify My Love," was banned.

Now, for the first time, the channel has decided to take a pass on a clip by pop music's hottest star.

For six years, this star has turned shock into success, consistently pushing the outer limits of the outrageous, of what is permissible and what is not. Madonna has attracted millions of fans around the world and offended many in the mainstream.

"Like a Prayer," for example, was criticized by religious groups as blasphemy, and because of this video, Pepsi-Cola canceled a Madonna TV commercial, despite having paid her $5 million.

Madonna: I wouldn't have turned out the way I was if I didn't have all those old-fashioned values to rebel against.

Kashiwahara: [voice-over] Madonna's career has been fashioned by her vision of sexuality, from her gyrations to her dress. Madonna underwear, worn as outerwear, became a fashion craze. Even her serious endeavors tend to be sexually suggestive—Madonna urging get out the vote.

Madonna: ["Rock the Vote" ad on MTV, with Madonna wrapped in the American flag, revealing a red bikini underneath] "And if you don't vote, you're going to get a spanking."

Kashiwahara: [voice-over] While MTV has banned "Justify My Love," the pay TV channel, Jukebox, has decided to show it.

Andrew Orgel, Video Jukebox Network: We're not a censor, and we don't position ourselves as a censor. I think we're very sensitive, though, to our audience.

Kashiwahara: [voice-over] So whether she is deliberately provocative and in bad taste, or performing within the limits of artistic expression, Madonna continues to carve out a career out of controversy. This is Ken Kashiwahara for "Nightline."

Sawyer: And now the video. Obviously, we are broadcasting it late at night and we expect that only adults are watching. You should know this video includes graphic portrayals of sexuality and nudity.

["Justify My Love," video and music, is aired, unedited, in its entirety.]

Sawyer: And when we come back . . . Madonna.

[Commercial break]

Sawyer: *She is certainly controversial, but she is also popular. Madonna's first four albums sold 48 million copies, and* Forbes *magazine calls her ". . . the top-earning female entertainer this year." Madonna joins us from Los Angeles.*

Am I correct in assuming that if an artist wants an album or a record to be very popular, you need to have airplay, or usually you need to have airplay on MTV?

Madonna: Yes, it's a very important marketing tool for an artist.

So I should assume, then, that you went through the ordinary process. With MTV in mind, you put together your video and simply submitted it to their standards committee, thinking it would get the clearance that it always has?

Yes, I did.

Well, you—or at least your record company—know that nudity is banned by MTV.

I'm not so sure about that because when I did my *Vogue* video there's a shot of me where I'm wearing a see-through dress and you can clearly see my breasts. They told me that they wanted me to take that out, but I said I wouldn't. They played it anyway. So I thought that once again I was going to be able to bend the rules a bit.

You certainly were bending the rules a lot more than you had in the past, or did you feel that you were well within the bounds that you had bent?

Half of me thought that I was going to get away with it, that I was going to be able to convince them; the other half thought there was going to be a problem [because of] the wave of censorship and the conservatism that is sweeping over the nation.

When you say you thought you could get away with it, haven't you pushed the envelope a little bit with each [video]?

I think that's what art is all about—experimenting. But it is an expression, my artistic expression, and for me a video is the filmic expression of the song—a visual that describes what the song is about. And you've got to listen to the words of the songs. It's about a woman who's talking to her lover and saying, "Tell me your dreams—am I in them? Tell me your fears—are you scared? Tell me your stories—I'm not afraid of who you are." We're dealing with sexual fantasies and being truthful and honest with our partner. These feelings exist and I'm just dealing with the truth here in my video.

Let me tell you why I asked that: there are a lot of people in the industry who have said, "Look, this is one of the best self-marketers in the business. We have never really seen anything like it, and she knows how to push right to that edge." And this was a win-win for you. If they put the video on, you would get that kind of play; if they didn't, you'd still make some money. It was all, in a sense, a kind of publicity stunt.

It may seem like it was a publicity stunt, and actually, I was very lucky, but I did not plan on selling this video. I just went in there to shoot it, and I said, "You know what? I'm not going to think about whether it's going to get played or not—I'm just going to do it. This is how I truly feel about this song, how I want to express myself."

And when we gave it to MTV, we asked them if they would play it. They came back a while later and they said no. I said, "Is there one scene or another that you specifically object to?" And they said, "No, it's the whole tone." So we didn't really even have a chance to try to make it viewable. They rejected it completely.

And so then I had to think, with my manager, what next? What should we do? And we decided, hell, let's sell it like a video single—it's never been done before.

The controversy wasn't planned; it just happened.

But in the end you're going to wind up making even more money than you would have.

Yeah, so lucky me.

But the question that I think a lot of people are concerned about is, you say you go into the studio—

Yeah.

—and you want to illustrate this song, and you're doing it in the way that you want.
Yeah.

But they see a kind of trend, where you are pushing the limits of sexuality. In this case, you have nudity and you have bisexuality and you have, apparently, group sex. And they're thinking that maybe you're pushing the limits of what's permissible, that you're carrying it a little further each time. And what people are asking, then, is where is that line? Where do you finally say, "Okay, this is far enough"?
That's a good question, but then, I would like to address the whole issue of censorship on television. Where do we draw the line in general?

Well, you can't go that far . . . first you have to tell me where you draw the line.
I draw the line in terms of what I think is viewable on television. I draw the line with violence and humiliation and degradation. And I don't think any of these issues are evident in my video. That's what I don't want to see.

Then one woman's art is another woman's pornography. I'm thinking of the "Express Yourself" video.
Mm-hmm.

I mean, there are images of you chained, there are images of you crawling under a table—
Yes, I am chained —

—and there are a lot of people upset by that.
—yes, yes. Okay, I have chained myself, though, okay? There wasn't a man that put that chain on me. I did it myself. I was chained to my desires. I crawled under my own table. There wasn't a man standing there making me do it. I do everything by my own volition—I'm in charge. Degradation is when somebody else is making you do something against your wishes.

I understand. Is the expression, then, of sexuality so long as it's two consenting adults—
Absolutely.

—any form of sexuality all right on television?
First I'd like to say I don't believe in censorship of any kind, but then I believe in labeling. I would believe in some kind of warning label that would say to adults [that] after a certain hour we're allowed to play these videos with adult themes.

So I've dealt with sexuality, but I also think that we should also have categories for the other issues that I think are not necessarily good for 10-year-olds to watch. I think MTV should have their violence hour, their degradation to women hour, and then we could have an hour where we deal with adult sexual themes. But if we're going to have censorship, let's not be hypocrites about this. Let's not have double standards.

Why is it okay for 10-year-olds to see someone's body being ripped to shreds or Sam Kinison spitting on Jessica Hahn? Why aren't we going to deal with these issues? Why do parents not have problems with those but do have a problem with two consenting adults, regardless of their sex, displaying affection for each other?

Madonna, you've raised about 30 important questions and I think we ought to get to those when we come back.

Well, I only have a few minutes, so—

We're going to come right back . . . and we'll explore those questions in just a moment.

[Commercial break]

Madonna, I wonder if you were being facetious a moment ago. You said despite your concerns about violence and degradation to women, maybe MTV should consider having an hour for violence, and an hour that displays degradation to women, despite the fact that it's broadcast right into people's homes where their children can see it.

I'm saying we already have these videos that display degradation to women and violence that are played 24 hours a day, yet they don't want to have a video playing that deals with sex between two consenting adults. So I'm saying, where do we draw the line? . . . Look, give me a chance, let me have my slot. Give me a warning label. Warn parents so it doesn't take them by surprise, so that they have a chance to take their child away from television, but also warn them about violence and warn them about scenes in videos that depict degradation to women.

But you know how very hard it is for a parent to control [their children] having access to TV; they sit there and watch MTV all day long. If you were in that parent's position and it was your 10- or 11-year-old, would you not be worried about their seeing this kind of stuff?

Personally, I wouldn't be worried about it. I think that sexuality is something that Americans would really rather just sweep up under the rug, and if my video provokes an open discussion about sex with their parents, I think this is a really good thing.

But, Madonna, you have to help me here. When a 10-year-old sees you chained to a bed or sees your boyfriend bound up, and another women comes by while you're there, maybe you know that that's a fantasy, and you know that other people are able to deal with all kinds of sexuality, but a 10-year-old's going to get awfully confused here.

Good. Then let them get confused and go ask their parents about it. Let their parents explain to them that it is a sexual fantasy and that these things exist in life, like violence. It's not necessarily a pretty picture—it's a frightening thing—

but it's reality. Why are we willing to deal with the realities of violence and sexism [but not] sexuality?

The networks won't even play ads on TV about condoms, about birth control, about practicing safe sex. We're pretending we don't have a lot of teenagers that are having sex in the world right now. Why are we subjecting ourselves to this kind of ignorance?

Look, I'll tell you what their answer is going to be to you. They're going to say, "We really are concerned about these issues, and we are concerned that our children understand them. But quite frankly, it's our job to instruct our children and we don't want you on television—in the kinds of ways that you're on television—giving those images to our children. Thanks, anyway."

Well, guess what? They're not doing their job. Because the teenage pregnancies in this country have reached a high. We have sophomores in high school who are having their second babies already. And the rate of AIDS is rising in the heterosexual community at a really frightening rate. So why is that? These parents are not doing their jobs.

What you're trying to tell me [is] that you're balancing between an artist's need for self-expression—an artist's need to explore any kind of issue, including sexuality— [and] the responsibility that comes along with your prominence. There is a responsibility that comes along with your position as a role model.

Okay. You know what? I feel that I am behaving in a very responsible way. If you say I have a responsibility as a mainstream artist, I feel that I am being responsible. As I said at the beginning of the interview, I'm talking about people being honest to each other about their sexuality. They're not alienating anyone; they're not degrading anyone. It's about honesty, it's about the celebration of sex. There is nothing wrong with that. I'm very responsible because I do deal with sexuality a lot in my shows and in my music. I promote safe sex whenever I can. I put literature in my albums about using birth control and using condoms.

But my point really goes back to that other question, and I'm not suggesting that you're not [responsible]. I'm just saying that you have to ask yourself when you go into the studio or when you put on your show, [that] you want to be able to explore these kinds of things because that's what art is.

Right.

But at the same time, you have to reflect on what's going to be responsible. So then, do you say, "Where do I draw the line?" Or does it keep going further and further?

As I said to you before, I *am* being responsible. Where I draw the line is what I said: I don't believe in gratuitous violence and I don't believe in degradation—the degradation of any human being. I would never promote those things in any of my art, and I don't.

I know you've taken some heat from some women who feel that maybe you're not expressing the values that they want feminism to express . . . all the way from way back when you wore the belt buckle that said "boy toy" to the "Material Girl" video, which they feel reflects old values of women, even if it was satirical to express yourself. Do you have an answer to them?

I would like to point out that they're missing a couple of things. I may be dressing like the typical bimbo, but I'm in charge. I'm in charge of my fantasies. I put myself in these situations with men. In terms of my public image: people don't think of me as a person who's not in charge of my career or my life. And isn't that what feminism is all about—equality for men and women? And aren't I in charge of my life, doing the things I want to do? Making my own decisions?

I don't think anybody would question whether you're in charge of your own life. . . . What is the next sort of thing that we could be looking forward to? Do you have it in mind already? Will you continue to explore sexuality in the fashion that you have?

Absolutely.

Will you try to carry it a little further?

I don't know. I can't predict what I'm going to feel artistically. I don't think anyone can. But it is a very important issue to me, and I'm sure I will be dealing with it more in the future.

Madonna's *Sex*

I think I've been terribly misunderstood because sex is the subject matter I so often deal with—people automatically dismiss a lot of what I do as something not important, not viable or something to be respected.

—MADONNA, in a *Vanity Fair* profile, 1992

Sex *by Madonna, edited by Glenn O'Brien. Warner Books, $50. Oversized book with aluminum covers with text by Madonna and photographs by Steven Meisel. No pagination. Sold in a plastic mylar bag labeled "Warning! Adults Only!"*

"This book is about sex. Sex is not love. Love is not sex. But the best of both worlds is created when they come together. You can love God, you can love the planet, you can love the human race and you can love all things, but the best way for human beings to show love is to love one another. It's the way we spread love through the universe: one to one."

And so begins *Sex,* the print equivalent of Madonna's music video "Justify My Love," both explorations of Madonna's sexual fantasies. Roundly condemned by book reviewers in general, *Sex* was impervious to the negative reviews: the half-million copies that made up the first printing sold briskly.

With photos by Steven Meisel that recall the work of Helmut Newton and Robert Mapplethorpe and prose by Madonna that reads like bad Henry Miller, *Sex* is—depending on your viewpoint—either a groundbreaking or a grandstanding work.

66

The Rev. Donald E. Wildmon's Crusade for Censorship, 1977–89

by Christopher M. Finan

> Still, although we were simply promoting the practice of selective buying, the networks constantly sounded a false alarm, crying "censorship." I say false alarm because I've always understood censorship to mean the silencing of free speech or the written word by government decree or judicial fiat. Yet we had not asked for a single law to be passed. I had also thought that censorship meant the *prohibition* of communication before the fact. Yet, we had advocated nothing of the sort.
>
> —DONALD WILDMON, from *Don Wildmon: The Man the Networks Love to Hate*

The Rev. Donald E. Wildmon has always claimed to be an "average guy." When he first came to the attention of the public, he was the leader of a boycott against advertisers who sponsored "sex, violence and profanity" on television. Wildmon insisted that he was not a censor but an outraged private citizen who was exercising his constitutional right to protest. But Wildmon is not an average citizen. His ambition is to remake American society. Nor is he content with the instruments of change provided by democratic institutions: he advocates the censorship of television, movies, books, and magazines. During his 12-year campaign for censorship, he has tried to suppress:

• Television shows like "Charlie's Angels," "Three's Company," "All in the Family," "Laverne and Shirley," "Love, Sidney," "Taxi," "WKRP in Cincinnati," "Hill Street Blues," "Moonlighting," "L.A. Law," "thirtysomething";
• Television dramas like "Roe v. Wade," Pete Hamill's "Flesh and Blood," Maya Angelou's "Sister, Sister," and "Portrait of a Rebel: Margaret Sanger";
• Movies like "The Last Temptation of Christ";
• Magazines like *Playboy, Penthouse,* and *Sassy.*

Wildmon is again engaged in a battle to change television. He announced in January [1989] that a group he has formed, Christian Leaders for Responsible Television (CLeaR-TV), will lead a boycott against the advertiser who sponsors the worst television shows during the May television ratings "sweeps." His aim in 1989 is the same as it has always been: censorship.

Wildmon's campaign began one night in December 1976. At the time, he was an obscure, 38-year-old United Methodist pastor, serving a church in Southaven, Mississippi. But, he had always been ambitious. "Back in my younger days I reached the conclusion that the worst thing that could happen would be to come to the time of death and realize that my life had made no difference," Wildmon said recently.[1] That night in 1976 as he sat watching television with his family, he found the vehicle for his ambitions. He later claimed that as he switched channels he was unable to find a single show that didn't feature sex, violence, or profanity.[2] Wildmon interpreted this as a calling from God to take up the fight for purer television. He resigned his job in June 1977 and moved to Tupelo, Mississippi, 50 miles outside of Memphis to establish the National Federation for Decency. The NFD struggled in the beginning. According to his son, Wildmon was able to pay himself only $1,800 in the first seven months of the organization's existence; his wife began working to help the venture survive.[3]

Wildmon struggled with the problem of how to establish an identity for the NFD. The first effort to attract national attention was a campaign called, "Turn the Television Off Week," which targeted mostly southern cities in July 1977. Wildmon claimed that his survey of television programming revealed that 54 percent of all shows had sexual content. Wildmon said such a high proportion of sexual programming distorted real life. He was also upset that 90 percent of the sex was adulterous. "The strategy of so much network programming is to appeal to the prurient interest of man and not to spend money for quality programming," Wildmon said.[4] Yet, while he received some press attention for his television boycott, there was no proof that anyone had actually turned off a set.

Wildmon's problem was how to exert power over the networks with an organization that claimed only 1,400 members. Boycotts of television programs would never work. The number of people who would turn off their sets at any one time would never be large enough to register in the ratings. Wildmon decided to try boycotts of advertisers. The sensitivity of advertisers to bad publicity had been established the year before in the controversy over the satire "Soap." Now, in the spring of 1978, Wildmon announced his first boycott of advertisers. He told Sears that his supporters would boycott its stores until it withdrew sponsorship of three shows at the top of his hit list—"Three's Company," "Charlie's Angels," and "All in the Family." Although his following was minuscule, Wildmon used it to maximum effect by staging demonstrations outside Sears stores in several parts of the country and in downtown

---

1. *AFA Journal*, January 1989, p. 2.
2. *Time*, July 6, 1981, p. 20.
3. Tim Wildmon fundraising letter, May 26, 1987.
4. Associated Press, July 21, 1977.

Chicago in front of the Sears building itself. The boycott worked. While denying it was acting under pressure, Sears canceled its ads on "Three's Company"
and "Charlie's Angels."[5]

During 1979, Wildmon continued to make his voice heard. He attacked "Flesh
and Blood," a television movie based on a novel by Pete Hamill, because it
dealt with the subject of incest.[6] He also attacked "Portrait of a Rebel: Margaret
Sanger," a movie about the leader of the movement for birth control. He struck
out at CBS, accusing it of complicity in the murder of a little girl in Wichita
Falls, Texas. The four-year-old was murdered by her mother, who had seen a
similar crime committed when CBS broadcast "Exorcist II." "CBS must accept
partial blame for her death," Wildmon insisted. "They were an accessory to the
murder." An NFD picket outside CBS headquarters in New York carried a sign
that insisted: "CBS Controlled by Satan."[7]

Yet the NFD was making little progress. It was firmly anchored on the
lunatic fringe of the hundreds of groups trying to change television to suit
their tastes. Wildmon had a new weapon in the advertiser boycott, but he had
been unable to secure the backing from larger, more established groups that he
would need to launch a national campaign. He began to think that his future
might lie in another direction. He ran for a seat in the Mississippi House of
Representatives in 1980 but finished a distant third, garnering only 921 votes
or 15 percent of the total cast.[8]

A month after his defeat in the Mississippi House race, Wildmon made another effort to win backing for his advertiser boycott. He met with the Reverend Jerry Falwell in Lynchburg, Virginia. Falwell, the leader of the Moral
Majority, was then at the peak of his career as a spokesman for the religious
right. As Wildmon later told the story, he held up before Falwell a dollar bill.
"The networks don't care about your moral values, but they do care about this,"
Wildmon told him. According to Wildmon, Falwell didn't require much persuading. "Great," he said. "Let's go with it." Wildmon said later that he
believed he had reached a turning point. As he sat in his motel room that
night, he was sure of victory. "Now I have the numbers," he recalled thinking.
"Now I have the clout. After three years of wandering in the wilderness, I've
found a road to the Promised Land."[9]

Two months later, in February 1981, Wildmon announced the organization
of the Coalition for Better Television (CBTV), the group that would bring him
national recognition. His alliance with Falwell enabled Wildmon to claim that
CBTV represented 200 organizations with a combined membership of over three

5. *Washington Post,* May 17, 1978, sec. B, p. 1.
6. Associated Press, October 15, 1979.
7. Ibid., July 7, 1980.
8. United Press International, November 5, 1980.
9. *Newsweek,* June 15, 1981, p. 101.

million. These three million people were prepared to back a boycott of the three advertisers who sponsored the worst programming on television, he announced. The targets of the boycott were to be selected following three months of monitoring by 4,000 members of the coalition. The monitors would catalogue the offending shows on the basis of "sex incidents per hour," scenes of violence and uses of profanity.[10]

Few people outside of employees of the television networks and, to a lesser extent, the advertising industry, attempted to answer Wildmon. One of them was Peggy Charren, president of Action for Children's Television, a strong critic of the networks. Charren accused Wildmon of wanting to censor television. Sex, violence, and profanity were only the beginning, she warned:

> What will be the next target of the CBTV's censorship crusade? A production of "A Streetcar Named Desire?" A documentary on teenage pregnancy? The news?[11]

For the most part, however, the networks were forced to defend themselves.

The networks struck back in the final weeks of the CBTV rating period by releasing the results of opinion polls that showed the public opposed the boycott. A poll commissioned by ABC showed that 64 percent believed that the popularity of a program should be the sole factor in determining what was on television. Only 1.3 percent said that they would consider backing a boycott. The poll also showed that Falwell and Wildmon had little support among their own constituents. It revealed that 55 percent of those identifying themselves as members of the Moral Majority opposed efforts to force their opinions on others. CBS News reported that one third of the organizations listed as sponsors of CBTV disavowed any connection with the group.[12]

Nevertheless, CBTV was beginning to harvest the fruit of its campaign. Advertisers had begun to crack under the threat of the impending boycott. The first important convert to the cause of CBTV-approved television was Owen B. Butler, the chairman of Procter and Gamble, the company that spent more on television annually than any other—nearly $500 million. In a speech to the Academy of Television Arts and Sciences on June 16, Butler announced that his company had withdrawn advertising from 50 television shows over the past year. Butler denied the company had been responding to pressure from Wildmon, but he left little doubt that Procter and Gamble would take his advice in the future:

> We think the coalition is expressing very important and broadly held views about gratuitous sex, violence and profanity. I can assure you that we are listening very carefully to what they say, and I urge you to do the same.

10. UPI, February 28, 1981.
11. *Newsweek,* June 15, 1981, p. 101.
12. AP, June 19, 1981; *New York Times,* June 30, 1981, sec. C, p. 15.

Television and advertising industry officials were shocked by Butler's admission. Charren had been expecting it. "Based on what TV advertisers did during the Red scares of the 50's, this is exactly what I expected," she said.[13]

Wildmon knew that he had Butler's ear. In remarks to reporters later, he revealed that Procter and Gamble had been speaking with CBTV for some time. "We've had dialogues with P&G over a period of many months," Wildmon said.[14] Nor was Procter and Gamble alone in seeking an accommodation with Wildmon. On June 26, the *New York Times* reported that several television advertisers had been invited to a meeting with CBTV officials "in the Memphis area." Wildmon confirmed that discussions were under way to reach a compromise that would prevent a boycott.[15] Wildmon told the Associated Press that the boycott threat was having a decided effect. "I've talked with six advertisers in the last week who have pulled 150 commercials off the air in the last four months," he said.[16]

On June 29, at a CBTV press conference that had been scheduled to announce the start of the boycott, Wildmon announced its cancellation. With Falwell and Phyllis Schlafly of the Eagle Forum looking on, Wildmon told the press that the boycott was no longer necessary because in their meetings with CBTV officials, advertisers had promised to help "clean up" television. Wildmon refused to identify the advertisers who had made these pledges. While he professed himself satisfied, Wildmon warned that CBTV might institute a boycott in the fall if the shows premiering then were objectionable. Falwell said his organization was "raising funds for a war chest to buy and assist others in buying full-page ads across the nation naming public enemy No. 1 or 2 or whoever they are and listing their products."[17]

Skeptics raised questions about the decision to cancel the boycott. They suggested that the networks' opinion polls had trumped Wildmon. They said he was afraid of losing. "Let me tell you something," Wildmon said, replying to his critics. "I was raised to know that it was not a disgrace to fight and get whipped."[18] But Wildmon had at least won a moral victory. The chairman of one of the nation's biggest corporations had promoted his views as important for the nation. Even those who opposed his tactics endorsed his claim that television needed better programming.

But "better programming" is a subjective judgment. Wildmon insisted that his opposition to shows was based solely on objectively measured levels of sex, violence and profanity. When Wildmon objected to a show because of its

13. *Newsweek,* June 29, 1981, p. 60.
14. Ibid., June 29, 1981, p. 60.
15. *New York Times,* June 26, 1981, p. 10.
16. AP, June 26, 1981.
17. *New York Times,* June 30, 1981, sec. C, p. 15.
18. UPI, July 14, 1981.

sexual content, however, it was not always because it was prurient but often because it presented sex in ways he disliked—outside marriage, between teen-agers or partners of the same sex. He also opposed the mention of birth control, abortion and, later, AIDS. His criticism of profanity often had more to do with offensiveness of the subject of discussion than the use of vulgar words. Wildmon's condemnation did not stop at shows like "Vegas" and "The Dukes of Hazzard," but extended to programs dealing with adult themes like "All in the Family," "Taxi," and "WKRP in Cincinnati." (See Addendum 1 for a full list of the television programs attacked by Wildmon.)

Wildmon's extremism clearly guided his attacks on programming during the balance of 1981. He was particularly unhappy about NBC's decision to develop a series based on a movie about an aging homosexual who permits a young woman and her daughter to move in with him. Wildmon, who saw the show as an attack on the institution of the family, said it was "utterly stupid" for NBC to undertake the series at the very moment when concern about television was at its peak. Tony Randall, the star of the proposed series, "Love, Sidney," defended his show. "It's about compassion. It's about love. It's about the need people have for family. And they're saying it's anti-family," Randall said.[19] As the preemptive strike on Randall's show indicated, Wildmon was not waiting for shows to be aired before attacking them. Wildmon condemned a fictionalized treatment of a series of murders of black children in Atlanta before the producer had decided to go ahead with the project.[20]

Wildmon's pose as a moderate was undermined later in the year when some of his followers pushed his views about sex on television to their logical extreme. He was forced to apologize to Phil Donahue, the talk show host, for a release issued by one of the chapters of his National Federation for Decency that described Donahue, whose show had won nine Emmy awards, as a "sex activist broadcaster." The release said many of Donahue's "sex shows" promoted ab-normal sex and threatened a boycott of Donahue's sponsors. In an appearance on "Donahue," Wildmon apologized for the release. He admitted that a program on breast-feeding should not have been characterized as a "sex program." But, Wildmon soon resumed the offensive, insisting that his monitoring showed that almost half of Donahue's shows dealt with sex. He charged that some urged acceptance of sex practices contrary to traditional Christian morality.[21]

Wildmon's appearance on "Donahue" showed how far he had come from Southaven, Mississippi. The threat of a boycott had given him national ex-posure. Now he was anxious to see what an actual boycott would achieve. In late 1981, Wildmon decided that the networks had not met his demands and that a boycott would be necessary after all. But, just as Wildmon was preparing

19. *Washington Post*, July 7, 1981, sec. C, p. 1.
20. UPI, July 29, 1981,
21. AP, September 29, 1981.

to realize his dream, Jerry Falwell withdrew his support for the tactic of boycotting advertisers. The division between Wildmon and Falwell had first become apparent in a television documentary, "Eye of the Beholder," broadcast in late 1981. It was this documentary that first reported Wildmon's determination to proceed with the boycott. It also revealed that Falwell was having second thoughts about boycotts against advertisers. He appeared to take to heart the survey results released in June that showed his own followers rejecting efforts to force the Moral Majority's views on others. Falwell told the interviewer that the Moral Majority had raised $2 million for the boycott but then suggested that his group would not back coercive efforts to change programming. The Moral Majority's resignation from the boycott was confirmed by a spokesman for the group in late January 1982. "Our feeling is that the networks are headed in the right direction," he said.[22]

In the absence of the Moral Majority, Wildmon changed his plans. Falwell had promised $2 million for publicity for the boycott before he backed out, and publicity was critical because the boycott depended upon the consumer's ability to recognize the target's products in the market place. Lacking funds, Wildmon abandoned the proposed boycott of advertisers. At a news conference in February 1982, he announced a boycott against RCA, the owner of NBC.

Wildmon also revealed new demands. "Our concerns have been too narrow and will be expanded," he explained. "Our concerns about sex, violence and profanity in programs is valid, but there will be more. We're going to surprise some people."[23] He demanded changes in the way NBC handled eleven subjects. Besides sex, violence and profanity, he wanted less drug abuse and "racial and religious stereotyping." The network would have to make an effort to portray life as it was lived by Christians, Wildmon said. "RCA-NBC has excluded Christian characters, Christian values and Christian culture from their programming," he charged. Wildmon also wanted to see an improvement in the portrayal of American business. Wildmon claimed that business executives had been painted as "crooks and con men."[24]

During his news conference, Wildmon had demonstrated again that he was not reluctant to criticize a popular show by singling out for attack NBC's award-winning dramatic series, "Hill Street Blues," which he said was full of sexual innuendo. Several months later, he showed that he was not afraid to attack a show with serious artistic intentions either. NBC was preparing to broadcast a movie that had been written by the poet Maya Angelou. "Sister, Sister" was the story of how three black sisters in North Carolina resolved the differences that separated them. Wildmon had not seen the movie. Apparently

22. UPI, January 27, 1982.
23. AP, February 23, 1982.
24. *New York Times,* March 5, 1982, sec. C, p. 28.

reacting to a part of the story in which a minister committed adultery and stole the church receipts, Wildmon claimed that "negative stereotyping of people identified as Christian in the film is an example of a continuing trend by RCA-NBC and an example of anti-Christian, anti-religious network programming."[25] The advertisers responded to his complaints: 12 of the 28 sponsors asked to see the program again, and one sponsor, Kodak, withdrew its ads after determining that the film was not sufficiently "family-oriented." Author Jessica Mitford rejected Wildmon's criticisms in a letter to the *New York Times*. She pointed out that "Sister, Sister" was the type of program that Wildmon had formerly said he approved:

> Psychological drama of the highest order, "Sister, Sister" achieves a stunning breakthrough as a sensitive portrait of a three-dimensional, non-stereotypical black family. No wild car chases, no prostitution, no drugs, no teen-age crime—in short, no sex or violence (sorry about that Mr. Wildmon).[26]

Wildmon had revealed himself for what he was: a Christian minister who believed that television should reflect his own world view, including his high opinion of Christian ministers. He had also shown himself as a man with an insatiable appetite for change, one change making him hungry for the next. He lost the support of many who had formerly sympathized with him. A day of reckoning was fast approaching.

Judgment day fell at the close of the third quarter of 1982. RCA reported earnings that demonstrated Wildmon's boycott had not had an effect. Third-quarter earnings were $47.6 million, an increase of $152.4 million over the third quarter of 1981 when the company had shown a loss.[27] Wildmon replied by pointing to RCA's weak consumer products division, insisting that this was the part of the corporation most likely to be hurt by the boycott. But if Wildmon had won a moral victory over the networks in 1981, there seemed little question that he had been defeated in 1982. By early 1983, "Love, Sidney," the series starring Tony Randall that Wildmon had attacked before its premiere, had become a success and was inching closer to acknowledgment of Sidney's homosexuality. Before it became the target of Wildmon's boycott, NBC had prevented Randall from striking back at Wildmon.[28] Now, Randall dismissed Wildmon as "that ignorant, cynical, Bible-thumping ass in Mississippi."[29] There was no lightning.

For his part, Wildmon had dropped any pretense of being a reformer. He no longer accused the networks of using sex, violence and profanity to gain

25. AP, June 7, 1982.
26. *New York Times,* June 11, 1982, p. 30.
27. Ibid., November 21, 1982, sec. 3, p. 21.
28. *Washington Post,* July 7, 1981, sec. C, p. 1.
29. *Time,* March 7, 1983, p. 120.

ratings. The problem with the networks was that they were dominated by a "humanist" view of society. "The humanist point of view is that man came from nowhere, is going nowhere and has no responsibility to others," Wildmon said. Wildmon professed himself an apostle of the Christian view. "The Christian view is that man was created by God and that there's somewhere to go— heaven or hell—and some moral absolutes and moral guidelines to follow," he said. The conflict between the two was irreconcilable. "You have a clash of two distinct value systems," Wildmon said. The networks were trying to remake society in line with humanist values. Wildmon acknowledged that they were winning. "I don't think we have more than five or six years left to stem the tide," he said. "Television is the most destructive force in our society."[30] It was clear that if Wildmon were in charge, television would be dominated by Christian values.

After the failure of the RCA boycott, the Coalition for Better Television lapsed. But while Wildmon had returned to obscurity, he had not abandoned his ambition to strike a devastating blow at the "humanist" media. He travelled tirelessly in an effort to make his National Federation for Decency a grass-roots organization. The major publication of his organization was the NFD *Journal*. The *Journal*, which has changed little in its 12-year history, carries detailed criticism of individual television shows and lists the names and addresses of their sponsors. Its columns explain the demise of American society as the result of divorce, women in the work force and other factors that are weakening the traditional family. It frequently attacks birth control and abortion. Nevertheless, the tone of the magazine is set by the somewhat lurid descriptions of crime that can allegedly be attributed to pornography, television or movie violence and rock and roll music. The April 1989 *Journal* carried a story in which a mother blames the rock band the Grateful Dead for the drug abuse problem that led her son to take hostages and be killed by the police.[31]

Wildmon knew that organizing local chapters of the NFD would occur more quickly if the organizing occurred within the context of a larger campaign. In 1984, the NFD began a fight to ban *Playboy* and *Penthouse* magazines. As always, Wildmon's tactic was not to attack the producers directly. He tried to strangle the magazines' circulation through boycotts aimed at chain stores, including drug and convenience stores, where they were sold from "blindered" racks behind the counter. He returned to the picketing tactic that he had used against Sears, sending demonstrators to 7-Eleven and other stores. While Wildmon experienced some success against the smaller chains, the Southland Corporation, which owned 7-Eleven, and most major chains held firm. Wildmon campaigned for two years with meager results.

30. UPI, May 20, 1983.
31. *AFA Journal*, April 1989, p. 12.

Wildmon's return to national prominence was largely the result of actions taken by the national administration in Washington. Wildmon and other "anti-pornography" activists had strongly supported the candidacy of Ronald Reagan because, among other things, they believed that he would take strong measures to curb sexually explicit material. They were disappointed when Reagan took little action during his first term. Wildmon and other advocates of stricter censorship visited Reagan following his reelection to urge him to fulfill the promise or his conservative "social agenda." The result was the appointment of the Attorney General's Commission on Pornography in 1985. The partisans of the new Commission were eager to see it rebut a previous commission's conclusion that sexually explicit material was not harmful to adults. The 1970 report by the President's Commission on Obscenity and Pornography recommended the abolition of obscenity laws. With the appointment of what became known as the Meese Commission in 1985, the anti-pornography activists acquired an important vehicle for their opinion and Wildmon found another national forum. The Commission was chaired by a former prosecutor who had made his reputation by prosecuting adult bookstores and movie houses.

Wildmon did not waste his opportunity. At a public hearing in Los Angeles in October 1985, Wildmon told the Meese Commission that it must attack not only organized crime, reputed to be the major producer of hard-core obscenity, but also major corporations that were involved in the sale of non-obscene, First Amendment protected material with sexual content. "The general public usually associates pornography with sleazy porno bookstores and theaters," Wildmon said. "However many of the major players in the game of pornography are household names."[32] Wildmon then proceeded to name names. Of course, the Southland Corporation was at the top of his list. But the list of 23 corporations that Wildmon alleged were involved in "pornography distribution" included CBS, Time, Ramada Inns, RCA, Coca-Cola, three national distributors of magazines and 11 chain stores, including Rite Aid, Dart Drug Stores and National Video, a chain of video stores.

Wildmon's testimony before the Meese Commission became national news when, without being identified as coming from Wildmon, it was incorporated into a letter that the Commission sent to the corporations named by Wildmon. The Commission informed the corporations that Wildmon's characterization of them as "distributors" of "pornography" would be included in the Commission's final report. They were invited to reply to the charge of their anonymous accuser. Instead, several lawsuits were filed to force the Commission to withdraw its letter. Among the plaintiffs filing suits were the American Booksellers

---

32. Donald E. Wildmon, "Pornography in the Family Marketplace," attached as an addendum to letter of Alan Sears, Executive Director, Attorney General's Commission on Pornography to various corporations, February 1986. However, the testimony was not attributed to Wildmon at the time. Wildmon's identity was revealed later.

Association, the Council for Periodical Distributors Associations, and the Magazine Publishers of America as well as *Playboy* and *Penthouse*. They accused the Commission of establishing a blacklist to coerce the corporations receiving the letter into withdrawing First Amendment–protected material. A federal judge ordered the Commission to retract the letter and barred it from issuing any lists of retailers.

But, the Meese Commission's letter had set in progress a chain of events that no judge's order could arrest. Wildmon's boycott campaign against the chain stores, like the campaign against the television advertisers, had made them extremely sensitive to adverse publicity. The Commission's letter was the straw that broke their backs. On April 10, 1986, the Southland Corporation announced that it was pulling *Playboy* and *Penthouse* from its 4,500 stores and recommending to 3,600 other 7-Elevens that were owned by franchisees that they get rid of them as well. The statement by Southland announcing the decision suggested that the chain was responding to evidence adduced by the Meese Commission that showed a link between "adult magazines and crime, violence, and child abuse."[33] But Wildmon questioned Southland's altruism. He claimed that Southland had bent under the boycott. "It is a good example of what can happen when the Christian community stands together with selective buying," Wildmon said. "It took us approximately two years, but our voice was heard."[34] By the time a federal judge issued an injunction against the Meese Commission in July, ordering withdrawal of the letter to the corporations, six of the chains targeted by the Commission had pulled *Playboy* and *Penthouse* and 34 smaller chains who didn't receive the letter had followed Southland's lead. More than 10,000 stores had stopped carrying the magazines.[35] By August, the number had grown to 17,000.[36]

The removal of *Playboy, Penthouse* and other men's "sophisticated" magazines from stores across the country had a domino effect, causing the removal of other magazines that were controversial for one reason or another. Magazines about rock and roll music, several teen magazines, the swimsuit issue of *Sports Illustrated,* and issues of *American Photographer* and *Cosmopolitan* were removed from sale in some parts of the country in the panic set off by the Meese Commission letter.

Wildmon kept his name in the headlines in 1987 by attacking a controversial disc jockey and a mainstream hotel corporation. Wildmon's complaint against "shock radio" personality Howard Stern was one fact that led the

33. The only magazines carried by 7-Eleven were *Playboy, Penthouse* and *Forum* magazines. But *Playboy* and *Penthouse* were explicitly excluded from the magazines examined by the Meese Commission. "Our study did not address magazines like *Playboy* and *Penthouse*," Commission Chairman Henry Hudson said on "Meet the Press," on July 13, 1986.

34. UPI, April 11, 1986.

35. *Washington Post,* July 23, 1986, sec. B, p. 3.

36. *Los Angeles Times,* August 25, 1986, p. 1.

Federal Communications Commission to expand its ban on "offensive" programming. At the same time, Wildmon was directing a boycott against the Holiday Inn hotel chain in an effort to stop it from making "R"-rated films available to guests in their rooms. However, demonstrations scheduled at 100 Holiday Inns across the country on April 18 failed to materialize. Only 13 hotels were picketed; the average demonstration numbered between five and 10 protesters and demonstrations lasted for only a few hours.[37]

It was at the time of the Holiday Inn boycott in mid-1987 that Wildmon began to make preliminary moves toward resuming his attack on television. He had never abandoned it entirely. The pages of the NFD *Journal* were full of condemnation for the current crop of programs and the people who sponsored them. In April 1987, Wildmon criticized the networks for dropping their ban on permitting bras to be modelled by live models. He predicted that the next step would be live underwear ads.[38] But Wildmon had refrained from announcing any boycott of advertisers since his RCA campaign. The first sign of a new campaign came with the organization of a successor to the Coalition for Better Television. Wildmon established Christian Leaders for Responsible TV (CLeaR-TV). Then, in June, CLeaR-TV announced its first boycott, targeting Mazda Motors and Noxell for their sponsorship of television programs allegedly featuring sex, violence and profanity.[39] Four months after declaring a boycott of Mazda and Noxell, CLeaR-TV announced that Mazda had agreed to reduce the amount of sex and violence it allegedly helped promote on network TV. Noxell had previously come to terms.[40]

With the first victories by CLeaR-TV, Wildmon was back on track for another major showdown with the networks. But there was a diversion on his return to the crusade. Wildmon became a leader in the fight to prevent Universal Pictures from releasing Martin Scorsese's film, "The Last Temptation of Christ." The film was opposed by many religious leaders because it portrayed Christ as a messiah struggling with human weaknesses, including sexual desire. While many Christian leaders condemned the film, Wildmon tried to suppress it. Wildmon asked his supporters to petition their local theaters in an effort to prevent the exhibition of the film and announced a boycott against companies owned by Universal's parent corporation, MCA. He also urged his followers to vote against the Democratic Party in the upcoming election because Lew Wasserman, the MCA chairman, was a major fundraiser for the Democrats.[41] Among the demonstrations against the release of the film, two held in Los Angeles in July were widely interpreted as anti-Semitic. Wildmon acknowledged the incidents as "very unfortunate."[42] However, he contributed to the

37. UPI, April 18, 1987.
38. *Advertising Age,* April 27, 1987, p. 75.
39. *Communications Daily,* June 1, 1987, p. 5.
40. Ibid., September 23, 1987, p. 7.
41. AP, August 5, 1988.
42. *Los Angeles Times,* July 23, 1988, pt. II, p. 1.

controversy by demanding to know how many Christians served in top positions at MCA and Universal.[43] The protests over the film culminated in demonstrations in seven cities on August 12, the day of the film's release. The largest demonstration, involving 500 people, occurred outside a theater in New York. Despite the fact that several theater chains refused to show the film, "The Last Temptation of Christ" set a box office record during its first week.

In the midst of the controversy over "The Last Temptation of Christ," Wildmon was able to claim a victory over the networks when the creator of the "Mighty Mouse" cartoon agreed to cut 3½ seconds of an episode that Wildmon had protested. The creator, Ralph Bakshi, had fallen under suspicion because of his role in making an X-rated animated feature, "Fritz the Cat." However, Bakshi had also won an award for "Mighty Mouse" from Action for Children's Television. In the disputed episode, Wildmon charged Bakshi with portraying Mighty Mouse as experiencing drug-induced exhilaration after inhaling the petals of a flower. Mighty Mouse had sniffed cocaine, Wildmon contended. Bakshi defended his cartoon, insisting that Wildmon had interpreted the scene out of context. However, Bakshi said he was removing the scene because of his concern that the controversy might lead children to believe that what Wildmon was saying was true. Wildmon interpreted the cut differently. "This is a de facto admission that indeed Mighty Mouse was snorting cocaine," Wildmon said. "We have been vindicated."[44]

The decisions by Mazda, Noxell, and CBS whetted Wildmon's appetite for another full-scale battle with the networks. For a time in mid-1987, Wildmon had been preoccupied with the financial problems that plagued the NFD in the wake of the scandal over evangelist Jim Bakker's sexual encounter with a Long Island church secretary. Like other organizations that depended for funds on evangelical Christians, the NFD was hurt by the drop in contributions that followed Bakker's disgrace. The problem became so critical for Wildmon that he quietly folded the NFD at the end of the year. As he closed the 10-year-old NFD, Wildmon opened the American Family Association and resumed business as usual. By the end of 1988, he had established AFA on a firmer footing than the National Federation for Decency had ever enjoyed. The AFA's first tax return, filed for 1988, revealed an income of $5,228,505. All of the funds came from contributions and gifts. In December, the representatives of CLeaR-TV, Wildmon's television group, agreed to announce a boycott of the worst advertiser at the conclusion of the sweeps period in May.

The announcement of the boycott threat in January had the same chilling effect on advertisers in the spring of 1989 that it had in 1981. Kimberly-Clark and Tambrands announced they would not advertise on the show "Married . . . with Children." An *Advertising Age* story reporting the controversy over "Married . . . with Children" noted that a growing number of companies were

---

43. Facts on File, *World News Digest,* September 9, 1988, p. 656 F3.
44. AP, July 26, 1988.

reviewing the programs they sponsored more carefully.[45] Less than two weeks after Kimberly-Clark and Tambrands acted against "Married . . . with Children," two advertisers who had been pressured by Wildmon pulled their ads from "Saturday Night Live." Ralston-Purina Company canceled $1 million in ads because one of the shows "crossed over the line of good taste." General Mills withdrew an undisclosed number of commercials.[46] A month later, Domino's Pizza also pulled out, citing the efforts of the American Family Association as a factor in its decision.[47] At about the same time, Wildmon scored a technical knock-out over Pepsi, which, after initial resistance, bent to a demand to sever its connection with Madonna because she had starred in a music video that used religious imagery in a way that he disliked.[48] Advertiser fear had grown to such an extent by May that ABC was unable to find sponsors for sequels to two shows that dramatized actual crimes and other real events. The original shows had received respectable ratings, and the inability to attract sponsors for the sequels was described as unprecedented by industry officials. Wildmon's blast at a movie dramatization of the *Roe* v. *Wade* case, which the critics praised for its even-handed treatment of the abortion controversy, cost NBC as much as $1 million in lost advertising revenue.[49]

Yet there are significant differences between 1981 and 1989. Existing anti-censorship groups have expanded and new ones have been created. One of the new groups, the Americans for Constitutional Freedom, which was organized in 1986 by the American Booksellers Association and the trade associations representing magazine distributors and wholesalers, promised a stiff fight against Wildmon. "Wildmon doesn't want to make television better," Oren Teicher, the executive director of ACF, said. "He wants to make it reflect his world view: he wants to make television in Donald Wildmon's image." Teicher observed that a major difference between 1981 and 1989 is that much more is known about Wildmon today. In 1981, he was able to pretend that he was only concerned about too much sex, violence, and profanity. "Today, we know what Donald Wildmon wants," Teicher said. "Donald Wildmon wants censorship."

• *Christopher M. Finan is Executive Director of Americans for Constitution Freedom.*

45. *Advertising Age,* March 6, 1989, p. 1.
46. AP, March 17, 1989.
47. *Advertising Age,* April 17, 1989, p. 81.
48. UPI, April 6, 1989.
49. *Newsday,* May 17, 1989, sec. II, p. 2.

Addendum 1
Television Programs Attacked by Wildmon Because of Their Content
Compiled by Christopher M. Finan

Alf
All in the Family
Almost Grown
Amen
Anything but Love
The A Team
Benson
Bronx Zoo
Cagney and Lacey
The Cavanaughs
CBS Schoolbreak Special
Channel 99
Charlie's Angels
Cheers
Crime Story
Dads
Dallas
Dear John
Designing Women
A Different World
Dukes of Hazzard
Dynasty
Empty Nest
The Equalizer
Facts of Life
Family Ties
First Impressions
Flamingo Road
Full House
Gimme a Break
Golden Girls
Growing Pains
Head of the Class
Heartbeat
Heart of the City
Highway to Heaven
Hill Street Blues
Hogan Family

Hooperman
Hotel
Houston Knights
In the Heat of the Night
Jack & Mike
Jake and the Fat Man
Johnny Carson
Kate & Allie
Knight Rider
Knots Landing
LA Law
Laverne & Shirley
Let's Make a Deal
Live-In
Love Boat
Love, Sidney
Magnum P.I.
A Man Called Hawk
Mary Hartman,
    Mary Hartman
Matlock
Matt Houston
Maude
Miami Vice
Midnight Caller
Mike Hammer
Moonlighting
Mr. Belvedere
Mr. T
Murder, She Wrote
Murphy Brown
My Two Dads
Nancy Walker Show
The Newlywed Game
Night Court
Nightingales
Outlaws
Remington Steel

Riptide
Sara
Saturday Night Live
Scarecrow and Mrs. King
Scooby Doo
Shadow Chasers
Simon & Simon
Slap Maxwell
Sledge Hammer
Smothers Brothers
Soap
Sonny Spoon
Spenser for Hire
St. Elsewhere
Stingray
Sweet Surrender
Tattinger's
Taxi
Thirtysomething
The Thorns
Three's a Crowd
Three's Company
T.J. Hooker
Tour of Duty
Trapper John, M.D.
TV 101
20/20
227
Under One Roof
Valerie
Webster
West 57th Street
Who's the Boss
Wiseguy
WKRP in Cincinnati
Wonder Years
World of Disney
A Year in the Life

Addendum 2

Corporations Criticized by Wildmon for Sponsoring Programs or Material Wildmon Has Opposed

Compiled by Christopher M. Finan

Abbot Labs
Ace Hardware
A.H. Robins
Airwick Corporation
Alberto-Culver
American Airlines
American Cynamid
American Express
American Home Products
American Motors
Anheuser Busch
Apple Computer
Armstrong Industries
ATT
Avon Products
Beatrice Foods
Beecham Corporation
Bristol-Meyers
Burroughs Wellcome
Cadbury-Schweppes
Campbell's Soups
Carter-Wallace
CBS
Chanel
Chesebrough-Ponds
Chrysler
Circle K. Corporation
Citibank
Clorox
Coca-Cola
Colgate Palmolive
Combe, Inc.
Corning Glassworks
Cosmair
CPC International
Cumberland Farms

Dairy Mart
Denny's Inc.
Domino's Pizza
Dow Chemical
Dunkin' Donuts
Eastman Kodak
Farly Industries
Ford Motor Co.
Fuji Film
Gallo Wines
General Electric
General Foods
General Mills
General Motors
Georgia Pacific
Gillette Corp.
Grand Met Consumer Prod.
Gulf and Western
Hallmark Cards
Heinz
Helene Curtis
Hershey Products
Hilton Hotels
H.I.S. Clothing
Holiday Corporation
Honda
Hormel
Hyatt Corporation
Hyundai
ITT Corporation
Johnson & Johnson
Johnson Wax Co.
Keebler
Kellogg's
Kimberly-Clark
K-Mart

Lever Brothers
Levi Strauss
McDonald's
Marriott Corp.
Mars Candy
Mastercard International
Mazda Motors of America
Mennen
Metropolitan Life
Miles Lab
Monsanto
Nestle
Nissan USA
North American Phillips
Noxell Corp.
Parker Bros.
Penney's
Pepsico
Pfizer
Phillip Morris
Pillsbury
Playtex
Procter and Gamble
Prudential Insurance
Quaker Oats
Quality Inn
Ralston-Purina
Ramada Inn

Rayovac
RCA
Revlon
Richardson Vicks
RJR Nabisco
Ryder Trucks
Sandoz
Sara Lee Corp.
Schering-Plough
Searle
Sears, Roebuck
Sharp
SmithKline Beecham
Sterling Drug
Tambrands
Time, Inc.
Topps Chewing Gum
Toyota
Tru-Value Hardware
Tyson Foods
Union Carbide
Warner Communications
Warner-Lambert
Wendy's
Wrigley's
Yamaha Motor Corp.
Zenith

The Music Industry

67

A Brief Overview of Explicit Lyrics and State Legislation

by Parents Music Resource Center

In a tongue-in-cheek article for the Washington Post *(July 12, 1992), Caleb Rossiter began "My Wicked, Wicked Songs" with a not-so-subtle reference to one of the founders of the Parents Music Resource Center:*

> *I've just been tipped off that Dan Quayle, Tipper Gore and the sheriff of Broward County, Fla., are raiding my house. It's part of their campaign against Sister Souljah, Ice-T and everyone who uses music to incite youngsters to kill white people and cops of all hues, to rape and pillage and worse.*

The Kingston Trio, he explains, was there first, with an old cowboy ballad (one verse: "I was feeling kind of mean—I shot a deputy down"*).*

At the center of the music-labeling controversy is the PMRC, which since its inception in 1985 "has been working to educate the public, especially parents, about the negative themes in music and its potential impact on child and adolescent behavior."

There's no denying that the PMRC has had an important impact on the music recording industry. Music labeling was "voluntarily" adopted by members of the Recording Industry Association of America, Inc., in preference to having a labeling system legislated. (This, of course, was what happened in the comic book industry in the 1950s.)

Ironically, though no federal legislation is pending, nearly two dozen states have jumped on the bandwagon, which highlights the traditional problem with censorship: once it starts, where does it end? Or is it better not to have forced the issue at all?

While music has almost always been a force for friction between generations of parents and children, never before has the music community sustained the assaults of the past two years. And while we have been able to claim victory in each of our battles, the coming year may prove especially challenging given that the issue has momentum and that it is an election year in 47 state legislatures.

History

By 1985, the Parents Music Resource Center (PMRC), a parental advisory group headed by Tipper Gore, had focused enough attention on the explicit lyrics of some pop music, that the record companies agreed to place parental advisory labels on those recordings that might warrant parental review prior to a child's purchase. Those stickers were of varying size, wording, and placement. For many consumers, these labels were not enough.

By 1989, explicit lyrics were again the topic of headlines and controversy. It became clear that the public's perception was that the record companies were simply giving "lip service" to their commitment to labeling explicit recordings.

Facing increasing pressure from state legislatures, the record companies adopted a voluntary uniform parental advisory logo in May of 1990. While each company retained discretion regarding the labeling of specific recordings, the size, placement, and wording of the logo were standardized. In this way, parents and other interested consumers could better determine which recordings may warrant parental review.

As a backdrop to all of this the "2 Live Crew" obscenity case was being played out in Florida. Accused of violating the state's obscenity laws at a live show, the rap group was put on trial. A separate case involving a Florida retailer's sale of the 2 Live Crew album was also in the headlines. These two cases simply added fuel to the bonfire.

Legislative Battles

In all, 22 states considered introducing legislation that would have required the record companies to place a specific sticker on sound recordings containing explicit lyrics. Moreover, these stickered recordings would have been prohibited for sale to minors. Penalties ranged from small fines on retailers to prison and heavy fines for retailers and record company executives alike.

Of the 22 states that considered these bills, 14 actually introduced them. In the end, 13 states defeated or withdrew the bills after lengthy meetings with representatives of the Recording Industry Association of America (RIAA) and others in the music community. Only one state, Louisiana, passed legislation requiring the labeling and prohibiting the sale to minors of certain sound recordings. After intense lobbying of Governor Buddy Roemer, we were able to convince him to veto the bill at the eleventh hour, giving the legislature no time to reconsider and override the veto.

In 1991, Louisiana was the only state to seriously consider similar legislation. After a series of defeats for record companies and retailers in the committees of the House and Senate and passage of the bill on the House floor, the Senate voted the bill down by one vote on the last day of the 1991 legislative session.

The Outlook

The 1992 state legislative calendar may be a full one for the record companies. Fueled by a generally conservative mood in the country and the histrionics of right wing groups such as the American Family Association and the Eagle Forum, we are likely to see even more legislative activity that would restrict First Amendment freedoms of artists, labels, songwriters, retailers and consumers. Some of this activity will likely be in the form of labeling bills similar to those we have seen in the past. In fighting this kind of legislation, the industry has had two years of experience. What is most alarming is that the legislators are becoming more sophisticated in their approach to this issue.

At present, we are facing legislation in Michigan that would allow each community to establish its own local standards for obscenity. Currently, communities in each state operate under a state-wide standard for obscenity. This means that one community may deem an album appropriate for sale to consumers while the neighboring community may restrict its sale to minors or attempt to ban its sale altogether. Obviously, this kind of atmosphere would wreak havoc on our companies at all levels of distribution and sales.

This kind of legislation and other changes to state obscenity standards will most likely be the focus of our state legislative activity over the coming year. And being an election year, 1992 may be the most challenging year we have yet seen.

68

PMRC Mission Statement

The Parents Music Resource Center is a non-profit organization created in May 1985 to address the issue of lyrics in some popular music which glorifies graphic sex and violence and glamorizes the use of drugs and alcohol. Founded by Tipper Gore, Susan Baker, Pam Howar and Sally Nevius, the PMRC's goals are to increase awareness through education and to promote responsibility and self-restraint within the record industry. The PMRC feels that the current levels of violence, racism, brutality toward women, and drug and alcohol glamorization in music lyrics, videos, and stage shows need to be addressed through public discussion and debate. We are engaged in an educational campaign designed to inform people about themes in the media.

1. The PMRC is currently in a coalition with the six-million member National Parents' Teachers' Association (PTA). The American Academy of Pediatrics (AAP) supports PMRC's educational initiatives. We have no other affiliations.

2. The PMRC does not support, condone or accept censorship. Our current agreement with the Recording Industry Association of America is a consumer information system that applies more information on a recording, rather than less. This is designed to allow a freedom of choice in the marketplace by employing truth-in-packaging.

3. The PMRC no longer supports a record rating system due to the difficulty in interpreting an artist's words. We support a generic warning label which reads, "Explicit Lyrics—Parental Advisory."

4. The PMRC is opposed to legislation in the area of record labeling. We support our current voluntary agreement with the Recording Industry Association of America—a self-regulating agreement that entails no government involvement.

5. The PMRC respects the rights of retailers to establish their own selling policies; however, we do not promote the restriction of sales of labeled recordings to minors. We encourage parents to work with community leaders and retailers to develop the appropriate standards for their community.

6. Recent public opinion surveys show that an overwhelming majority of the public, both young and old, favor the current changes within the record industry. A recent Gallup poll found that 64 percent of the 16–24-year-olds surveyed thought recorded music with explicit lyrics should have warning labels. Over 74 percent of the parents polled in a 1990 ICR survey commissioned by the Recording Industry Association of America favored some form of warning label system with over two-thirds preferring a voluntary system.

Beyond Voluntary Labeling
by Gwen Ifill

Recording industry representatives and record-labeling advocates like Tipper Gore are in agreement: Voluntary labeling of albums has eliminated the need for state legislation outlawing lewd lyrics.

Problem is, no one told the state legislators. When they got that word today, at their annual convention here, they were less than delighted.

"I think that when my forefathers wrote the First Amendment," said Kentucky state Rep. Paul Clark (D), "they never dreamed that the record industry would let someone say the F word. It's dangerous stuff we're talking about."

Clark tongue-lashed industry representatives attending a panel discussion at the National Conference of State Legislatures: "You people," he said, "are ruining our children."

Several of the legislators who have introduced their own unsuccessful record-labeling bills this year, carrying criminal penalties for noncompliance, questioned the record industry's ability to police itself. They pointed out that the industry must rely on more, not fewer, record sales to survive. . . .

"Thirty years ago there was a fear over Elvis Presley and Little Richard," said William Wasserman, national field director of People for the American Way. "People raised on a different generation of music called it too loud, too fast, too vulgar. And a lot of these songs are now jukebox standards across the country."

Gore, whose Parents Music Resource Center helped craft the voluntary agreement with the record industry and whose activities helped spur the first wave of labeling legislation five years ago, said freedom of expression must be protected.

The burden, however, she said, should remain on the industry, not the government.

"I think who makes that decision is extremely important, and it is incumbent on the industry to provide that information," she said. . . .

• Gwen Ifill is a *Washington Post* staff writer.

69

The Recording Industry's
Voluntary Lyrics Labeling Program

by Recording Industry Association of America

In its 1991 Annual Report, the RIAA recounted its lobbying efforts to combat restrictive music labeling on a state-by-state basis—notably the hard-won battle in Louisiana where, according to the RIAA, "the legislature considered a law that would have undermined the effectiveness and value of the standardized logo. An effort led by the RIAA prevented this bill from becoming law (see sidebar). The RIAA mailed over 2,000 letters in a grassroots effort to marshal opposition. . . ."

The proposed law on music labeling in Louisiana was voted down . . . by one vote.

As the RIAA has pointed out, "Since 1992 is an election year, we anticipate that restrictive legislation could be proposed in many more states."

On May 9, 1990, RIAA unveiled the industry-wide uniform voluntary logo that is now used for recordings deemed by the record company and recording artist to have "explicit lyrics."

The black-and-white logo, which reads "Parental Advisory: Explicit Lyrics," is affixed to the permanent packaging on the bottom right corner of records, tapes and CD's. Easily identifiable, the logo is being used by RIAA member companies which produce some 95 percent of all recorded music in America today, as well as by non-member companies. Consumers, parents, retailers and the media have all been made aware of its implementation.

RIAA recognized that there was a fairly low level of awareness about its earlier voluntary labeling program and hopes that the new standardized logo will overcome that problem by providing an easily recognizable tool for those parents who wish to monitor what their kids are buying.

Each recording company retains responsibility for deciding which recordings will have the standard logo applied. Those decisions are made by each company in discussion with its artists.

An independent national survey of parents conducted for RIAA in April of 1990 showed that there is a minority opinion that the government should be involved in making decisions about music. A comparable group does not support any program of labeling at all, while a majority (52 percent) support voluntary labeling; three out of four parents (76 percent) agreed they didn't want the government meddling in decisions about what music their children should listen to.

Accepting a difference of values among people is part of living in a free society. Voluntary labeling is a program that provides information, without infringing on the rights of all citizens to express themselves through music and to listen to whatever they choose.

"One Vote in a Hot Spot"
by Michael Cover

Louisiana has been a hot spot for us for a few years now. The legislation proposed last year would have made it a crime for minors to purchase recordings that are voluntarily labeled by our members. The easiest way to comply with such a law would have been to take the logo off!

So our job was to educate people about what the industry was already doing. We worked with members of the music community. We worked with First Amendment groups—the libraries, the booksellers, the newspapers. I did interviews all over the state. I talked to anybody I could talk to, because that personal contact is what changes people's minds.

And of course, I talked with the legislators—on the phone, in their offices, walking down the hall on the way to a vote, wherever I could—and I'd say, "Look, if your aim is to protect the public, to give them information, we're already doing that." But despite all our work, the votes went against us—in House committee, on the House floor, in Senate committee.

It was the last day of the session, and the full Senate still hadn't voted. I'd come back to Washington to prepare our next line of defense. And late that night, at home, I got a call from our state counsel, and he said the vote was taken, and I just held my breath.

And he said, "We won by one vote."

I was ecstatic, because it said we as an industry were doing the right thing.

• Michael Cover is the director of state relations for the RIAA.

70

Mythical Beasts

by Frank Zappa

In his testimony before Congress, musician Frank Zappa spoke out against the PMRC's initial proposal on record labeling, which involved a ratings system like that of the movie industry. Though the idea of the ratings system later fell by the wayside, the notion of "voluntary" labeling became the industry practice: "voluntarily" put labels on, or have labels legislated. Just as the comics book industry regulated itself with the comics code in the fifties, the record industry followed suit.

These are my personal observations and opinions. They are addressed to the PMRC as well as this committee. I speak on behalf of no group or professional organization.

The PMRC proposal is an ill-conceived piece of nonsense which fails to deliver any real benefits to children, infringes the civil liberties of people who are not children, and promises to keep the courts busy for years, dealing with the interpretational and enforcemental problems inherent in the proposal's design.

It is my understanding that, in law, First Amendment issues are decided with a preference for the least restrictive alternative. In this context, the PMRC's demands are the equivalent of treating dandruff by decapitation.

No one has forced Mrs. Baker or Mrs. Gore to bring Prince or Sheena Easton into their homes. Thanks to the Constitution, they are free to buy other forms of music for their children. Apparently they insist on purchasing the works of contemporary recording artists in order to support a personal illusion of aerobic sophistication. Ladies, please be advised: the $8.98 purchase price does not entitle you to a kiss on the foot from the composer or performer in exchange for a spin on the family Victrola. Taken as a whole, the complete list of PMRC demands reads like an instruction manual for some sinister kind of toilet training program to house-break *all* composers and performers because of the lyrics of a few. Ladies, how *dare* you?

The ladies' shame must be shared by the bosses at the major labels who, through the RIAA, chose to bargain away the rights of composers, performers, and retailers in order to pass H.R. 2911, the Blank Tape Tax: a private tax, levied by an industry on consumers, for the benefit of a select group within that industry. Is this a "consumer issue"? You bet it is. PMRC spokesperson Kandy

Stroud announced to millions of fascinated viewers on last Friday's "Nightline" debate that Senator Gore, a man she described as "a friend of the music industry," is co-sponsor of something she referred to as "anti-piracy legislation." Is this the same tax bill with a nicer name?

The major recording labels need to have H.R. 2911 whiz through a few committees before anybody smells a rat. One of them is chaired by Senator Thurmond. Is it a coincidence that Mrs. Thurmond is affiliated with the PMRC? I can't say she's a member because *the PMRC has no members.* Their secretary told me on the phone last Friday that the PMRC has *no members, only founders.* I asked how many other D.C. wives are *non-members* of an organization that raises money by mail, has a tax-exempt status, and seems intent on running the Constitution of the United States through the family paper-shredder. I asked her if it was a cult. Finally, she said she couldn't give me an answer and that she had to call their lawyer.

While the wife of the Secretary of the Treasury recites "Gonna drive my love inside you . . ." and Senator Gore's wife talks about "Bondage!" and "Oral sex at gunpoint" on the CBS Evening News, people in high places work on a tax bill that is so ridiculous, the only way to sneak it through is to keep the public's mind on something else—"Porn Rock."

The PMRC practices a curious double standard with these fervent recitations. Thanks to them, helpless young children all over America get to hear about oral sex at gunpoint on network TV several nights a week. Is there a secret FCC dispensation here? What sort of end justifies *these* means? Parents should keep an eye on these ladies if that's their idea of "good taste."

Is the basic issue morality? Is it mental health? Is it an issue at all? The PMRC has created a lot of confusion with improper comparisons between song lyrics, videos, record packaging, radio broadcasting, and live performances. These are all different mediums, and the people who work in them have a right to conduct their business without trade-restraining legislation, whipped up like an instant pudding by The Wives of Big Brother.

Is it proper that the husband of a PMRC *non-member/founder/person* sits on any committee considering business pertaining to the Blank Tape Tax or his wife's lobbying organization? Can any committee thus constituted "find facts" in a fair and unbiased manner? This committee has three. A minor conflict of interest?

The PMRC promotes their program as a harmless type of consumer information service, providing "guidelines" which will assist baffled parents in the determination of the "suitability" of records listened to by "very young children." The methods they propose have several unfortunate side effects, not the least of which is the reduction of all American music, recorded and live, to the intellectual level of a Saturday morning cartoon show.

Teenagers with $8.98 in their pocket might go into a record store alone, but "very young children" do not. Usually there is a parent in attendance. The $8.98

is in the parents' pocket. The parent can always suggest that the $8.98 be spent on a book.

If the parent is afraid to let the child read a book, perhaps the $8.98 can be spent on recordings of instrumental music. Why not bring jazz or classical music into your home instead of Blackie Lawless or Madonna? Great music with *no words at all* is available to anyone with sense enough to look beyond this week's platinum-selling fashion plate.

Children in the "vulnerable" age bracket have a natural love for music. If, as a parent, you believe they should be exposed to something more uplifting than "Sugar Walls," support Music Appreciation programs in schools. Why haven't you considered your child's need for consumer information? Music Appreciation costs very little compared to sports expenditures. Your children have a right to know that something besides pop music exists.

It is unfortunate that the PMRC would rather dispense governmentally sanitized Heavy Metal Music, than something more "uplifting." Is this an indication of PMRC's personal taste, or just another manifestation of the low priority this administration has placed on education for the Arts in America? The answer, of course, is *neither.* You can't distract people from thinking about an unfair tax by talking about Music Appreciation. For that, you need *sex*—and lots of it.

Because of the subjective nature of the PMRC ratings, it is impossible to guarantee that some sort of "despised concept" won't sneak through, tucked away in new slang or the overstressed pronunciation of an otherwise innocent word. If the goal here is total verbal/moral safety, there is only one way to achieve it: watch no TV, read no books, see no movies, listen to only instrumental music, or buy no music at all.

The establishment of a rating system, voluntary or otherwise, opens the door to an endless parade of Moral Quality Control Programs based on "Things Certain Christians Don't Like." What if the next bunch of Washington Wives demands a large yellow "J" on all material written or performed by Jews, in order to save helpless children from exposure to "concealed Zionist doctrine"?

Record ratings are frequently compared to film ratings. Apart from the quantitative difference, there is another that is more important: People who act in films are hired to "pretend." No matter how the film is rated, it won't hurt them personally. Since many musicians write and perform their own material and stand by it as their art—whether you like it or not—an imposed rating will stigmatize them as *individuals.* How long before composers and performers are told to wear a festive little PMRC arm band with their Scarlet Letter on it?

The PMRC rating system restrains trade in one specific music field: Rock. No ratings have been requested for comedy records or country music. Is there anyone in the PMRC who can differentiate *infallibly* between rock and country music? Artists in both fields cross stylistic lines. Some artists include comedy material. If an album is part rock, part country, part comedy, what sort of label would it get? Shouldn't the ladies be warning everyone that inside those country albums with the American flags, the big trucks, and the atomic pompadours there lurks a fascinating variety of songs about sex, violence, alcohol, and *the devil,* recorded in a way that lets you hear *every word,* sung for you by people who have been to prison and are *proud of it?*

If enacted, the PMRC program would have the effect of protectionist legislation for the country music industry, providing more security for cowboys than it does for children. One major retail outlet has already informed the Capitol Records sales staff that it would not purchase or display an album with *any kind of sticker on it.*

Another chain with outlets in shopping malls has been told by the landlord that if it racked "hard-rated albums" they would lose their lease. That opens up an awful lot of shelf space for somebody. Could it be that a certain Senatorial husband and wife team from Tennessee sees this as an "affirmative action program" to benefit the suffering multitudes in Nashville?

Is the PMRC attempting to save future generations from sex itself? The type, the amount, and the timing of sexual information given to a child should be determined by parents, not by people who are involved in a tax scheme cover-up.

The PMRC has conducted a Mythical Beast, compounding the chicanery by demanding consumer guidelines to keep it from inviting your children inside its sugar walls. Is the next step the adoption of a "PMRC National Legal Age for Comprehension of Vaginal Arousal"? Many people in this room would gladly support such legislation, but before they start drafting their bill, I would urge them to consider these facts:

• There is no conclusive scientific evidence to support the claim that exposure to any form of music will cause the listener to commit a crime or damn his soul to hell.

• Masturbation is not illegal. If it is not illegal to do it, why should it be illegal to sing about it?

• No medical evidence of hairy palms, warts, or blindness has been linked to masturbation or vaginal arousal, nor has it been proven that hearing references to either topic automatically turns the listener into a social liability.

• Enforcement of anti-masturbatory legislation could prove costly and time-consuming.

• There is not enough prison space to hold all the children who do it.

The PMRC's proposal is most offensive in its "moral tone." It seeks to enforce a set of implied religious values on its victims. Iran has a religious government. Good for them. I like having the capital of the United States in Washington, D.C., in spite of recent efforts to move it to Lynchburg, Virginia [home of Rev. Jerry Falwell].

Fundamentalism is not a state religion. The PMRC's request for labels regarding sexually explicit lyrics, violence, drugs, alcohol, and especially occult content reads like a catalog of phenomena abhorrent to practitioners of that faith. How a person worships is a private matter, and should not be inflicted upon or exploited by others. Understanding the fundamentalist leanings of this organization, I think it is fair to wonder if their rating system will eventually be extended to inform parents as to whether a musical group has homosexuals in it. Will the PMRC permit musical groups to exist, but only if gay members don't sing, and are not depicted on the album cover?

The PMRC has demanded that record companies "re-evaluate" the contracts of those groups who do things on stage that they find offensive. I remind the PMRC that groups are comprised of individuals. If one guy wiggles too much, does the whole band get an "X"? If the group gets dropped from the label as a result of this "re-evaluation" process, do the other guys in the group who weren't wiggling get to sue the guy who wiggled because he ruined their careers? Do the founders of this tax-exempt organization with no members plan to indemnify record companies for any losses incurred from unfavorably decided breach of contract suits, or is there a PMRC secret agent in the Justice Department?

Should individual musicians be rated? If so, who is qualified to determine if the guitar player is an "X," the vocalist is a "D/A," or the drummer is a "V"? If the bass player (or his Senator) belongs to a religious group that dances around with poisonous snakes, does he get an "O"? What if he has an earring in one ear, wears an Italian Horn around his neck, sings about his astrological sign, practices yoga, reads the *Quaballah,* or owns a rosary? Will his "occult content" rating go into an old CoIntelPro computer, emerging later as a "fact," to determine if he qualifies for a home-owner loan? Will they tell you this is necessary to protect the folks next door from the possibility of "devil-worship" lyrics creeping through the wall?

What hazards await the unfortunate retailer who accidentally sells an "O"-rated record to somebody's little Johnny? Nobody in Washington seemed to care when Christian terrorists bombed abortion clinics in the name of Jesus. Will you care when the "Friends of the Wives of Big Brother" blow up the shopping mall?

The PMRC wants ratings to start as of the date of their enactment. That leaves the current crop of "objectionable material" untouched. What will be the status of recordings from that Golden Era prior to censorship? Do they become collector's items . . . or will another "fair and unbiased committee" order them destroyed in a public ceremony?

Bad facts made bad law, and people who write bad laws are, in my opinion, more dangerous than songwriters who celebrate sexuality. Freedom of speech, freedom of religious thought, and the right to due process for composers, performers and retailers are imperiled if the PMRC and the major labels consummate this nasty bargain. Are we expected to give up Article One [of the Constitution] so the big guys can collect an extra dollar on every blank tape and 10–25 percent on tape recorders? What's going on here? Do *we* get to vote on this tax? There's an awful lot of smoke pouring out of the legislative machinery used by the PMRC to inflate this issue. Try not to inhale it. Those responsible for the vandalism should pay for the damage by *voluntarily rating themselves*. If they refuse, perhaps the voters could assist in awarding the Congressional "X," the Congressional "D/A," the Congressional "V," and the Congressional "O." Just like the ladies say: these ratings are necessary to protect our children. I hope it's not too late to put them where they *really* belong.

o   o   o

Okay, the "hearing" is over. . . . The good news is the PMRC has given up on all demands *except* that *some kind of symbol appears on the front of an album with "undesirable" content*. . . . Is this too much to ask? You bet it is!

That "tiny little symbol" still requires somebody else to decide what those lyrics mean, and whether or not they are "filthy." This determination is the responsibility of individual parents making decisions based on standards in their community, not those of a record executive in New York or Hollywood. . . .

. . . Senator Hollings . . . said in the hearing, on the record, that he preferred my proposal to the PMRC rating idea. You never heard about it, did you?

This revolutionary proposal is very simple. No rating. No sticker. No committee decisions. Let the parent decide after reading the lyrics. The lyrics would be printed on a sheet of white paper (preferably with a First Amendment Reminder at the top of the page), under the shrinkwrap on the back of the album. For cassettes, an accordion-fold. . . .

Any kind of warning system is going to cost money. This one puts the responsibility for the decision of what is clean or dirty where it belongs: in the hands of the parents. If millions of parents really want this, then funding it should not be a problem. If not, remember: most record stores still have a children's section. You can always shop there.

o   o   o

As the wife of a senator, Tipper Gore was able to focus attention on the agenda for the PMRC in a way that someone else, without political affiliations, could not. In light of the recent presidential election, however, fears of music censorship have begun anew, as musicians wonder what effect Tipper Gore—as the wife of the vice president—will have on the industry.

• *Called "the most original mind in rock music" by* Playboy, *Frank Zappa is the 43rd inductee into the* Playboy *Music Hall of Fame, voted upon by its readership.*

71

Sound Off!

by Mary Morello

. . . Elites seek to rule and impose social stability by the application of "traditional values"—of authority, profit, family hierarchy, moral rigidity and class domination.

—*Nation*, February 11, 1991

A law of physics: For every action, there's an equal but opposite reaction. This, it seems, is the nature of censorship; some rise up to censor, others to defend. Censorship is proactive, anticensorship is reactive.

Unlike the PMRC—well funded, highly organized, and politically empowered— Parents for Rock and Rap is a grassroots organization that operates with a staff of one.

Parents for Rock and Rap was formed as a counter-force to Parents Music Resource Center and some of the fundamentalists who attempt to control people's lives. In the United States, freedom is guaranteed to every citizen by the First Amendment. As one of our members wrote when he joined (a father, a U.S. Army sergeant, stationed in Berlin), "The First Amendment is not negotiable." PFRR works for freedom of expression for artists in the music industry, but we cross over into all of the arts if and when necessary. Our organization includes not just parents, but anyone interested in fighting censorship and repression of musicians. Music censorship consists of record labeling, either self-imposed or legally mandated, communities regulating which artists may or may not perform, age restrictions on concert goers and record buyers, and record stores refusing to store certain "objectionable" albums.

Censorship is on the rise. Contradictory to what the far right says, the majority of Americans want their arts to be free. PFRR members include: students of all ages, parents, grandparents, college professors, representatives of news media, lawyers, veterans, artists in the music community (rock, rap and metal), writers, editors, ad infinitum. PFRR is beginning to have power and clout because at the present time we have hundreds of active members in the United States, Canada, England, Germany and even one member from Nigeria. We keep growing.

The purpose of our organization is to target any censorship of artists in the music industry. We work as a total organization, or the seventeen regional representatives work with their members, or we work individually. We call members of Congress, governors, assemble people, record chains, write letters when there is censorship. When something happens in your area you have many options. If the problem is a city board regulating who can and cannot view a concert, or which groups can or cannot perform in your community, attend board meetings and protest (call your municipal building to find out when and where they are held). If there is police harassment during or after a concert you can call the chief of police to protest, contact the mayor of the community, write letters to the editors of the local papers. If you think your state legislature or Congress is attempting to censor, the Congress opinion number is (202) 224-3121; ask the operator for a specific Senator or Representative. You have a state assembly person representing the area where you live. Find out who it is and contact him with your opinion. Type up a petition, get signatures, send it to the person or persons involved. Write and call record store owners and owners of other chains and tell them you will boycott their shops if they continue to practice censorship. Write record company presidents who attempt to censor their own artists.

I must mention my great disappointment with record companies and artists who have succumbed to the pressure of censorship. Not all! The owners of record companies have enough money and clout that they could have fought the labeling and won, especially since they have the First Amendment on their side.

This brings us around to parents. Parents, not the government nor outside forces, should help their children make decisions. Parents have to realize that they don't belong to the generation their children have joined, just as they were different from their parents' generation. They can listen to their children's albums and discuss the lyrics if they don't approve. Many parents would not think of interfering in their young person's choice of music. They look upon music as a good outlet. Parents should love their children, give them what advice they can and set them free. If they falter, be there for them. Parental neglect and abuse are a far worse and damaging problem for young people.

I want to at least mention the racism that has always entered the picture when Afro-Americans are involved. Those who are white, bigoted parents resent their young enjoying the music of Afro-Americans. The negativism against rap was and is pure racism. . . .

You don't have to be a teenager to be alarmed by music censorship. I am 67 years old and the mother of a rock musician. I do not have money nor am I famous but I am never frightened of any opposition. I believe an artist is not an artist if he or she is not free to express herself or himself in an art. Whether we enjoy rap or rock, reggae or even country music, as Americans, if we are to be free, we have to fight against censorship and to uphold the First Amendment.

Peace.

• *Mary Morello is the founder of Parents for Rock and Rap.*

72

Corporate Censorship
He Who Pays the
Piper Calls the Tune

by George Beahm

The Iceman cometh . . . and, as *Newsweek* explained in its story on rapper Ice-T, ". . . concedeth." Ice-T's song "Cop Killer" will not be on future albums of "Body Count," and Time Warner is recalling all existing albums.

At the center of the controversy: black rapper Ice-T, who in the August 10, 1992, *Newsweek* story is shown pointing to his T-shirt bearing the words: "L.A.P.D./ We Treat You Like a King," a mocking reference to the LAPD that converged with nightsticks on motorist Rodney King and—let's be honest here—beat the living crap out of him.

In the wake of the acquittal of the LAPD officers in the King case, "Cop Killer" is, depending on your viewpoint, social commentary, an assault of words, or (as police see it) inflammatory lyrics, an invitation to declare open season on cops.

To paraphrase an old nursery rhyme: Nightsticks and stones may break my bones, but words will never hurt me.

Not surprisingly, Ice-T found himself (along with the company that produced it, Time Warner) targeted for criticism. As *Newsweek* reported:

> Police groups, 60 members of Congress, an attorney general, Oliver North, even the president and the vice president of the United States accused Time Warner of, in essence, advocating the murder of police officers. Police unions threatened to divest their pension funds of several hundred million dollars in Time Warner stock and to boycott all Time Warner products. (The 30,000-member National Black Police Association opposed it.) More than 1,400 stores dropped the album.

Newsweek also reported that within two weeks after a Time Warner board meeting at which "Cop Killer" was the topic of discussion, a decision was made to pull it from the album permanently.

"But even as 'Cop Killer' disappears," notes *Newsweek*, "a troubling question raised in the turmoil remains: who controls what we see or hear? Is it the artistic community or the corporate one?"

Unfortunately, the corporate community will decide in the end, for it pays the pipers that play the tunes. Just as the controversy surrounding the obscenity charges catapulted Luther Campbell's 2 Live Crew to national prominence, "Cop Killer" brought Ice-T to the attention of an audience that, without the controversy, might never have noticed him.

The media, of course, are quick to capitalize on such news stories. Awash with coverage on Ice-T and his rap song, the critics came out in force and, in the end, self-interests became self-censorship. Put differently, when the artistic impulse—however offensive—is subverted by financial considerations of big business sensitive to public opinion, it's economic censorship, pure and simple. *To no one's surprise, Ice-T and Time Warner subsequently parted company.*

Perspectives on Ice-T's "Cop Killer"

Ice-T: "The police ain't shit to me and never will be. They're a Gestapo organization in L.A., and until you start takin' them cops down out there in the street, then ya'all are really still [unintelligible] in the wind. And when brothers get ready to do that, I'll be right in the front, you know what I'm sayin'? But niggers ain't ready to smoke . . . pig[s]. I personally would like to blow up some fucking police stations. And if it was up to me, I would burn the White House down, you know, because I'm an anarchist. I'm ready to do this shit, but some people gotta die. And if you ain't ready to spill no blood, then, you know, go on outa here. You know what I'm sayin'?" (Ice-T, quoted in *AIM Report,* August-A 1992; Ice-T's comments from an amateur videotape made in a radio parking lot during the L.A. riots.)

Willie D (former member of Geto Boys): "We're living in a Communist country and everyone's afraid to say it." (*USA Today,* July 13, 1992.)

Havelock Nelson (*Billboard* rap columnist): "The issue isn't *Cop Killer,* it's killer cops." (*USA Today,* July 13, 1992.)

Charlton Heston: "The new version [of the album] will still contain songs disgustingly demeaning to women. . . . They still think it's okay to sing about raping women, murdering mothers and sodomizing little girls."

Charles Meeks (head of the National Sheriffs Association): "We hope corporate America has got the message that advocating the death of anyone for the purpose of making money is not acceptable in this country." (*Washington Post,* July 29, 1992.)

Part 5
Sex and Censorship

The First Amendment is there to protect speech that some-body thinks is dangerous. Speech that we all agree is okay doesn't need the First Amendment because no one is going to attack it. But through the ages there is always speech, there are always pictures, there is always some kind of magazine or book that somebody is going to decide is going to fell western civilization. They are going to blame all the problems on pornography, on political dissent, on something. The First Amendment is there to protect that very speech that somebody thinks is dangerous.

—MARCIA PALLY, from "Donahue" (1986)

Adult entertainment, X-rated material, or pornography, no matter what you call it, is at the center of the debate on censorship. On one hand, there are those who feel strongly that, regardless of whether it's soft-core "porn" (like Playboy *or* Penthouse*), or more hard-core "porn," societal ills can be blamed on the forbidden fruit. On the other hand, there are those who feel just as strongly that all, except the clearly obscene, adult material is protected under the First Amendment, and any attempt to suppress it will have a chilling effect on publishing.*

In recent years the distinction between what is permissible and what is out of bounds has been blurred. The explosion of sex in the media is at an all-time high, movies are increasingly dependent on sexual content to attract audiences, and fairly explicit sexual material is available in mainstream bookstores. (Who, for instance, would have thought to find Madonna's explosive Sex *in chain bookstores nationwide?)*

Opponents of sexual freedom in all its varied expressions point to the rise in AIDS, the emergence of gays and lesbians seeking their place in society, women's liberation with its emphasis on sexual freedom and self-expression, and the rise in violent crimes against women as counterarguments against sexual permissiveness at a time when unsafe sex can kill.

Unfortunately, attempts to legislate morality have failed to clarify the issue. The findings of the Meese Commission lent fuel to the argument that there is a causal link between pornography and violence. Then, too, the Pornography Victims' Com-

pensation Act—informally dubbed the Bundy bill—was defeated, but only by a slim margin; it will likely reemerge in the near future.

Can pornography lead to violence? Does pornography have any place in our society? Or does the specter of censorship overshadow the detrimental aspects of pornography?

73

Debunking Misinformation About Pornography and Obscenity Law

from Morality in Media, Inc.

Morality in Media, with forty-five chapters and state affiliates, is a national, inter-faith organization that was founded in 1962. It works in the areas of public information and the law. A division of Morality in Media is the National Obscenity Law Center, a clearinghouse of legal information on obscenity cases and materials for prosecutors and other law-enforcement officials.

When you begin an organized effort against the illegal pornography trafficking in your community, certain cliché arguments will be brought out to weaken your effort. You will hear them in private conversation, in public debate and in the media.

These cliches and answers should be studied and mastered so that the truth will be brought out.

Myths About Pornography, Obscenity Law

1. You are advocating censorship by urging enforcement of state and federal obscenity laws.

Absolutely not. Censorship is illegal and unconstitutional. Censorship is prior restraint of First Amendment rights by government. No American would stand still for this. However, there are constitutional laws prohibiting the dissemination of obscene materials in order to preserve public health, safety and morals. Individuals may produce anything they please, but they are responsible after the fact if they violate local, state or federal obscenity laws.

2. But freedom of expression is protected by the First Amendment.

It most certainly is. But the United States Supreme Court consistently has held that obscenity is not protected by the First Amendment any more than libel, perjury, slander, contempt of court, false advertising or copyright violations are. Obscenity is *not* a First Amendment issue. It is a *crime,* and 90 percent of the traffic in hardcore pornography in the country is controlled by *organized* crime.

3. Pornography is thriving, so the American people must want it or accept it.

(a) Certainly there are some who want it. That's what makes it so profitable. But all surveys show that the majority of Americans are vehemently opposed to the traffic in pornography and want it stopped. The majority *do* care, but they are confused and discouraged in the face of a highly organized industry and the loud prophets of false freedom.

This is the reason that Morality in Media exists: to expose the false prophets, to vindicate the true freedom of responsibility under law, and to raise in an organized way the voice of the majority who care very much about standards of public morality.

One of the major factors in the growth of the pornography traffic is the lack of vigorous enforcement of obscenity laws, particularly at the county level.

(b) "Community standards" cannot be measured by the number of patrons of an "adult" bookstore. Because pornography is so available does not mean it is acceptable to the people. The U.S. Supreme Court said in 1974, "Mere availability of similar materials by itself means nothing more than that other persons are engaged in similar activities."

(c) The illegal drug industry also is thriving, but obviously that does not mean that the majority of Americans accept this heinous traffic.

4. Pornography is a victimless crime.

(a) There is no such thing as a victimless crime. In every crime there is a victim and a victimizer. The victims of the pornography industry are strewn from coast to coast and include corrupted children, degraded women, addicted men, broken marriages, invaded communities, and ultimately, the very humanity— the soul—of a nation.

(b) Victims of "copycat rape" are not uncommon: easily accessible, hardcore pornographic materials are known to ignite rapists and provide them with blueprints for brutal sexual assaults on women and children.

(c) Children are victimized in a myriad of ways. Some are used in child pornography. Others are exposed to pornographic materials to "soften them up" for incest or other sexual molestation. A growing number of children today are sexually molesting other children in imitation of what they've seen. "Throwaway" teenagers are being lured into performing before the pornographer's camera. And finally, every child in America today risks exposure to materials which distort human sexuality and which can lead to a lifetime of sexual dysfunction.

5. Obscenity is difficult to define; there is no clear definition on the books.

False. The United States Supreme Court defined obscenity quite adequately in its 1973 landmark *Miller v. California* case. According to the High Court, material is considered obscene if it meets the following three criteria: (1) the average person, applying contemporary community standards, would find that the work, taken as a whole, appeals to prurient interest; (2) the work depicts or describes in a patently offensive way, sexual conduct specifically defined by the applicable state law; and (3) the work, taken as a whole, lacks serious literary, artistic, political and scientific value.

This definition is as clear as other concepts which the law engages in every day such as "the reasonable person" or "good faith."

6. But the Supreme Court left it to communities to decide what is obscene.

This is an oversimplification and a misleading one. "Community Standards" is not *the* test for obscenity, but a *part* of the test, and has been part of the test for obscenity since 1957. It is a judge or jurors who decide what is obscene under the guidelines, putting themselves in the place of the average person to determine or apply community standards.

7. When "consenting adults" watch obscene videocassettes at home, no one is being harmed.

Regarding so-called consenting adults, the U.S. Supreme Court said in its 1973 *Paris Adult Theatre I* v. *Slaton* case: "We categorically disapprove the theory that obscene films acquire constitutional immunity from state regulation simply because they are exhibited for consenting adults only. Rights and interests other than those of the advocates are involved. These include the interest of the public in the quality of life, the total community environment, the tone of commerce and possibly, the public safety itself."

As for the defense that "no one is being harmed," the moral values of the "consenting adults" themselves will insidiously be eroded by continued exposure to pornographic material which devalues human sexuality.

8. I have a right to watch what I choose in my own home.

There is no such thing as a constitutional right to obtain illegal pornographic films. The obscenity laws, however, are not aimed at you in the privacy of your home (unless child pornography is involved). No one can be prosecuted for watching obscenity. The law puts the penalty on the purveyor.

9. If you don't like obscene films and books, you don't have to see them or buy them, but don't interfere with my right to buy them.

My like or dislike for obscenity is irrelevant. The fact is that it is illegal. You do not have a right to obtain illegal materials. Obscenity laws have been consistently upheld by the U.S. Supreme Court. They are intended to protect the common good from prurient, offensive materials lacking in literary, artistic, political, and scientific value—materials which do, in fact, have a destructive effect on individuals and society (see #4).

10. You cannot legislate morality.

(a) On its face this cliche is absurd and an argument against the democratic process itself. All law rests on moral assumption, and every law legislates morality. Defining what is morally right and wrong is and always has been the essence of the legislative function.

(b) One of the major freedoms of any viable society is the freedom to choose to protect public morality. Public morals are the business of the entire community, and it is public morality that obscenity laws are designed to safeguard.

11. Obscenity is in the eye of the beholder. What is obscene to you may not be obscene to me.

This implies that obscenity is subjective. It is not. It is the hardcore pornographic description or depiction of specific sexual activity—the description or depiction of which is prohibited by law to protect the common good.

12. Who are you to tell me what I can see or read? You are imposing your morality on me.

(a) Nobody can tell you what to see or to read but the community can tell you what commercial materials cannot be sold to you if you choose to live in that community. The community sets up standards for itself and has a right to legislate to protect those standards.

(b) With pornography now invading the sanctity of the home in the form of dial-a-porn, cableporn, video porn, computer porn, radio porn, satellite-to-dish porn and rock music porn, it's more accurately a case of the sex industry's trying to impose its immorality on an entire nation and an entire generation of children.

(c) In any society, someone's morality (or immorality) must prevail. The real question becomes, "Whose will prevail in America?" The pornographer's, leading to anarchy and decadence? Or the moral principles of those who honor the Judeo-Christian code—a code which has been embraced, not imposed, as the cornerstone of Western civilization!

13. Pornography is harmless. The 1970 Presidential Commission Report said so.

(a) The 1970 Majority Report of the Presidential Commission on Obscenity and Pornography was called a "scientific scandal" by many in the scientific community. It was rejected by the U.S. Senate by a vote of 60 to 5. The Hill-Link Minority Report of that Commission was read into the record in both Houses of Congress as a "responsible position on the issues." The Hill-Link Report cited numerous instances where evidence was suppressed when it went counter to the predetermined "findings" of the majority report. In addition, studies in the Hill-Link Report show linkages between exposure to obscene material and sexual deviancy and promiscuity. However, pornographers and their defenders who want obscenity laws repealed will continue to resurrect this discredited Report.

14. The findings of the 1986 Attorney General's Commission on Pornography, concluding that pornography is harmful, have been totally discredited.

Absolutely untrue. After the findings were made public, there was a high-priced campaign conducted in an effort to discredit the Commission, but it proved unsuccessful. The Commission found that a causal link exists between sexually violent material and antisocial and sometimes unlawful acts of sexual violence. The Commission also found that "non-violent materials depicting degradation, domination, subordination or humiliation" bore some causal relationship to the level of sexual violence, sexual coercion, or unwanted sexual aggression in the population so exposed. The findings affirmed what common sense has told Americans since the founding of this nation.

15. Why bother enforcing the law? The "Adult" bookstores keep operating while their owners are in the courts.

(a) Occasional law enforcement is ineffective. Continuous, vigorous enforcement of the law is the answer. When arrests and prosecutions begin, the sex industry is put on warning. Prison sentences, fines and legal fees can eventually put the pornographers out of business. Atlanta, Jacksonville, and Cincinnati are clean cities because of vigorous, continuous enforcement of the law.

(b) RICO (Racketeer Influenced and Corrupt Organizations) laws provide the ultimate weapon against the illegal pornography industry. Besides imposing stiff penalties, RICO laws can force the forfeiture of all assets of a business, including cars, homes and bank accounts, acquired through obscenity-related activities. This is what breaks the racketeer's financial back. The federal government and approximately 30 percent of the states have their own RICO statutes including obscenity. Every state should be armed with such a law.

16. It is impossible for the owners and managers of stores selling pornographic videos and magazines to know if the material is obscene.

(a) The U.S. Supreme Court said in its landmark *Miller* decision when it defined obscenity: "We are satisfied that these prerequisites (the three part test) will provide fair notice to a dealer in such materials that his public and commercial activities may bring prosecution."

(b) It is the responsibility of the owners and managers to know the content and character of the material they're selling. It is also their responsibility to be familiar with both the federal and state obscenity laws.

17. Why be concerned about obscenity when there is so much violent crime?

They're related. Pornography denies human dignity and often stimulates the user into violent acts. Its outlets breed and attract violent crime. It is no coincidence that when "adult" bookstores are closed down, violent crimes decrease in that neighborhood due to an exodus of prostitutes, drug pushers and criminally prone who are attracted to pornography outlets.

18. If you'd let pornography flow freely, people would get bored and the problem would take care of itself.

(a) This boredom or satiation theory is invalid. Many users of pornography do not get bored, but rather become addicted, seeking more and more bizarre materials. For many, also, the passivity of pornography must eventually give way to action. In the unstable, it often triggers sexual abuse, rape and sometimes even murder.

(b) Remember that new markets for the industry are being created every day as children and teenagers are lured by the pornographer's siren song into becoming consumers of pornographic material.

19. I'd rather see people making love than making violence.

There is no love in pornography. It is totally loveless, debasing women, children and all humanity. In addition, violence is inherent in all pornography, even in that described as "non-violent." Violence against the mind and spirit can be as devastating—sometimes more so—as violence against the physical body.

20. War, poverty, hunger, the homeless are the real obscenities which you should be fighting.

There are many noble causes to which we may be able to contribute financially. In terms of time, however, it is not possible for one person to fight all the evils of the world. Each person should select his or her own battlefield in the fight for a decent society. Hardcore pornography—dehumanizing, depraved, and an assault upon the sacredness of the person in the most intimate sanctuary of his or her being—is a true obscenity. The war against it is worthy, and winnable at that.

21. What next? Where do you draw the line? A ban on obscene materials today will lead to real censorship tomorrow with maybe the Bible or Michelangelo's statue of David being banned next.

(a) That we have for two centuries enjoyed political and religious freedom is the clearest proof that enforcement of long-established obscenity laws does not threaten our First Amendment freedoms.

(b) The American people are too intelligent to fall for the "slippery slope" scare tactics that would have you believe that a prohibition against obscenity today will ultimately lead to a ban against everything from the Sistine Chapel to a diaperless Donald Duck. Such absurdities are somewhat like being asked to believe that a ban against playing loud rock music at 3 A.M. in the midst of a residential street would lead to a ban on the right of the Philharmonic to perform in Carnegie Hall.

(c) The question "What next?" should be asked in the context of what next will happen to our society if the obscenity laws are not enforced, and dehumanizing, depraved materials are allowed to spread with dazzling speed by means of high-tech advances.

(d) Where do you draw the line? Most state legislatures and the U.S. Congress have already drawn that line, and the U.S. Supreme Court has upheld its constitutionality. Furthermore, our entire society is made viable by the drawing of lines in every aspect of life.

22. People who fight pornography are anti-sex, prudish, and sexually repressed.

(a) Anti-sex? It's just the opposite. It's the pornography industry which is anti-sex and the porn fighters who are pro-sex. Pornography takes something beautiful and converts it into commercialized slime. The porn-fighters are out there protecting healthy sexuality with the key ingredients of love, tenderness, commitment and privacy of intimate moments.

(b) If "prudish" and "sexually repressed" are the labels attached to those who oppose the depictions of sadomasochism, gang rape, sexual orgies, bestiality, ad infinitum, then those labels should be worn proudly.

23. All of our law enforcement resources today should be used to fight a far greater menace than obscenity—illegal drugs!

(a) It is the height of folly to regard the drug explosion as existing in a vacuum—the merest of abstractions unrelated to the dehumanizing milieu fostered by the sex industry—and attempt to eradicate it as though it were not a many-headed hydra. Obscenity and drugs march hand in hand to the deadly tune of the organized crime industry. To ignore the commercial distribution of obscene materials and indeed, by lack of law enforcement, assign it a protected status is much like repairing faulty electrical wires in a home to prevent a fire while deliberately ignoring the army of termites gnawing away at the foundation.

(b) Organized crime launders its profits from pornography and pumps the money into the illegal drug trade. By fighting one, you are fighting both.

(c) Drugs can lead to a physical addiction; pornography to a psychological addiction. Both are destructive not only to the hooked individual, but eventually to the entire moral fabric of any society.

24. Pornography is beneficial to the lonely, the sexually confused, and to those who believe they are hopelessly unattractive; in fantasy, it gives them some relief from their sexual frustration.

The consumption of pornography can lead to a detrimental addiction, and the type of person just described—one who can't relate—is the most vulnerable to becoming a slave to pornography. Pornography can provide him with anti-social sexual imagery which becomes locked into his mind and returns again and again to haunt.

Dr. Victor Cline, psychologist at the University of Utah, has found a near universal four-step syndrome associated with immersion in the world of pornography: addiction; escalation (more deviant material is needed to attain the same sexual stimulation); desensitization (the shocking has become acceptable); and finally, acting out. The last step may result in violent as well as illegal sexual activities.

25. District attorneys and U.S. attorneys have good reason for not enforcing the obscenity laws—mainly "limited resources and more important priorities."

This cliche, year after year, has become the standard excuse of delinquent prosecutors who do not enforce the obscenity laws. Their reasons vary. Some are simply ideologically opposed to the law itself. Others with political aspirations find it more politically popular to prosecute Wall Street white collar crime than Times Square obscenity. Note that white collar crime robs the public's pocketbooks, but obscenity robs the very humanity—the soul—of a community. Violations on Wall Street and in Times Square both need to be prosecuted.

Some district attorneys actually are uneducated on the pernicious impact of illegal pornography on communities; however, the most prevalent reason why some prosecutors have been ignoring the obscenity law is that they misinterpret the silence of the community as acceptance.

District attorneys and U.S. attorneys who are not enforcing the obscenity laws need to hear from the public with reminders that pornography outlets serve as magnets for the sexually deranged and drug-crazed population. They will make obscenity a priority and will find the resources to do so if they receive enough encouragement and enough complaints about an illegal industry which threatens to corrupt our entire value system.

Obscenity Statute Utilizing *Miller* Standard

Material is obscene if:

(1) to the average person, applying contemporary community standards, taken as a whole, it predominantly appeals to a prurient interest in nudity, sex or excretion;

(2) the material, taken as a whole, lacks serious literary, artistic, political or scientific value, and

(3) the material depicts or describes, in a patently offensive way, sexual conduct specifically defined in subparagraphs (i) through (v) below:

(i) acts of sexual intercourse, heterosexual or homosexual, normal or perverted, actual or simulated;

(ii) acts of masturbation;

(iii) acts involving excretory functions or lewd exhibition of the genitals;

(iv) acts of bestiality or the fondling of sex organs of animals;

(v) sexual acts of flagellation, torture or other violence indicating a sadomasochistic sexual relationship.

From *Attorney General's Commission on Pornography: Final Report, July 1986,* p. 1805.

74

Can Pornography Lead to Violence?

by Wendy Melillo

> To defend society from sex is no one's business. To defend it from officiousness is the duty of everyone who values freedom—or sex.
>
> —BRIGID BROPHY, British novelist and critic, from *The Observer* ("Sayings of the Week"), August 9, 1970

The camera focuses on the couple in bed, having sex.

Picking up a white silk scarf, the woman slowly ties the man's hands to the headboard.

As he achieves orgasm, she stabs him repeatedly with an ice pick.

Plots mixing sex with violent death—once the domain of a small number of X-rated movies known as "snuff" films—are now a routine part of what Hollywood offers. Some argue that this stabbing scene, from the R-rated movie *Basic Instinct,* is pornographic and has no business being so easily accessible. Conservatives say any explicitly sexual scene, whether it is violent or not, is inappropriate for Americans to watch.

Others say that censorship of erotic material will only result in dangerous precedents that limit freedom of choice. They argue that graphic sexual scenes reflect the real lives of many people.

At the heart of the debate is whether pornographic material can lead to violent crimes. From family living rooms and research laboratories to Congress and the courts, the battle rages over the impact of "dirty pictures" on society.

Religious leaders and conservatives blame pornography for a host of societal ills, from promoting violence to encouraging unusual sex practices such as voyeurism or sexual relations with animals. Joining their argument are many liberal feminists, like Catharine MacKinnon, a professor of law at the University of Michigan Law School, and the writer Andrea Dworkin. They argue that any images that depict women engaged in sexual activity are harmful because such graphic displays objectify and degrade all women.

On the other side are researchers and social scientists who dispute the link between erotic material and sexual assaults. They are joined by those in the pornography industry—publishers, owners of adult video and book stores—who turn to First Amendment rights for adults, arguing that what Americans do in their own privacy is no one else's business.

At issue is whether banning pornography will successfully lead to fewer acts of rape, incest, battery and sexism. Many find it an appealing notion. But can it work?

Social scientists define pornography as writings, drawings, pictures or films designed to arouse sexual desire. Pornography can generally be divided into four categories: sexually explicit material that includes violence; nonviolent pornography that depicts degradation, humiliation, subordination or domination; pornography that is not violent or degrading (erotica); and nudity.

Currently, it is illegal to produce or distribute any film that shows children or teenagers under 18 engaged in sexual acts.

Other pornography is legal if it has not been declared obscene by the local community. The Supreme Court, in 1973, adopted the following criteria to determine obscenity: if an average person would find the work "patently offensive"; if the work appeals to "morbid or shameful" interest in sex when judged against community standards; and if the work "lacks serious literary, artistic, political or scientific value."

In bookstores, video outlets and adult sex shops that dot the Washington areas's commercial landscape, pornographic material is an increasingly popular staple.

Last year, Americans rented 410 million adult tapes, an increase of 15 million from 1989, according to a study by *Adult Video News,* an industry trade publication in Upper Darby, Pa. Pornography is still stereotypically associated with male customers, but in reality the demographics are changing. The study found that nearly half of those renting adult films were either individual women or women accompanying men.

Sex therapists and industry specialists point to the increase in adult material made specifically for women and couples as one reason for the growing interest. Such material is also much more accessible.

Women no longer have to go to an adult store located in a part of town that makes them uncomfortable, said Sandra S. Cole, president of the American Association of Sex Educators, Counselors and Therapists. "Now you can go to your local shopping mall with your kids in tow, leave them in the Disney section and rent an adult tape with your head held high."

Yet the increase in popularity has also spurred concern among conservatives and helped lead to the formation by the Reagan administration of a controversial commission that studied the impact of pornography on society. The commission concluded that pornography had become more violent since 1970 and that sexually explicit material can significantly change men's attitudes about women and thereby promote sexual assault and crime. It called for local and federal authorities to crack down on pornography.

Park Elliott Dietz, a forensic psychiatrist who was part of the commission, said that although he did not at first view pornography as a moral issue, after viewing a number of hard-core, violent sexually explicit tapes, magazines, books and photos, "I was astonished to find that by the final meeting of the commission, pornography had become a matter of moral concern to me." Critics, however, complained that the commission had little research evidence on which to base its finding that pornography is harmful.

"There are lots of people who don't like this stuff and that is their constitutional right," said Marty Klein, a family counselor and sex therapist in Palo Alto, Calif. "But the intuitive belief that people have that pornography contributes to violence has not been proved. What people are saying is 'I feel bad that other people are watching this stuff and I want that to stop' and that is being translated into policy statements."

The controversy now has moved to Congress. Legislation, introduced last year by Sen. Mitch McConnell (R-Ky.), would allow victims of a sexual crime to recover damages from "commercial producers, distributors, exhibitors, and sellers of obscene and child pornographic material" if they prove that the pornographic material "was a substantial cause of the offense." The proposal has been passed by the Senate Judiciary Committee and is expected to be considered by the full Senate before the end of the year.

Meanwhile, across the country, battles are being waged in communities where conservative groups seek to limit the public's access to pornographic material. One of the leaders in these fights, the American Family Association, a Mississippi based pro-family organization, works with local attorneys to file lawsuits against pornographic material that it believes should be declared obscene.

"Our perspective is pornography is a destructive medium," said Donald E. Wildmon, the group's president. "It is not love, but sex and violence. If you look at these materials, the woman is an object to be used and discarded after you get through with her."

The federal government, social scientists and courts have all grappled with the issue of whether viewing pornography can prompt an individual to commit a violent sexual crime such as rape or child molestation.

President Lyndon Johnson considered the question in 1968 when he appointed a commission to examine the relationship between material that included sexually explicit images and violent, antisocial behavior. In its final report in 1970, the commission found "no reliable evidence to date that exposure to sexual materials plays a significant role" in delinquent or criminal sexual behavior.

In the 1980s, however, concern grew about child pornography and an increasing amount of sexual violence in adult films. Then-Attorney General Edwin Meese appointed his commission on pornography in 1985.

The commission did not fund new research but held public hearings to review current studies and information about the manufacture and distribution of pornographic material.

The Meese commission requested an independent review of the social science data on pornography and its effects on violent behavior. The review, conducted by Edna Einsiedel, a social scientist at the University of Calgary, found no link between sexually explicit material and violent sex crimes.

The commission then asked Surgeon General C. Everett Koop to collect more data. Koop gathered a group of experts in medicine, sociology and psychology to investigate the effects of pornography, especially on children and adolescents. The group reported that "children and adolescents who participate in the production of pornography experience adverse, enduring effects," but found no evidence that exposing adults to nonviolent sexual material leads to crime.

Despite the independent reviews, the commission concluded that the material was harmful. But that conclusion seemed to overstate some of the findings within the report itself. For example, after stating a link between pornography, aggressive sexual fantasies and aggressive behavior, the commission said: "What role pornography, particularly violent pornography, plays in the construction of these fantasies remains to be answered."

At the time, Henry E. Hudson, who chaired the commission, said the members used "common sense" when linking pornography to violence.

The issue has sparked a great deal of interest among social scientists. Marcia Pally, a social science researcher in New York, in *Sense and Censorship: The Vanity of Bonfires,* her review of sexually explicit and violent material, says that violence in sexually explicit material has actually decreased since the 1970 commission report.

Sexually explicit violence is also a very small part of the script of most adult films. Her book cites a 1990 study analyzing the content of current adult films, which found that in videos depicting explicit pornography, sexual behavior accounted for 41 percent of all scenarios presented, while sexual violence accounted for 4.73 percent and nonsexual violence for 4.73 percent. The authors, Ni Yang and Daniel Linz, at the University of California at Santa Barbara, also reviewed R-rated videos and found that sexual behavior was depicted in 4.59 percent of the scenes, while sexual violence made up 3.27 percent and nonsexual violence 35 percent.

The consensus among these researchers is that sexual images do not cause sexual crimes—and that pornography is only a small source of violent scenes in the film media.

The effect of violent sexual scenes is still uncertain. The report by Surgeon General Koop concluded that "in laboratory studies measuring short term effects, exposure to violent pornography increased punitive behavior toward women." Because the effect has only been measured in a laboratory setting, researchers are undecided about whether this effect can be translated to real world situations.

"We must be cautious when attempting to generalize beyond the limits of the laboratory to other domains," wrote social scientists Edward Donnerstein and Daniel Linz of the University of California at Santa Barbara, in a letter to Sen. Joseph R. Biden (D-Del.) protesting the McConnell bill.

"Without supporting evidence from field studies (which at this time do not exist), and research demonstrating that the measures of aggression collected in the laboratory are valid predictors of real world aggression, the current state of laboratory research is best described as strongly suggestive."

Researchers point to violent images as more likely candidates to foster aggression than sexual images. A 1980 study by Donnerstein measured aggressiveness by asking participants to deliver simulated shocks. If a person was angered and then shown violent, sexual images, he was more likely to deliver a shock that was about two points higher than people who were not exposed to such material.

After a review of several studies of this type, Donnerstein concluded: "It is the aggressive content of pornography that is the main contributor to violence against women. In fact, when we remove the sexual content from such films and just leave the aggressive content, we find a similar pattern of aggression and asocial attitudes."

Some mental health experts contend that the violence depicted throughout the mass media, not just in pornography, has a great deal of influence on the small percentage of the population that is likely to commit a crime. They believe a violent movie can provide people who are already predisposed to crime—like sex offenders—with a script that they can imitate. Even so, they say, it is difficult to prove with conventional research tools.

"I have seen rapes inspired by a particular piece of pornography and I have also seen mass murders inspired by *Time* magazine and suicides inspired by *The Deer Hunter* and violent crime inspired by R-rated films," said forensic psychiatrist Dietz, who practices in Newport Beach, Calif.

Dietz says the social science studies that would convincingly show a relationship between violence in the media and crime don't exist because the funding for research on the media's effects has always come from the media itself.

To prove harm, the media demands that the most rigorous tests be used, argues Dietz. But what ends up being studied is the effect of the media on normal, average people, and he thinks that is the wrong question to ask. "You are not going to find a professor of psychology who shows the most damaging films to a group of unincarcerated sex offenders or criminally insane men because the effect it would have would be so obvious that no human subjects review committee would permit such a dangerous experiment," he said.

"So instead, he shows his movies to a group of college freshmen required for credit to be research subjects. Well, no one is worried about the effects on bright, educated, mentally stable, good people."

Dietz also contends that society should concern itself with the media's effects on the segment of the population that is most vulnerable to crime. Take the opening scene in the R-rated movie *Basic Instinct,* as an example.

"That scene is done in a way that every red-blooded American male has an erection by the time the man in the movie does," said Dietz. He is concerned about the sexual arousal of the viewer who is already predisposed to committing a crime because such a scene can act as a trigger. "There is no question that [this] type of scene does more harm than a gentle, lovemaking scene however sexually explicit it might be," he said.

Attempts to link sexually explicit material with criminal acts such as rape and murder grew significantly after serial killer Ted Bundy, in an interview before his execution in 1989, blamed pornography for his violent behavior.

Bundy said, "The FBI's own study on serial homicide shows that the most common interest amount serial killers is pornography."

Bundy was referring to a series of interviews the FBI conducted from 1979 to 1983 with 36 male, incarcerated murderers. All the murders were sexual, based on evidence gathered at the crime scene—the victim's attire or lack of attire, positioning of the body, presence of foreign objects in body cavities and signs of sexual intercourse.

The report, which did not focus on pornography, concluded that the murderers' background experience, a "combination of low social attachment, physical, emotional, and/or sexual abuse, and a dominance of a violent, sexually fantasized life sets in motion the attitudes and beliefs that trigger the deviant behavior of rape, mutilation, torture and murder."

Yet researchers argue that other aspects of Bundy's life must be weighed against his avowed interest in pornography. Dorothy Lewis, a clinical professor at Yale University's Child Study Center, who conducted several interviews with Bundy and his family, found a troubled childhood. For a time, Bundy and his mother lived with a grandfather, who was reported to be extremely violent. The grandfather "beat and tortured animals, threw Bundy's aunt down a flight of stairs and generally terrorized the rest of the family," according to researcher Pally's review of Lewis's work.

Gene Abel, a professor of psychiatry at Emory University School of Medicine in Atlanta, wrote: "What we find is that sex offenders have rationalizations and justifications for their behavior. And Ted Bundy, like most of the sadists we've dealt with, had a lot of false beliefs or rationalizations to explain his behavior. What he said, in essence, was, 'It isn't my fault, these are pornographic things that I've seen.' And we just don't see that relationship."

The subject of pornography and violence has also received considerable scrutiny in other countries. Commissions in Britain, Canada and Denmark investigated the effects of sexually explicit material and found no link to violence.

In countries where pornography is legalized, the crime rates for rape and sex offenses have actually decreased, according to a Danish report. A study of reported rape cases from 1964 to 1984 in four countries—Denmark, Sweden, West Germany and the United States—found that the only country that reported increases in rape incidents was the United States, where local obscenity laws can be much stricter.

The increase in U.S. rapes was attributed by the researchers to rape being more an act of violence than a sex crime. "Most other research data we have about pornography and rape suggest that the link between them is . . . weak," writes Berl Kutchinsky, professor of the Institute of Criminal Science at the University of Copenhagen, in his report. "And our knowledge about the contents and the uses of pornography suggests that pornography does not represent a blueprint for rape, but is an aphrodisiac, that is, food for the sexual fantasy of persons."

Meanwhile, efforts to restrict pornography continue. Last February, the Supreme Court of Canada ruled that the country's anti-obscenity law was vital to protecting women and children from the harm caused by degrading magazines and films.

Canada's obscenity law does not prohibit nonviolent, sexually explicit material that would be considered erotica.

Many professionals and women's groups were in favor of maintaining the obscenity law when it was challenged by a Winnipeg adult pornography store owner. He was charged with violating the law by selling and renting material that depicted sexual degradation and violence.

"We wanted the court to see [pornographic] material in the content of women's lives," said Kathleen Mahoney, a professor of law at the University of Calgary. "We had the court look at the types of videos and magazines that in our view did degrade women and show violence and sex combined."

For Evelina Giobbe, the pornography debate is more personal and painful. As founder and program director of Women Hurt in Systems of Prostitution Engaged in Revolt (WHISPER), a nonprofit group in St. Paul, she encounters daily the role pornography plays in keeping women in prostitution.

For all the commission reports and studies that show there is no link between violence and pornography, Giobbe has facts and figures of her own. She bases her data on interviews with 19 women, ages 19 to 37, who worked as prostitutes in the Twin Cities area.

Among some of her findings were that pornography plays a significant role in teaching prostitutes what pimps expect of them, and clients often use pornographic films and magazines to illustrate the kind of activity they want the women to engage in.

Giobbe, who works to get women out of prostitution, said that the more egregious types of pornographic material can bring demands for "sado-masochistic acts, bondage, anal intercourse, acts involving urination and defecation and the shaving of genital hair to give the appearance of prepubescence."

That is a far cry from the glamorized vision of prostitution that is often portrayed in sexually explicit material, on television and R-rated movies, she said.

"The movie *Pretty Woman* was nothing more than a Cinderella prostitution story that reflected nothing about the reality of these women's lives," said Giobbe. "If you think you will be an escort, chatting away in French and English with international businessmen and you later find out your role is to allow a man to use your body in any way he wants, you have to know what lifestyle you are choosing."

But for Marcia Pally, the New York researcher, the premise that getting rid of dirty pictures will make the world a better, safer place is misguided. "To blame social evils on sexual material is so appealing because it is much easier to ban pornography than to deal with the real triggers of violence against women," she said.

To reduce violence, Pally maintains that parents have to examine how they teach children to deal with anger and aggression.

"Real life violence is learned in the nonfantasy, three-dimensional pedagogy of family and community. In every nuance and gesture, one generation instructs the next in the sorts of contempt and violence that are acceptable and expected. However popular it is today to blame two-dimensional media, basic values about men and women, race and religion, sex, money, work and the mores of violence are learned early, at home."

- *Wendy Melillo writes for the* Washington Post.

The Meese Commission

75

"This Week with David Brinkley" A Roundtable Discussion on the Meese Commission

(June 1, 1986)

Interviewers: David Brinkley, Sam Donaldson, George Will.

Participants: Jody Powell. *Guests:* Deanne Tilton (member of the attorney general's Commission on Pornography), Barry W. Lynn (legislative counsel, the American Civil Liberties Union), Rev. Jerry Falwell (from the Liberty Federation), and Bob Guccione (founder and publisher of *Penthouse* magazine).

Reports from ABC Correspondents: Karen Stone and Jack Smith.

David Brinkley: A place calling itself the world's largest retailer of pornography is two blocks from the White House, and, it seems, everywhere else. Magazine racks, movie theaters, videotapes, cable television—a revolution, it is said. But a revolution not everyone has joined, and a commission set up by the U.S. Department of Justice after a long study is about to issue a report saying pornography is harmful and can lead to violence. Is that true? We'll ask today's guests. . . .

Sixteen years ago we had a presidential commission on pornography. It did a long study and then issued a report saying it could find no connection between pornography and violent or criminal behavior. Well, Richard Nixon, who was then president, disliked the finding and disowned the report. Now the new commission says that report is obsolete. It's a different world now and the findings are the opposite. So the argument rages.

Background

Jack Smith: It wasn't very long ago that books we now find in the classics section of our stores, titles like *Ulysses* and *Lady Chatterley's Lover,* were banned as obscene. It is astonishing to reflect how much standards have changed in such a short time. *[Voice-over] Nowadays, almost anything goes and pornography has become a $10-billion-a-year industry. But for many people it has moved too fast and gone too far.*

Leigh Ann Metzger (Eagle Forum): Photographs and depictions of people being victimized, literally abused, women being raped—and this is sold as pornographic material; children being molested and sexually exploited. I think there's got to be a line drawn somewhere.

Pat Fagan (Free Congress Foundation): I do think the fruits of the sexual revolution are sort of apparent to most people, and most people don't like a lot of the fruits.

Smith: Increasingly today, sexual themes are also violent, with women as the victims. And that has split the feminist movement.

Evelina Kane (Women Against Pornography): We feel that pornography is a central element not only in the social subordination of women, but that it's an active element in the sexual abuse of women.

Smith: The Supreme Court placed the burden of defining obscenity on local standards. Since local juries, though, can't decide what these are, pornography is rarely prosecuted. Some cities recently have begun sidestepping the court's ruling by using zoning laws to shut down porn stores; others have successfully jailed the makers of porno films for soliciting prostitution. And the public seems to approve. In an ABC News–*Washington Post* poll this year, 57 percent of Americans said the laws were not strict enough. And that worries legal scholars.

Geoffrey Stone (University of Chicago Law School): A society that values free speech, values free speech not because it's harmless, but values free speech even when it is harmful.

Metzger: I'm really kind of tired of that argument. The First Amendment belongs to all Americans and it doesn't belong just to broadcasters or certainly not just to the pornographers. And there is no First Amendment right to obscenity.

Edwin Meese (U.S. Attorney General, May 1985): We are dealing with a general tendency that is pervading our entire culture.

Smith: Attorney General Meese last year decided a commission was in order to study pornography, and after a year of holding hearings it will publish its report in July. It's expected to recommend tightening the obscenity laws and prosecuting stores that sell obscene material and will encourage citizens' groups to monitor newsstands, video stores and even local judges. But its most controversial and damaging conclusion is a finding that substantial exposure to most pornography today bears some causal relationship to sexual violence or rape.

Barry Lynn: This commission was truly stacked from the beginning.

Smith: The commission's objectivity has been challenged, because many of its members have backgrounds in law enforcement. And its conclusions linking pornography to rape have been questioned even by some on the commission itself.

Judith Becker (commission member): If you're talking purely about scientific data showing that you expose somebody to something and absolutely that is the only cause of why they engage in that type of behavior, I have not seen any definitive proof.

Smith: Nevertheless, liberals are alarmed because they fear the report will become the foundation for new attacks on the First Amendment.

Alan Dershowitz (Harvard Law School): The issue here is not pornography. The issue here is choice. The issue is whether somebody tells us what we can read.

Smith: This already appears to be happening.

Jerry Falwell: No, we don't thank heaven for 7-Eleven; we will no longer purchase your products until you respect our families.

Smith: Anti-porn groups have recently been trying to force major chains to stop selling men's magazines like *Playboy* and *Penthouse*. And two months ago the nation's 7-Eleven stores caved in.

Jerry Thompson (president of Southland Corporation, which owns 7-Eleven): We made the decision to discontinue selling these magazines in our company-operated stores.

Smith: But civil libertarians say the real reason was pressure from Washington.

Dershowitz: The Meese Commission sent out a letter to 7-Eleven and other stores, threatening them with inclusion on a blacklist to be published by the government unless they stopped selling *Penthouse* and *Playboy* magazine.

Smith: The commission denies it and says it simply felt obliged to let companies who had been named in testimony respond before that testimony got published. Nevertheless, *Playboy* and *Penthouse* are suing the commission.

Burton Joseph (attorney for Playboy Enterprises): It is an attempt at intimidation to affect perfectly legal, perfectly constitutional, perfectly lawful books and magazines and films.

Fagan: The free speech argument—again, I come back to the present lawsuit being brought against the commission—is a fraud, because those who have been saying it all the time are now trying to block free speech of a very public document.

Smith: First Amendment disputes are as old as the Republic, but there's something new in this one. If pornography does indeed cause injury, that might, as with libel, justify limits to free speech. This is why the commission has caused such an uproar, for by linking pornography to violence it could change the terms of a very old debate.

The Roundtable Discussion

Brinkley: Now, Ms. Tilton, you are a member of the commission whose report we're going to be discussing here, the report of the attorney general's Commission on Pornography. Now, you have numerous critics, as you're well aware, many of whom say that you did not get a full spectrum of opinion in putting together this report, that you had too many law enforcement people and too few social scientists who have studied this problem. What would you say to that?

Tilton: We had many social scientists that studied this problem. We did have a great number of law enforcement officers. We did offer opportunity to those who were not in either of those fields to testify. Most of what we received, the predominance was written material, although we did hear from both sides, and the responsibility was really on us to weigh that accordingly.

Brinkley: Mr. Lynn, are you one of those making this criticism? I think you are.

Lynn: I certainly am. I think that this commission began with most of its members being highly biased against pornography and in favor of censorship long before they were appointed to the commission, and they then engaged in a process of data-gathering that included national hearings from which they held testimony, 77 percent of which was from anti-pornography zealots of one kind or another. So basically what we've had is a biased group looking at the evidence of anti-pornography groups and individuals. They did hear from social scientists. Most of the social scientists, however, begged them not to take very limited studies and use that as the basis for developing public policy that would lead to censorship. . . . [T]he commission . . . called for a real crackdown on sexually oriented material and made the utterly unsubstantiated claim that somehow science proves a connection between consumption of sexual material and sexual violence. The scientists asked them not to do that. They've subsequently criticized the report, and I think what we really have is a commission that cannot honestly say that if pornography disappeared tomorrow, this would be much of a safer society for women or children in our country today.

Will: Mr. Lynn, let's take as given the fact that science can neither establish nor disprove a connection between violence and pornography and move on to another question: In your opinion, or the opinion of your organization, is there anything the government or the community is allowed to do about pornography? That is, is it reasonable or, in your view, inherently unreasonable for any government at any level to do anything to restrict the distribution of pornography in the name of affirming certain community values, using the law in an expressive function?

Lynn: I think occasionally that the law can be utilized to help parents control the kind of material that comes into their home—for example, mandating lock boxes on cable television so that parents can keep out of their home the things that they do not want their children to see. But beyond that I think any government action, any censorship at all, is always the wrong solution for any perceived problem. Now—

Will: But Mr. Lynn, the existence of Times Square, for example—is sort of a public phenomenon. That results from treating pornography, does it not, as a private transaction between a consumer and a buyer. By treating pornography that way, all of a sudden you have enormous manifestations like Times Square.

Lynn: There are very few manifestations like that, however. You really find that you can walk down 99.9 percent of the streets in this country and never come across a sexually explicit image. You can find a lot of sexist images in advertising and on television, but you don't see pornography. Pornography does not come out and literally or figuratively assault most people. I think that what you're concerned about is the general level of the attitude that's fostered by pornography. And I don't think, however, that we can use the powers of the state or federal governments to suppress bad attitudes, the creation of unpleasant ideas or images. And much of the pornography's view is certainly, to my way of thinking, morally and aesthetically, very offensive. But I don't think the power of the state can be used to suppress that.

Donaldson: Ms. Tilton, let me ask you about a letter the commission wrote to a number of organizations, companies that sell *Penthouse*, *Playboy*, and other magazines [see sidebar]. It's said that this letter was an attempt to put them on a blacklist and to threaten them by commission action even before you had examined the subject.

Tilton: Yes. I would very much like to respond to that, but I'm afraid I cannot because there is pending litigation at this time. I would like to respond to that at a future date. But may I respond to some of the statements made by Mr. Lynn?

Donaldson: Please.

Tilton: Our report does not call for a tightening of obscenity laws. It does not state that there is a cause-and-effect relationship between all pornography and crime. If one reads the report, one can see that the body of the report is informational and provides information on both sides. There are 92 recommendations that are included in this report, and over half of them deal with child pornography. And I am concerned that most of the media coverage on this report focuses on a very small portion of what is included and does not include some very substantial, important recommendations for the protection of children both from accessing pornography or obscenity and also from participating or being used as victims in the production. Certainly the report states that there are potential harms that may result to a vulnerable population. My personal opinion is that that is primarily in the violent pornography category. We did not scientifically show that there was a cause-and-effect relationship. I want to clarify that, because it was not shown. It was a totality of the evidence that led the commission to state that violent pornography may have an effect on the behavior of some people. I would very clearly not want the public to take this as a mandate to run forward for stricter prosecution, because we did not change the obscenity laws or intend to.

Lynn: Ms. Tilton—

Tilton: This is absolutely true. And all of the recommendations merely deal with enforcing the existing obscenity laws.

Lynn: But as this commission realized from hearing from law enforcement people, for example, in Cincinnati and Atlanta, you can use the existing laws to remove virtually all sexually oriented material from a city with vigorous prosecution. So when this report calls for a massive effort at the state, local and federal level against all kinds of sexually oriented material, I'd say that's pretty dramatic. And I also would have to dispute the conclusion that most of this has something to do with violence or children or this kind of pornography. What this report does is to call for a crackdown even on that material that is not violence, that is not—even in Ms. Tilton's words—harmful. It is a crackdown even on mutual, loving, consensual portrayals of explicit sexual conduct. They didn't say exempt that from prosecution under obscenity laws. They said full steam ahead with obscenity laws to get rid of all kinds of sexually-oriented material in our society. And I think that's dramatic. I also think it's unusual—

Brinkley: Ms. Tilton, I'll give you the last word. Our time is about up.

Tilton: Yes, I disagree with Mr. Lynn that it calls for a crackdown on non-obscene material. I want to point out that there are recommendations for national forums to look at the extent of molestation of children in the production of pornography and the effects of pornography on children. There are many recommendations trying to bring to the public's attention that there is victimization, that our criminal court system does not respond to the needs of children who are exploited, and the body of the report dealing with law enforcement merely speaks to those issues regarding prosecution of existing obscene material, and that information is just that. It is information that is provided to the public. I hope the public takes it in that light.

Brinkley (to Falwell): The Supreme Court and others have said in so many words that they cannot say what pornography is. One court ruling, as I recall it, said, "I can't define it but I know it when I see it." Can you define it?

Falwell: Well, I've said repeatedly that I think pornography is the literature of deviants. But beyond that the Supreme Court also has ruled that communities may set their own standards and may in fact do just what the Meese Commission is recommending—take a very clear stand against what offends that particular community. And I commend Mr. Meese.

Brinkley: Mr. Guccione, can you define it?

Guccione: No. I don't think anybody can define it. And the Meese Commission itself, incidentally, agreed that trying to find the definition for pornography was futile.

Donaldson: Mr. Guccione, you print a lot of stuff that a lot of people think is dirty. How do you defend printing it?

Guccione: I don't think anything that we publish is dirty. When you talk about pornography, what exactly are we talking about? There is no definition. There is no legal content of the term "pornography."

Donaldson: Does anything go, then?

Guccione: You have to say—

Donaldson: Any sort of pictures, any sort of—

Guccione: Certainly not, because there is a legal question, and that is called obscenity. If anything that I or anyone else publishes can be called obscene under our laws, we have the court system to deal with that problem. We don't need Jerry Falwell or the Meese Commission to make recommendations dealing with some question as obscure as the word "pornography." There are guidelines to tell us what obscenity is. As I say, it could be dealt with in the courts.

Donaldson: Well, Mr. Guccione, you once printed an interview with Rev. Jerry Falwell, and he sued you for $50 million.

Guccione: And he lost.

Donaldson: Well, Reverend Falwell, what was wrong with the interview that was printed in *Penthouse* magazine?

Falwell: Oh, there wasn't a thing wrong with the interview. The interview was accurate. It was stolen, of course. Two writers who purported to be writing for other publications were in fact selling it to Mr. Guccione. But, nevertheless, it was a very accurate interview. The only thing I objected to was casting pearl among swine and having my interview sandwiched in among some of the garbage that Guccione prints.

Guccione: Well, who's the pearl and who's the swine, Mr. Falwell? We did not steal the interview. We paid for it. It was offered to us for sale and we purchased it.

Will: Mr. Falwell, in response to David's question about what pornography is, you took a complicated term, pornography, and substituted another difficult one; that is, you said it is the literature of deviants. Now, this is a country in which 75 million people rented pornographic—adult, as they're called—tapes last year to show in their own living rooms. Pornography is a multi-billion-dollar industry. Given this, the fact that Americans are sort of voting with their dollars in a way that conservatives say a market is, after all, a form of democratic voting, why isn't it fair to say that pornography now is accepted as part of the recreation of this nation, as demonstrated by market spending?

Falwell: Well, I haven't been very involved in the legal side of this. Frankly, we have been going at this from the free enterprise perspective; that is, we have mobilized millions of Americans—even feminists are working with us who may not agree on other issues—who do believe that pornography is demeaning to women whose bodies are exploited for commerce. We've been working together with millions of families, men, women, young people, to talk and discuss with the chief executive officers in major corporations like Southland, like Thrifty, like Rite-Aid, and now there are 24,000 such retail outlets that no longer sell Mr. Guccione's product—

Guccione: Let me—can I—

Falwell: That has nothing to do with legality. It had to do with free enterprise. If we do not wish to buy at a place that sells the garbage, we just simply advise the people of that and then they make their own decisions.

Will: Well, we come up against this problem. For example, you're targeting, and I guess your greatest success so far is to get *Playboy* and similar magazines off, say, the newsstands of 7-Eleven. The President's son is a contributing editor of *Playboy*. William Buckley writes for *Playboy*.

Guccione: And *Penthouse*.

Will: And *Penthouse,* I am now told. Are you quite sure that you are representing community values, and if so, what community?

Falwell: Well, may I say that no owner or stockholder or CEO of a grocery outlet or chain of stores need respond if they do not think we represent a community. The fact is that 24,000 outlets the last five years have listened to what Don Wildmon, the National Federation for Decency, Moral Majority,

Liberty Federation, and PTA and other groups have said to them—that we do not want pornography at the eye-level of a five-year-old child in a grocery store, a convenience store, or we don't want to support those outlets that are making their money off demeaning the women of this country.

Brinkley: Mr. Guccione, you want to get into this?

Guccione: Yes, I'd certainly like to respond. Firstly, Mr. Falwell is correct when he says that he and the Reverend Donald Wildmon have been bringing extreme pressure against these retail chains for a number of years. They've been picketing them, barraging them with hate mail, boycotting them, and so on, but this hasn't made a single scintilla of difference. Those stores continue to stock *Penthouse, Playboy,* and other magazines. It was not until the attorney general's letter signed by Sears and sent out under the stationery of the Justice Department reached these various chains that caused them within five or six weeks of the receipt of this letter to drop *Penthouse, Playboy, Forum,* and other magazines. So to me that's too coincidental. It is not the work of Jerry Falwell. It is the work of the Meese Commission conspiring with Falwell, Wildmon, and others. Let me just throw in one interesting fact. *Newsweek* recently conducted a Gallup poll on porn. They asked the question—and this was a national poll—how many of you have ever read *Penthouse* or *Playboy?* Sixty-seven percent, or two out of every three Americans, said yes. That means 84 percent of all men and 50 percent of all women. Now, that's a pretty big constituency, and when you stop to think that *Penthouse* is seen by 24 million people every single month in this country, let Jerry Falwell tell me that he has mustered a bigger class of people than those.

Falwell: Well, I would say to this, Bob, that I would think the percentages would be larger if you asked, "How many of you have ever seen or read one," because I have personally read your magazine so that I know what I am talking about. I would imagine most ministers have. That does not mean that many people find their newsworthy information in your magazine. Going to *Penthouse* or *Playboy* to get good journalism is like going to the city dump to buy your groceries, and I don't believe for a moment that people do that.

Guccione: People's Drugstores in Washington conducted a similar poll. They found out that of all the people that patronized their stores, only 4 percent disapproved of the magazines—

Falwell: Well, why did they stop selling the magazine?

Guccione: Because they also received the attorney general's letter, the infamous letter, a copy of which I hold in my hands right here.

Brinkley: George, you started a question?

Will: Yes, Mr. Falwell, the letter that Mr. Guccione is concerned about alarmed some other people, and I'd like your opinion of it as a conservative who is sort of against intrusive and coercive government. The letter contained the implied threat that distributors of *Playboy* and *Penthouse* might be listed as distributors of pornography, identified that way. Does that alarm you a bit when the government goes beyond, say, your private citizen's action and also becomes the encourager of the kind of boycotts that you're conducting?

Falwell: I think that's rather good, and I would support that by saying that for the same reason we have found it necessary to have government intrusion in the drug market. For example, heroin is illegal. Narcotics are illegal in this country. I hope they always are. I hope that marijuana is always illegal to sell or distribute or use. And I don't think that's intrusion. I think that is the protection, as the Constitution says, of the general welfare; likewise, pornography, obviously, having no redemptive value whatsoever, is damaging to the public and I think government has a right to protect the general welfare.

Donaldson: Explain your view that pornography has no redemptive value. Why would people buy it, then?

Falwell: Well, people buy heroin. I don't think anybody thinks that heroin has redemptive value. We live in a race of men and women who are capable of breaking the law, of doing things that are not good for themselves or others. And government is supposed to be that organization, that entity that protects people from themselves and from others.

Donaldson: Well, of course, one definition—

Guccione: May I say something, please?

Donaldson:—of redemption is in the eye of the beholder. Heroin produces a medical problem which kills people; heroin is as well an addiction.

Falwell: Well, so does pornography, and my personal opinion—and I think there's definite support for it, and I know Mr. Guccione knows this—is that even though Mr. Johnson's commission did not come out the way most people would like for it to have come out, it did in fact prove that over 50 percent of all persons in prison for having committed a sex crime admitted that they did that immediately after an experience with pornography. Now, if that isn't a causal relationship, I don't know what is.

Donaldson: Well, Reverend Falwell—

Brinkley: Mr. Guccione?

Donaldson: May I just follow that up? Reverend Falwell, a lot of the people who go to church commit crimes and I don't think that it's fair to blame the fact that they went to church on the fact that they commit crimes. Why do you make this association?

Falwell: Well, I don't think in church, in a congregation, anyone gets up as a pastor, whether Catholic or a rabbi in a synagogue, and suggests that you go out and rape a little girl or molest a little boy or show things that arouse people sexually.

Donaldson: Mr. Guccione, does your magazine suggest that you go out and rape someone or molest a little boy?

Guccione: Certainly not, and may I say that the argument that Mr. Falwell presented a moment ago was extremely stupid and fallacious, to compare something like heroin with magazines like *Penthouse* and *Playboy*. Heroin is certainly illegal and it is certainly harmful. But *Penthouse* and *Playboy* are neither illegal nor are they harmful, and they are protected by the First Amendment. They are protected by the Constitution of the United States, and certainly drugs are not protected by the Constitution. So that it is typical of the Falwell argument, to make and say anything which suits his own ends, which serves his purposes.

Falwell: Bob, I'm not suggesting—

Brinkley: Hold on. Let him finish, Mr. Falwell, let him finish.

Falwell: Fine.

Guccione: And also, just to clear the matter a little further, two of the four women on the Meese Commission—Dr. Judith Becker and Ellen Levine—have both said in their dissenting remarks that no self-respecting investigator should rely on this, the Meese report. And Dr. Donnerstein, who is this country's leading authority on sexual violence and upon whom the Meese Commission relied entirely, commented that the commission's conclusions were bizarre.

Brinkley: Mr. Falwell, now.

Falwell: I was in a meeting Friday with Mr. Alan Sears, the executive director of the Meese Commission, in which he pointed out that not just that those two persons just mentioned were in dissent but nine others were very much supportive of what Mr. Meese is saying and what the commission is in the majority saying. And the fact is that pornography is not good for public health. Now, I'm not suggesting that we stop—

Guccione: It simply isn't true.

Falwell:—Mr. Guccione from printing his salacious magazine. I'm simply saying that we out in the private sector have a right, whether we be PTA members or church members or whatever, to decide where we buy our goods. And if we decide that we don't want to buy our goods the same place that Mr. Guccione's goods are sold, that is our constitutional right and we've decided that, and the industries around the country.

By the way, Bob, there are a dozen other major retail outlets that will be announcing the removal of your material in the next three weeks. And so the worst is yet to come, as far as you're concerned.

Donaldson: Mr. Guccione, do you think that Reverend Falwell can put you out of business?

Guccione: Absolutely not. And let me say something else, too. When he continually talks about free enterprise and that he and others like him have the right—

Donaldson: Could I just follow that up? You say absolutely not.

Guccione: Of course not.

Donaldson: That's very brave talk. But in fact, if you can't distribute your magazine, how are you going to be able to—

Guccione: But he's talking about the retail chains, the people most likely to give in to something like this blacklist threat.

Falwell: That's where you sell most of your magazines.

Guccione: But there are something like 75,000 to 80,000 retail outlets in which we are in, owned independently by people who are not going to be persuaded either by Falwell or the Meese Commission. Now, we brought our lawsuit against the Meese Commission for this very purpose, to show that they have been using the offices of the government and the power of the attorney general's office to influence people, to intimidate.

Will: Mr. Guccione, some people will say Mr. Falwell may draw the line in the wrong spot, but at least he knows that drawing lines is important. Do you draw the line anywhere?

Guccione: Of course we do.

Will: Where?

Guccione: When you talk about child pornography, that is something that would never appear in *Penthouse,* certainly never appear in *Playboy* or any of the other mainstream men's magazines. And that, as I said before, can be dealt with through the courts. If someone were to print child pornography, he can be successfully prosecuted. He could be incarcerated and fined and done away with—

Will: Because it's dangerous?

Guccione: And that's how you handle it.

Will: Because it's dangerous?

Guccione: Because child pornography can be dangerous, not because it would be read by children or looked at and understood by children, but because children are being used against their will. But the girls who appear in *Penthouse* and *Playboy* are girls who are appearing there because they want to, because they are being paid to, because they believe it's a step into show business and in most cases it is. And everybody is happy. The readers are happy, we're happy. Everybody but Jerry Falwell is happy.

But in dealing with children or people who cannot defend themselves or cannot speak up for their own rights, that is an intrusion on their privacy, and that is something that should be dealt with legally.

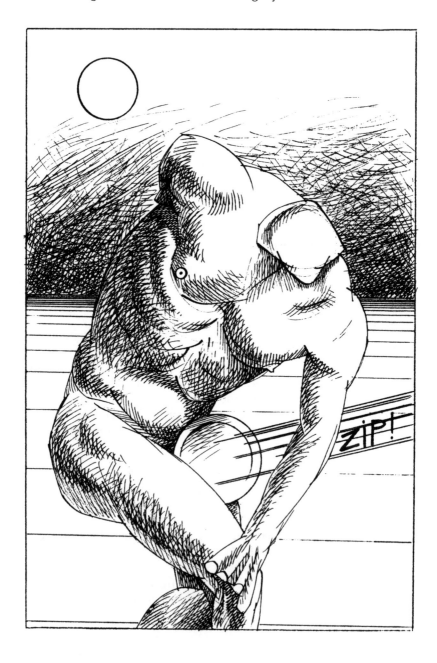

Letter from the Attorney General's Commission on Pornography

As Porteous wrote in Jesus Doesn't Live Here Anymore, *this letter, typed on Department of Justice stationery, signed by Alan Sears (executive director of the Attorney General's Commission on Pornography), was sent out in 1986 "to the heads of convenience stories and other chains which sold magazines such as* Playboy *and* Penthouse.*"*

The Attorney General's Commission on Pornography has held six hearings across the United States during the past seven months on issues related to pornography. During the hearing in Los Angeles, in October 1985, the Commission received testimony alleging that your company is involved in the sale or distribution of pornography. The Commission has determined that it would be appropriate to allow your company an opportunity to respond to the allegation prior to drafting its final report section on identified distributors.

You will find a copy of the relevant testimony enclosed herewith. Please review the allegations and advise the Commission on or before March 3, 1986, if you disagree with the statements enclosed. Failure to respond will necessarily be accepted as an indication of no objection.

Thank you for your assistance.

Porteous, commenting on the letter, wrote in Jesus Doesn't Live Here Anymore:

The "relevant testimony" mentioned in the letter was actually a report titled "Pornography in the Family Marketplace," prepared by Donald Wildmon. The report opened with: "Few people realize that 7-Eleven convenience stores are the leading retailers of porn magazines in America." It continued to say that if 7-Eleven discontinued the sale of porn, "*Playboy* and *Penthouse* would be seriously crippled financially."

Of course, Rev. Wildmon wasn't mentioned in the Justice Department letter, or the report enclosed with the letter. A letter of this type from the U.S. Department of Justice is certain to have a chilling effect on its recipients. And, indeed, it did. Shortly afterward, the Southland Corporation, with 8,100 company-owned 7-Eleven convenience stores, announced that it was pulling the magazines. Other companies did likewise.

Several months earlier, I had spoken to an official at Southland who assured me that the company would not bow to these self-styled censors. Well, they bowed all right, after the U.S. Department of Justice played into the hands of the censors. What is ironic is that the two magazines mentioned in Wildmon's report [*Playboy* and *Penthouse*] are constitutionally protected. Even Wildmon agrees with that.

76

"The Risks of Abuse"

from *Attorney General's Commission on Pornography Final Report, July 1986* (pp. 269–75)

Although we are satisfied that there is a category of material so overwhelmingly preoccupied with sexual explicitness, and so overwhelmingly devoid of anything else, that its regulation does no violence to the principles underlying the First Amendment, we recognize that this cannot be the end of the First Amendment analysis. We must evaluate the possibility that in practice materials other than these will be restricted, and that the effect therefore will be the restriction of materials that are substantially closer to what the First Amendment ought to protect than the items in fact aimed at by the *Miller* definition of obscenity. We must also evaluate what is commonly referred to as the "chilling effect," the possibility that, even absent actual restriction, creators of material that is not in fact legally obscene will refrain from those creative activities, or will steer further to the safe side of the line, for fear that their protected works will mistakenly be deemed obscene. And finally we must evaluate whether the fact of restriction of obscene material will act, symbolically, to foster a "censorship mentality" that will in less immediate ways encourage or lead to various restrictions, in other contexts, of material which ought not in a free society to be restricted. We have heard in one form or another from numerous organizations of publishers, booksellers, actors, and librarians, as well as from a number of individual book and magazine publishers. Although most have urged general anti-censorship sentiments upon us, their oral and written submissions have failed to provide us with evidence to support claims of excess suppression in the name of the obscenity laws, and indeed the evidence is to the contrary. The president of the Association of American Publishers testified that to his knowledge none of his members had even been threatened with enforcement of the criminal law against obscenity, and the American Library Association could find no record of any prosecution of a library on obscenity charges. Other groups of people involved in publishing, bookselling, or theatrical organizations relied exclusively on examples of excess censorship from periods of time no more recent than the 1940s. And still others were even less helpful, telling us, for example, that censorship was impermissible because "This is the United States, not the Soviet Union." We know that, but we know as well that difficult issues do not become easy by the use of inflammatory rhetoric. We wish that many of these people or groups had been able to provide concrete examples to support their fears of excess censorship.

Throughout recent and not so recent history, excess censorship, although not necessarily prevalent, can hardly be said not to have occurred. As a result we have not been content to rest on the hollowness of the assertions of many of those who have reminded us of this theme. If there is a problem, we have our own obligations to identify it, even if witnesses before us have been unable to do so. Yet when we do our own researches, we discover that, with few exceptions, the period from 1974* to the present is marked by strikingly few actual or threatened prosecutions of material that is plainly not legally obscene. We do not say that there have been none. Attempted and unsuccessful actions against the film *Caligula* by the United States Customs Service, against *Playboy* magazine in Atlanta and several other places, and against some other plainly non-obscene publications indicate that mistakes *can* be made. But since 1974 such mistakes have been extremely rare, and the mistakes have all been remedied at some point in the process. While we wish there would be no mistakes, we are confident that application of *Miller* has been overwhelmingly limited to materials that would satisfy anyone's definition of "hard core."

Even absent success or seriously threatened prosecutions, it still may be the case that the very possibility of such an action deters filmmakers, photographers, and writers from exercising their creative abilities to the fullest. Once it appears that the likelihood of actual or seriously threatened prosecutions is almost completely illusory, however, we are in a quandary about how to respond to these claims of "chilling." We are in no position to deny the reality of someone's fears, but in almost every case those fears are unfounded. Where, as here, the fears seem to be fears of phantom dangers, we are hard pressed to say that the law is mistaken. It is those who are afraid who are mistaken. At least for the past ten years, no even remotely serious author, photographer, or filmmaker has had anything real to fear from the obscenity laws. The line between what is legally obscene and what is not is now so far away from their work that even substantially mistaken applications of current law would leave these individuals untouched. In light of that, we do not see their fears, however real to them, as a sufficient reason now to reconsider our views about the extent of First Amendment protection.

Much more serious, much more real, and much less in our control, is the extent to which non-governmental or governmental but non-prohibitory actions may substantially influence what is published and what is not. What television scriptwriters write is in reality controlled by what television producers will buy, which is in turn controlled by what sponsors will sponsor and what

---

*1974 seems the most relevant date because that was the year in which the Supreme Court, in *Jenkins* v. *Georgia*, 418 U.S. 153 (1974), made it clear that determinations of obscenity were not primarily a matter of local discretion.

viewers will view. Screenwriters may be effectively censored by the extent to which producers or studios desire to gain an "R" rating rather than an "X," or a "PG" rather than an "R," or an "R" rather than a "PG." Book and magazine writers and publishers are restricted by what people are willing to buy. Writers of textbooks are in a sense censored by what school districts and librarians are willing to offer, and librarians are censored by what boards of trustees are willing to tolerate.

In all of these settings there have been excesses. But every one of these settings involves some inevitable choice based on content. We think it unfortunate when *Catcher in the Rye* is unavailable in a high school library, but none of us would criticize the decision to keep *Lady Chatterley's Lover,* plainly protected by the First Amendment, out of the junior high schools.

We regret the legitimate bookstores have been pressured to remove from their shelves legitimate and serious discussions of sexuality, but none of us would presume to tell a Catholic bookseller that in choosing books he should not discriminate against books favoring abortion. Motion picture studios are unable to support an infinite number of screenwriters, and their choice to support those who write about families rather than about homosexuality, for example, is not only permissible, but is indeed itself protected by the First Amendment.

Where there have been excesses, and we do not ignore the extent to which the number of those excesses seems to be increasing, they seem often attributable to the plainly mistaken notion that the idea of "community standards" is a carte blanche to communities to determine entirely for themselves what is obscene. As we have tried once again to make clear in this report, nothing could be further from the truth. Apart from this, however, the excesses that have been reported to us are excesses that can only remotely be attributed to the obscenity laws. In a world of choice and of scarce resources, every one of these excesses could take place even were there no obscenity laws at all. In a world without obscenity law, television producers, motion picture studios, public library trustees, boards of education, convenience stores, and bookstores could still all choose to avoid any mention or discussion of sex entirely. And in a world without obscenity laws, all of these institutions and others could and would still make censorious choices based on their own views about politics, morals, religion, or science. Thus, the link between obscenity law and the excess[ive] narrowness, at times, of the choices made by private industry as well as government is far from direct.

Although the link is not direct, we are in no position to deny that there may be some psychological connection between obscenity laws and their enforcement and a general perception that non-governmental restriction of anything dealing with sex is justifiable. We find the connection unjustifiable, but that is not to say that it may not exist in the world. But just as vigorous and vocal enforcement of robbery laws may create the environment in which vigilantes feel justified in punishing offenders outside of legal processes, so too may obscenity law create an environment in which discussions of sexuality are effectively stifled. But we cannot ignore the extent to which much of this stifling, to the extent it exists, is no more than the exercise by citizens of their First Amendment rights to buy what they want to buy, and the exercise by others of First Amendment rights to sell or make what they wish. Choices are not always exercised wisely, but the leap from some unwise choices to the unconstitutionality of criminal laws only remotely related to those unwise choices is too big a leap for us to make.

77

On the Meese Commission and the First Amendment

by Kurt Vonnegut

> Everyone has the right to freedom of opinion and expression; this right includes freedom to hold opinions, without interference and to seek, receive, and impart information and ideas through any media regardless of frontiers.
>
> —Article 19, United Nation's Universal Declaration of Human Rights

I have read much of the heart-rending testimony extracted from victims of sexual abuse at meetings of the Attorney General's Commission on Pornography. It is clear to me that our government must be given the power to suppress the words and images which are the causes of sexually motivated insanity and crimes. As the Bible says: "In the beginning was the word."

I myself make my living with words, and I am now ashamed. In view of the terrible damage freely circulated ideas can do to a society, and particularly to innocent children, I beg my government to delete from my works all thoughts which might be dangerous. I want the help of our elected leaders in bringing my thoughts into harmony with their own and thus into harmony with the thoughts of those who elected them. That is democracy.

Attempting to make amends at this late date, I call to the attention of the Attorney General's Commission on Pornography, and God bless the attorney general, the fundamental piece of obscenity from which all others spring, the taproot of the deadly poisonous tree. Kill the taproot and the tree dies, and with it its deadly fruits, which are rape, sodomy, wife-beating, child abuse, divorce, abortion, adultery, gonorrhea, herpes, and AIDS.

I will read this most vile of all pieces of so-called literature aloud, so that those who dare can feel the full force of it. I recommend that all persons under 14, and all persons under 30 not accompanied by an adult, should leave the room. Those remaining who have heart trouble or respiratory difficulties, or who are prone to commit rape at the slightest provocation, may want to stick their fingers in their ears. And what I ask you to endure so briefly now is what the selfless members of the pornography commission do day after day for the good of our children. I am simply going to dip you in filth, and pull you out of it and wash you off immediately. At terrible risk of infection, they have to wallow in pornography. They are so fearless. We might think of them as sort of sewer astronauts.

All right. Everybody ready? Tighten your G-strings. Here we go:

> Congress shall make no law respecting an establishment of religion, or prohibiting the free exercise thereof; or abridging the freedom of speech, or of the press; or the right of the people peaceably to assemble, and to petition the Government for a redress of grievances.

That Godless loop of disgusting sexuality, friends and neighbors, happens to be a basic law of this country. How could this have happened? Some communistic, pederastic, wife-beating congressman, while we weren't watching, must have tacked it onto the Rivers and Harbors bill. It should be expunged with all possible haste, in order that innocent children can be safe again.

Adolf Hitler blamed the Jews for inspiring every sort of sexual ugliness in Germany, so he tried to kill them all. Say what you like about him, incidentally, it can't be denied that he led an exceedingly clean life sexually. In the end, he made an honest woman of his only sexual partner, Eva Braun.

Oh dear—have I slipped into pornography yet again? It is so easy to do.

Hitler was wrong about the Jews. It is unclean images which are responsible for unclean sexuality.

In order to protect innocent German children, all he had to do was get rid of the First Amendment. In no way can this be interpreted as an anti-Semitic act. The authors of that amendment, Thomas Jefferson and James Madison, were not Jews.

It is not enough that sex crimes of every sort are already against the law, and are punished with admirable severity. It is up to our leaders, and particularly to our attorney general, to persuade a large part of our citizenry that even the most awful sex crimes are perfectly legal, and even celebrated in some godless quarters, because of the permissiveness of our Constitution. Only then will an aroused and thoroughly misinformed citizenry rise up in righteous wrath to smash the First Amendment—and many other only slightly less offensive parts of the Bill of Rights.

Once the findings of the Attorney General's Commission on Pornography are published for all to see, whether they can read or not, what sort of American would dare to defend liberty, whose cost is so horrible? I'll tell you what kind of an American, friends and neighbors: the sort of American who would rape a three-year-old girl, drench her in lighter fluid, set her ablaze, and throw her off a fire escape.

As we used to say in geometry class back in public school when I was a boy: "Q.E.D.—quod erat demonstrandum."

I thank you for your attention.

Sexuality: Different Voices

78

On Women and Pornography

by Anne Rice

In recent years several anthologies of erotica by women for women have been published. In the best of these anthologies, like Yellow Silk, *the exploration of female sexuality is a far cry from male pornography with its male-subordinating-female fantasies; instead, women's erotica tends to be more dreamy, evocative; clearly sensual, and unabashedly sexual.*

Although it has become politically correct to endorse feminists like Andrea Dworkin and Catherine McKinnon who take the position that all pornography debases women, other women are justifiably concerned that Dworkin and McKinnon's voices are taken as representative for all women. The writers of an antipornography bill that has yet to be adopted in the U.S., Dworkin and MacKinnon's draconian recommendations foreshadowed the Bundy bill; both would have a chilling effect on the publishing climate, and for that reason neither to date has passed.

Anne Rice has written her version of Lolita (Belinda), *a trilogy of erotic fiction under the pen name A.N. Roquelaure, soft-core mainstream bondage novels, and the lush and sensual Vampire Chronicles featuring the Vampire Lestat. In this excerpt from an interview, she speaks for all those women who feel female sexuality must seek full expression, and the militant feminists be damned.*

Women as sexual beings haven't been out of the closet for more than about twenty years. What I see now is the closet door being slammed back in our face by an alliance of feminists, Moral Majority conservatives, and old-guard liberals who seek more to protect women as victims of male sexuality than to argue for equal rights or the rights of women to express themselves sexually. To me this is very frightening. . . . I largely see feminists as my enemy. Although I see myself almost as a radical feminist, at this point in history there are many vocal reactionary, repressive feminists who are trying to get pornography banned and trying to interfere with the expression of sexual desire in art. . . . [Andrea

Dworkin and Catharine MacKinnon] have been indulged. If the kind of anti-pornography legislation which they advocate were pushed by two fundamentalist Baptist ministers from the Bible Belt, it would be laughed out of the public arena overnight. But because Dworkin and MacKinnon are women and are supposed to be feminists, they have confused well-meaning liberals everywhere. People have bent over backward to understand their position when they don't deserve any leeway—because Dworkin and MacKinnon have no respect for free speech, for the Constitution of the United States, or for rights that have mattered to the rest of us for hundreds of years, rights that have evolved out of English common law.

If you link pornography to rape, then, as I understand it, a woman would have the right to sue *Playboy* magazine if she felt *Playboy* incited some man to rape her. But then, logically, the man could turn around and sue *Playboy* for making him rape her. Or he could say, "The movie made me do it. I was so obsessed after viewing *The Tool Box Murders* that I couldn't stop myself." Once you place blame outside the man for the rape, it's only one jump to sticking it right back on provocative clothing: "She made me do it because she wore a red dress and gold bracelets."

Dworkin and MacKinnon are really questioning whether people have free will. This is as true for the rapist as for the porn star. But I think people must be held responsible for their actions. When Dworkin and MacKinnon say that a woman who has signed a contract to be in a porn film should not be held to it, what does this mean? That women don't have free will to sign contracts? If it is a question of coercion, fine. Coercion happens. But there are already laws on the books for that.

Americans don't really want censorship from their government. They don't want Linda Lovelace to be hurt either, but they want to be able to go to that corner video store and rent *Deep Throat* and find out what it's about. Middle-class Americans are renting these tapes by the millions. To me, that shows the sexual revolution is still going on to a large extent, and I think that's healthy and wholesome. The Meese Commission made noise but had little impact.

79

Interview: William Margold

Conducted by George Beahm

A twenty-year veteran of the adult entertainment film industry, William Margold is the industry spokesman for the Adult Video Association. Through FOXE (Fans of X-rated Entertainment), the organization which he founded and which now has 1,200 members, Margold is (as he puts it) "the first X-rated evangelist in history, preaching the gospel of X."

Margold, who holds a degree in journalism, emphasizes that he has worked in "every" capacity in the industry: as actor, writer, director, critic, publicist, and most recently spokesperson. On talk shows and on the lecture circuit, Margold, as he explains, "keeps abreast of our enemies—the sexually guilty moralists who seek to crucify the creativity of consenting adults."

Quick to coin phrases, Margold is most proud of the ad line to a movie he wrote, directed, and starred in. The movie was Lust Inferno, *the subject was televangelists, and the ad line simply said, "He brought them to their knees, but not to pray." Shot in 1982, it predated by three years the scandals that erupted when Jim Bakker and Jimmy Swaggart discovered their human frailties; their flesh was weak and the spirit all too willing. . . .*

Though the adult entertainment industry has had more than its share of controversy, particularly from the religious community, the real danger the industry faces, says Margold, is "from the government, which cannot define obscenity yet uses the court system to drain the profits generated by an industry that annually sells and rents millions of dollars' worth of videos to much of the American public."

Margold may have a point there. In Daytona Beach, Florida, public prosecutor and State Attorney John Tanner is, according to the National Coalition Against Censorship, "trying to get the names of people who have rented sexually explicit videos from two retail stores." To the media, Tanner explains that "I don't think nice, decent people rent these types of tapes." A "born-again" Christian, Tanner points to pornography as "one more area in which the world and Satan himself are eating away the fabric of American life—the family."

Just as few can define "family values" to the general satisfaction of the public, few can define the parameters of pornography. Margold is quick to point out that the adult video industry wants to make a distinction: It does not produce hard-core material for cult audiences—"snuff" films (which he maintains don't exist, since he's never seen one and knows of no one who has persuasively explained to him that they've seen one), "child porn" (illegal and in execrable taste), and bestiality.

Instead, the adult video association's members produce videotapes that are mainstream and thus necessarily conservative. "Probably the most aberrant thing we film is anal sex." The outer limits of hard-core pornography, exploring themes like bestiality and sexual torture, are not within the adult video association's purview, according to Margold. (A 1986 Gallup poll showed that 62 percent of the respondents did not favor a ban on the sale or rental of X-rated videocassettes for home viewing.)

Another frequent criticism he hears: charges of exploitation of women. As adult film star Stacey Nichols told Ed Koch of the Las Vegas Sun *at the Consumer Electronics Show in 1992, "Exploitation occurs when people are forced to do something they don't want to do, but that's not the case with me because I know what I'm doing and I enjoy it."*

Frequently attacked by several comers, Margold likes to point out that "no one ever died from an overdose of pornography."

Beahm: *As you know, public prosecutor John Tanner is trying to get the names of customers who rent X-rated videotapes. Your observation?*

Margold: Welcome to invasion of privacy. The intimidation factor reigns supreme.

What's the market for X-rated entertainment?

Approximately 85–90 percent is for the video market. On occasion films are made for theatrical release or for cable; we shoot a "hard X" and a "soft X (devoid of male genitalia)."

What figures do you have on tape rentals?

A half-billion tapes are rented or sold each year; ours is a billion-dollar business.

Any demographics available?

No. The 1,200 members of FOXE are incredibly diverse—lawyers, bakers, butchers, and candlestick makers, a real cross section of America.

Since its inception twenty years ago, the industry has gone through a great deal of change. You are an insider; what are your observations about the current status of the industry and the direction it is headed?

To me, the industry's rather tame. I've been in it so long, it's become mundane. But to the general public, I still think they are titillated by "X," perhaps by the idea that they are watching something that perhaps goes against the grain. I think that is what keeps the adult industry viable, though it is now practicing self-censorship—the worst type of censorship.

We are no longer willing to take any kind of entertainment chances, catering to a white bread mentality. In order to survive, we have become homogenized, producing pornographic pabulum. We have gone mainstream.

Your industry is frequently under attack; generally, on moral grounds; specifically, on subject matter: child porn, bestiality, snuff films—the worst examples imaginable. How accurate are those perceptions?

Kids are very hard to control, animals will bite you, and if I really beat somebody up, I can't use them the next day; and if I kill them, then I don't have them around the next day, and that's not good.

That's what I told the Meese Commission, in exactly that terminology.

The truth is, the X-rated industry censors itself from within. For example, there's a $10,000 bounty out from the Adult Video Association leading to the arrest and conviction of any child pornographer. We are *totally* opposed to that kind of material. It exists, perhaps, in some form of underground material; but I represent, through the AVA and FOXE, the *mainstream* entertainment industry.

From your viewpoint, what's the value of X-rated videotapes?

We simply provide a sexual catharsis for the masses. Our whole reason for existing is to encourage society to alleviate their sexual frustration and guilt.

There are a lot of ways to mollify your own sexual guilt. A lot of people can't deal with their own sexuality; therefore, they don't want anyone else to enjoy it, either.

Would you say that for the actors and actresses in your industry, they are consensual adults performing adult acts for an adult viewership?

Yes. They know exactly what is happening; they want to perform and are being paid as well as we can pay them. Just like professional football or baseball players, they are catered to as working professionals.

You talk frequently on radio shows with your opponents. What observations have you made about them?

I really believe that many of our biggest enemies are also our most closet fans. These people who rail against us are often the most pious. They are loathsome; in some cases, after the public discussion is over, they ask about their watching our production of X-rated material, which I find rather amusing.

I ask them: Why are you against us? They say, "It's the wrong type of entertainment." My response is that we should let the public decide, so why are you deciding for them? They usually don't have an answer to that.

Any final thoughts?

First, I don't really see what we do as detrimental to society.

Second, here's a slogan I came up with for rap artist Aja: "Rap may be crap, but censorship is horseshit."

80

"Trampling Basic Rights"

by George Beahm

Your attempt to obtain names of individuals . . . is a profound interference with basic values protected by the First Amendment and . . . a dangerous opening to religious, political, artistic and intellectual repression. This action is an escalation of your ongoing vendetta against these video stores because they refuse to ban material of which you personally disapprove. That it is directed to expressive materials which are frequently attacked—in this case apparently subject to prosecution by you in an effort to prove they are "obscene"—makes your action more, not less, intolerable. To hope to intimidate people because the content of the expression is often stigmatized is to push cynicism and opportunism to its limits.

—LEANNE KATZ, NCAC Director, letter to John Tanner
(from *Censorship News,* September 1992)

In the "Forum" section of the September 1992 issue of *Playboy,* Ken Presti of Winter Park, Florida, writes that "State's Attorney John Tanner has asked for a court order forcing video stores to identify people who rent *Drillers, Men in Motion No. 6, Spank Me, Daddy,* and *Who Reamed Rosie Rabbit No. 2* (four adult films he wants banned under obscenity laws). Tanner claims he won't prosecute the customers but may call them to the witness stand in his civil suit against store operators. . . ."

As the National Coalition Against Censorship pointed out, "It is an outrageous—and unprecedented—invasion of the viewers' privacy and First Amendment rights. It is truly a dangerous opening to religious, political, artistic, and intellectual repression."

In an editorial ("Trampling Basic Rights") in the *Daytona Beach Journal* (May 10, 1992), the subhead says it all: "Tanner takes porn war into private homes." The paper elaborates:

Faced with election-year pressure to show results in his four-year-war on pornography, State Attorney John Tanner is doing what he said he wouldn't—taking the war into private homes.

Defending his expenditure of money and man hours on getting nasty videotapes off rental shelves, Tanner has said he was going only after pur-veyors of sexually explicit tapes and not individual renters.

Now, however, Tanner wants names of renters for his suit against two video store owners.

He claims he won't prosecute the renters. Even so, making the names of renters a public record and threatening to haul them into court could subject them to justifiable worry and considerable public embarrassment.

The renters broke no law when viewing the tapes. These may have been sexually explicit films, but they are not necessarily legally obscene. That's still for a jury to decide.

o   o   o

People expect when renting a tape, checking out a book, or viewing a movie that it is nobody's business but their own. They don't need to explain their actions or tastes to Tanner or anyone else in government.

Being left alone in one's private life is a fundamental expectation of every American. That right enjoys broad protections under the U.S. Constitution's First and Fourth amendments, and is protected explicitly in Florida's privacy amendment.

But Tanner knows one doesn't have to prosecute anyone successfully to win a war against sexually oriented videotapes. You simply threaten a few small-business owners who don't have the means to fight back, and intimi-date everyone else.

Intimidation is what the request for the list of renters' names is really all about. Scare people into censoring themselves. Put the thought in people's heads that their film tastes just might be put on public display. Make people worry that they may be called into court. Make people wonder if uniformed officers will come knocking on their doors.

It's an effective tactic. Tanner already has said he might use it again. It's a kind of demand-side censorship.

o   o   o

This is hardly the first time Tanner has resorted to questionable practices in his all-consuming mission against pornography. He already has misused the grand jury process and attempted to bully store owners with threatening letters.

Tanner's request for customer lists is one more act of a man more inter-ested in pursuing his own private moral crusade than in upholding the Constitution. This prosecution has gone on far too long, and once again Tanner has gone too far.

The citizenry apparently agreed, for Tanner lost his reelection bid in the September 1991 Republican primary.

81

The Devil Made Me Do It: The Bundy Bill

by George Beahm

Dr. James Dobson, head of Focus on the Family, videotaped an exclusive interview with convicted serial killer Ted Bundy. According to the liner notes accompanying the videotape, *Fatal Addiction,* the cost to produce the tape was substantial:

> Focus on the Family spent more than $40,000 to produce this video. In addition to flying members of our staff to Florida for the interview itself, we retained a professional video crew, leased equipment and rented editing facilities in Jacksonville [Florida]. *We also provided hundreds of preliminary copies of the Bundy interview to the news media* [italics mine]. Furthermore, Focus incurred significant expenses in shooting additional footage for the introduction, and in packaging and duplicating thousands of VHS format cassettes like this one for those who requested it.

We can only speculate as to why Ted Bundy agreed to the one-hour interview: A desire to come clean? The final confessional? Or, perhaps, one last chance to stir the soup, fuel the fires of dissent, and manipulate society through his disingenuousness? Ted Bundy, perhaps, having the last laugh on society?

One fact, though, is clear: special-interest groups, especially those of the religious right, would have powerful ammunition in the form of propaganda if Bundy, a hapless "victim," cited pornography as the proximate cause for his crimes. His "admission" would conveniently shift the blame away from himself and attempt to fix it on the "pornographers."

As actor Dana Carvey (of "Saturday Night Live") in his role as the Church Lady would say, with a smirk, "How conve-e-e-nient."

The liner notes for *Fatal Addiction* paint a vivid word picture of the evils of pornography:

> In this video . . . Bundy takes viewers back to his roots, explaining the development of his compulsive behavior. He reveals his addiction to hard-core pornography and how it fueled the terrible crimes he committed. *Bundy warns that within our society are men like him, whose violent tendencies are being encouraged by pornography* [italics mine]. A controversial presentation, "Fatal

Addiction" is the story of a tormented man, a man caught between the right and wrong he learned as a child and his plunge into the dark world of hard-core, violent pornography.

In the interview, published in *Physician* (a house publication), Bundy tells Dobson that as a young teenager, he encountered "soft-core pornography," then subsequently came across "a pornographic book in someone's trash that was harder, more graphic, more explicit."

Admitting to pornography addiction, Bundy explained that he wasn't "some helpless victim" but, instead, "a normal person" who simply couldn't resist the siren of pornography—a seduction of the innocent.

No sane person can feel sympathy for Bundy, who, as the liner notes for *Fatal Addiction* points out, "admitted murdering more than two dozen young women but is widely believed to have killed many more." Our hearts go out to families of the helpless victims of his heinous crimes, but not to Bundy, who would lead us to believe that he was seduced by the dark side.

In the interview from *Physician*, Bundy admitted that he didn't want to die, that he deserved the maximum punishment under the law, and that society at large "deserved to be protected from me and from others like me." Few would disagree (some, in fact, felt quite strongly about the issue, wearing T-shirts bearing the simple words, "Fry Ted Bundy.")

The next day, at 7:00 A.M., on January 24, 1989, Ted Bundy was put to death by electrocution in Florida.

Not surprisingly, two years later when the Pornography Victims Compensation Act of 1991 (S. 983) was introduced by Sen. Mitch McConnell (R–Ky.), the bill was informally dubbed the Ted Bundy bill.

In an op-ed piece for *USA Today* published in April 1992, Senator McConnell defended his rationale: "The porn lobby denies there could ever be any causal link between sadistic, hard-core porn and sexual crimes. If that's true, pornographers have nothing to worry about: Under my bill, if you can't *prove* the link, you don't get a dime."

The problems inherent in the bill, as *USA Today* pointed out, are three-fold: "Proving pornography caused an attack would be virtually impossible. . . . Not even the Supreme Court can agree on a definition of obscenity. Obscenity in one community would be considered art in another. . . . Freedom of expression guaranteed by the First Amendment would be compromised with no tangible gain."

USA Today concluded: "The sex-crime victims compensation act will not prevent assaults, nor contribute to any understanding of the causes and prevention of sex crimes. It would be a dangerous distraction."

The Media Coalition, Inc., an association representing book and magazine publishers, distributors, and booksellers, elaborated:

> The Pornography Victims Compensation Act . . . authorizes victims of rape and other sexual crimes to sue producers and distributors of any "sexually

explicit" material that was "a proximate cause" of the attacks upon them. The bill provides that the testimony of the rapist is an acceptable means for determining proximate cause. Media Coalition believes that the bill would have a chilling effect on the distribution of all works with sexual content, including both classic and contemporary novels, art and photography books, and health and sex education materials.

While the debate rages on in the Senate, a similar debate is raging in Massachusetts. Catharine MacKinnon (a Michigan law professor) and author Andrea Dworkin (*Pornography: Men Possessing Women*) have proposed a similar anti-pornography bill, an ordinance so strict that, as *Time* pointed out, it has yet to be passed anywhere in the U.S.A.: "The two activists have been campaigning in tandem against pornography since the early '80s; city ordinances they devised for Minneapolis, Indianapolis and Bellingham, Wash., all similar to the Massachusetts bill, were rejected by courts or local officials."

A law school professor at Yale, Thomas I. Emerson, wrote in *Censorship: Opposing Viewpoints* that "the sweep of the Minneapolis Ordinance is breathtaking." He elaborated:

It would subject to government ban virtually all depictions of rape, verbal or pictorial, and indeed most presentations of sexual encounters. More specifically, it would outlaw such works of literature as D.H. Lawrence's *Lady Chatterley's Lover,* Henry Miller's *Tropic of Cancer,* William Faulkner's *Sanctuary,* Ernest Hemingway's *For Whom the Bell Tolls,* and Norman Mailer's *Advertisements for Myself,* to name but a few. The ban would indeed extend as far as Shakespeare, and perhaps to the Bible, in one direction and to the millions of copies of the "romance novels" now being sold in the supermarkets in the other. It would embrace much of the world's art, from ancient carvings to Picasso, well-known films too numerous to mention, and a substantial part of commercial advertising. . . .

The nearest analogy to what is proposed in the Minneapolis ordinance would be an official enactment prohibiting all expression that promoted or encouraged racism in our society. The laws, constitutional and statutory, that attempt to eradicate racism in our national life have never been carried to such a point. They deal with discriminatory acts, not the expression of discriminatory beliefs, opinions, ideas or attitudes. And it is hard to believe that the Supreme Court would permit their extension into such areas. . . .

Professor Emerson is not alone. *Time* magazine points out that several groups voiced concerns, including the American Civil Liberties Union and Feminists for Free Expression. Their concerns were echoed by Marilyn Fitterman of the New York State chapter of the National Organization for Women, who told *Time,* "We feel this bill is censorship. It takes the onus off the criminal and blames the publishers and artists."

MacKinnon and Dworkin, according to *Time,* have cause for celebration. It seems they are not alone:

> MacKinnon and Dworkin believe theirs is an idea whose time has come at last. As evidence, they can cite [a February 1992] unanimous ruling by Canada's Supreme Court—endorsing MacKinnon's argument—that pornography harmful to women can be outlawed even though freedom of expression is infringed.

The battle lines have been drawn, the defensive positions occupied, and the war over words (and images) will very likely produce numerous casualties—possibly the First Amendment.

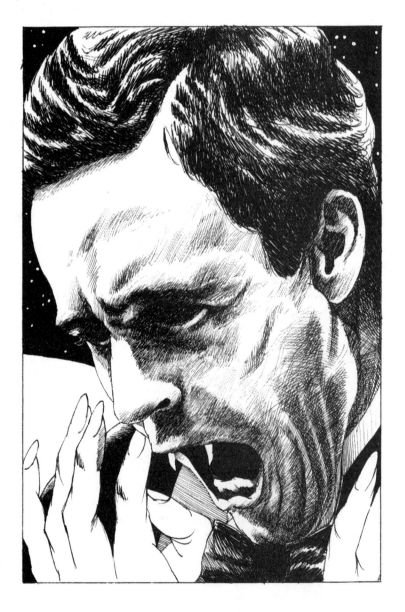

82

Pornography Victims' Compensation Act

Statement by Sen. Mitch McConnell before Senate Judiciary Committee, July 23, 1992

Two years ago, I introduced the Pornography Victims' Compensation Act, to provide victims of sex crimes, whose offenders were incited or influenced by pornography, with a civil cause of action against its producers and purveyors.

The support for that bill has been extraordinary. An array of organizations including the Family Research Council, Feminists Fighting Pornography, the American Family Association, victims rights groups, and dozens of National Organization for Women chapters nationwide, all joined together in calling for action on this anti-porn, pro-victim legislation.

These diverse groups coalesced around the Pornography Victims' Compensation Act because they shared a goal—to hold pornographers liable for the harm they cause. They also share a belief—that crime is fostered by a culture in which the sexual degradation, abuse, and murder of women and children are a form of entertainment.

That belief is shared by most Americans. Earlier this year, the National Victim Center released a study that found 93 percent of Americans believe violence in the media impacts violence in society.

The pornographic media is increasingly violent, and dangerous. A 1988 study by the FBI found that 81 percent of violent sexual offenders regularly used violent pornography. A study by the Michigan State Police found that of 48,000 sexual crimes committed over a 20-year period, pornography was used just prior to or during 41 percent of them.

Mr. Chairman, violent pornography played a role in one of the most notorious killers your state of Delaware has ever experienced. "Prime Time Live" recently profiled Steven Pennell, the so-called "Corridor Killer," who preyed on women along a stretch of the U.S. 40-U.S. 13 corridor in the late 1980s. Pennell was a cruel and sadistic serial killer, torturing his victims until they died.

When he was caught by police they discovered in his possession a variety of violent pornography. Particularly notable was a violent pornographic videotape, entitled "The Taming of Rebecca." It was queued to a scene strikingly similar to mutilation he performed on his victims. That tape was entered as evidence by the prosecution.

Mr. Chairman, "The Taming of Rebecca" is obscene, hard-core pornography. It will not be found at the local 7-Eleven, Blockbuster Video, or even the Playboy Channel. It would be actionable under the Pornography Victims' Compensation Act.

A columnist wrote in *U.S. News & World Report:* "The connection between the amount of violent entertainment and the amount of real-life violence is no longer seriously doubted among social scientists."

Women in this country are scared, and with good reason. The Judiciary Committee reported on May 21, that "American women are in greater peril now from attack than they have ever been in the history of our nation."

The U.S. rape rate—4 times that in Germany, 8 times France's, 15 times England's, and 20 times Japan's—is on the rise. In 1990, reported rapes in this country exceeded 100,000 for the first time. Last year's increase was three times that of the year before. In my home state of Kentucky, reported rapes increased 43 percent last year. A 43 percent increase in *one* year.

Experts in the field believe that number vastly understates the true magnitude of the problem as thousands of rapes go unreported, out of fear of reprisal and stigmatization.

Some telling statistics: the rape rate is increasing four times as fast as the overall crime rate; one in five adult women has been raped, one in six by someone she knows; a woman is raped every 6 minutes; 3 to 4 million women are beaten each year, 1 million so severely they seek medical help; more than half of all homeless women are fleeing domestic violence; and the leading cause of death on the job for women is homicide (for men, accidents).

Another horrifying fact—only 29 percent of rapists are sentenced to a year or more behind bars.

All women are victims in this culture of sexual violence. Millions of American women are afraid to walk from their offices to their cars. They are afraid to go outside at night. They are afraid within their own homes.

The National Victims Center reported this spring that

> The fear of crime restricts the freedom of Americans to go where they want, when they want. Because of the threat of crime, the lifestyles of many Americans are restricted. *The freedom of women is particularly restricted by this threat.*

The center's survey found that 73 percent of American women limit the places they will go by themselves.

There is another dimension to pornography and crime—the extent to which they affect children. Each year, one million children from 6 months to 16 years old are sexually molested and then filmed or photographed. There is a large audience for this filth, many of whom are themselves child molesters.

Children are particularly vulnerable in this culture of sexual violence. And their predators are prolific. The typical child molester abuses 117 children.

The pornography industry trades in the abuse, exploitation and degradation of women and children. Pornography is not an expression of speech—it is a business.

This bill hits pornographers where it hurts them most: their wallets.

Victims of sexual crimes in our nation currently have no legal recourse other than a justice system which frequently lets offenders go free. The Pornography Victims' Compensation Act provides victims of sex crimes with a civil cause of action against pornographers if the victim can prove a link between the crime and specific pornographic material.

The bill does not dictate what pornographers may produce—it simply holds them liable for it.

The original Pornography Victims' Compensation Act drew opposition from the entertainment industry. I believe some of their claims over the scope of the material the original bill would have covered were exaggerated. Nevertheless, I have carefully considered the points they raised and incorporated many of them into the re-draft.

The latest version of the bill, which I along with Senators Grassley, Thurmond and Packwood, introduced yesterday, would cover only that material which the Supreme Court *already* has said is not protected speech under the First Amendment. Under this modified version of the Pornography Victims' Compensation Act, only *obscene* material and *child pornography* would be actionable.

The United States Supreme Court has been unequivocal in its view that the First Amendment does *not* protect obscene material or child pornography. In case after case, the court has carefully distinguished between such worthless forms of expression and the free speech guaranteed by the Constitution, which ought to have the broadest latitude possible. I agree with that distinction— after all, pornography is a business, not a belief. Its chief motivation is profits, not principles. And its methodology is exploitation, not expression.

The Supreme Court could not be much clearer on this issue. It said in *Miller* v. *California,* "This much has been categorically settled by the Court, that obscene material is unprotected by the First Amendment." It went on to describe the kind of material it was talking about:

> . . . [W]orks, which, taken as a whole, appeal to the prurient interest in sex, which portray sexual conduct in a patently offensive way, and which, taken as a whole, do not have serious literary, artistic, political or scientific value.

That is the standard I adopt in my bill.

The Supreme Court has been even more emphatic in the area of child pornography. In *New York* v. *Ferber,* the court upheld restrictions on child pornography that went well beyond the narrow test enunciated in *Miller* v. *California.* The court said, "It is evident beyond the need for elaboration that a state's interest in safeguarding the physical and psychological well-being of a minor is compelling." Further, the court argued, "The prevention of sexual exploitation and abuse of children constitutes a government objective of surpassing importance."

The reason for the court's exclusion of child pornography from First Amendment protection is that child pornography is child abuse, in two fundamental ways identified by the court:

First, the materials produced are a permanent record of the children's participation and the harm to the child is exacerbated by their circulation. Second, the distribution network for child pornography must be closed if the production of material which requires the sexual exploitation of children is to be effectively controlled.

I would add a third way that child pornography is child abuse: most consumers of child pornography are child abusers who use this material to legitimize their sexual activities—not only to validate these activities with themselves, but to persuade their child victims that adult-child sexual contact is somehow normal, simply because it is depicted in a magazine or video.

For these reasons, I believe the Supreme Court is completely justified in separating the perverse world of obscenity and child pornography from the vital free speech values which our country's founders enshrined in the Constitution.

There are many who would like to go further, but I believe it is important to pass a bill which is constitutional and addresses the danger presented by the most extreme pornography.

The bill will give victims of sex crimes a civil recourse against that most extreme pornography—obscenity and child pornography.

The modified bill incorporates many of the concerns raised by representatives of the entertainment industry. I do not expect to win their endorsement, but this should mute their criticism and alleviate concerns of those engaged in legitimate publishing, motion picture, and television enterprises.

I would like to work in good faith with the opponents of this bill, and hope that we can achieve something more than stonewalling on one of the most dangerous threats to women today.

Pornography is fueling violence in this country, and it is time pornographers were held accountable for the harm they cause. If we are to protect women and children from sexual predators, we must recognize that sex crimes do not occur in a cultural vacuum. It is time to hold accountable those who are getting rich off veritable how-to manuals and films for rapists and child abusers.

S. 1521—Pornography Victims' Compensation Act
Sponsored by Sen. Mitch McConnell (R-Ky.)

Victims' Right of Action
The Act provides a private right of action to victims of sexual crimes and their guardians and estates. It would allow them to sue the commercial producers, distributors, exhibitors, and sellers of obscene and child pornographic material if the person bringing suit can prove that the defendant's material was a substantial cause of the offense.

Elements of the Cause of Action
In order to recover damages, the person bringing suit would have to prove, by a preponderance of the evidence, that:

• the victim was a victim of a forcible sexual crime, as defined under state law, whether or not such crime has been prosecuted or proven in a separate criminal proceeding;
• the material is obscene or child pornography;
• the defendant should have reasonably foreseen that the material would create an unreasonable risk of such a crime;
• the material was a substantial cause of the offense, i.e., a direct motivating factor in causing the offender to commit the offense.

Proof of Causation
In determining whether the material was a substantial cause of the offense, the finder of fact may consider any evidence admissible under the Federal Rules of Evidence, except the testimony of the offender shall not be considered.

Damages and Liability
If the person bringing suit meets the requirements of proof, he or she is entitled to full recovery for economic loss, pain and suffering, and attorneys' fees. The producer, distributor, exhibitor, and seller of the material each shall be held jointly and severally liable for the damages.

Statute of Limitations
The Act imposes a statue of limitations, barring suits more than two years after the commission of the criminal offense or one year after conviction for the offense.

Effective Date
The Act applies to materials produced after the date of enactment, or any commercial distribution, exhibition, or sale of material after the date of enactment.

83

Pornography and the New Puritans

by John Irving

John Irving's essay was originally published in the New York Times Book Review, *March 29, 1992.*

These are censorial times. I refer to the pornography victims' compensation bill, now under consideration by the Senate Judiciary Committee—that same bunch of wise men who dispatched such clearheaded, objective jurisprudence in the Clarence Thomas hearings. I can't wait to see what they're going to do with this maladroit proposal. The bill would encourage victims of sexual crimes to bring civil suits against publishers and distributors of material that is "obscene or constitutes child pornography"—*if* they can prove that the material was "a substantial cause of the offense," *and if* the publisher or distributor should have "foreseen" that such material created an "unreasonable risk of such a crime." If this bill passes, it will be the first piece of legislation to give credence to the unproven theory that sexually explicit material actually *causes* sexual crimes.

At the risk of sounding old-fashioned, I'm still pretty sure that rape and child molestation predate erotic books and pornographic magazines and X-rated video-cassettes. I also remember the report of the two-year, $2 million President's Commission on Obscenity and Pornography (1970), which concluded there was "no reliable evidence . . . that exposure to explicit sexual material plays a significant role in the causation of delinquent or criminal sexual behavior." In 1986, not satisfied with that conclusion, the Meese commission on pornography and the Surgeon General's conference on pornography also failed to establish such a link. Now, here they go again.

This time it's Republican Senators Mitch McConnell of Kentucky, Charles Grassley of Iowa and Strom Thurmond of South Carolina; I can't help wondering if they read much. Their charmless bill is a grave mistake for several reasons; for starters, it's morally reprehensible to shift the responsibility for any sexual crime onto a third party—namely, *away* from the actual perpetrator.

And then, of course, there's the matter of the bill running counter to the spirit of the First Amendment of the United States Constitution; this bill is a piece of backdoor censorship, plain and simple. Moreover, since the laws on obscenity differ from state to state, and no elucidation of the meaning of obscenity is presented in the bill, how are the publishers or distributors to know in advance if their material is actionable or not? It is my understanding, therefore, that the true intent of the bill is to make the actual creators of this material think very conservatively—that is, when their imaginations turn to sex and violence.

I recall that I received a lot of unfriendly mail in connection with a somewhat explicit scene in my novel, *The World According to Garp*, wherein a selfish young man loses part of his anatomy while enjoying oral sex in a car. (I suppose I've always had a fear of rear-end collisions.) But thinking back about that particular hate mail, I don't recall a single letter from a young woman saying that she intended to rush out and *do* this to someone; and in the 14 years since that novel's publication, in more than 35 foreign languages, no one who actually *has done* this to someone has written to thank me for giving her the idea. Boy, am I lucky!

In a brilliant article on the Op-Ed page of the *New York Times,* Teller, of those marvelous magicians Penn & Teller, had this to say about the pornography victims' compensation bill: "The advocates of this bill seem to think that if we stop showing rape in movies people will stop committing it in real life. Anthropologists call this 'magical thinking.' It's the same impulse that makes people stick pins in voodoo dolls, hoping to cripple an enemy. It feels logical, but it does not work." (For those of you who've seen these two magicians and are wondering which is Penn and which is Teller, Teller is the one who never talks. He *writes* very well, however.)

"It's a death knell for creativity, too," Teller writes. "Start punishing make-believe, and those gifted with imagination will stop sharing it." He adds, "We will enter an intellectual era more insipid than the one we live in."

Now *there's* a scary idea! I remember when the film version of Günter Grass's novel *The Tin Drum* was banned in Canada. I always assumed it was the eel scene that offended the censors, but I don't know. In those days, a little naked sex—in the conventional position—was permissible, but unpleasant suggestiveness with eels was clearly going too far. But now, in light of this proposed pornography victims' compensation bill, is there any evidence to suggest that there have been *fewer* hellish incidents of women being force-fed eels to women in Canada than in those countries where the film was available? Somehow, I doubt it. I know that they're out there—those guys who want to force-feed eels to women—but I suspect they're going to do what they're going to do, unaided by books or films. The point is: let's do something about *them,* instead of trying to control what they read or see.

It dismays me how some of my feminist friends are hot to ban pornography. I'm sorry that they have such short memories. It wasn't very long ago when a book as innocent and valuable as *Our Bodies, Ourselves* was being banned by school boards and public libraries across the country. The idea of this good book was that women should have access to detailed information about their bodies and their health, yet the so-called feminist ideology behind the book was thought to be subversive; indeed, it was (at that time) deplored. But many writers and writers' organizations (like PEN) wrote letters to those school boards and those public libraries. I can't speak to the overall effectiveness of these letters in regard to reinstating the book, but I'm aware that some of the letters worked; I wrote several of those letters. Now here are some of my old friends, telling me that attitudes toward rape and child molestation can be changed only if we remove the offensive *ideas*. Once again, it's ideology that's being banned. And although the movement to ban pornography is especially self-righteous, it looks like blacklisting to me.

Fascism has enjoyed many name changes, but it usually amounts to banning something you dislike and can't control. Take abortion, for example. I think groups should have to apply for names; if the Right to Life people had asked me, I'd have told them to find a more fitting label for themselves. It's morally inconsistent to manifest such concern for the poor fetus in a society that shows absolutely no pity for the poor child after it's born.

I'm also not so sure that these so-called Right to Lifers are as fired up about those fetuses as they say. I suspect what really makes them sore is the idea of women having sex and somehow not having to *pay* for it—pay in the sense of suffering all the way through an unwanted pregnancy. I believe that is part of the loathing for promiscuity that has always fueled those Americans who feel that a life of common decency is slipping from their controlling grasp. This notion is reflected in the unrealistic hope of those wishful thinkers who tell us that sexual abstinence is an alternative to wearing a condom. But I say how about *carrying* a condom, just in case you're moved to *not* abstain?

No one is coercing women into having abortions, but the Right to Lifers want to coerce women into having babies; that's why the pro-choice people are well named. It's unfortunate, however, that a few of my pro-choice friends think that the pornography victims' compensation bill is a good idea. I guess that they're really not entirely pro-choice. They want the choice to reproduce or not, but they *don't* want too broad a choice of things to read and see; they know what *they* want to read and see, and they expect other people to be content with what they want. This sounds like a Right to Life idea to me.

Most feminist groups, despite their vital advocacy of full enforcement of laws against violence to women and children, seem opposed to Senate Bill 1521. As of this writing, both the National Organization for Women in New York State and in California have written to the Senate Judiciary Committee in opposition to the bill, although the Los Angeles chapter of NOW states that it has "no position." I admit it is perverse of me even to imagine what Tammy Bruce thinks about the Pornography Victims' Compensation Bill; I hope Ms. Bruce is not such a loose cannon as she appears, but she has me worried. Ms. Bruce is president of L.A. NOW, and she has lately distinguished herself with two counts of knee-jerk overreaction. Most recently, she found the Academy of Motion Picture Arts and Sciences to be guilty of an "obvious exhibition of sexism" in not nominating Barbra Streisand for an Oscar for best director. Well, maybe. Ms. Streisand's other talents have not been entirely overlooked; I meekly submit that the academy might have found *The Prince of Tides* lacking in directorial merit—it wouldn't be the first I've heard of such criticism. (Ms. Bruce says the L.A. chapter received "unrelenting calls" from NOW members who were riled up at the perceived sexism.)

Most readers will remember Tammy Bruce for jumping all over that nasty novel by Bret Easton Ellis. To refresh our memories: Simon & Schuster decided at the 11th hour not to publish *American Psycho* after concluding that its grisly content was in "questionable taste." Now please don't get excited and think I'm going to call that censorship; that was merely a breach of contract. And besides, Simon & Schuster has a right to its own opinion of what questionable taste is. *People* magazine tells us that Judith Regan, a vice president and senior editor at Simon & Schuster, recently had a book idea, which she pitched to Madonna. "My idea was for her to write a book of her sexual fantasies, her thoughts, the meanderings of her erotic mind," Ms. Regan said. The pity is, Madonna hasn't delivered. And according to Mitchell Fink, author of the "Insider" column for *People*, "Warner Books confirmed it is talking about a book—no word on what kind—with Madonna." I don't know Madonna, but maybe she thought the Simon & Schuster book idea was in questionable taste.* Simon & Schuster, clearly, subscribes to more than one opinion of what questionable taste is.

But only two days after Mr. Ellis's book was dropped by Simon & Schuster, Sonny Mehta, president of Alfred A. Knopf and Vintage Books, bought *American Psycho*, which was published in March 1991. Prior to the novel's publication, Ms. Bruce called for a boycott of all Knopf and Vintage titles—except for books by feminist authors, naturally—until *American Psycho* was withdrawn from publication (it wasn't), or until the end of 1991. To the charge of censorship, Ms. Bruce declared that she was *not* engaged in it; she sure fooled me.

But Ms. Bruce wasn't alone in declaring what *wasn't* censorship, nor was she alone in her passion; she not only condemned Mr. Ellis's novel—she condemned its availability. And not only the book itself *but its availability* was severely taken to task in the very pages in which I now write. In December 1990—three months before *American Psycho* was published, and at the urging of *The Book Review*—Roger Rosenblatt settled Mr. Ellis's moral hash in a piece of writing prissy enough to please Jesse Helms. According to Mr. Rosenblatt, Jesse Helms has never engaged in censorship, either. For those of us who remain improperly educated in regard to what censorship actually *is*, Mr. Rosenblatt offers a blanket definition. "Censorship is when a government burns your manuscript, smashes your presses and throws you in jail," he says.

Well, as much as I may identify with Mr. Rosenblatt's literary taste, I'm of the

---

*Editor's note: On October 21, 1992, Warner Books published *Sex*, a book of Madonna's sexual fantasies.

opinion that there are a few forms of censorship more subtle than that, and Mr. Rosenblatt has engaged in one of them. If you slam a book when it's published, that's called book reviewing, but if you write about a book three months in advance of its publication and your conclusion is "don't buy it," your intentions are more censorial that critical.

And it *is* censorship when the writer of such perceived trash is not held *as* accountable as the book's publisher; the pressure that was brought to bear on Mr. Mehta was totally censorial. *The Book Review* is at its most righteous in abusing Mr. Mehta, who is described as "clearly as hungry for a killing as Patrick Bateman." (For those of you who don't know Mr. Ellis's book, Patrick Bateman is the main character and a serial killer.) Even as reliable a fellow as the editorial director of *Publishers Weekly,* John F. Baker, described *American Psycho* as a book that "does transcend the boundaries of what is acceptable in mainstream publishing."

It's the very idea of making or keeping publishing "acceptable" that gives *me* the shivers, because that's the same idea that lurks behind the pornography victims' compensation bill—making the *publisher* (not the perpetrator of the crime or the writer of the pornography) responsible for what's "acceptable." If you want to bash Bret Easton Ellis for what he's written, go ahead and bash him. But when you presume to tell Sonny Mehta, or any other publisher, what he can or can't—or should or shouldn't—*publish,* that's when you've stepped into dangerous territory. In fact, that's when you're knee-deep in blacklisting, and you ought to know better—all of you.

Mr. Rosenblatt himself actually says, "No one argues that a publishing house hasn't the right to print what it wants. We fight for that right. But not everything is a right. At some point, someone in authority somewhere has to look at Mr. Ellis's rat and call the exterminator." Now this is interesting, and perhaps worse than telling Sonny Mehta what he should or shouldn't publish—because that's exactly what Mr. Rosenblatt *is* doing while he's *saying* that he isn't.

Do we remember that tangent of the McCarran-Walter Act of 1952, that finally defunct business about ideological exclusion? That was when we kept someone from coming into our country because we perceived that the person had *ideas* that were in conflict with the "acceptable" ideas of our country. Under this act of exclusion, writers as distinguished as Graham Greene and Gabriel García Márquez were kept out of the United States. Well, when we attack what a publisher has the right to publish, we are simply applying the old ideological exclusion act at home. Of all people, those of us in the idea business should know better than that.

As for the Pornography Victims' Compensation Bill, the vote in the Senate Judiciary Committee will be close. As of this writing, seven senators have publicly indicated their support of the bill; they need only one more vote to pass the bill out of committee. Friends at PEN tell me that the committee has received a lot of letters from women saying that support of the bill would in some way "make up for" the committee's mishandling of the Clarence Thomas hearings. Some women are putting the decision to support Justice Thomas alongside the decision to find William Kennedy Smith innocent of rape; these women think that a really strong antipornography bill will make up for what they perceive to be the miscarriage of justice in both cases.

The logic of this thinking is more than a little staggering. What would these women think if lots of men were to write the committee and say that because Mike Tyson has been found guilty of rape, what we need is *more* pornography to make up for what's happened to Iron Mike? This would make a lot of sense, wouldn't it?

I conclude that these are not only censorial times; these are stupid times. However, there is some hope that opposition to Senate Bill 1521 is mounting. The committee met on March 12 but the members didn't vote on the bill. Discussion was brief, yet encouraging. Colorado Senator Hank Brown told his colleagues that there are serious problems with the legislation; he should be congratulated for his courageous decision to oppose the other Republicans on the committee, but he should also be encouraged not to accept any compromise proposal. Ohio Senator Howard Metzenbaum suggested that imposing third-party liability on producers and distributors of books, magazines, movies and recordings raises the question of whether the bill shouldn't be amended to cover the firearms and liquor industries as well.

It remains to be seen if the committee members will resist the temptation to *fix* the troubled bill. I hope they will understand that the bill cannot be fixed because it is based on an erroneous premise—namely, that publishers or distributors should be held liable for the acts of criminals. But what is important for us to recognize, even if this lame bill is amended out of existence or flat-out defeated, is that *new* antipornography legislation will be proposed.

Do we remember Nancy Reagan's advice to would-be drug users? ("Just say no.") As applied to drug use, Mrs. Reagan's advice is feeble in the extreme. But writers and other members of the literary community *should* just say no to censorship in any and every form. Of course, it will always be the most grotesque example of child pornography that will be waved in front of our eyes by the Good Taste Police. If we're opposed to censorship, they will say, are we in favor of filth like this?

No, we are not in favor of child pornography if we say no to censorship. If we disapprove of reinstating public hangings, that doesn't mean that we want all the murderers to be set free. No writer or publisher or *reader* should accept censorship in any form; fundamental to our freedom of expression is that each of us has a right to decide what is obscene and what isn't.

But lest you think I'm being paranoid about the iniquities and viciousness of our times, I'd like you to read a description of Puritan times. It was written in 1837—more than 150 years ago—and it describes a scene in a Puritan community in Massachusetts that you must imagine taking place more than 350 years ago. This is from a short story by Nathaniel Hawthorne called "Endicott and the Red Cross," which itself was written more than 10 years before Hawthorne wrote

The Scarlet Letter. This little story contains the germ of the idea for that famous novel about a woman condemned by Puritan justice to wear the letter *A* on her breast. But Hawthorne, obviously, had been thinking about the iniquities and viciousness of early New England morality for many years.

Please remember, as you read what Nathaniel Hawthorne thought of the Puritans, that the Puritans are not dead and gone. We have many new Puritans in our country today; they are as dangerous to freedom of expression as the old Puritans ever were. An especially sad thing is, a few of these new Puritans are formerly liberal-thinking feminists.

In close vicinity to the sacred edifice [the meeting-house] appeared that important engine of Puritanic authority, the whipping-post—with the soil around it well trodden by the feet of evil doers, who had there been disciplined. At one corner of the meeting-house was the pillory, and at the other the stocks; . . . the head of an Episcopalian and suspected Catholic was grotesquely incased in the former machine; while a fellow-criminal, who had boisterously quaffed a health to the king, was confined by the legs in the latter. Side by side, on the meeting-house steps, stood a male and a female figure. The man was a tall, lean, haggard personification of fanaticism, bearing on his breast this label,—A WANTON GOSPELLER,—which betokened that he had dared to give interpretations of Holy Writ unsanctioned by the infallible judgment of the civil and religious rulers. His aspect showed no lack of zeal . . . even at the stake. The woman wore a cleft stick on her tongue, in appropriate retribution for having wagged that unruly member against the elders of the church; and her countenance and gestures gave much cause to apprehend that, the moment the stick should be removed, a repetition of the offence would demand new ingenuity in chastising it.

The above-mentioned individuals had been sentenced to undergo their various modes of ignominy, for the space of one hour at noonday. But among the crowd were several whose punishment would be life-long; some, whose ears had been cropped, like those of puppy dogs; others, whose cheeks had been branded with the initials of their misdemeanors; one, with his nostrils slit and seared; and another, with a halter around his neck, which he was forbidden ever to take off, or to conceal beneath his garments. Methinks he must have been grievously tempted to affix the other end of the rope to some convenient beam or bough. There was likewise a young woman, with no mean share of beauty, whose doom it was to wear the letter A on the breast of her gown, in the eyes of all the world and her own children. And even her own children knew what that initial signified. Sporting with her infamy, the lost and desperate creature had embroidered the fatal token in scarlet cloth, with golden thread and the nicest art of needlework; so that the capital A might have been thought to mean Admirable, or anything rather than Adulteress.

Let not the reader argue, from any of these evidences of iniquity, that the times of the Puritans were more vicious than our own.

In my old-fashioned opinion, Mr. Hawthorne sure got that right.

o   o   o

Not surprisingly, Irving's essay generated considerable controversy. In a letter to the editor, published in the June 7, 1992, issue of the New York Times Book Review, *Irving responded to his critics:*

As for those letters that expressed the frightening majority opinion—that pornography is to blame for sexual violence against women—I must unhappily revise my estimation that only some feminists are persuaded by this lunatic logic; it appears that some wishful thinking appeals to more than "some." Therefore, let us ban everything pornographic—and by all means we must include as "pornographic" everything that these women deem distasteful (or even remotely unflattering)— and let us then bask in the miraculously violence-free society that would doubtless be created. I suppose this new society would resemble a virtual return to the Stone Age, wherein, we have it on good authority, there was absolutely no sexual abuse of women—at least not until there emerged the first of those nasty cave drawings, which we all agree gave everyone such bad ideas.

• *John Irving is a novelist whose works include* The World According to Garp.

84

Sense and Censorship
The Vanity of Bonfires

by Marcia Pally

> . . . [T]he worst, most insidious effect of censorship is that, in the end, it can deaden the imagination of the people. Where there is no debate, it is hard to go on remembering, every day, that there is a suppressed side to every argument. It becomes almost impossible to conceive of what the suppressed things might be. It becomes easy to think that what has been suppressed was valueless anyway, or so dangerous that it needed to be suppressed. And then the victory of the censor is total. . . .
>
> —SALMAN RUSHDIE, "Casualties of Censorship," in
> *They Shoot Writers, Don't They?*

Acknowledgments

I would like to thank Americans for Constitutional Freedom and the Freedom to Read Foundation for their support and encouragement throughout all stages of this project. Thanks also to Cleo Wilson for picking up all the dropped stitches, to John Dixon for his elegant design, to Cindy Rankowitz, Jennifer Maguire and Jill Chukerman for their attention to public relations, to Carmen Armillas for her computer and inputting skills, to Arlan Bushman for proofreading, and to Sue Dickey for her administrative assistance. Special gratitude goes to Bari Nash for her tireless fact-checking, to Pam for sticking by me through all the trials, errors and paper, and to the bracing vision of the Constitution, which continues to inspire and cheer me.

What Is "Censored"?

"The First Amendment was designed 'to invite dispute,' to induce 'a condition of unrest,' to 'create dissatisfaction with conditions as they are,' and even to stir 'people to anger.'

"The First Amendment was not fashioned as a vehicle for dispensing tranquilizers to the people. Its prime function was to keep debate open to 'offensive' as well as to 'staid' people . . . the materials before us may be garbage. But so is much of what is said in political campaigns, in the daily press, on TV, or over the radio. By reason of the First Amendment . . . speakers and publishers have not been threatened or subdued because their thoughts and ideas may be 'offensive' to some." (Justice William O. Douglas, *Miller* v. *California,* June 6, 1973, 413 U.S. 15, p. 1453)

In the above quote, Supreme Court Justice William Douglas takes it as an obvious good that "speakers and publishers have not been threatened or subdued." Yet from time to time, participants in public life, legislators and community groups, believe there is benefit to subduing them and the material they bring before the nation. Society will profit, it is reasoned, from shaping for the good the ideas its people encounters.

A decade ago during the first Reagan administration, such beneficial shaping found new support. Enthusiasts for the idea promised society would not lose anything of value. In fact, they assured the public that restricting "bad" images, especially sexually explicit material and rock 'n' roll, would improve life. It would reduce drug abuse, teen pregnancy, and especially sexual violence: rape, incest, and wife battery. They professed to target "the really gruesome, horrible stuff."

This book will take a cursory look at their promise since they have been trusted with the "really gruesome, horrible stuff."

Recent Censorship Cases

By 1989, book banning had increased to three times the levels of 1979, according to the Office for Intellectual Freedom of the American Library Association. The most censored books now are *The Diary of Anne Frank, To Kill a Mockingbird, Of Mice and Men, 1984, Slaughterhouse-Five, Catcher in the Rye, The Adventures of Huckleberry Finn,* all the works of Stephen King and Judy Blume, especially Blume's *Are You There, God? It's Me, Margaret* for mentioning menstruation. Also on the most-censored list is the children's book *The Sisters Impossible* for the words *hell* and *fart,* as well as Studs Terkel's *Working,* Desmond Morris's *The Naked Ape,* and Alice Walker's *The Color Purple.* Dictionaries now on the most-censored list include *Webster's Seventh, Random House, Doubleday,* and *American Heritage,* for including definitions of "dirty" words.

Among the films that have been removed from library and store shelves since 1980 are *A Passage to India, Victor/Victoria, A Clockwork Orange,* Zeffirelli's *Romeo and Juliet* and *Splash!*

Efforts to restrict material have come not only from the conservative right. The National Coalition on Television Violence (NCTV), a group with liberal credentials, has been active in ferreting out material it believes endangers the public. Not only does the NCTV censure such movies as *The Texas Chainsaw Massacre Part 2* but also lists in its bulletins films such as *Star Trek IV: The Voyage Home* for "chasing, gun threat, and one Vulcan nerve pinch." NCTV lists the animated cartoon *Lady and the Tramp,* and the popular Christmas ballet *The Nutcracker* for its "battle between soldiers and mice." Additionally, the NCTV compiles lists of objectionable books including the works of Stephen King, Robert Ludlum, Frederick Forsyth, Mario Puzo, James Clavell, Helen MacInnes, John le Carré and Leon Uris.

Late in 1990, the National Coalition on Television Violence and two Christian media monitoring groups, the American Family Association and Good News Communications, organized a conference for media surveillance groups. Their goals include establishing a Christian Film and Television Commission and "reestablishing the presence of the church in Hollywood."

According to the American Library Association, the fastest growing area of book censorship cases is the occult. The second fastest-growing sector of censorship is health and family life issues, particularly materials focusing on AIDS education, sex education and drug abuse.

The censors who began with the "really gruesome, horrible stuff" appear to have extended their platform.

To bring the roster up to the present: in 1989, Terry Rakolta tried to remove the television program, *Married . . . With Children* from the air. In 1990, the rock group 2 Live Crew was indicted for obscenity, which carried not only a fine but a jail term, for an adults-only concert; admission was permitted only to those over 21. ("Art and the Oeuvre of 2 Live Crew," Jonathan Yardley, *Washington Post,* October, 10, 1990)

Nineteen-ninety also saw the Federal Communications Commission seek to expand its ban on adult programming from the hours when children might see such programs—6A.M. to 8P.M.—to 24 hours a day. Under such a ruling, at no time could an adult hear a radio or see a television program that was more sophisticated or controversial than what is appropriate for children. ("Government Seeks to Extend Ban on Broadcast of Offensive Shows," *New York Times,* July 13, 1990)

Also in 1990, the Cincinnati Contemporary Arts Center and its director were indicted on obscenity charges for exhibiting Robert Mapplethorpe's photography retrospective, "The Perfect Moment," though in that city no public monies were used to fund the show and no children under 18 were permitted entrance. Each visitor to the Cincinnati museum chose to attend the exhibit and paid for admission; each chose again to view the photographs of nudity and sexual material cordoned off in a special section that attracted the longest lines.

Early in 1991, the American Family Association launched a letter-writing campaign and boycott against Blockbuster Video, the largest video rental-and-sales chain in the country, demanding that Blockbuster drop all NC-17 films. Although Blockbuster said that none of the protests came from its video club members, the chain scotched NC-17 material. (Blockbuster told the press it dropped NC-17 videos independent of the AFA campaign, though only days before, it announced that it would evaluate NC-17 tapes on a title-by-title basis.) (*Billboard* magazine, January 1991)

Also in 1991, bills were introduced in several state legislatures that make it a crime to sell sexually explicit lyrics to minors. This is the first time a government body has tried to define prerecorded lyrics as legally obscene, making it the responsibility of local store owners and sales clerks to know the content of all the songs on all the records, tapes and compact discs they sell, and to know in advance of selling them whether they might be harmful to minors according to state law. (*Hollywood Reporter,* March 15, 1991)

In the last several years, the National Endowment for the Arts (NEA) has suffered repeated attacks, including the requirement that artists receiving NEA grants sign a pledge that their art would not address a list of forbidden subjects. Prohibited subject matter included not only obvious horrors such as the sexual exploitation of children but also depictions of sex and homoeroticism—not specifically homosexual sex acts but anything that might be considered suggestively homoerotic. Because of the many attacks on the NEA, the New York City Opera (an NEA recipient) considered dropping scenes from its production of Arnold Schönberg's opera *Moses und Aron* from the 1990-91 season because they included the appearance of three naked virgins. ("Arts Agency Voids Pledge on Obscenity," *New York Times,* February 2, 1991; "Nude Characters to Remain in City Opera Production," *New York Times,* July 21, 1990)

In March 1991, the American Family Association lobbied in Congress against the NEA funding of Todd Haynes's film *Poison,* which had won first prize at the Sundance Film Festival the preceding January. This experimental film assails prejudice and the persecution of those who are different from the mainstream. It employs three allegorical stories about oppression, one about a homosexual man in prison based on the writings of the French writer Jean Genêt. Calling this pornography, the American Family Association attacked the NEA for awarding Haynes a small grant. ("Support for Avant-Garde Film Defended," *New York Newsday,* March 30, 1991)

Also in March 1991, the American Family Association tried to persuade advertisers to pull their ads from the television program "Absolute Strangers." Based on the story of Martin Klein whose pregnant wife fell into a coma as a result of an auto accident, it follows Klein's efforts to abort the fetus, on doctors' advice, in order to save her life. He was taken to court by anti-abortion groups—the "absolute strangers" of the title—who sought to prevent the abortion. When Klein finally obtained court permission for the abortion, his wife regained consciousness within hours. ("Group Targets 'Absolute Strangers'" *New York Newsday,* March 18, 1991)

Ever busy, the American Family Association targeted the advertisers of yet another television program throughout the spring of 1991. Titled "Our Sons," the program starred Julie Andrews and Ann-Margret as two mothers, one of whose sons is dying of AIDS. (*New York Newsday,* March 18, 1991)

Earlier, in 1989, Artists Space in New York lost its NEA funding because, according to the NEA, the catalog for a show on AIDS criticized the public policies of elected and public figures. It seemed to some at the time that such criticism was at the heart of the democratic process ("Arts Endowment Withdraws Grant for AIDS Show," *New York Times,* November 9, 1989). Artist Andres Serrano's work was also removed from exhibition in 1989 on charges of blasphemy. On a day somewhat before the Serrano incident, a work by Thomas Jefferson was banned on the same grounds. On that occasion, Jefferson wrote,

"Are we to have a censor whose imprimatur shall say what books may be sold, and what we may buy? . . . Whose foot is to be the measure to which ours are all to be cut or stretched? Is a priest to be our inquisitor or shall a layman simple as ourselves set up his reason as the rule. . . . It is an insult against our citizens to question whether they are rational beings or not, and [an insult] against religion to suppose it cannot stand the test of truth and reason."

The Costs of Censorship

Thomas Jefferson thought censorship an insult; it is also a danger. When the state, church or private group restricts books, movies and music from the public, the nation loses the right and gradually the *ability* to make up its mind about the information and entertainment it sees and hears, about the ideas it encounters now and what will be available for future use. Historian Henry Steele Commager wrote, "Censorship . . . creates the kind of society that is incapable of exercising real discretion . . . it will create a generation incapable of appreciating the difference between independence of thought and subservience."

Censors always promise an improvement in life: rid yourselves of pornography, of *Das Kapital, Catcher in the Rye,* or *The Sisters Impossible* and life will be safer, happier, more secure. Yet no matter where the "promise" starts—no matter what material censors begin with—once a nation surrenders the right to choose its books, music and films, it has given away the right to mosey around in art, popular entertainment and "trash." Some may argue that pornographic magazines or rock 'n' roll are worthless and can well be done without. Others may say the same of detective novels, horoscope charts or fashion magazines. The idea behind the freedom to read and view is that one makes that determination for oneself.

It's the Picture that Causes the Crime: The Great Soothing Appeal of Censorship

The promise of a better life if only society banishes some book, magazine or movie is the great soothing appeal of censorship. Currently the most popular version vows that banning sexually explicit material and rock will reduce drug abuse, teen pregnancy and sexual violence—get rid of pornography, get rid of rape. It seems pertinent to ask if it will. Alternately, the pornography/rock-causes-harm idea is a quick fix that kids the public into thinking that the solution to society's ills is merely a matter of banning offensive pictures.

In the last decade, those who would restrict such material have masked traditional religious arguments against sexual imagery with the patina of social-benefit reasoning. The pornography/rock-causes-harm argument makes the banning of books, movies and music seem reasonable to many who would dismiss threats of brimstone and hellfire. Dr. Larry Baron, one of the leading authorities on pornography and violence (Yale and the University of New Hampshire), wrote in the journal *Society* in 1987,

"A particularly insidious aspect of the [Meese Commission's] *Final Report* is the commission's use of feminist rhetoric to attain its right-wing objective. Replacing the outmoded cant of sin and depravity with the trendier rhetoric of harm, the commission exploited feminist outrage about sexual violence in order to bolster oppressive obscenity laws."

The pornography/rock-causes-harm argument is easy to understand, easy to sell. It claims that sexual imagery degrades and violates women; men look at it and emulate what they see. So the course of action seems short, direct, and has the lure of peace in our time.

It also has the cachet of feminist tradition. Over the last 20 years, women and some men examined images in all sectors of culture, from television commercials to the films shown in medical school. This investigation became a tool for identifying sexism and exposing its pervasiveness. It made sense to apply this technique to sexual material. Yet in the process, a confusion arose between examining images for their insights about society and calling those images *sources* or *causes* of social injustice. (See Ellen Willis, "Feminism, Moralism, and Pornography," in *Beginning to See the Light,* 1981, Alfred A. Knopf, New York; M. Pally, "Ban Sexism Not Pornography," *The Nation,* June 29, 1985)

The mass-market pornography and rock industries took off only after World War II. Prior to the twentieth century, few people save the wealthy elite saw any pornography whatsoever; certainly they heard no rock 'n' roll. Yet violence and sexism flowered for thousands of years before anybody had commercialized images to show them how to do it. (For an historical overview of the censorship of sexually explicit material see, Walter Kendrick, *The Secret Museum: Pornography in Modern Culture,* 1987, Viking Press, New York.) Drugs have been used for centuries without rock lyrics as a guide—and in some cultures, like Chinese and American Indian, commonly by large sectors of the population. Teenagers have somehow managed to become pregnant for thousands of years without the aid of pornography or rock. According to historians John D'Emilio and Estelle Freedman, up to one third of births in colonial America occurred out of wedlock or within eight months of hurried marriages. (*Intimate Matters: A History of Sexuality in America,* Harper & Row, 1988.)

Most of history's rapists, child abusers and drug addicts read nothing at all; they were illiterate and technology had not yet provided them with magazines or movies. Societies today where no sexual material or Western music is permitted, like Saudi Arabia, Iran and China (where sale and distribution of pornography is now a capital offense), do not boast social harmony and strong women's rights records (*New York Times,* December 29, 1990 and January 15, 1991).

In light of the historical success of sexual and drug abuses, it seems unlikely that pornography or rock is fundamental to their flourishing. It is improbable that banning rock or sexually explicit material will reduce those abuses or assist women and children. (See Varda Burstyn, editor, *Women Against Censorship,* 1985, Douglas & McIntyre Ltd., Vancouver, British Columbia.)

The media are besieged today with claims of increasing violence. This mayhem-escalation theory reasons that while sexual and drug abuses have run through history, they are more rampant now as a result of sexually explicit material and rock. Yet D'Emilio and Freedman's data belie such claims about teen pregnancy, and rape rates may be not be increasing, in spite of the availability of sexual images.

The Bureau of Justice Statistics reports that between 1973 and 1987 the national rape rate of 0.6 per 1,000 remained steady and the rate of attempted rape decreased 46 percent from 1.3 to 0.7 per 1,000. These data were gathered from household surveys rather than from police statistics where rapes are famously underreported. They identify at least some of the rapes that never reach police files because women are afraid to report them (especially in cases of domestic rape) or suspect the police will treat lightly their complaints. Additionally, these data cover the decades when feminists brought rape to the attention of the nation and created the social climate and structures—hotlines, police department task forces, and the like—to encourage women to bring rape into the open. This has led to an overall increase in rape reporting. One would expect rape rates to increase, not remain steady or decrease as is reported here.

The recent increase in media attention to rape, including date rape and marital rape, may not reflect an increase in rape as much as an increase in sensitivity to it and decreasing tolerance for this sort of violence. The July 1991 issue of *Pediatrics* reports similar findings for child abuse. Over the last four decades, child abuse "appears to have remained steady at about 12 percent for females." As in the rape studies above, these data were gathered from personal surveys rather than from police files where until recently, child abuse, like rape, was significantly underreported. Recent increases in child abuse reporting is attributed, in *Pediatrics,* to the legal requirement to report child abuse and to attitudinal changes toward women and children.

A 12 percent rate of child abuse is a grave social problem, as is the incidence of rape and wife battery. A one percent incidence of such violence would demand remedy. Yet the bumper-sticker cry "It's worse now than ever before" may not only be a misinterpretation of facts but an exploitation of them as a scare tactic, not so much to aid women and children as to provide justification for censorship measures that the public might otherwise not tolerate.

The last few decades, with the marketing of sexual material and rock, have ironically seen the greatest advances in sensitivity to violence against women and children. Before the pelvic-wriggler Elvis and mass publication of sexual images, there were no rape or incest hotlines and battered-women's shelters; date and marital rape were not yet gleams in a feminist's eye. Should one conclude, then, that the presence of pornography or rock has benefitted women and children? More likely, pornography, rock and the quality of women and children's lives are not causally related but are expressions of more basic forces in society, as are drug abuse and teen pregnancy. It is these issues that need addressing.

In a June 1991 article, *New York Times* rock critic Jon Pareles examined two videotapes that attribute social harms to MTV. "Rising to the Challenge" is sold by the Parents Music Resource Center (PMRC), the group founded by Tipper Gore that persuaded record companies to put warning labels on their product. It was written by former PMRC executive director Jennifer Norwood and Robert DeMoss, youth-culture specialist for Focus on the Family, a Christian fundamentalist group. The second tape, called "Dreamworlds," was made by Sut Jhally, professor of communications at the University of Massachusetts, and is being sold for classroom use.

Pareles discovered, upon investigating "Rising to the Challenge," that the violent incidents allegedly inspired by rock video occurred before most of the albums mentioned were released, "suggesting," noted Pareles, "that the music reflects the culture instead of driving it." On examining "Dreamworlds," Pareles found that the images of women were ripped out of context without indicating what proportion they form of all music video images or even what videos they come from. In actual MTV, viewed in full and in context, Pareles found about one in six clips with "ornamental" or "sexy" women and "two minutes per hour of female bimbofication, along with such various nonbimboes as moms, teachers, old women and children." Music video also includes female singers and bands.

Pareles concludes with this observation: "When a teenager sees some guy with waist-length two-tone hair, wearing leopard-print spandex and studded leather standing in a spotlight holding a guitar, he or she can probably figure out that it's a performance, a show, a fantasy—part of a privileged arena far away from daily life. Given the evidence, I wish I could say the same about their elders." (*New York Times,* June 2, 1991)

Violence Against Women—Sources and Remedies

If pornography and rock do not cause violence, public attention needs to turn to what does. Leading feminists and the U.S. Commission on Civil Rights suggest that violence against women begins with educational and economic discrimination including a sex-segregated labor market and devaluation of traditional "women's work." Men learn to consider women burdens, stiflers and drags on their freedom. Women, in turn, do not have the economic independence and access to day care that would enable them to leave abusive settings. Feminists also suggest that violence begins with the infantilization of women so that men hold them in contempt and see them as easily dismissed or lampooned and ready targets for anger. (See U.S. Commission on Civil Rights, *Women in Poverty,* 1974; *Women Still in Poverty,* 1979; and *Child Care and Equal Opportunity for Women,* 1981)

Yet another factor in violence against women is the domestic arrangements that leave mom as the prime, often only, caretaker of small children. Even in progressive households, women continue to do most of the child care. To the infant and small child, mom is the font of affection, food and warmth. It's on mom that all one's infantile expectations for care are foisted, and all one's earliest disappointments blamed. An infant gets wet, cold or hungry, and learns to expect succor from mom and only mom; when these needs are not immediately met, the infant gets angry at mom. (See Nancy Chodorow, *The Reproduction of Mothering: Psychoanalysis and the Sociology of Gender,* 1978, University of California Press; Dorothy Dinnerstein, *The Maid and the Minotaur: Sexual Arrangements and Human Malaise,* 1976, Harper & Row, New York)

Under mom-only (or mostly) child care, one learns to act out one's desire for mom's attention, and one's rage that she's not always there, on all the women in the rest of one's life. Add to this "boy training" that makes aggression a daily project of masculinity—that says aggression is not only acceptable but impressive and manly. From such child rearing, most people feel ambivalent about women, and men feel free to say so with force.

This psychological swirl surfaces in pornography, just as it does in our private sexual fantasies, music, novels, and plastic arts, in advertising and fashion. Because pornography is fantasy, a genre of extremes like science fiction and gothic horror, it shows up in rude and blunt ways. Yet pornography did not invent rage at women and banning pornography won't end it. Like rock 'n' roll, it reflects rather than drives one's experience with the world. (See *amici curiae* brief of the Feminist Anti-Censorship Taskforce et al., by Nan Hunter and Sylvia Law, in *American Booksellers et al.* v. *William Hudnut III et al.,* United States Court of Appeals for the Seventh Circuit, 1985; M. Pally, paper, Harvard-MIT colloquium on Pornography, October 1985)

"Pornography is not the ultimate citadel of sexism," wrote Dr. William Simon, professor of sociology at the University of Houston and author of *The Post-Modernization of Sex.* "At best, it is a shadow cast by more important, more affluent, and far more powerful institutions."

Consider which more effectively teaches boys to have contempt for women: pictures of nudity and sex or hearing their fathers say to their mothers "Aw, shut up." If society wishes to reduce violence against women or improve the quality of family life, it is chasing after shadows until it eliminates that "Aw, shut up."

In his essay in *Society* magazine (July/August 1987), Dr. Larry Baron wrote, "The [Meese] commission would have us believe that sexual aggression can be controlled through the strict regulation of obscene materials, an illusion that shifts our attention away from the structural sources of rape . . . such issues as sexism, racism, poverty and a host of other factors ignored in the [Meese Commission] *Final Report.*"

Drs. Simon and Baron expose the irony of the last decade. The administrations that have been most active in restricting sexual material in the name of benefitting women and children have at the same time reduced funding for the Women, Infant and Children nutrition program, for pre- and postnatal care, day care and child health and education programs. The fundamentalists who work tirelessly to ban books, music and TV in the name of protecting women would return them, according to religious doctrine, to the economic and social dependence women have struggled to overcome.

In view of violence's excellent record for centuries before the production of commercialized images, the restriction of sexual imagery or rock 'n' roll seems to offer only negative results: Were this country to ban them tomorrow, it would still be plagued with sexual and drug abuses. It would have succeeded only in establishing dangerous precedents for stifling work such as *The Diary of Anne Frank, The Sisters Impossible* and the photographs of Robert Mapplethorpe.

Women should be especially keen to the value of constitutional protections against censorship. They allow the publication of ideas and images that some people, even most people, believe are dangerous—the "offensive" and angering material of Justice Douglas's quote. When feminists began their social critique 25 years ago, many Americans felt their platform was anarchic and possibly evil. Freedom to promote their ideas, including those about female sexuality, has been the linchpin of the modern women's movement. (See *amici curiae* brief of the Feminist Anti-Censorship Taskforce et al., by Nan Hunter and Sylvia Law, in *American Booksellers et al.* v. *William Hudnut III et al.,* United States Court of Appeals for the Seventh Circuit, 1985; for an expanded discussion of female sexual fantasy, see *Pleasure and Danger: Exploring Female Sexuality,* Carole Vance editor, 1984, Routledge & Kegan Paul, Boston, Massachusetts; *Powers of Desire: The Politics of Sexuality,* Ann Snitow, Christine Stansell and Sharon Thompson editors, 1983, Monthly Review Press; *Heresies,* 1981, vol. 3, no. 4, issue 12)

Women are ill-advised to abandon free speech rights for a supposed quick fix to sexism and violence. Should the freedom to express unpopular ideas be quashed, feminist works might well be among the first to go. One need only consider the recent Supreme Court decision in *Rust v. Sullivan,* upholding regulations that prohibit discussion of abortion in federally funded Title X family planning clinics. It has been another irony of the decade that women such as Catharine MacKinnon, Andrea Dworkin and Women Against Pornography believe censoring books, magazines and films will advance women's cause.

Society might do better to take the advice of Drs. Simon and Baron, and that of thousands of feminists and social science professionals, and address the fundamental sources of violence. The red herring of book, music and film banning flatters the public into thinking it is doing good while it is ignoring the substantive causes of social ills. Controlling the viewing and listening habits of the nation might not be the best way to use the country's funds and resources.

Every hour well-wishers spend attacking *Playboy,* "Married . . . With Children" or 2 Live Crew is an hour they might spend improving the economic options of minorities and women. They might develop police and community programs to aid abused women and children. To address the emotional fuel behind sexual abuses, one might create the social structures at home and in the workplace that would balance the skew of mom-only parenting. One might do better not banning Mapplethorpe or Madonna, but getting mom out of the house at least half the time, and dad back in. (See National Advisory Council on Economic Opportunity, *Final Report: The American Promise: Equal Justice and Economic Opportunity,* 1981; *Bruno v. McGuire,* 4 Family Law Reporter, 3095, 1978; A. Boylan and N. Taub, *Adult Domestic Violence: Constitutional, Legislative and Equitable Issues,* 1981; S. Schechter, *Women and Male Violence: The Visions and Struggles of the Battered Women's Movement,* 1982, South End Press)

Drs. Edward Donnerstein, Daniel Linz and Steven Penrod are leading researchers of the relationship between sexual and violent images and social harm. In their 1987 book *The Question of Pornography: Research Findings and Policy Implications* (New York, Free Press, a division of Macmillan Inc.), they wrote,

"Should harsher penalties be leveled against persons who traffic in pornography, particularly violent pornography? We do not believe so. Rather, it is our opinion that the most prudent course of action would be the development of educational programs that would teach viewers to become more critical consumers of the mass media. . . . Educational programs and stricter obscenity laws are not mutually exclusive, but the legal course of action is more restrictive of personal freedoms than an educational approach. And, as we have noted, the existing research probably does not justify this approach."

The Social Science Data

(For an expanded review of the social science research on sexually explicit material and aggression, see *Sense and Censorship: Resource Materials*)

Between 1968 and 1970, the President's Commission on Obscenity and Pornography studied the relationship between sexually explicit material and antisocial behavior. Over a two-year period with a budget of $2,000,000 (in 1970 dollars; contrast with the $500,000 in 1985 dollars allotted the Attorney General Meese's Commission on Pornography), it conducted national surveys on pornography consumption and crimes rates, as well as controlled laboratory studies. The 1970 commission concluded,

"Empirical research designed to clarify the question has found no reliable evidence to date that exposure to explicit sexual materials plays a significant role in the causation of delinquent or criminal sexual behavior among youths or adults." (1970 Commission, p. 139)

"Studies of juvenile delinquents indicate that their experience with erotica is generally similar to that of nondelinquents. . . . There is no basis in the available data, however, for supposing that there is any independent relationship between exposure to erotica and delinquency." (1970 Commission, p. 242)

"If a case is to be made against pornography in 1970, it will have to be made on grounds other than demonstrated effects of a damaging personal or social nature." (1970 Commission, p. 139)

In the years since 1970, two notions have again become popular: that pornography has become more violent and more widespread; as a result, it is responsible for antisocial behavior, specifically sexual perversions and violence against women and children. In 1985, Attorney General Edwin Meese formed another commission to study the social and psychological effects of sexually explicit material. The publicity surrounding the Meese Commission led to the belief that the pornography-causes-harm hypothesis was confirmed, yet the Meese Commission's investigation of the science does not support this conclusion. (See Resource Materials, sections 1B and 1E, Meese Commission)

In the 20 years since the 1970 commission—and especially since the mid-eighties when the pornography-causes-harm idea made pornography research legitimate grounds for tenure—the social sciences have produced a sizable literature of pornography studies. Certain methodological problems limit the findings, most importantly: generalizing from the laboratory to life; the "sexual bravura" skew implicit in the responses of college males (most commonly the subjects of research experiments) who are asked questions about sex; the "experimenter demand" effect, where subjects guess at the experimenter's hypothesis and then, even unconsciously, try to fulfill it; and the implausibility of all studies involving electrical "shocks" as a measure of aggression. Subjects in laboratory experiments know that researchers cannot allow their participants to be hurt in college labs. Nevertheless, the social science data might shed some light on the pornography-causes-harm debate. (Surgeon General Koop's Report on Pornography, 1986, pp. 5–11; Becker and Levine dissenting report to the Meese Commission; see also Resource Materials, section 1G, Methodological issues in social science research)

The idea that sexually explicit material has become more violent appears to be unfounded (See Resource Materials, section 2A, Prevalence of violence in sexually explicit material). Reviewing the literature on violence in sexually explicit material, Drs. Edward Donnerstein (University of Wisconsin, University of California), Daniel Linz (University of California), and Steven Penrod (University of Wisconsin) wrote in a 1987 *American Psychologist* article ("The Findings and Recommendations of the Attorney General's Commission on Pornography: Do the Psychological 'Facts' Fit the Political Fury?" (vol. 42, no. 10), that "We cannot legitimately conclude that the Attorney General's first assumption about pornography—that it has become increasingly more violent since the time of the 1970 Pornography Commission—is true. . . . The available data might suggest that there has actually been a decline in violent images within mainstream publications such as *Playboy* and that comparisons of 'X'-rated materials with other depictions suggest there is in fact far more violence in the *non*pornographic fare."

Dr. Joseph Scott and Steven Cuvelier (Ohio State University) ran a content analysis of *Playboy* over a 30-year period and found an average of 1.89 violent pictorials per year, with violence *decreasing* through the eighties. ("Sexual Violence in Playboy Magazine: A Longitudinal Content Analysis," *Journal of Sex Research,* 1987, vol. 23, no. 4; "Violence in *Playboy* Magazine: A Longitudinal Analysis," *Archives of Sexual Behavior,* 1987, vol. 16, no. 4)

They wrote, "Although the overall number and ratio of violent cartoons and pictorials in *Playboy* over the 30-year period examined [were infrequent], a major question addressed was whether the amount of violence was increasing. Rather than a linear relation, a curvilinear relationship was observed with the amount of violence on the decrease. . . . Those who argue for greater censorship of magazines such as *Playboy* because of its depictions of violence need a new rationale to justify their position." (*Archives of Sexual Behavior,* 1987, vol. 16, no. 4)

In his study of XXX video cassettes, Dr. Ted Palys of Simon Fraser University found a *decrease* in violence in sexually explicit videos. ("Testing the Common Wisdom: The Social Content of Video Pornography," *Canadian Psychology,* 1986, vol. 27)

In a 1990 content analysis of current videotapes, Drs. Ni Yang and Daniel Linz (University of California) found that in XXX explicit pornography, sex accounted for 41 percent of all behavioral sequences, sexual violence for 4.73 percent and nonsexual violence for another 4.73 percent. In R-rated films, sexual behavior accounted for 4.59 percent of all sequences, sexual violence accounted for 3.27 percent and violence accounted for 35 percent. ("Movie Ratings and the Content of Adult Videos: The Sex-Violence Ratio," *Journal of Communication,* 1990, vol. 40, no. 2)

Laboratory Studies

The Meese Commission idea that sexually explicit material yields social harms also seems unwarranted. Almost no legitimate researcher now gives credence to the notion that nonviolent sexual material causes anything but sticky paper. They have uncovered no substantive link between sex crimes and sexual images, much less rock 'n' roll. (See Resource Materials, sections 1B and 1E, Meese Commission)

Upon the release of the Meese Commission's *Final Report,* Dr. Park Dietz, a Meese Commission member and medical director of the Institute of Law, Psychiatry and Public Policy at the University of Virginia, said,

"I believe that *Playboy* centerfolds are among the healthiest sexual images in America, and so are many of Mr. Guccione's centerfolds."

Henry Hudson, chairman of the Meese Commission, said, "A lot of critics think that our report focuses on publications like *Playboy* and *Penthouse* and that is totally untrue."

During the year of its investigations, the Meese Commission asked Dr. Edna Einsiedel (University of Calgary) to write an independent review of the social science literature. Her report also found no link between sexually explicit material and sex crimes. The Meese Commission then asked then-Surgeon General C.E. Koop to gather additional social science data. Koop conducted a conference of researchers and practitioners in the medical and psychological fields. His report also found no link between sexual material and violence. (See Resource Materials, sections 1C, Einsiedel Report, and 1D, Surgeon General's Report)

The Meese Commission nevertheless recommended the restriction of sexually explicit material in its *Final Report.* Two commissioners, Ellen Levine and Dr. Judith Becker, so disagreed with the recommendations that they issued a dissenting report (see Resource Materials, section 1E, Meese Commission). Lambasting the commission for a "paucity of certain types of testimony including dissenting expert opinion" they concluded, "No self-respecting investigator would accept conclusions based on such a study." (Becker and Levine, Dissenting Report, pp. 4, 7)

Dr. Becker, director of the Sexual Behavior Clinic at New York State Psychiatric Institute, told the *New York Times* (May 17, 1986), "I've been working with sex offenders for 10 years and have reviewed the scientific literature, and I don't think a causal link exists between pornography and sex crimes."

Dr. Edward Donnerstein called the Commission's conclusions "bizarre"

(*New York Times,* May 17, 1986; see also his overview of the effects of sexually explicit material in *The Question of Pornography: Research Findings and Policy Implications,* with Daniel Linz and Steven Penrod, 1987, New York, Free Press, a division of Macmillan Inc.). He and other researchers such as Drs. Neil Malamuth (University of California) and Daniel Linz found no change, even in attitudes about women, when men were shown nonviolent sexual images that comprise the bulk of the pornography market.

In his November 1990 testimony before the Indecent Publications Tribunal of New Zealand, Donnerstein commented on the idea that sexually explicit materials might act as a trigger to sexual aggression. Donnerstein said he was "of the view that the vast majority of studies indicated that no such trigger mechanism or capacity existed."

In *American Psychologist,* Linz, Donnerstein and Penrod wrote, "To single out pornography for more stringent legal action is inappropriate—based on the empirical research. . . . If the Commissioners were looking for ways to curb the most nefarious media threat to public safety, they missed it." ("The Findings and Recommendations of the Attorney General's Commission on Pornography: Do the Psychological 'Facts' Fit the Political Fury?" 1987, vol. 42, no. 10)

In 1985, the Institute of Criminal Science, University of Copenhagen, reported that in European countries where restrictions on sexually explicit materials have been lifted, incidence of violent sex crimes over the last 20 years has declined or remained constant. Neither the Canadian nor the British commissions on pornography found any link between sexual material and sex crimes. (See Resource Materials, section 1F, Danish, Canadian, British and Australian investigations of pornography; section 4E, Crosscultural correlation studies of rape rates and availability of sexually explicit materials)

The British Inquiry into Obscenity and Film Censorship wrote, "We unhesitatingly reject the suggestion that the available statistical information for England and Wales lends any support at all to the argument that pornography acts as a stimulus to the commission of sexual violence." (P. 80)

Having found no substantive evidence of negative effects from exposure to nonviolent sexual material, researchers investigated material that is "degrading"—that depicts women in subordinate positions or in unusual sex practices. (See Resource Materials, section 2B, Effects of exposure to nonviolent and "degrading" sexual material.) This research is rife with problems of definition. Is a woman inviting intercourse subordination, love or domination? Is oral or anal sex "normal"? Researchers proceeded in their investigations with their ideas of non-normative sexual images.

These studies found no link between "degrading" pornography and aggression against women (D. Zillmann and J. Bryant, "Effects of Massive Exposure to Pornography," 1984, in *Pornography and Sexual Aggression,* New York, Academic Press). At hearings before the New Zealand Indecent Publications Tribunal in 1990, Donnerstein stated that any reasonable review of the research literature would not conclude that exposure to "degrading" pornography yields anti-social behavior.

Additionally, several researchers found that viewing sexual material produced a *decrease* in aggression in male subjects. (D. Zillmann and B. Sapolsky, *Journal of Personality and Social Psychology,* 1977, vol. 35; R. Baron, *Journal of Personality and Social Psychology,* 1974, vol. 30 (3); R. Baron, *Human Aggression,* 1977, New York, Plenum Press; R. Baron and P. Bell, *Journal of Personality and Social Psychology,* 1977, vol. 35; N. Malamuth "Erotica, Aggression and Perceived Appropriateness" 1978, presented at the 86th convention of the American Psychological Association; L. White, *Journal of Personality and Social Psychology,* 1979, vol. 37)

Neither the Surgeon General's report on pornography nor the Einsiedel review of the scientific literature showed any reliable link between "degrading" pornography and sex crimes or aggression.

The final category of sexual material investigated is violent pornography. (See Resource Materials, section 3A, Effects of exposure to sexually violent material.) These research results are the most inconsistent and confusing. Donnerstein, Linz et al., have found that exposure to violent imagery increases aggression in male subjects in laboratory settings (E. Donnerstein and D. Linz, "The Question of Pornography: It Is Not Sex but Violence That Is an Obscenity in Our Society," *Psychology Today,* December 1986). Drs. Neil Malamuth and Joseph Ceniti (University of California) found no effects from exposing subjects to violent pornography. (N. Malamuth and J. Ceniti, "Repeated Exposure to Violent and Nonviolent Pornography: Likelihood of Raping Ratings and Laboratory Aggression Against Women," *Aggressive Behavior,* 1986, vol. 12)

Donnerstein and Linz attribute the aggressive effects in their experiments to the violent content of images, not the sexual content. When they and other researchers showed subjects sexual imagery with no violence, they saw no aggressive effects. When they showed subjects violent imagery with no sex, they saw the most aggressive results.

In their December 1986 *Psychology Today* article, Donnerstein and Linz wrote, "The most callous attitudes about rape . . . were found among those men who had seen only the violent coercion. Subjects who saw the X-rated version without violence scored lowest."

Dr. Suzanne Ageton is one of the few scientists to investigate attitudes about women and aggression in life situations (*Sexual Assault Among Adolescents,* 1983, Lexington, Massachusetts, Lexington Books). She found that involvement in a delinquent peer group appeared consistently as the most powerful factor in determining violence, accounting for 76 percent of sexual aggression. Three other factors, including attitudes about women and violence, accounted for 19 percent altogether.

After Surgeon General Koop's 1986 conference for the Meese Commission, Malamuth wrote a letter to *American Psychologist* to correct misstatements published there about material that "portrays sexual aggression as pleasurable for the victim." He wrote,

"We [the Surgeon General's conference] did not reach the consensus that 'this type of pornography is at the root of much of the rape that occurs today' . . . We also agreed that 'acceptance of coercive sexuality appears to be related to sexual aggression,' but we did *not* conclude that 'if a man sees a steady stream of sexually violent material . . . he begins to believe that coercion and violence are acceptable . . . and may himself become the perpetrator.'" (Emphasis added)

In 1990, Donnerstein and Linz wrote this warning about research on violent images and aggression toward women,

"The findings are accurate as long as we are referring to laboratory studies of aggression. . . . Whether this aggression, usually in the form of delivering [mock] electric shocks, is representative of real world aggression, such as rape, is entirely a different matter." (1990 report to the government of New Zealand)

Explaining the research on violent material, Donnerstein told the District Court of Ontario (in *Her Majesty the Queen Against Fringe Product Inc.,* 1989),

"The measure is simply arousal, not sexual arousal. The Zillmann research strongly shows that once you get arousal up—the measures could be heart rate, galvanic skin response, blood pressure is the common one—if arousal is high and subjects are aggressing, it's going to facilitate aggressive behavior, independent of where the arousal comes from. And yes, there are studies where males bicycle ride and then are more aggressive when they are angered."

In sum, subjects in laboratory experiments will aggress if they are angered. If they are additionally "worked up" or aroused in any way, they will increase their aggression. These results will occur if men are exercised by aerobics and are not limited to their viewing sexual or violent imagery.

Another area of the psychological research investigates the formation of paraphilias, or unusual sexual practices, including pedophilia and sexual murder. (See Resource Material, section 5, Sexual materials and paraphilias.) At the time of the Meese Commission, Commissioner Dr. Park Dietz said, "No sprinkling of images, however deviant, can render an otherwise normal man either paraphiliac or criminal."

Dr. John Money, director of the Psychohormonal Research Unit at Johns Hopkins University School of Medicine, is likely the world's expert on the subject. In his 1989 book *Vandalized Lovemaps* (with Dr. Margaret Lamacz, Prometheus Books), he writes that the derailed sexual impulses of rapists, child abusers, exhibitionists, and the like result from childhood traumas, usually with the child's family, including incest, physical abuse or neglect, or emotional indifference.

His research found no evidence that sexually explicit material causes or maintains sexual crimes or aberrations. "The fantasies of paraphilia are not socially contagious," Money wrote in the *American Journal of Psychotherapy* (1984, vol. 38, no. 2). "They are not preferences borrowed from movies, books or other people." People who seek out specialty pornography are attracted to it because the sorts of behavior depicted are already of interest to them.

Dr. Money also found that the majority of people with unusual or criminal sexualities were raised with strict antisexual, repressive attitudes, and he predicted in a *New York Times* article (January 23, 1990) that the "current repressive attitudes toward sex will breed an ever-widening epidemic of aberrant sexual behavior."

Correlation Studies on Pornography and Rape

Researchers have investigated the relationship between sales of sexually explicit material and rape rates. (See Resource Materials, section 4D, Correlation studies of rape rates and sales of sexually explicit material.) According to the 1984 studies of Drs. Larry Baron and Murray Straus (Yale University, University of New Hampshire) and 1988 studies by Dr. Joseph Scott and Loretta Schwalm (Ohio State University), communities with more sales of pornography report more rapes. Yet Scott and Schwalm also found higher incidences of rape in areas with strong sales of any men's magazine, such as *Field & Stream.* ("Pornography and Rape: An Examination of Adult Theater Rates and Rape Rates by State," 1988, in *Controversial Issues in Crime and Justice,* Beverly Hills, California, Sage)

When Baron and Straus introduced into their data a "hypermasculinity" rating called the Violence Approval Index, the relationship between pornography circulation and rape disappeared. ("Sexual Stratification, Pornography, and Rape in the United States," 1984, in *Pornography and Sexual Aggression,* Orlando, Florida, Academic Press)

Baron explained at the Meese Commission hearings that "The relationship . . . may be due to an unspecified third variable. It is quite plausible that the findings could reflect state-to-state differences in a hypermasculated or macho culture pattern." (For an overview of the Baron and Straus studies see, L. Baron and M. Straus, *Four Theories of Rape in American Society: A State-level Analysis,* 1989, Yale University Press, New Haven, Connecticut)

In later studies, the correlation between rape rates and pornography sales disappeared when the number of young men living in a given area was factored into the data.

There is "no evidence of a relationship between popular sex magazines and violence against women," wrote Dr. Cynthia Gentry (Wake Forest University) in her 1989 study reviewing the data on the relationship between pornography sales and rape. The only factor that predicted the rape rate in a given locale was the number of men between the ages of 18 and 34 residing there. ("Pornography and Rape: An Empirical Analysis," 1991, *Deviant Behavior,* vol. 12)

In 1988, Scott and Schwalm reported similar findings in their correlation studies on rape rates and sexually explicit material. ("Rape Rates and the Circulation Rates of Adult Magazines," *Journal of Sex Research,* 1988, vol. 24)

Perhaps most interesting is Baron's 1990 study that found a *positive correla-*

tion between sales of sexually explicit material and high gender equality, suggesting that both flourish in politically tolerant areas. In the Baron study, *the best predictor of gender inequality was the presence and number of fundamentalist groups.* ("Pornography and Gender Equality: An Empirical Analysis," *Journal of Sex Research,* 1990, vol. 27)

Popular "Truths": The Media and Minors

Any investigation of the pornography/rock-causes-harm theory must consider its more popular arguments. Perhaps the most serious charge is that dangerous images fall into the hands of minors and so should be restricted from general distribution. (See Resource Materials, section 7C, Effects of media on minors)

Although the Surgeon General's report found little evidence that children ages 10–17 view X- or XXX-rated material, parents cannot watch their children all of the time and children undoubtedly find books, TV programming and music that their parents dislike. The great difficulty in trying to restrict such material is that adults hardly agree on the materials suitable for minors of different ages. One parent's literature, popular entertainment or music is another parent's trash. Some parents would encourage their minor children to see "Married . . . With Children" or *Last Tango in Paris* while others would prohibit them from reading *The Diary of Anne Frank.* One only need think of the debate over sex and AIDS education classes or of the controversy that began in 1990 over the Impressions reading series. What some teachers and parents consider a syllabus that sparks students' interest in reading others believe contravenes their religious beliefs. The series' section on Halloween, which includes ghost and goblin stories, has been attacked for teaching witchcraft. At least two suits against school districts using the series were filed in Willard, Ohio, and Sacramento, California.

Should some parents be successful in eliminating the materials they believe are harmful to minors by removing them from libraries, shops or television, they would keep that material from other adults and other people's children—a determination most Americans would rather make themselves.

Dr. Beverly Lynch, a former president of the American Library Association (ALA), suggests that guiding the reading and viewing of minors is the job of parents, not of local groups or government. It is ALA's position that most parents would prefer to supervise their children's reading and viewing—not only about sex but about religion, politics, money and most other aspects of life—rather than have those decisions made for them by state authorities or other parents, however well-meaning. In 1986, Dr. Lynch told the Meese Commission,

"The American Library Association opposes restricted access to material and services for minors, and holds that it is *parents*—and only parents—who may restrict their children—*and only their children*—from access to library materials. We not only defend the right of parents to supervise and guide the reading habits of their children, but we assert that it is their responsibility."

Children encounter people and ideas in life that contradict their parents' beliefs. In such circumstances, parents rely on the values they have imparted to their children to be a foundation for their children's developing views. Most parents also allow their children to play out of doors even though they might run into busy streets. They have taught their children to keep away from traffic, and trust that their teaching will prevail. So, too, with books, music and movies. No idea, no matter how offensive, can maim as thoroughly and quickly as an oncoming car.

Testifying to the Ontario District Court in 1989, Dr. Edward Donnerstein reported that should the media have negative effects on viewers, particularly minors, those effects are mitigated by parents and community values.

"There are the parental values, their church values, what they learn about in school or what they learn from mom and dad. And, in fact, I think the most interesting thing about all the research is that it tends to indicate that . . . if we as parents only sit down with those children and talk about violence on television, and talk about objectification in films, we actually mitigate the [negative] effects."

Parents have the right and the tedious responsibility to judge art, entertainment and even trash for themselves and their families without the sanctimony of strangers. Like most hypocrisies, censorship provisions are empty flattery. They create the illusion of virtue when one is relying on the "virtue" of others.

Similar to the parents' protest against offensive material is the "taxpayer's revolt," most evident in the NEA controversy and the 1991 *Rust* Supreme Court decision (upholding government regulations that prohibit discussion of abortion in federally funded family planning clinics). Its advocates argue that although artists may produce what their muses inspire and the public may purchase the art or information of its choice, taxpayers should not be forced to pay, through government funding agencies, for art or information they do not like.

Yet not all taxpayers agree on what art or information is worth funding. Taxpayers such as Senator Jesse Helms would not support Mr. Mapplethorpe's photographs, while thousands of taxpayers in Ohio, Pennsylvania, Massachusetts, California, Connecticut and New York not only favored paying for his work through the NEA but paid for it a second time in admission fees to his exhibition. Some taxpayers believe information about abortion or career opportunities in the military is poisonous and should not be disseminated; others believe it is crucial to the quality of American life.

To support the art and information one admires, one might need to tolerate support for art or information one dislikes but that others believe is worthy. Adlai Stevenson II wrote poetically, "The sound of tireless voices is the price we pay for the right to hear the music of our own opinions."

Another popular argument against sexually explicit material and rock is that men get ideas from them and force women to do what the photos or lyrics depict. The danger to women here is not sex, the positions or costumes, but in the *force*—economic, psychological and physical. Coercion is much older than rock or pornography, and women's intimidation begins not with the commercialized image but with confusion and powerlessness. Those who wish women well are wasting their time until they help women acquire the emotional means to know their sexual desires and the emotional and economic means to say "no" when they mean "no" and make it stick.

Another popular line is that taken by the rapists and wife batterers who tell their court-appointed social workers that they learned their ways from pornography. Ted Bundy, before his execution, graced us with such revelations. (See Resource Materials, section 8A, Ted Bundy: Pornography made me do it)

It's a clever ploy. Just look at who gets off the hook. First it was the Devil that made them do it, now it's Miss Jones. In their dissenting report to the Meese Commission, Dr. Judith Becker and Ellen Levine wrote, "Information from the sex-offender population must be interpreted with care because it may be self-serving." (Becker and Levine, Dissenting Report, p. 11)

Dr. Gene Abel (professor of psychiatry, Emory University School of Medicine) said at the time of the Bundy execution, "What we find is that sex offenders have rationalizations and justifications for their behavior. And Ted Bundy, like most of the sadists we've dealt with, had a lot of false beliefs or rationalizations to explain his behavior. What he said, in essence, was, 'It isn't my fault, these are pornographic things that I've seen.' And we just don't see that relationship."

Bundy's lawyer, James Coleman, said of Bundy's final interview, "It was vintage Bundy. It was Bundy the actor. He didn't know what made him kill people. No one did."

Beneath the pornography-made-me-do-it argument is the traditional blame-the-woman line. Men used to get away with rape and assault with the "tight sweater" excuse. A skirt too short, a neckline too low made rape the woman's fault. According to antipornography logic, it is still the woman's fault—if not the woman in the sweater then the woman in the magazine. If not the woman in the room, then the woman on the screen, calendar or wall. Attorneys Nan Hunter and Sylvia Law wrote in the Feminist Anti-Censorship Taskforce brief to the U.S. Court of Appeals, "Individuals who commit acts of violence must be held legally and morally accountable. The law should not displace responsibility onto imagery." (in *American Booksellers Association et al.* v. *William Hudnut III et al.*)

Also popular today is the claim that men rape because they learned from pornography that it's permissible or that women like it. There is something amiss with the idea that men rape to *please* women. To the rapist facing his terrified victim it has always been clear that she didn't "want it." Men rape because it hurts and they do it to hurt women. If society wants to reduce rape, it must address the psychological, economic and social conditions that make men want to inflict such pain.

Finally, one comes across the argument that nobody likes pornography and that communities have the right to rid themselves of the junk that nefarious and sleazy outsiders bring in. No one should be made to read, look at or buy what they don't want. Yet perhaps one should not determine what other people read or view by making sure it's not available in local libraries and stores. The retrospective of Robert Mapplethorpe photographs earned the Cincinnati Contemporary Arts Center a record number of visitors and new museum members. A jury of local residents judged it fit for public exhibition. One wonders who was the community whose standards these photographs offended.

Those who wish to restrict sexual material would have one believe that only unhealthy, troubled characters use it, and certainly no women. From this they reason the women must be protected from it. Relying on traditional notions of female asexuality and "purity," this reasoning promotes sexism more thoroughly than much of the material women's protectors would ban. (See Feminist Anti-Censorship Taskforce *amici curiae* brief in *American Booksellers et al. v. William Hudnut III et al.*)

The sales receipts of sexually explicit material tell a different story. (See Resource Materials, section 9B, Community values and sales of sexually explicit materials.) Nineteen eighty-nine saw 395 million rentals of adult video tapes, most of which were watched by two or more people. Forty-seven percent of these rentals were made by women in couples or women alone. The figure in 1988 was 398 million. Reagan's 1984 election was considered a landslide with 54 million votes. These figures do not include adult-video sales, cable TV viewing, mail-order sales, adult-theater attendance or adult-video viewing in private clubs. In a related area, phone sex in 1987 was a $2.4 million business—up from $1 million four years earlier ("Charting the Adult Industry," *Adult Video News Buyer's Guide*, 1991; *Sexuality Today*, May 4, 1987).

If pornography is an $8 billion a year industry, as those who wish to restrict it say it is, surely that doesn't mean eight perverts are each spending one billion dollars a year. Whose "community values" does sexually explicit material contravene? In the last five years, when antipornography legislation has come before state governments or before the public in local referenda, it has been voted down or killed in the legislatures in Michigan, Maine and Cambridge, Massachusetts.

Sex Industry Workers

Feminists who work with abused women have turned the country's attention to the mistreatment of models and actors performing in sexually explicit photographs, films and videos. It seems more than obvious to say that anyone who commits fraud or violence—in the production of sexual material or in any other industry—should be vigorously prosecuted under laws against intimidation, assault, false imprisonment, battery and rape. Special programs are needed to aid police officers working with those abused in the production of sexual material and to help them take seriously the charges of models and actors.

The most effective guarantee of safety for sex-industry workers would be provisions making those industries legitimate retail businesses. The more legitimate, the more accountable to law, from sanitation codes and work-for-hire contracts to criminal codes. Any activity is more dangerous on the black market. A woman cannot go to the police and complain about being cheated of her pay, let alone raped, if her job is illegal. She cannot bring her rapist to trial if the cops think she's "cheap" and laugh her out of the station house.

Many people reasonably feel that work in the sex industries is not the ideal job for either men or women. The remedy is economic. Until better jobs are available and accessible, do-gooders are being sanctimonious at the expense of the actors and models who need the work. Closing down the sex industries wipes out a source of income that's crucial to industry employees, no matter how dismaying those jobs seem to others. It closes down options. Education and job training expand them.

At their July 1991 convention, the National Organization for Women considered launching a national campaign against sexually explicit material. Performers from the sex industries attended the convention and lobbied against the campaign, arguing that restrictions on pornography aggravated rather than improved their lives. The sex workers prevailed and the antipornography proposal failed.

Why Does Censorship Feel So Right?

A question still nags: why does the antipornography/antirock argument feel so right? Why is it persuasive to so many men and women? One of its appeals is activism. Since sexual images and heavy rock are visible and somewhat illicit, one can easily organize against them. Witness the renown that Women Against Pornography, the American Family Association and the Parents Music Resource Center have achieved in the last decade. The participants believe they're doing something to better life, and it is rewarding to feel effective.

Pornography and rock 'n' roll are small issues compared with a vast system of kneejerk sexism or the unsettling economic and social changes of the last quarter century. One feels one can get on top of them, beat 'em, win. After years of exhaustion fighting a sexist economy and politics, after years of feeling at a loss in an inflationary, shrinking market or in the face of rapid changes in gender roles and parenting, the "decency" movements are a boon to many people who want to feel they control their lives. (M. Pally, "Ban Sexism Not Pornography, *The Nation,* June 29, 1985)

Psychologist Paula Webster suggests yet another idea. She writes that the antipornography argument feels right because it carries "the voice of mom" (paper to Women and the Law Annual Conference, March 1985). Most people in Western societies grow up with the feeling that sex is dirty and that abandon is dangerous. Most women grow up with the assurance that men are dangerous. They heard it indirectly or they heard it point blank, but the message becomes a lens through which they see the world.

In later years, most adults manage to develop the sexual aspects of life. Yet the old lessons remain embedded in the imagination and at the core of the emotions. So when one is told that pornography is dirty and makes men dangerous, it "clicks." When one hears in adult language and political terminology the things one absorbed when one was young, it sounds infallible. Already suspicious of sex, one calls it culprit. Suspicious of dark nights with loud music and hectic dancing, one calls it *Walpurgisnacht* and blames the witches for one's woes.

Consider the parents who claimed the rock group Judas Priest made their sons commit suicide. To prove their point and collect damages, they went to court, where other information about the boys came to light. Ray Belknap was 18; his parents separated before he was born. His mother married four times and her last husband regularly beat Ray. He also threatened Ray's mother with a gun in front of the boy, according to the police. Ray had quit high school after two years and was a heavy user of hallucinogens and cocaine. But the rock lyrics made him do it. James Vance, Ray's friend, was born when his mother was 17. She beat him when he was a child and when he got older, he beat her in return. He also had a history of drugs and boasted of drinking two six-packs of beer a day. But the rock lyrics made him do it. (*New York Times,* September 20, 1990)

Would that the cure to society's troubles were a matter of eliminating pornography and rock 'n' roll. Would that it were so single-issue or so easy. The words of Drs. Morris Lipton and Edward Greenwood, members of the 1970 commission on pornography, come to mind,

"We would have welcomed evidence relating exposure to erotica to delinquency, crime and antisocial behavior, for if such evidence existed we might have a simple solution to some of our most urgent problems. However, [this] . . . is not only to deny the facts, but also to delude the public by offering a spurious and simplistic answer to highly complex problems." (*Psychiatric News,* March 15, 1972)

Censorship has always been more problem than solution. It purges society of books, movies, and music, leaving hate, racism, sexism, drug abuse, poverty, and violence flourishing as they did before the printing press, phonograph and camera.

Reacting to Offensive Speech: Persuasion Over Repression

In the instance that one sees or hears ideas that are offensive or dangerous, the least productive tactic is to invoke censorship. Thomas Paine wrote, "He that would make his own liberty secure, must guard even his enemy from opposition; for if he violates this duty, he establishes a precedent that will reach to himself." The tough part about free speech is enduring it when the other guy is talking.

Rather than silence one's opponents, one would do better to use the offensive speech to get one's own voice heard, to add to the debate. "Bad" ideas are best used as an occasion to attract attention to "good" ones, with the understanding that one's adversaries will try just as energetically to get their points across. Student groups and university administrations who seek to rid their campuses of prejudice would do better to use this approach than to ban so-called "hate-speech." Colleges and universities, with their continuing hubbub of rallies, meetings and debates, seem ideal places to learn how to use offensive views to spur discussion and promote better ideas.

This add-to-the-debate approach is more daunting outside the university, where individuals or small groups face wealthy, vertically integrated media conglomerates. It's the old problem of trying to speak when one doesn't own the presses. Yet 25 years ago, what began as a small ragtag group of student loudmouths slowly convinced the public and media of the folly of the Vietnam war. At the start of the 1960s, most people and members of the press were in favor of the U.S. presence in Southeast Asia; by the end of the '60s, most, including mainstream news commentators, were against it. The campaign against smoking, 20 years ago the effort of a small, curious group, has persuaded millions of Americans to quit. More recently, inexperienced groups of gay men protested against a dearth in AIDS funding and have grown into impressive lobbying forces with considerable budgets in half a dozen or so years.

Feminists and civil rights activists made nuisances of themselves till they were heard. No public figure says "nigger" today and few say "girl" not because the words were banned but because blacks and women convinced the country that racism and sexism were wrong. Women and minorities aired their ideas, both in the mainstream media and in the publications, galleries, and theaters that they built. Writers, theorists and artists rode the coattails of a political effort and, in turn, provided a spin for the politics to go another round. The supposedly quicker solution of silencing "bad" speech gives up the game. Having established the precedent of censorship, there is nothing to stop one's views from being silenced next.

The people who own the presses worked hard for that privilege. They did, or their fathers or grandfathers; someone put in a good deal of time and effort. Power never cedes. To promote new ideas, one has to do the work that persuades people to pay attention. One has to not only think, write, or perform but also set up the structures, political and financial, to help unorthodox voices be heard. It is a double load, it takes its toll, and it has taken up lifetimes. The advantage of having an uncensored marketplace of ideas is that one gets to make one's bid.

The principle behind freedom of expression is not that it automatically secures what one thinks is good or true, but that it is society's best chance at truth in the long run. The nation bats ideas back and forth in public, advancing and modifying its opinions. The alternative is to let someone appoint himself king and have his way. In 1947, Winston Churchill told parliament, "It has been said that democracy is the worst form of government, except all those other forms that have been tried."

Democracy takes time and it is a contact sport. One has to be there and there's no automatic pilot. "The right to differ on things which do not matter much is the mere shadow of freedom," wrote the Supreme Court. "The test of substance is the right to differ on things which touch the very heart of existing order."

• *Marcia Pally is a social scientist who writes frequently on censorship issues. For an expanded review of the social science research on sexually explicit material, see* Sense and Censorship: The Vanity of Bonfires, Resource Materials on Sexually Explicit Material, Violent Material and Censorship: Research and Public Policy Implications, *available from Americans for Constitutional Freedom.*

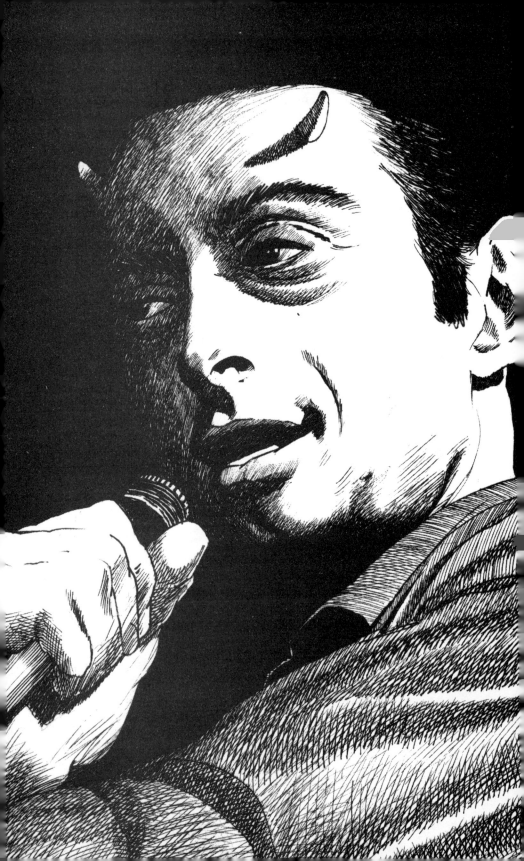

Appendices

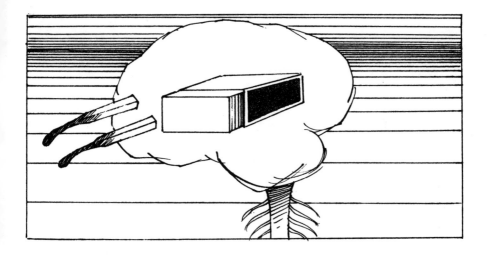

1

Waldenbooks—
A Position Statement

by Susan Arnold

Like its counterpart B. Dalton Bookseller, Waldenbooks is oftentimes asked for a comment when books and censorship make the news, for an obvious reason: What Waldenbooks carries in its stores is, to a large extent, what America is reading. If you don't find it at Waldenbooks, you may find it in an independent bookstore, or in B. Dalton Bookseller.

As far as adult material goes, there's very little to be found on their shelves: Magazine selection is limited to Playboy *(and its various pictorial collections) and* Penthouse *(but none of its various publications, like* Variations *or* Forum*). In short, soft-core material.*

In fiction, adult erotica are for the most part not available in the Waldenbooks chain. Although it carries the Anne Rice Beauty *trilogy, under the pen name A.N. Roquelaire, and the occasional erotic mainstream novel (like* Vox *or* Damage*), adult erotica like Barney Rossett's Blue Moon Books can't be found on its shelves anymore.*

The following is our position on the sale of adult fiction and magazines:

The shelves of our 1,150 stores hold a wide array of titles containing ideas as diverse as the world in which we live. We sincerely believe that it is in everyone's best interest to make ideas of all kinds available to interested individuals, regardless of what our own tastes might be.

In that spirit, Waldenbooks believes in the right of the individual to make his or her own choice with regard to reading material. We selectively carry adult titles (fiction and magazines) as part of our overall responsibility as America's leading bookseller to provide choice, diversity and selection that respond to the needs and preferences of the reading public. As a matter of policy, we comply with all local laws and ordinances in the display and sale of adult titles—sale of these titles is restricted to adults only.

Of course, everyone makes personal choices about the values of particular books. We believe that it is not our role as booksellers to make these choices for our customers. Our role is not and should not be that of a censor.

We take our position as a member of your community seriously. And we listen to our customers. When they are concerned, we are concerned. We believe that we have an obligation to make available constitutionally protected reading material which has significant appeal to a wide variety of Americans.

We review our policies on a regular basis to ensure that Waldenbooks remains a respected general interest bookstore, and our customers' comments are included in this process.

2

The Ten Best Censored Stories of 1992

Compiled by Project Censored

The brainchild of Dr. Carl Jensen, Project Censored has, since its inception in 1976, explored and publicized "the extent of censorship in our society by locating stories about significant issues of which the public should be aware, but is not, for a variety of reasons."

Dr. Jensen, a 1992 recipient of the HMH [Hugh M. Hefner] First Amendment Award, is the author of Censored: The News That Didn't Make the News and Why *(the 1993 Project Censored yearbook), published by Shelburne Press. Dr. Jensen also edits the monthly newsletter* Censored, *available for $30 in the U.S. ($45 for foreign subscriptions); write to* Censored *Newsletter (P.O. Box 310, Cotati, CA 94931).*

1. The Great Media Sell-Out. This quid pro quo between major media monopolies and the Reagan/Bush administrations silenced the nation's watchdogs. Source: *Mother Jones,* May/June 1992, "Journalism of Joy," by Ben Bagdikian.

2. Corporate Crime Dwarfs Street Crime. While the press frightens the public with headlines about street crime, corporate crime grows at an accelerated pace. Source: *Multinational Monitor,* December 1991, "Corporate Crime & Violence in Review," by Russell Mokhiber.

3. Censored Election Issues. Under-reported issues during the election year included: Bush and Iran-contra; Bush's Team 100; Homelessness; Dan Quayle's Council on Competitiveness; The Death Rate of Iraqi Children After the Gulf War; and What Happened in Mena, Arkansas, While Bill Clinton Was Governor. Sources: *Common Cause* magazine, April/May/June 1992, "George Bush's Ruling Class"; *Washington Post,* 1/9/92, "A Profound Silence on Homelessness," by Mary McGrory; *The Progressive,* May 1992, "Deregulatory Creep," by Arthur E. Rowse; *This World, San Francisco Examiner,* 10/11/92, "46,900 Unspectacular Deaths," by Mike Royko; *Unclassified,* February/March 1992, "The Mena, Arkansas, Story."

4. World's Leading Merchant of Death. How the United States became the world's leading producer and supplier of weapons. Source: *World Press Review,* September 1992, "The World's Top Arms Merchant," by Frederick Clairmonte; *The Human Quest,* July/August 1992, "War 'Dividends'—Military Spending out of Balance with Needy," by Tristam Coffin.

5. Iraqgate & the Watergate Law. The Bush Administration stalls Iraqgate probe and Senate Democrats, fearing an independent investigation of their activities, join Republicans to defeat the Watergate Law. Sources: *Covert/Action Information Bulletin,* Fall 1992, "Bush Administration Uses CIA to Stonewall Iraq-gate Investigation," by Jack Calhoun; *War and Peace Digest* (NY), August 1992, "BNL-Iraqgate Scandal"; *The Paper* of Sonoma County (CA), 10/22/92, "Is Bush a Felon?" by Stephen P. Pizzo; *New York Times,* 10/20/92, "The Patsy Prosecutor," by William Safire.

6. Winning the War on Drugs. Drug statistics reveal that President Bush lied when he announced we were winning the war on drugs. Sources: *In These Times,* 5/20/92, "Drug Deaths Rise As the War Continues," by Mike Males; *Extra!* September 1992, "Don't Forget the Hype: Media, Drugs and Public Opinion," by Micah Fink.

7. Trashing Federal Regulations for Profit. An extraordinary correlation between major campaign contributions and federal regulatory relief is revealed. Sources: *The Nation,* 3/23/92, "Bush's Regulatory Chill: Immoral, Illegal, and Deadly," by Christine Triano and Nancy Watzman; *The Progressive,* May 1992, "Deregulatory Creep," by Arthur E. Rowse.

8. Government Secrecy Makes a Mockery of Democracy. The nation's information policy is totally out of control with widespread over-classification. Source: *Issues in Science and Technology,* Summer 1992, "The Perils of Government Secrecy," by Steven Aftergood.

9. Advertising Pressure Corrupts a Free Press. The subtle, but pervasive, influence of advertisers on the content of the news. Source: *The Center for the Study of Commercialism,* 1992, "Dictating Content: How Advertising Pressure Can Corrupt a Free Press," by Ronald K.L. Collins.

10. Pentagon's Post Cold War Black Budget. Despite the end of the cold war, $100 million a day still goes to support the national-security machinery in the U.S. Source: *Mother Jones,* March/April 1992, "The Pentagon's Secret Stash," by Tim Weiner.

Fifteen Other Censored Stories of 1992

The fifteen other underreported stories of 1992 were: Solar Power Eclipsed by Oil, Gas, and Nuclear Interests; What Happened to the EPA? The Specter of Sterility; News Media Lose the War with the Pentagon; Plutonium Is Forever; America's Killing Ground: Dumping on Native American Lands; Norplant: Birth Control or Social Control? The Censored News About Electric Automobiles; Poison in the Pacific; Black Gold Conquistadors Invade Ecuador; How to Sell Pollution for Profit; Clear-Cutting the World's Rainforests; Censorship Through Bribery; The No-Pest Shell Game; University of Arizona Desecrates Sacred Native American Site.

3

Arts Censors of the Year

(In Observance of Banned Books Week 1992)
by the American Civil Liberties Union

Long-time moral crusader Donald Wildmon, rap music detractor Oliver North, anti-pornography feminist Catharine MacKinnon, and acting NEA chair Anne-Imelda Radice are among the individuals that have been chosen as Arts Censors of the Year by the American Civil Liberties Union's Arts Censorship Project.

The ACLU announced its Arts Censors of the Year as Americans observed Banned Books Week—a time when we pause to celebrate literature and art and also to examine the strains of intolerance and repression that still haunt our society. Since its founding in 1920, the ACLU has fought for freedom of artistic expression, and that fight continues to this day as government officials, prosecutors and self-appointed guardians of public morality seek to inhibit artists, and to restrict access to words or images they deem "offensive."

Censorship comes in many forms and guises. Several of the ACLU's Arts Censors are public officials who have used the weight and authority of their offices to wage campaigns against musicians, painters, sculptors, and writers. Their historical antecedents include John Michael Casey, the Boston City Censor whose banning of 65 books in 1926 popularized the phrase "Banned in Boston," and Postmaster General Arthur Summerfield, who in 1959 prosecuted the American publisher of D.H. Lawrence's *Lady Chatterley's Lover.*

The remaining Arts Censors cited by the ACLU are private individuals and pressure groups that have advocated censorship in an effort to impose their morality and cultural tastes on the rest of society. Private groups and individuals, of course, have a First Amendment right to advocate censorship, but when they urge actions that result in diminishing the rights of other Americans to read, hear, or view expressions of their choice, the content of their advocacy—and the consequences of their efforts if successful—must be opposed. Today's private censors follow in the footsteps of Anthony Comstock and his Society for the Suppression of Vice, whose pro-censorship activism led to the passage of the Comstock Law in 1873 and the subsequent destruction of tens of thousands of "improper" pictures and books.

Intolerance for diverse ideas, beliefs, and lifestyles has been a strong theme in the politics of this election year. The groups and individuals chosen by the ACLU as Arts Censors of the Year have, by their actions, helped set the stage for this repressive climate.

The ACLU's Arts Censors of the Year are:

Government Arts Censors

• **Anne-Imelda Radice,** acting chair of the National Endowment for the Arts, who stated in testimony before Congress that she would veto any grants for sexually explicit art or other projects that deal with "difficult subject matter." One week later, she kept her word, vetoing grants to two galleries that were planning exhibitions of nationally recognized artists who used nude images in their work.

• **The Duval County, Florida, Public School District,** which has censored more than sixty books over the years and which, this past year, purged the county's school libraries of titles by Stephen King and African-American poet Nikki Giovanni, not to mention the classic fairy tale *Snow White,* banned because of its "graphic violence."

• **Omaha City Councilman Steve Exon,** and members of a local organization called Omaha for Decency, who together organized a private sting operation resulting in prosecutions against four local record stores for selling 2 Live Crew's "Sports Weekend" album to teenagers.

• **The Maryland State Legislature's Frederick County Delegation,** which reversed its plans to seek $500,000 in state funding for a local arts center after the museum displayed a satiric, anti-Persian Gulf War painting.

• **The Washington State Legislature and Governor Booth Gardner,** who passed a law imposing a mandatory labeling system, with criminal penalties, for musical recordings deemed "erotic" by a state court.

Anne-Imelda Radice

In retrospect, it seems like an obvious scenario: Ideologues in Washington, thwarted in their efforts to control the content of NEA-funded artworks through legislation, plant a mole inside the agency and let her do their work for them. This, with only a few added complexities, is the story of Anne-Imelda Radice's rise to the chairmanship of the National Endowment for the Arts, where she quickly established her intentions this spring by unilaterally vetoing a pair of grants that might have proved politically controversial.

Radice, who former NEA chair John Frohnmayer says was "taking orders from the White House" throughout her year-long tenure as Frohnmayer's second-in-command, made her plans for the agency clear in a House subcommittee meeting held during her first week as chair. Accepting the mantle of "decency czar," Radice promised that the Endowment no longer would fund "sexually explicit" artworks, and said she had no qualms about overturning decisions made by the NEA's peer panels of artists and art administrators or by the Endowment's oversight body, the National Council on the Arts. "The last stop is with the chairman," she told the congressmen, "who has to reflect on Congress, on the American people, on the future of the Endowment. . . ."

In other words, she was willing to deny grants to artists, museums, or other awardees on the basis of political expediency. She also said, "if we find a proposal that does not have the widest audience [in other words, that might offend religious-right critics], we just can't afford to fund that." One week later she kept her word, rejecting grants to the List Gallery at the Massachusetts Institute of Technology and the Anderson Gallery at Virginia Commonwealth University. Both were planning exhibitions of nationally recognized artists, some of whom employ nude images in their work. In rejecting the grants, she ignored the expertise of both the NEA's museum panel and the National Council, both of which had already approved the proposals.

The peer panels, each made up of experts in a particular art form, were mandated by the Endowment's authorizing legislation as a way to insulate grant decisions from political pressures. Not surprisingly, several other panels found it difficult to complete their work in the wake of Radice's reversals, since all standards for the legitimacy of their efforts had been thrown into question. Two panels resigned in protest; but rather than respond to their concerns, Radice transferred their funds to other programs.

Radice's abandonment of the peer panel process, which has worked well for a quarter-century, and her explicitly stated willingness to satisfy right-wing censorship pressures by vetoing controversial grants, further politicized the NEA and made the agency captive to ideological manipulation. Whether Radice will continue to sacrifice artistic freedom in order to maintain the Endowment's political stability remains to be seen.

Duval County School District, Florida

Censorship of textbooks and other publications is commonplace in America's public and private schools. Each year, dozens of school districts decide that their children's minds must not be corrupted by offensive books, from literary masterpieces that contain mild love scenes to science texts that teach theories of evolution. In Louisiana this year, a book titled *Hoodoo and Voodoo* was taken off library shelves because "it tells you ways to give people evil thoughts"; in California, a teacher assigned her class to read Ray Bradbury's *Fahrenheit 451,* but when students opened their books they found that all uses of the words "hell" and "damn" had been blacked out.

One school district that has made a science of book banning is Duval County, Florida, where students' access to more than 60 different books has been restricted or banned over the years. This year's additions to the list include, for junior high and high schools students, best-selling author Stephen King's *The Dead Zone* and *The Tommyknockers,* as well as acclaimed poet Nikki Giovanni's *My House,* and *Skateboarding* magazine; for elementary school children, this year's biggest threat was . . . *Snow White.*

A group of parents and "media specialists" in the county have determined that the classic Brothers Grimm fairy tale is too violent for its audience; after all, the story features a hunter killing a wild boar and a wicked witch ordering Snow White's heart torn out. Elementary school children now must receive a parent's permission before checking the book out of the school library. The same goes for high school students who wish to read one of the Stephen King novels, which also were relegated to the back rooms of Duval County's libraries after parental complaints.

County administrators take a book off the shelves as soon as they receive a complaint, instead of allowing continued access until a detailed review can determine whether or not the book is suitable for students. This places the burden of proof on the book's defenders, rather than on its attackers, and has resulted in the restriction or banning of an unusually high number of books in the county.

Other novels placed behind the librarians' desks at Duval's secondary schools include William Faulkner's *As I Lay Dying* and J.D. Salinger's *Catcher in the Rye;* in the elementary schools, Shel Silverstein's much-loved *A Light in the Attic* was removed temporarily because it includes a drawing of a bare-bottomed man being stung by a bee. ("Slight nudity," the school board noted.)

"Now where does this stop?" a Duval County science teacher recently asked. "I have this sense that a small, vocal minority is doing the community a big disservice." Unfortunately, it appears that Duval's book-banning tradition is not on the wane, but on the rise: during the last school year, 17 books were restricted or banned, setting a new record.

Steve Exon, Omaha Councilman, and Omaha for Decency

Last fall, in a campaign of harassment of the type that happens too often around the country, Nebraska Attorney General Don Stenberg wrote letters threatening seven video stores near Omaha with prosecution unless they stopped renting X-rated tapes. Stenberg's threat was the result of lobbying by members of Omaha for Decency, a local pressure group; he wrote the letters even though he knew that most, if not all, of the sexually oriented tapes rented by the stores were protected by the Constitution. Most of the stores refused to take the tapes off their shelves, and Stenberg eventually backed down. Still, the owner of one of the stores was certain that Omaha for Decency was not finished. "If they can do this," said the owner, Derek McMains, "it could lead to censorship of other things like rock music tapes, which we also sell." Six months later, his words proved prophetic.

Attacks on artistic freedom often begin at a grass-roots level, when like-minded residents of a community decide that art and entertainment products they do not like should be eliminated from their town. Of course, pro-"decency" groups have as much right to advocate their opinions as anyone else does. Sometimes, however, a group goes beyond advocacy and decides to take law enforcement into its own hands.

In the spring of 1992, Omaha for Decency conducted a private "sting" operation against nine music stores, with the help of City Councilman Steve Exon. Their intent was to stop sales of 2 Live Crew's "Sports Weekend" album to teenagers, an act which they hoped would be found illegal under Nebraska's "harmful to minors" law. The group sent teenagers into the stores to purchase the album, then submitted their "evidence" to Omaha prosecutor Gary Bucchino, who pressed charges against four of the stores.

The "harmful to minors" law, which criminalizes a broader range of materials for minors than Nebraska's obscenity law restricts for adults, encompasses materials that are "patently offensive to prevailing standards in the adult community as a whole with respect to what is suitable material for minors." Attorneys for the record stores argued that the law, like similar statutes in 35 states, is unconstitutionally vague, and provides merchants and consumers with insufficient information regarding the types of materials that are prohibited. As a result, prosecutors often are able to suppress materials for purely ideological reasons, by threatening merchants with fines or prison.

By early summer of 1992, when a court in Florida determined that 2 Live Crew's previous album, "As Nasty As They Wanna Be," was *not* obscene, it had become apparent to Bucchino that his case would be difficult to win, so he dropped the charges. Nevertheless, organizations such as Omaha for Decency no doubt will continue to use "harmful to minors" laws to deprive both parents and their children of musical choices, and to push their own ideological and religious agendas on the rest of society.

Maryland State Legislature, Frederick County Delegation

More than a year after the Gulf War, state legislators in Maryland showed this winter that anti-war sentiment remains politically unacceptable, voting to delay state funding for an arts center that exhibited a satiric artwork depicting President Bush, Gen. Norman Schwarzkopf, and others in the nude.

The painting, titled "A Peace Treaty and a New World Order," was created by Austrian artist Josef Schutzenhofer. It generated immediate attention and controversy upon its unveiling last January at the Delaplaine Visual Arts Center in Frederick. In the painting, Bush stands naked next to entertainer Dolly Parton (also nude). Behind them, Schwarzkopf and Sen. Jesse Helms (R-NC) wear Roman breastplates and no pants; Schwarzkopf has his foot on the back of Saddam Hussein, who kneels on a prayer rug, and Schwarzkopf holds a shield emblazoned with the face of Adolf Hitler.

The painting is a satirical take-off of a Rubens sketch titled "The Peace Treaty of 1630." As a result of the controversy that surrounded the painting, the Frederick County delegation to the state legislature decided not to submit a bill authorizing a $500,000 bond issue for a new building for the arts center. The center had requested the funds, in the form of a matching grant, in order to renovate an old mill; before the painting was mounted, the delegates had expressed no reservations about seeking the funding.

However, several of them said the painting had probably offended enough of the community to rule out public support for the funding bill. "It totally has nothing to do with whether we like or dislike any of the art exhibits," said Del.

George H. Littrell, Jr. "It's a matter of making an educated decision on the facts of life in Annapolis in getting funding."

Another delegate, J. Anita Stup, was less diplomatic. "Call me a fuddy-duddy if you will, but I don't approve of it," she said. "I don't approve of pornography."

The legislators may have thought the painting would hurt public support for the arts center, but its presence certainly didn't hurt the center's attendance figures. In fact, patrons lined up around the block to get a look at Schutzenhofer's work, disregarding signs warning them of the painting's potentially offensive subject matter. The signs were mandated by the arts center's board of directors, who also required that the painting be quarantined within its own room, away from other works in the exhibit.

Washington State Legislature and Gov. Booth Gardner

The issue of record labeling has perplexed state governments and private citizens since 1985, when the Parents Music Resource Center first demanded that the recording industry adopt "parental advisory" labels for albums containing "explicit lyrics." The PMRC's success in coercing the industry into "voluntary labeling" of potentially offensive recordings has led numerous state governments to try to impose their own labeling systems, and to restrict teenagers' access to "explicit" recordings.

So far, most governmental attempts to impose labeling systems have either failed in state legislatures or been vetoed by governors. This spring, however, the State of Washington passed an "erotic music" law that could severely limit the range of constitutionally protected recordings available to minors in that state.

The law allows a county prosecutor who finds a potentially offensive recording in a local store to ask a judge whether that album is "erotic" under the terms of the statute. If the judge makes such a determination, all copies of that recording distributed for sale in the state must be stickered "adults only," and must be exhibited in special locations within record stores. Anyone who sells a stickered recording to a minor can be fined or jailed.

Because the judicial hearing on a recording's status under the law must take place within five days of a prosecutor's request, the law deprives the recording's defenders of the opportunity to mount a convincing argument. To make matters worse, the state requires only that the store originally named by the prosecutor be notified of the hearing; thus, other stores around the state have no opportunity to defend the recording, but are forced to abide by the judge's decision. More than two dozen musicians, record companies, and consumers have brought a lawsuit against the state, arguing that these breaches of due process, in addition to the vagueness of the law's definition of "erotic" recordings, violate the First and Four-teenth Amendments to the U.S. Constitution as well as the Washington State Constitution. (In the fall of 1992, a state court judge struck down the law as unconstitutional.)

The PMRC may have believed that labeling musical recordings would simply help parents make decisions about their children's listening habits, but the "voluntary" labels instituted by the record industry have served as an inspiration for states like Washington to restrict public access to works that are deemed offensive. And the haphazard process by which record companies decide which albums will be labeled has resulted in a more structured blacklisting of albums and artists, both by fearful music store owners and by crusading government officials. All in all, record labeling has evolved into an exotic form of censorship, disguised as "consumer information" but resulting in the suppression of artistic works.

Private Arts Censors

• **Oliver North and Jack Thompson,** who led a campaign of prosecution and harassment against musicians and record companies over Ice-T's song, "Cop Killer," and other music with messages they dislike.

• **Catharine MacKinnon and Andrea Dworkin,** for drafting and advocating legislation that would allow lawsuits to ban sexually oriented entertainment, and to allow victims of sexual crimes to collect damages from the producers and distributors of such entertainment.

• **Rev. Donald Wildmon,** for a lifetime of disservice to the fundamental values of the Bill of Rights in his pursuit of one overarching goal: the restructuring of American law to reflect his own moral code through an unrelenting campaign against artistic expression he deems to be "pornographic" or "blasphemous."

Oliver North and Jack Thompson

"We have only two lines of defense, our military and our police," says Iran-Contra figure Oliver North. "During the Gulf War, Freedom Alliance supported our troops. Now it's time to support our overworked, underpaid, and outgunned police."

For what Gulf War–like cause did America's police require North's support? The defense against rap music, of course. The above quote appeared in a letter asking members of North's Washington-based advocacy group, Freedom Alliance, to encourage state governments to prosecute media conglomerate Time Warner for distributing Ice-T's song "Cop Killer." And this summer, North hired Florida attorney Jack Thompson, a man already notorious for his unsuccessful attempts to prosecute 2 Live Crew on obscenity charges, to see if sedition statutes or other laws could be used to punish Time Warner executives and freeze the company's assets.

American sedition laws, the earliest of which were written in the late 1700s to stifle dissenting speech, have long since fallen into disuse. But North and Thompson argued that "Cop Killer," a provocative song about one man's decision to take revenge for acts of police brutality, was illegal because it "advocated violence against police officers."

North and Thompson certainly weren't "Cop Killer"'s sole attackers, but their threats of legal action were among the most foolhardy aspects of the "Cop Killer" controversy. Eventually, after an extensive campaign of attacks that ranged from bomb threats against Time Warner to calls by Vice President Quayle for "Cop Killer"'s defenders to "stop hiding behind the First Amendment," Ice-T pulled the song from his album. But even after Ice-T agreed to withdraw the song, North and Thompson continued to press prosecutors and police groups to initiate criminal or civil actions against the singer and Time Warner. Eventually they cajoled the leaders of the Boston Police Patrolmen's Association into announcing plans for a civil suit against Ice-T and a Boston rap group also affiliated with Time Warner. The suit was dropped after a coalition of Boston civil rights groups denounced it as frivolous, and after the BPPA's rank-and-file members voted to reject the North/ Thompson tactics.

Although North and Thompson so far have been unsuccessful in provoking a lawsuit against Time Warner, they succeeded this summer [1992] in exploiting North's notoriety to stir up racial hatred and misunderstanding. They may think they are defending police officers by scapegoating musicians for the potential crimes of others, but their continued attempts to undermine our constitutional rights may leave the police with little to defend in return.

Catharine MacKinnon and Andrea Dworkin

For more than a decade, Catharine MacKinnon and Andrea Dworkin have been among the most outspoken leaders of the fight to ban pornography. MacKinnon, a noted legal scholar, and Dworkin, author of numerous novels and non-fiction works, have helped draft legislation in several states that would sacrifice the First Amendment rights of filmmakers, video store owners, and consumers by eliminating sexual materials that they mistakenly claim lead to sexual violence against women.

Although courts and local officials in Indianapolis, Minneapolis, and Bellingham, Washington, recognized the folly in anti-porn bills that were proposed there during the 1980s, MacKinnon and Dworkin's efforts have borne fruit again in a bill currently being considered in Massachusetts. And an alliance of anti-porn feminists and religious fundamentalists has convinced Congress to consider the so-called Pornography Victims Compensation Act, which passed the Senate Judiciary Committee in July and now awaits action by the full Senate. (The bill was voted out of committee but not acted on in 1992.)

The PVCA—which MacKinnon and Dworkin have not directly supported, primarily because it is not restrictive enough—arises from the faulty assumption that consuming sexually oriented materials can lead directly to criminal acts (hence the misnomer "pornography victims"). It would make producers and distributors of books, magazines, films, and videos liable for the deeds of criminals supposedly influenced by those materials. The proposal often is called the "Bundy bill," after serial killer Ted Bundy, whose claim that "porn made me do it" lent weight to a porn-causes-violence theory unsubstantiated by any credible scientific evidence.

In order to pass the Judiciary Committee, the PVCA was narrowed to allow lawsuits only in cases in which the pornography cited by a sex offender as playing a "substantial" role in his crime has already been found obscene in court. MacKinnon and Dworkin advocate even broader bills, like the one being considered in Massachusetts, that would encompass sexually oriented materials that are protected by the Constitution, but that they claim depict the "subordination of women." The Massachusetts bill also would allow *anyone* offended by a pornographic work—not just victims of supposedly related crimes—to sue for damages on claims that the materials violated their civil rights.

Shifting the burden of liability for sex crimes onto filmmakers and video store owners allows criminals to escape responsibility for their actions. It also distracts our attention from the *real* causes of hostility and violence toward women in our society—problems reflected, not caused, by pornography. Unfortunately, Canada's Supreme Court ignored these facts recently, ruling that pornography could be outlawed, despite the harm done to free expression, if it depicts the subordination of women. The government's brief supporting the ban was coauthored by MacKinnon.

Rev. Donald Wildmon

Of all the men and women who have tried to force their own narrow viewpoints upon the rest of us over the past decade, no one approaches the sheer diligence of the head of the American Family Association, the Rev. Donald Wildmon. Perhaps no other private citizen of his generation has dedicated so much time and energy to the cause of depriving others of their First Amendment rights. Wildmon's crusades against American culture have attacked products of nearly every artistic medium, from "Charlie's Angels" to "The Last Temptation of Christ" and from Madonna's "Like a Prayer" to Andres Serrano's "Piss Christ."

From his modest beginnings, attempting to organize boycotts of major television advertisers with a tiny following, Wildmon built the National Federation for Decency in the early 1980s with the help of televangelist Jerry Falwell. Soon he escalated his boycotts against supposedly "anti-Christian" television programs, and against convenience stores that sold *Playboy* and *Penthouse* magazines. And after urging President Reagan to form the "Meese Commission" on pornography, Wildmon's testimony claimed that the list of American "distributors of pornography" included CBS, RCA, Time, Inc., Ramada Inns, Coca-Cola, and other major corporations.

Wildmon's career as the nation's most prominent censor has been dotted with both successes and failures. He succeeded in pressuring 7-Elevens and other stores to remove sexually oriented magazines, and his threats of boycotts persuaded advertisers to withdraw their sponsorship of "Three's Company" and "Charlie's Angels." But some of his efforts have backfired publicly: his attacks on Martin Scorsese's film "The Last Temptation of Christ" and Robert Mapplethorpe's "The Perfect Moment" exhibit brought tens of thousands of patrons into theaters and museums. Nevertheless, Wildmon has been effective in framing the debate on his terms, with the result that much of the public seems to believe that artists such as

Mapplethorpe and Serrano are "pornographic" or "blasphemous," and are unworthy of public support.

Some of Wildmon's tactics are at once laughable and distressing. Most recently, Wildmon claimed that a contract he had signed with the producers of a British documentary about censorship, *Damned in the USA,* allowed him to forbid distribution of the film in the United States. Wildmon, who is interviewed in the film, dislikes it because it contains footage of artworks he has fought against; this may be the first time a film about censorship has itself been censored by one of its stars. In September 1992, a Mississippi court ruled that he had no right to ban the film.

Former NEA chair John Frohnmayer once noted that men like Wildmon "come across as good old boys who don't know much, but know what's right. But don't think for a moment that they're bumpkins, or that they're just after the arts. Their agenda is suppression of thought with which they don't agree, and that's as un-American as anything I can think of."

4

Fighting Censorship
What You Can Do

By its very nature, censorship is proactive, whereas anticensorship efforts are reactive.

It becomes important, then, to raise your voice when the voices of censorship are heard.

In *Banned Books Week 1991: A Resource Book,* the American Library Association offers many ideas that you can implement; I've added some additional information, where appropriate. Also useful: *Fifty Ways to Fight Censorship* by Dave Marsh.

In no particular order:

1. Teachers: assign censorship as research paper topic. (The annual Banned Books Week celebration is a good time for this activity.)

2. Display a bumper sticker informing the world that you are anticensorship.

3. Retailers: print "freedom to read" messages on merchandise bags.

4. Teachers/local groups: discuss banned books as a topic.

5. Publish flyers, posters, newsletters, and lists of books with the titles of banned books.

6. Wear buttons that promote anticensorship (like "I Read Banned Books").

7. Teachers: stage a mock trial for a banned book.

8. Retailers: construct window displays to showcase banned books.

9. Teachers: have a film festival on the theme of censorship.

10. Teachers: screen a banned film.

11. Individuals: march in a community parade.

12. Retailers: sponsor a poster contest for children to promote free speech.

13. Retailers: print "freedom to read" bookmarks.

14. Individuals: wear a banned books T-shirt.

15. Retailers: display banned books in the store window.

16. Retailers: display book jackets of banned books.

17. Teachers: reenact the signing of the Constitution, wtih a discussion to follow.

18. Individuals: keep current on anticensorship efforts and read up on the subject.

19. Retailers: put up an eye-catching poster to promote banned books in the store window.

20. Libraries: rope off an area of the library to highlight the inaccessibility of banned books.

21. Local groups: commission a local storyteller or theater group to dramatize the subject of banned books by putting on a show for schools, libraries, and other public centers.

22. Librarians: schedule speakers to discuss First Amendment issues.

23. Retailers and librarians: use Bradbury's *Fahrenheit 451* as the theme for a window display. ("The system was simple. Books were for burning . . . along with the houses in which they were hidden," wrote Bradbury in the novel.)

24. Individuals: buy manuals, books, book bags, and other material that heighten awareness and publicize anticensorship efforts.

25. Groups: learn about the legislative process; spend a day at the state capitol to see democracy in action.

26. Administrators and teachers: include banned books in the curriculum.

27. Individuals: wear anticensorship pins.

28. Individuals: distribute anticensorship bumper stickers and decals.

29. Newspapers: run a feature story on Banned Books Week. (School or community newspapers could, perhaps, use Banned Books Week as a theme for one issue.)

30. Groups: sponsor a "read out" dramatizing the dangers of censorship.

31. Book dicussion groups: discuss banned books or banned authors.

32. Individuals and groups: promote Banned Books Week by ensuring that your community and local media are aware of the event; also, efforts should be made to promote it on a statewide basis.

33. Organizations: for public parades with floats, use banned books as the theme.

34. Individuals: join anticensorship organizations.

35. Organizations: print a Banned Books Week calendar.

36. Schools: give away banned books. (For instance, in Richmond, Virginia, copies of Stephen King's *'Salem's Lot* were given away after the local school district banned the novel.)

37. Teachers: show anticensorship videos like *Bags: Books Under Fire* and *Censorship in a Free Society.*

38. Organizations: circulate a petition challenging specific censorship efforts; afterward, send copies to local and state governments.

39. Organizations: contact a local cable TV station to put on a program on First Amendment issues.

40. Organizations, retailers: send local media press releases highlighting your anticensorship efforts, and efforts to promote Banned Books Week.

41. Libraries/bookstores: try to get public service announcements regarding Banned Books Week on the air. (The ALA offers sample PSAs for public use.)

42. Individuals: get on the mailing lists of censorship groups, to stay current of their activities.

5

Resources

The information in this appendix is subject to change without notice. When ordering by mail, I recommend you write to get the current price; always enclose a self-addressed, stamped envelope (no. 10, standard business size) for a response.

Books

A complete listing of books available on censorship, requiring a separate book in itself, is beyond the scope of this book.

For an annotated listing of some books consulted during the course of this project, see the Bibliography. For the most part, however, I relied heavily on more current material: newspapers, magazines, and newsletters—far too numerous to mention.

For the most current and complete listing of books on censorship, consult Melissa Mytinger's excellent bibliography, reflecting books in print, published in *Censorship and First Amendment Rights: A Primer,* published at $10 by American Booksellers Foundation for Free Expression (560 White Plains Road, Tarrytown, NY 10591).

For an annotated listing of banned books, listed alphabetically by author, consult *Banned Books Week '92: Celebrating the Freedom to Read,* "A Resource Book and Promotion Guide," edited by Robert P. Doyle, published by the American Library Association. (An annual, this resource guide is available only by mail; write to the ALA for its free publications list.)

For information on books in print, consult the R.R. Bowker reference work, updated annually, *Books in Print,* which is available at your local library and at most bookstores. Listing books by author as well as subject, *Books in Print* and its companion book, *Forthcoming Books in Print,* are indispensable.

If you want to order a book, chances are you'll have to special-order it from a bookstore. To facilitate ordering, provide the title, author, and ISBN (an identifying number assigned to each book—a book's social security number, so to speak).

Alternatively, check out your local library. A good place to start is the reference librarian, who can guide you in the right direction.

If your local library does not have the book you want, it can usually locate it at another library and obtain it through the Interlibrary Loan program. Typically, it takes two to three weeks for a book to arrive. (Because these books are shipped via U.S. mail, some libraries pass on the postage costs to you.)

Keep in mind that because a half year to a year (or more) will elapse between the time a book is submitted to a publisher and when it is published, the information may be somewhat dated.

Publications

Magazines are a good source of information, offering up-to-date information. *Playboy* magazine, published monthly, examines censorship in its monthly feature "The Playboy Forum." Similarly, *Penthouse* covers the censorship scene.

I also recommend *Gauntlet: Exploring the Limits of Free Expression* (309 Powell Road, Springfield, PA 19064). Published biannually, this no-holds-barred anticensorship journal will generally not be found in libraries or chain bookstores, since its editorial policy of publishing controversial art is at odds with mainstream sensibilities. Editor-publisher Barry Hoffman, working on a modest budget, offers subscriptions as well as back issues.

For coverage of censorship in TV and the film industry, *Entertainment Weekly* is a good place to look.

In searching for articles on censorship in popular magazines, consult the *Readers' Guide to Periodical Literature* (from R.W. Wilson Company; published bimonthly, with quarterly and yearly updates). This reference work, available at your local library, covers approximately 300 magazines.

Alternatively, many libraries have computerized databases that can search by author or subject, or both. (Our local library subscribes to "Magazine Articles Summaries," which covers approximately 500 magazines. A noteworthy feature of this database: it provides a précis for each entry.)

For a more focused look at censorship, the best sources include the newsletters, pamphlets, and publications from organizations devoted to First Amendment issues. (See the listing under "Organizations" in this appendix.)

Newspapers

The debate about NEA appropriations continues, and for this reason the *Washington Post* is invaluable for its continuing coverage. For a broader perspective, *USA Today* is helpful.

Television Programs

For transcripts of TV programs, contact Journal Graphics, Inc. (1535 Grant Street, Denver, CO 80203). Providing "every word that was spoken on a program," the transcripts are available by subject, from more than seventy program series, including all the major news programs on the three networks and CNN. "Transcripts may be delivered via fax, overnight courier or regular mail. Videotapes, audiotapes, and books are delivered via United Parcel Service."

Organizations

This list of organizations is, obviously, tentative. I contacted virtually every organization listed in other directories; some responded with information, others refused to participate, and some had closed down and their forwarding addresses had expired.

In cases where organizations were contacted but never responded to basic requests for information, I have so noted in a separate listing.

When contacting organizations, always enclose a self-addressed, stamped envelope, with the return address (preferably) typed, or printed neatly. Especially with organizations that have a modest operating budget, postage is a big expense.

Because phone numbers often change, I have not listed them; call long-distance directory assistance for information.

Accuracy in Media (1275 K Street, N.W., Washington, DC 20005).

"Investigates complaints of serious media misdeeds; takes proven cases to the top officials of media organizations, asking for corrections; publicizes the most serious cases and mobilizes public pressure to bring about remedial action; works for adoption by the media of higher standards of reporting, editing, and a responsible approach to news."

AIM publishes twice a month a newsletter, the *AIM Report* ($22.95, third class). Also reaches the public through: a weekly newspaper column in over 100 papers, "Media Monitor" (a radio commentary, five days a week), space advertising in newspapers and magazines, speakers for organizations, and AIM conferences.

Publishes a book and tape catalogue, available for free.

Dues and contributions are tax-deductible.

Adult Video Association (270 North Canon Drive, Suite 1370, Beverly Hills, CA 90210).

The AVA was founded by David Kastens, and its administrative director is Gloria Leonard. This industry organization of approximately 500 members is "dedicated to preserving your right to create and/or enjoy adult entertainment."

Membership fees are restricted to those who are in the industry, but an associate membership is available for the general public through its public relations affiliate, FOXE (Fans of X-rated Entertainment), which has approximately 1,200 members.

FOXE publishes a newsletter keeping members abreast of the Adult Video Association activities and offers for sale merchandise to raise money for its

> war chest to fund the many ongoing legal battles and legislative skirmishes right here on the homefront. Defend your constitutional right to see, hear, read, and learn *or* pay the price of losing your fundamental freedoms to the Troops of Tyranny!

The Adult Video Association offers a full-color poster, 24 × 28 inches, depicting six scantily clad women raising the flag—recalling the famous Iwo Jima image. This "Fighting for Your Freedom" poster, writes Margold, "was created to combat the small-minded and self-righteous who have forgotten what the American flag really stands for." Its cost is $13 (postage and handling included).

Other licensed products, available from various publishers, are a "Hot Dates" calendar for 1993, Adult Video Star Trading Cards ("Video Vixens"), T-shirts, etc. Discounts available on some products for FOXE members (write for membership information).

American Booksellers Association (137 West 25 Street, New York, NY 10001-7296).

The trade organization for booksellers, the ABA hosts the annual bookseller's convention at which a benefit for its Foundation for Free Expression is hosted.

Censorship news is often covered in their weekly *ABA Newswire* ($30 for members, $50 for nonmembers; add $10 for foreign orders).

American Booksellers Foundation for Free Expression (560 White Plains Road, Tarrytown, NY 10591).

Established in 1990, this organization is affiliated with the American Booksellers Association, which hosts the annual book trade convention, the ABA, and is principally concerned with book censorship.

Its goal: "To inform and educate booksellers, other members of the book industry and the public about the deleterious effects of censorship; to actively promote and protect the free expression of ideas, particularly freedom in the choice of reading material . . . .

"In continued cooperation with the American Library Association, [we] will sponsor the annual Banned Books Week observance to help focus . . . attention on the myriad efforts to interfere with the availability of constitutionally protected material."

Publications include: *Free Expression,* a quarterly newsletter, and *Censorship and First Amendment Rights: A Primer* (1991, 163 pp., $10).

Membership fees vary: contributor (less than $25), member ($25), supporter ($50), patron ($100), company and/or store member ($100), donor ($250), benefactor ($500+).

American Civil Liberties Union (Membership Department, 132 West 43 Street, New York, NY 10109-0592).

As Samuel Walker, author of *In Defense of American Liberties,* explains:

> The essential feature of the ACLU is its professed commitment to the nonpartisan defense of the Bill of Rights. This means defending the civil liberties of everyone, including the free speech rights of Communists, Nazis, and Ku Klux Klan members. It means defending the due process rights of even the most despicable criminals. . . . The ACLU's "absolutist" position on freedom from censorship and separation of church and state has led it to oppose censorship of pornography and, every winter at holiday time, to fight religious displays on government property.

Established in 1920, the ACLU has over 270,000 members. According to Walker, the ACLU is far-reaching:

In addition to a national office in New York and a large legislative office in Washington, D.C., it maintains staffed affiliates in forty-six states. The often feisty and independent affiliates handle 80 percent of the ACLU's legal cases. With some justification, the ACLU calls itself "the nation's largest law firm." At any given moment it is involved in an estimated one thousand cases, and it appears before the Supreme Court more often than does any other organization except the federal government.

In addition to an *Arts Censorship Project Newsletter* (its first issue was published in 1991), the ACLU publishes *Civil Liberties* (a newsletter "on current ACLU cases, and other legal and political developments, affecting your civil liberties") and also offers a wide range of briefing papers, public policy reports, pamphlets, posters, and books. For a free copy of its "Literature and Publications List/Order Form (item no. 3000), send a SASE to: ACLU, Dept. L., P.O. Box 794, Medford, NY 11763.

Membership fees (not tax-deductible) vary: limited income ($5), individual ($20), joint ($30).

American Family Association (Rev. Donald Wildmon, Box 2440, Tupelo, MS 38803).

Originally the National Federation for Decency, the AFA was founded by Rev. Donald Wildmon, who, as the *Washington Post*'s David von Drehle wrote, "is a familar figure in censorship controversies, leading boycotts and writing angry letters and raising some $6 million a year to clean up smut."

Drehle adds: "He has some strong opinions about the media, which can be summed up by saying that the media are choked with filth and ruining the country." Concludes Drehle: "Which is why Wildmon does not like to give interviews."

Not surprisingly, the AFA did not respond to any of my requests for information on the organization and its publications, or to an offer to publish, unedited, whatever Wildmon wanted to say about himself or his organization.

Those wanting a unique look at Wildmon should read his book, *Don Wildmon: The Man the Networks Love to Hate,* coauthored with Randall Nulton.

In the context of this book, one quote by Wildmon from the book is particularly illuminating:

> Taking their cue from the network brass, local television and radio stations frequently repeated the sweeping accusations, many of them false, against the NFD. But again, I was almost never allowed to answer the charges. As far as I was concerned, this use of a public medium to condemn a group of people without permitting them to respond was censorship in its ugliest form.

To which I'd add: *self*-censorship is far uglier.

American Humanist Association (7 Harwood Drive, P.O. Box 146, Amherst, NY 14226-0146).

According to the AHA, its philosophy

> holds that human beings determine the moral principles by which they live. . . . Humanists recognize that it is only when people feel free to think for themselves as individuals, using reason as their guide, that they are best capable of developing values that succeed in satisfying human needs and serving human interests. . . .

Humanists, out of respect for science, are skeptical of paranormal claims and have no belief in the supernatural. They see insufficient reason to believe in life after death and put no reliance upon supposed cosmic guarantees, rewards, or punishments.

But most importantly, Humanists take responsibility for their lives and their world. As a result, they are concerned and involved in efforts to solve the many problems that plague humanity. . . . Humanism is a philosophy of worldly concern and action.

Basic information about humanism is explained in "What Is Humanism?" a reprint from *The Humanist*, "The Humanist Philosophy in Perspective" by Frederick Edwords, and "Humanist Manifestos I & II," affirmations of their philosophy.

Publications include: *The Humanist* (a bimonthly magazine) and *Free Mind* (an association membership magazine).

The AHA also publishes books through its Humanist Press, produces audiotapes, videotapes, and films, and offers lecturers.

The AHA has over seventy chartered chapters that meet monthly.

Members receive: a one-year subscription to *The Humanist* and *Free Mind, The Philosophy of Humanism* by Corliss Lamont, "invitations to and discounts on national and regional conferences, discounts on books, pamphlets, cassettes, voting privileges within the AHA and the opportunity to hold office and become a Humanist Counselor or Advocate."

Membership fees ($9.98 goes toward the one-year subscription for *The Humanist;* the remainder is tax deductible): Regular membership ($39), joint membership ($49), low-income membership ($19), joint low-income membership ($24), committee of 1,000 membership ($100).

American Library Association (Office for Intellectual Freedom, 50 East Huron Street, Chicago, IL 60611).

Established in 1967, the Office for Intellectual Freedom is "charged with implementing ALA policies concerning the concept of intellectual freedom as embodied in the Library Bill of Rights, the Association's policy on free access to library and library materials. The goal of the Office is to educate librarians and the general public about the importance of intellectual freedom in libraries. Toward this goal, the Office provides information and support to the library community, coordinates educational activities, and publishes the *Newsletter on Intellectual Freedom*."

Publishes the bimonthly *Newsletter on Intellectual Freedom* ($30 a year), which reports censorship incidents through the U.S., summaries of recent court rulings, original articles, and reviews of books on censorship.

The Office for Intellectual Freedom offers many censorship resources, including material to promote Banned Books Week. (Recommended reading: *Banned Books Week*, a resource book; $13.)

Through its Freedom to Read Foundation, it publishes a quarterly newsletter, *Freedom to Read Foundation News*. The foundation was "established in 1969 as an independent organization dedicated to the legal and financial defense of intellectual freedom, especially in libraries." Membership fees (tax-deductible): student member ($10), regular member ($25), contributing member ($50), sponsor ($100), patron ($500), and benefactor ($1,000).

The Freedom to Read Foundation "works hand in hand with librarians, authors, booksellers, and civil libertarian groups to ensure that YOU decide what YOU want to read, and that others aren't making that decision for you. By joining . . . you will:

"Defend the First Amendment before the U.S. Supreme Court.

"Support librarians around the country who are besieged by attempts to restrict library materials and services.

"Expand the freedom to read by offering legal and financial help in cases involving libraries and librarians, authors, publishers, and booksellers."

American Society of Journalists and Authors, Inc. (1501 Broadway, Suite 302, New York, NY 10036).

An organization for writers and journalists, ASJA "has launched a campaign to speak out against the rising incidence of book censorship." To promote the cause, ASJA offers buttons ("I Read Banned Books," $1 each), a T-shirt (the text of the First Amendment, $16), and a *Censorship Resource List* ("a helpful list of sources for information on censorship and First Amendment issues"; send a no. 10 envelope with first-class postage for two ounces).

Americans for Constitutional Freedom (900 Third Avenue, Suite 1600, New York, NY 10022).

Publishes *Sense & Censorship: The Vanity of Bonfires* by Marcia Pally. (Composed of two pamphlets—the main text and resource materials—*Sense & Censorship* is available for its shipping charge of $1.50.)

Americans for Reponsible Television (P.O. Box 627, Bloomfield Hills, MI 48303).

Founded by Ms. Terry Rakolta, ART advocates restoring "'family viewing' to television" and "taking action against the sponsors of Trash TV."

ART's purpose is "to encourage and promote the responsible use of our public airwaves by its license-holders," writes ART's vice president, Terry Merritt.

States Rakolta, "ART dislikes being cast in the role of a citizen pressure group. But it was our duty to speak for the millions registering a public outcry against the persistent over-emphasis of sex and violence on TV and radio."

ART publishes a quarterly newsletter, *Americans for Responsible Television;* a one-year subscription is available for a $15 membership donation. Accepts donations in varying amounts. Fields requests for information on starting a local ART Chapter.

Association of American Publishers, Freedom to Read Committee (220 East 23 Street, New York, NY 10010; 1718 Connecticut Avenue, N.W., Washington, DC 20009-1148).

From *This Is AAP: An Introduction to the Association of American Publishers:* "The Freedom to Read Committee is the center of AAP activities to protect and strengthen

First Amendment rights. The committee plays a major educational role, promoting through its reports and public programs an understanding and appreciation of these rights. Intervention in court cases, testimony before Congress, and coordinated action with other organizations . . . are some of the ways in which the committee meets threats of censorship and other encroachments on First Amendment freedoms."

Publishes "Read All About It! Current Books About Your Bill of Rights." *Free* for a SASE. Bulk copies are also available; 10 copies for $2; 25 copies for $5; and $5 for each additional 25 copies.

Barfko-Swill (P.O. Box 5418, North Hollywood, CA 91616-5418).

Concerned about music censorship, particularly Tipper Gore's organization Parents Music Resource Center, Frank Zappa publishes a packet of information called the "Z/PAC," which includes photocopies of letters he's written to the president, published editorials, news stories, and an ordering form for records and other products. It is available for a SASE and $1.50 ("and any extra stamps or other contributions are gratefully accepted"); in it Zappa seeks to zap PMRC, which, as he explains,

> has a lot of nerve to ask for money. They are already very well funded, well connected, and seem to have the entire U.S. news media in their back pocket. This mailing, all legal fees, phone bills, and travel costs connected with fighting this issue have been paid for out of profits from Barking Pumpkin record sales, and from Barfko-Swill mail order funds. We thank you for buying these items. Without the orders you have already placed, a real opposing view to this issue would never have been heard.
>
> Okay, it's up to you now. Don't let yourselves down. Take some time and help protect *your* constitutional rights. You know how to use a phone. You know how to write letters. Make some noise about this issue. Use *your* imagination. DON'T BEND OVER FOR THE WIVES OF BIG BROTHER.

Christian Broadcasting Network, Inc. (1000 Centerville Turnpike, Virginia Beach, VA 23465-9989).

Christian Broadcasting was founded by Marion Gordan "Pat" Robertson in 1961. "The mission of CBN and its affiliated organizations is to prepare the United States of America and other nations of the world for the coming of Jesus Christ and the establishment of the Kingdom of God on earth.

"We are achieving this end through the strategic use of mass communication, especially radio, television and film; the distribution of cassettes, films and literature; and the educational training of students to relate biblical principles to those spheres of human endeavor that play a dominant role in the world.

"We strive for innovation, excellence and integrity in all that we do. We aim always to glorify God and His Son Jesus Christ."

Write for a complete list of publications available.

Christian Coalition (P.O. Box 1990, Chesapeake, VA 23327).

Founded in 1989 by Pat Robertson (see CBN, above), Christian Coalition is a well-organized, well-funded political organization that, according to *Christian*

American (the CC newpaper), gives Christians a voice in their government again. Its director is Ralph Reed, Jr.

Current "member and activist base" exceeds 200,000; circulation of the bi-monthly *Christian American* exceeds 400,000; over 3,500 people have attended Christian Coalition training seminars. With 475 chapters in 47 states, the Christian Coalition is a powerful political voice for evangelical Christians.

Also publishes a newsletter, *Religious Rights Watch,* highlighting stores of national interest; topics in a recent newsletter included criticism of Martin Scorsese's *Cape Fear,* concern over the University of North Florida's showing two lesbian films for Women's History Month, and the controversy surrounding the Auburn Gay and Lesbian Association in Auburn, Alabama.

Coalition Against Lyrics Legislation (Recording Industry Association of America, Inc., 1020 Nineteenth Street, N.W., Suite 200, Washington, DC 20036).

The RIAA's mission is "to create a better business environment for American recorded music." Among the growing issues facing the industry is music censorship. The RIAA notes that in 1990, "22 states considered laws that would have required special labeling or expanding the definition of obscenity, either of which would have created de facto censorship."

Comic Book Legal Defense Fund (P.O. Box 501, Princeton, WI 54968).

Specializing in protecting First Amendment rights nationwide on behalf of comic book publishers and retail stores, the Comic Book Legal Defense Fund accepts donations for its comic-book-related product as its major source of funding. Products available include: a button ("I Read Banned comics"; $2), and a T-shirt depicting a creature taped down to a table whose voice is being silenced by tape over his mouth ($18; large and extralarge sizes). Donations are tax-deductible. (Previously, this organization published a limited edition, numbered "Benefit" portfolio, with artwork by cartoon greats Sergio Aragones, Richard Corben, Robert Crumb, Will Eisner, and others.)

Educational Freedom Foundation (20 Parkland Place, Glendale, MO 63122).

EFF was founded in 1963 "to educate the public as to the importance and requirements of educational freedom, and to assist defense of the latter in court cases. . . . Among activities supported by the Foundation are research, publication of articles, pamphlets, and books, lectures, discussions, radio and television programs, meetings, and legal counsel, treatises, and briefs, all relating to the value and needs of educational freedom, particularly freedom of choice in education. . . . Non-political, non-partisan, and nonsectarian, the EFF work is mainly educational and informative. Its principal function is to obtain and disseminate information concerning freedom of education, particularly as it relates to the survival and welfare of non-governmental (including church-related) education."

Publishes a periodical, *Educational Freedom,* available for $5 a year; accepts donations. Also publishes a wide range of publications.

It is affiliated with the Citizens for Educational Freedom (927 South Walter Reed Drive, #1, Arlington, VA 22204), which is "primarily a political action association of parents and other citizens concerned with the survival of real freedom of choice in education. Membership costs $10 a year, which includes a subscription to its bimonthly newsletter.

CEF accepts contributions in varying amounts ($15 for families, up to $100 for supporting organizations).

Educational Research Analysts (Mel and Norma Gabler, P.O. Box 7518, Longview, TX 75607).

Described in their literature as a "vital ministry" by its Christian founders, ERA began when the Gablers' teenage son, then sixteen, "asked where he could find the truth if not in the textbooks. Upon reviewing some of the books, the Gablers found so many irrelevant and immaterial topics that they decided someone should per-haps act as sort of a censor and make sure a textbook is, in reality, a textbook," wrote Larry Dumas for the *Vermont Sunday News* (Sept. 30, 1973).

"[T]he Gablers feel there is too much sex, violence, and anti-Americanism already in textbooks which have become required reading for many grammar school children," wrote Dumas.

Publishes a monthly newsletter, *The Mel Gablers' Educational Research Analysts Newsletter,* available for a minimum pledge of $10.

Publishes a wide range of handbooks on school-related topics: humanism, values clarification, censorship, creation science, MACOS (Man, A Course Study), information against "value-free" sex education, etc. Handbooks are not priced individually; instead, the Gablers solicit contributions. They explain that if they were to sell them outright, the cost would be approximately $15 per handbook. As they explain: "Our material is designed to help you win victories, and is furnished to help you win victories, and is furnished on the basis of contributions to the work we are accomplishing in the area of textbook reform."

States Mel Gabler: "Norma and I contribute our time as our ministry to help rescue the hearts, minds, and souls of children. However, most of our time is required to answer telephone calls, letters, and to speak at conferences. As a result, most of our textbook reviewing, filling of orders, filing, photocopying, etc., must be done by our six staff members who depend upon us to eat, pay their rent, etc. Add to this expenses for paper, printing, postage, rent, utilities, two photocopy machines, and three personal computer systems. Contributions are our only source of income."

Requests tax-deductible donations in amounts varying from $25 to $1,000 or greater, and requests monthly pledges.

Focus on the Family (Colorado Springs, CO 80995; in Canada, P.O. Box 9800, Vancouver, BC V6B 4G3).

As James Dobson wrote, "Our objective is, quite simply, to reconnect families with the ageless wisdom of Judeo-Christian values. . . . We strongly believe that only a return to time-honored, traditional principles of morality, fidelity and commitment will save the family."

Focus on the Family is "a non-profit Christian organization. Our only reason for existence is to contribute to the stability of the family in our society. That purpose is based on a foundation of four guiding philosophies:

"1. *Our Christian Mission:* We believe that the ultimate purpose in living is to glorify God and to attain eternal life through Jesus Christ our Lord. This begins within our own families. From there we are committed to reaching out to a suffering humanity that does not know of His love and His sacrifice.

"2. *The Marital Bond:* We believe that the institution of marriage is a permanent, lifelong relationship between a man and a woman. This holds true regardless of trials, sickness, financial woes or emotional stresses that may ensue.

"3. *The Value of Children:* We believe children are a gift of God. A heritage from the Lord. Therefore, we are accountable to God for molding, shaping and preparing them for a life of service to Him and to their fellow man.

"4. *The Sanctity of Life:* We believe that human life is of inestimable worth and signifiance in all its dimensions. This includes the unborn, the aged, the widowed, the mentally retarded, the unattractive, the physically challenged and every other condition in which humanness is expressed from conception to the grave.

"We stand committed to these principles at every level of the organization. So does each member of our staff. The values and techniques we share with parents are drawn from the wisdom of the Bible and the Judeo-Christian ethic—an alternative to the humanistic relativism typical of today's theorists.

"God ordained the family. He gave it His blessing. Focus on the Family attempts to be a reflection of what we believe to be the recommendation of the Creator Himself."

With its operating budget estimated at $70–$80 million a year (according to Ralph Reed's Christian Coalition), Focus on the Family spreads the word through an extensive publications program:

• According to Dobson, 1,800 radio stations carry his daily program, a 30-minute broadcast, "Focus on the Family."

• A monthly magazine, *Focus on the Family,* which reaches nearly two million homes, has the third largest circulation of any religious publication. (The organization also publishes magazines for a diverse audience—children to adults; *Clubhouse Jr., Brio, Breakaway, Parental Guidance, Citizen, Physician,* and *Youthwalk.*)

• *Dr. James Dobson's Focus on the Family Bulletin,* published by Tyndale House, appears monthly in church bulletins nationwide—over three million.

• Its book publishing division, created in 1986, publishes Ruth Bell Graham, Gary Smalley, John Trent, and others.

• Focus on the Films produces Christian films that have been shown through network TV and local cable programming.

• Focus' Educational Resources division produces books, films, magazines, and audiocassettes, reaching "nearly four million teachers and students from elementary grades to university campuses."

"Another facet of our ministry is in the public policy area—both in the U.S. and Canada. In 1988, the Family Research Council in Washington, D.C., merged with Focus. This provided a base for influence and research efforts on behalf of the home. Our approach is nonpartisan, and its intended outcome is a social and political environment beneficial to growing families."

The organization accepts tax-free donations, monthly pledge gifts, and contributions ($10 to $100, or more); additionally, a wide range of products is available, with "suggested donation" amounts for each item.

Freedom Forum (The Freedom Forum World Center, 1101 Wilson Boulevard, Arlington, VA 22209).

Founded in 1935 by Frank E. Gannett, the Freedom Forum is "a financially independent [$700 million in assets], nonpartisan, international organization dedicated to free press, free speech, and free spirit for all people."

Its priorities are journalism education, professional development of journalists, and First Amendment rights of free press and free speech, "supported and advanced by programs, projects, publications and grants; international initiatives; the Freedom Forum Media Studies Center; and the Freedom Forum First Amendment Center."

Fund for Free Expression (Human Rights Watch, Publications Department, 485 Fifth Avenue, New York, NY 10017-6104).

Founded in 1978 "to monitor and promote observance of internationally recognized human rights," the Fund is a division of Human Rights Watch and focuses on "freedom of expression around the world and in the United States. . . . The Fund emphasizes the connection between freedom of expression and global social problems such as AIDS, famine and attacks on the environment, in order to establish censorship and information policies as an important element in the debate about these issues."

Prominent members include Arthur Miller, Toni Morrison, John Updike, and Kurt Vonnegut, Jr.

The Fund has recently published *Off Limits: Censorship and Corruption,* which "documents the extent to which a taboo topic for the press in many countries is the wealth accumulated by heads of state—and their family and associates—during their terms in office."

Publications of interest include (from 1991) "Muzzling Student Journalists" (article reprint), "The Threat Against Salman Rushdie," "Writers and Human Rights in Africa," "The Supreme Court and Free Speech," *Restricted Subjects: Freedom of Expression, Off Limits: Censorship and Corruption,* "Secret Trials in America?" "Managed News, Stifled Views," and "Freedom of Expression and the War."

It also publishes a newsletter, *News from the Fund for Free Expression.* Write for a free copy of its publications list.

Institute for Creation Research (10946 Woodside Ave N., Santee, CA 92071; P.O. Box 2667, El Cajon, CA 92021).

Founded in 1970, originally a division of Christian Heritage College, ICR has been an independent organization since 1981. "Our goals are to promote scientific creationism, Biblical creationism and related fields by various means, including pubications, research, seminars and other public meetings, and in particular by providing graduate training in the sciences, through our Graduate School."

Publishes a free monthly news journal focusing on creationism, *Acts and Facts.* ICR also has an extensive publications program, including books, cassettes, and videos. Write for a free copy of its publications list.

Institute for First Amendment Studies, Inc. (P.O. Box 589, Great Barrington, MA 01230).

An educational organization founded by Skipp Porteous, a former fundamentalist preacher turned First Amendment advocate, with a special interest in the separation of church and state.

The institute publishes two newsletters: *The Freedom Writer,* bimonthly; and *Walk Away,* quarterly ($10).

A membership costs $25 and includes a subscription to *The Freedom Writer* (nonmembers pay $30); a 10 percent discount is offered on books they sell, including Porteous's own story, *Jesus Doesn't Live Here Anymore: From Fundamentalist to Freedom Writer.* (Porteous has recently published *Challenging the Christian Right: The Activist's Handbook,* available from his institute.)

The institute accepts tax-deductible contributions in varying amounts: $36, $50, $100, $500, and more.

Media Coalition (900 Third Avenue, Suite 1600, New York, NY 10022).

An "association that defends the First Amendment right to publish and sell books and magazines that contain some element of sexual explicitness but are not obscene under U.S. Supreme Court standards," the Coalition was founded in 1973 and "represents most of the booksellers, book and periodical publishers, and periodical wholesalers and distributors in the U.S.," including the American Booksellers Association, the Association of American Publishers, the Council for Periodical Distributors Associations, the International Periodical Distributors Association, the Magazine Publishers of America, and the National Association of College Stores.

The Media Coalition:

• Distributes to members regular reports that outline the activities of state legislatures with respect to works of sexual content;

• Writes local government officials and state legislators in an effort to advise them on proposed legislation;

• Files *amicus curiae* briefs in First Amendment cases involving material with sexual content.

Morality in Media, Inc. (475 Riverside Drive, New York, NY 10015).

"A national, interfaith organization founded in 1962 to stop the illegal traffic in pornography constitutionally. Morality in Media works in the areas of public information and the law.

"There are 45 chapters and state affiliates of Morality in Media throughout this nation. Morality in Media coordinates the growing annual WRAP (White Ribbon Against Pornography) Campaign held during Pornography Awareness Week. In 1989, an estimated five million Americans participated.

"A division of Morality in Media is the National Obscenity Law Center, a clearinghouse of legal information on obscenity cases and materials for prosecutors and other law enforcement officials."

The $20 annual membership fee includes a one-year subscription to its bimonthly newsletter, *Morality in Media Newsletter.*

The organization accepts tax-deductible donations and encourages gifts in wills and trusts.

National Campaign for Freedom of Expression (918 F Street, N.W. #506, Washington, DC 20004; 1402 Third Avenue, #421, Seattle WA 98101).

This organization "is an educational and advocacy network of artists, arts organizations, audience members and concerned citizens formed to protect and extend freedom of artistic expression and fight censorship throughout the United States.

"The Campaign's work is committed to the understanding that true democracy is dependent on the right to free artistic expression for all, including those censored due to racism, sexism, homophobia and all other forms of invidious discrimination.

"The National Campaign for Freedom of Expression works to empower artists in the political process at every level of public enterprise."

The NCFE has twenty active affiliates nationwide and publishes a newsletter, the *NCFE Quarterly Bulletin,* "to keep the membership and constituency informed about the current status of NEA issues, legal defense issues, censorship in the arts, and affiliate news."

NCFE membership costs vary; all include a one-year subscription to *NCFE Quarterly Bulletin:* $15 for a one-year membership; $25 for a one-year membership and a copy of *Fifty Ways to Fight Censorship* by Dave Marsh; $50 for the membership, the Marsh book, and a First Amendment T-shirt.

In addition, NCFE accepts contributions to its Legal Offense Fund, and patron gifts to "support the fight against censorship" in the amounts of $100, $250, $500, and $1,000.

Formed in 1990 in response to the passage of the Helms amendment in July 1989, the NCFE has monitored NEA legislation, produced an art censorship video, sponsored festivals to focus attention on artists, generated letters to members of Congress, established liaisons, through its affiliates, with local media and national media, monitored NEA funding decisions, established a phone hotline on reauthorization efforts of NEA funding, gathered and disseminated censorship data across the country, provided legal defense for artists and art organizations under attack, and assisted artists nationwide in organizing local responses to censorship efforts.

Future programs include establishing a computerized censorship database, working with the media "to reframe the debate from obscenity and pornography to the issues of freedom of expression and cultural democracy," publishing the *Bulletin,* establishing a speakers' bureau, working on advocacy efforts (voter education, registration, grassroots organization), and continuing to provide legal defense support or referrals to artists, art organizations, and individuals under attack.

National Coalition Against Censorship (275 Seventh Avenue, New York, NY 10001).

For concerned citizens that want to fund a general-purpose, anticensorship group, this is a logical choice.

NCAC's Statement of Concern:

> Freedom of communication is the indispensable condition of a healthy democracy. In a pluralistic society it would be impossible for all people at all times to agree on the value of all ideas; and fatal to moral, artistic and intellectual growth if they did.
>
> Some of the Coalition's participating organizations reject all barriers abridging access to any material, however controversial or even abhorrent to some. Others reject barriers for adults, so long as their individual right of choice is not infringed. All of us are united in the conviction that censorship of what we see and hear and read constitutes an unacceptable dictatorship over our minds and a dangerous opening to religious, political, artistic, and intellectual repression.

NCAC "is an alliance of national organizations, including religious, educational, professional, artistic, labor and civil rights groups. United by a conviction that freedom of thought, inquiry, and expression must be defended, they work to educate their own members about the dangers of censorship and how to oppose it. As a Coalition, they strive to create a climate of opinion hospitable to First Amendment freedoms in the broader community."

The NCAC:

• Collects and disseminates information about censorship efforts throughout the country, working with organizations, individuals, and the media.

• Conducts meetings for discussion and debate of difficult First Amendment issues.

• Sponsors and cosponsors major conferences on freedom of expression.

• Acts as a resource and catalyst by making available a wide variety of educational materials and programming resources.

• Serves as a unique national clearinghouse on book-banning litigation in public schools.

Publications include: *Censorship News* (a quarterly newsletter, $25 a year), *The Meese Commission Exposed* ($6), and *Books on Trial* ($5). (Send a SASE for a listing of publications available.)

NCAC has recently begun a special program to counter censorship in schools, which "advises and gives direct assistance to schools and citizens in local communities when censorship controversies erupt; works through our Participating Organizations to stimulate and assist them in anticensorship activities; informs and educates the wider public about the dangers of censorship and how to oppose it; and researches and publishes *Books on Trial,* a report on school book-banning court cases, through its national Clearinghouse on Book-Banning Litigation."

To join the Coalition and become a "Friend," which entitles you to *Censorship News* and various reports, tax-deductible contributions in varying amounts are accepted: $25, $35, $50, $100, $250, $500, $1,000, and more.

National Coalition Against Pornography (800 Compton Road, Suite 9224, Cincinnati, OH 45231).

Founded in 1983, N-CAP is "an alliance of representatives from over 70 religious denominations and private organizations united to eliminate illegal, dangerous hard-core pornography from our society . . .

"N-CAP opposes censorship (prior restraint by the government)."

Its objectives are:

• To educate the public about the prevalence and severity of illegal obscenity and child pornography in America today—its physical, psychological and sociological harm.

• To mobilize and assist citizen groups who support enforcement of existing laws against the production, distribution and sale of illegal obscenity and child pornography.

• To support and assist government agencies entrusted with enforcing constitutional laws that prevent sexual violence, and to support and help draft legislation that strengthens or initiates such laws.

• Provides on request "Resources for Concerned Citizens" (photocopied information on combating pornography, on working with the media, and on ways of stopping receipt of mail-order porn, and factsheets on N-CAP, etc.).

• Sells many resources (books, booklets, audiotapes, videotapes, reports, etc.) about pornography and its effects.

• Accepts tax-deductible donations.

National Coalition on Television Violence (P.O. Box 2157, Champaign, IL 61825).

Monitors television violence and rates television shows and TV films with their own ratings system, modeled after the MPAA standards.

As NCTV explains, its editor and research director, Dr. Thomas E. Radecki, advocates "the establishment of municipal, state and national public film ratings boards for movie theater and videocassette distribution. Radecki said schools and churches should establish regular programs to teach the careful selection of programming and should monitor the successfulness of these efforts. Radecki also asked for support for the American Medical Association ban on amateur and professional boxing, and recommended warnings on all violent toys and video games."

Publishes a quarterly newsletter, *NCTV News,* available to members ($25 annual fee); donations are tax-deductible. Publishes several bibliographies (violent video-games, cartoon violence, TV violence, war toys, boxing and sports violence), viewing guidelines, monitoring report forms, and other material.

No More Censorship Defense Fund (P.O. Box 424756, San Francisco, CA 94142).

Originally founded to bring attention to music censorship, this organization is composed entirely of volunteers, working on a bare bones budget. Its scope has expanded to include censorship in general. It publishes *No More Censorship,* as funding permits.

Parents for Rock and Rap (P.O. Box 53, Libertyville, IL 60048).

Aptly located in Libertyville, this grassroots organization was founded by a retired schoolteacher and mother, Mary Morello, to oppose Tipper Gore's PMRC. As noted in "Roadkill" (a music column by Michael C. Harris), Parents for Rock and Rap advocates freedom for musical artists, particularly rap music, which Morello feels has received a bum rap.

States Morello: "You know why my neighbors back me? Because they don't want one person in this world interfering in the way that they raise their children, or choosing anything for their children."

A tax-deductible organization, Parents for Rock and Rap publishes a newsletter, *P.F.R.R.* (Write for subscription information.)

Parents Music Resource Center (1500 Arlington Blvd., Arlington, VA 22209).

Founded in 1985 by Susan Baker, Tipper Gore (wife of then Senator Al Gore), Pam Howar, and Sally Nevius, the PMRC was created "to address the issue of lyrics in some music which glorifies graphic sex and violence and glamorizes the use of drugs and alcohol . . . .

"The PMRC does not support, condone or accept censorship."

Publishes a bimonthly newsletter, *The Record,* available for $25 for a one-year subscription. Its publication program includes: a 38-minute video "highlighting current trends within the recording industry" ($24.95), a "Satanism Research Packet" ($15), handbooks for parents, information packets about PMRC, a color slide show on rock music, and community action kits for concerned parents. (Note: On its National Advisory Board is NCTV's Thomas Radecki.)

PEN American Center (Freedom-to-Write Program; 568 Broadway, New York, NY 10012).

An international organization of literary writers and editors, PEN "acts against censorship worldwide and cooperates closely with the network of human rights groups, including Amnesty International and Human Rights Watch. Some 150 cables and letters are sent annually to responsible governments, signed by prominent American authors, and PEN members conduct missions to countries where problems of censorship arise. . . . Freedom-to-Write holds frequent public events on freedom-of-expression themes . . . ; publishes case sheets, country reports, and monthly bulletins; generates ongoing press converage [recently, rallying to Rushdie's cause]; and initiates letter-writing campaigns by PEN's membership through rapid-action appeals. Violations of free expression at home and abroad are brought to the attention of State Department officials as well as members of Congress, before whom PEN members are invited to testify on matters of particular urgency. Amicus curiae briefs on First Amendment rights are submitted in behalf of cases filed by other groups or individuals, and libraries and schools around the United States are regularly monitored for book-banning and similar abuses. Two annual Freedom-to-Write Awards of $3,000 each are given to writers who have courageously defended the right to free expression."

PEN publishes a bimonthly newsletter, *Freedom-to-Write Bulletin,* available to Friends of PEN (affiliation costs $35 for the supporter level to $1,000 for the benefactor level).

Several publications are available from PEN, including *Liberty Denied: The Current Rise of Censorship in America,* by Donna A. Demac (201 pp., paperback, $10.95).

People for the American Way (2000 M. Street, N.W., Suite 400, Washington, DC 20036).

Publishes a wide range of material of interest, including *Attacks on the Freedom to Learn* (an annual that details state-by-state censorship attempts in schools), videotapes (*Redondo Beach: A Stand Against Censorship* and *Censorship in Our Schools: Hawkins County, TN*), *The Postcard Activist: Ban Censorship* (30 preaddressed postcards to "corporations, major networks, government officials and publishers [to let] them know that you oppose censorship"), art posters on censorship, and *Congressional Directory.*

PAW also publishes *Right-Wing Watch* (10 issues a year, $15), a newsletter that "by reviewing conservative direct mail appeals and scanning Religious Right television programs and activities, tells you what the Right is currently up to, whether the focus is fund-raising, education or art censorship efforts, or even internecine disputes."

Project Censored (P.O. Box 310, Cotati, CA 94931)

Started in 1976, Project Censored is the brainchild of Professor Carl Jensen. As Jensen explains: "Project Censored is an annual national media research project with an innovative approach to constructive media criticism which hopes to improve print and broadcast journalism. *At issue:* Whether or not the news media provide the public with all the information needed to make informed decisions. . . . The primary objective of Project Censored is to explore and publicize stories on important issues that have been overlooked or under-reported by the news media."

Publications include an annual censorship yearbook and a pamphlet (available for a SASE) discussing the top ten censored stories.

Project Censor's national newsletter, *CENSORED,* is $30 for a one-year subscription ($45, foreign subscriptions), and contains "the latest censored news nominations; reports on censored books and films; profiles on censored investigative journalists; updates on issues censored years ago; tips on how to learn more about censorship and censored issues."

Rock Out Censorship (P.O. Box 147, Jewett, OH 43986).

"Dedicated to crushing the hypocritical thought police who want to decide what is best for all of us," Rock Out Censorship—if nothing else—has a sense of humor, obvious in its newspaper, *The ROC: Voice of Rock Out Censorship!* ($10 for a one-year subscription; $13 for foreign subscriptions). Its subscription form has two blocks:

> • **YES!** "I want to help protect my right in this supposedly free country to watch, read or listen to anything I damn well please."
> • **NO!** "I really enjoy oppression and wouldn't mind too terribly having all my decisions made for me by a bunch of fascist bible-thumpers. So screw your stupid organization while I get a lobotomy and listen to some Amy Grant."

The organization cheerfully accepts donations (in amounts from $10 to $1,000, or more) to fight "the growing drive toward fascism in America." Among other purposes, the money will go toward printing (for instance) a quarter-million copies of *Rock Out Censorship* for free distribution at Guns 'n' Roses/Metallica concerts.

Rutherford Institute (P.O. Box 7482, Charlottesville, VA 22906-7482).

Founded in 1982 by constitutional attorney John W. Whitehead, the Rutherford Institute offers legal and educational services to: "preserve free speech in the public arena, including public schools; protect the right of churches, church schools, home schools, and other religious organizations to operate freely without improper state intrusion; defend parental rights and family autonomy; support the sanctity of all human life; assist individuals oppressed for their beliefs in totalitarian countries."

Although perceived to favor evangelical Christians, the Rutherford Institute "has and always will defend any group or individual regardless of their religious affiliation."

Publishes several newsletters: the *Religious Liberty Bulletin* (monthly; sold in bulk to churches), *Home School Brief* ($25 a year), and their mainstay publication, *Rutherford* (monthly).

The annual membership fee of $25 includes a one-year subscription to *Rutherford* and a 10 percent discount off publications.

Truth About Rock (Box 9222, St. Paul, MN 55109).

Founded by Steve Peters in 1979, Truth About Rock "helps you educate young people and parents in making reasonable moral choices about rock music." Wrote Peters, "Hot-rockin' groups [are] pushing drugs, illicit sex, violence, rebellion, suicide, murder, satanism and other x-rated values on a young and unsuspecting but very loyal audience."

Offers extensive products ("combat equipment you need for Rock's World War III"), including books, tracks, videos, and color T-shirts ("Jesus Christ . . . He's the Real Thing," using the Coca-Cola logo, and "God's Last Name is not Dammit").

Its quarterly newsletter, *Truth About Rock Report,* costs $20 for six issues.

Video Software Dealers Association (303 Harper Drive, Moorestown, NJ 08057-3329).

This organization represents the home video industry. Its membership includes 4,500 companies that represent over 25,000 video stores. VSDA lobbies on issues like censorship legislation "to diminish their potentially negative impact on the video retail industry."

It publishes an "educational products catalog" with publications available to the general public (members pay less). Of interest: "Child Protection and Obscenity Enforcement Act of 1988/1991 Update" ($25 members, $100 nonmembers).

Washington Coalition Against Censorship (6201 Fifteenth, N.W., #640, Seattle, WA 98107).

This coalition consists of "a group of organizations joined together to preserve and protect the freedom of expression guaranteed by the First Amendment of the United States Constitution. We support the diversity and freedom of a pluralistic society; we advocate the freedom to learn and to express ideas not always supported by the majority; we oppose censorship whenever and wherever it arises.

"WCAC is not an individual membership organization. You can support WCAC's work by purchasing our products or making a donation, by speaking out against censorship, and by keeping us informed of local problems."

Products available include: four T-shirt designs ($10 each), canvas book bags ($13), a lapel pin ($5), a portfolio by Seattle cartoonist Tom Whittemore (10 prints, letter size, $10), and *School Censorship: An Emergency Response Manual* ($15; currently under revision).

Bibliography

Alderman, Ellen, and Kennedy, Caroline. *In Our Defense: The Bill of Rights in Action.* New York: William Morrow and Company, 1991.

American Booksellers Foundation for Free Expression. *Censorship and First Amendment Rights: A Primer.* Tarrytown, NY: American Booksellers Foundation for Free Expression, 1992. ($10; 560 White Plains Road, Tarrytown, NY 10591.) *An excellent general interest book on the subject with a historical perspective, current events, and numerous resources.*

American Library Association. *Banned Books Week 92: Resource Book and Promotion Guide.* Chicago: American Library Association, 1992. *Updated annually, this publication provides a wealth of information, especially useful for librarians, bookstores, and teachers: a list of banned books (from 387 B.C. to present), a list of challenged books, notable First Amendment cases, quotes on the First Amendment, suggested anticensorship activities, clip-out ad slicks for print media to promote Banned Books Week, and scripts for public service announcements for radio and TV stations. Indispensable.*

Bradbury, Ray. *Fahrenheit 451.* New York: Del Rey, Ballantine, 1972. *The classic anticensorship novel, originally published in 1953, more relevant than ever today.*

Burress, Lee. *Battle of the Books: Literary Censorship in the Public Schools, 1950–1985.* Metuchen, NJ: Scarecrow Press, 1989.

Chapple, Steve, and Talbot, David. *Burning Desires: Sex in America.* New York: Doubleday, 1989.

Clarkson, Frederick, and Porteous, Skipp. *Challenging the Christian Right: The Activist's Handbook* (Institute for First American Studies, P.O. Box 589, Great Barrington, MA 01230), 1992. *Indispensable handbook for any organization or individual wishing to combat the Christian Right on its home turf.*

D'Emilio, John, and Freedman, Estelle. *Intimate Matters.* New York: Harper & Row, 1988.

Downs, Robert, ed. *The First Freedom.* Chicago: American Library Association, 1960. *A compilation celebrating freedom of speech and the press, and "liberty and justice in the world of books and reading."*

Downs, Robert., and McCoy, Ralph E., eds. *The First Freedom Today: Critical Issues Relating to Censorship and to Intellectual Freedom.* Chicago: American Library Association, 1984. *An updated compilation celebrating the freedom to write and read.*

Ernst, Morris L., and Schwartz, Alan U. *Censorship: The Search for the Obscene.* New York: Macmillan Company, 1964. *A history of censorship law in the U.S. and Great Britain.*

Haney, Robert W. *Comstockery in America: Patterns of Censorship and Control.* Boston: Beacon Press, 1960.

Journal Graphics, Inc. *1991 Transcript/Video Index.* Denver: Journal Graphics ($11.95;

1535 Grant Street, Denver, CO 80203), 1992. *An annual index to TV news and public affairs programming, "television good enough to read," as JG puts it.*

Marsh, Dave. *50 Ways to Fight Censorship.* New York: Thunder's Mouth Press (54 Greene Street, Suite 4S, New York, NY 10013), 1991. *Music critic Dave Marsh offers his laundry list of 50 anticensorship activities that make good common sense ("#1—Speak Out! #2—Register and Vote!")*

National Coalition Against Censorship. *The Meese Commission Exposed* (Proceedings of a National Coalition Against Censorship Public Information Briefing on the Attorney General's Commission on Pornography, January 16, 1986). New York: National Coalition Against Censorship, 1987 ($6; NCAC, 132 West 43 Street, New York, NY 10036). *As NCAC points out, the Meese commission "took no initiative in inviting writers and artists, or others who might help them assess the impact of censorship on creativity and communication. Few witnesses explored the implications of censorship." This book records the voices of celebrated figures from the creative community—Kurt Vonnegut, Colleen Dewhurst, Betty Friedan, et al.— taking the Meese commission to task for its egregious oversight. Subjects addressed include: writing, drama, civil liberties, sex education, psychology, feminism, psychiatry, family planning, booksellers, publishing, religion, and feminism.*

National Endowment for the Arts. *Guide to the National Endowment for the Arts: 1992-1993.* Washington, DC: National Endowment for the Arts, 1992 (free publication; NEA, National Hanks Center, 1100 Pennsylvania Avenue, N.W., Washington, DC 20506). *An excellent overview of the Endowment's goals, its various programs, and its staffing.*

————. *National Endowment for the Arts: 1990 Annual Report.* Washington, DC: National Endowment for the Arts, 1991. *The companion to the NEA guidebook, this book provides specific information on projects funded.*

New York Public Library. *Censorship: 500 Years of Conflict.* New York, NY: Oxford University Press, 1984. *A catalogue to the New York Public Library exhibit on censorship through the ages, celebrating "the sharing of a vast body of thought preserved in the books, prints and manuscripts that record our civilization, and which it is the Library's privilege and mission to preserve."*

Noble, William. *Bookbanning in America: Who Bans Books?—and Why.* Middlebury, VT: Paul S. Eriksson, Publisher, 1960.

O'Neill, Terry. *Censorship: Opposing Viewpoints.* St. Paul: Greenhaven Press (577 Shoreview Park Road, St. Paul, MN 55126), 1985. *On the premise that "those who do not know their opponents' arguments do not completely understand their own," this book, one in a series on diverse subjects, presents the issue in a pro/con format, drawing from "magazines, journals, books, and newspapers, as well as statements and position papers" to cover the subject.*

Pipes, Daniel. *The Rushdie Affair.* New York: A Birch Lane Press Book, published by Carol Publishing Group, 1990. *Eminently qualified to write about the Middle East, Pipes gives us an insightful look at the circumstances surrounding the Rushdie controversy. Required reading for anyone interested in Rushdie.*

Porteous, Skipp. *Jesus Doesn't Live Here Anymore: From Fundamentalist to Freedom Writer.* Buffalo, NY: Prometheus Books, 1991. *A fascinating recounting of Porteous's walk away from his fundamentalist faith to becoming a First Amendment purist. Especially revealing: his visit to Tupelo, Mississippi, where he toured Donald Wildmon's American Family Association headquarters.*

Smolla, Rodney A. *Free Speech in an Open Society.* New York: Alfred A. Knopf, 1992.

———. *Jerry Falwell v. Larry Flynt: The First Amendment on Trial.* New York: St. Martin's Press, 1988. *A blow-by-blow account of the legal battle between Moral Majority founder Jerry Falwell and* Hustler *publisher Larry Flynt, in a classic confrontation highlighting freedom of the press.*

Stanmeyer, William A. *The Seduction of Society: Pornography and Its Impact on American Life.* Ann Arbor: Servant Books (Box 8617, Ann Arbor, MI 48107), 1984.

U.S. Department of Justice. *Attorney General's Commission on Pornography.* 2 vols. Washington, DC: U.S. Government Printing Office, 1986.

Vizzard, Jack. *See No Evil: Life Inside a Hollywood Censor.* New York: Simon & Schuster, 1970. *A fascinating look at censorship in Hollywood, citing specific movies.*

Wagman, Robert J. *The First Amendment Book.* New York: Pharos Books, 1991. *An overview on the subject of censorship.*

Walker, Samuel. *In Defense of American Liberties: A History of the ACLU.* New York: Oxford University Press, 1990.

Washington Coalition Against Censorship. *School Censorship: An Emergency Response Manual.* Seattle: Washington Education Association and the National Educational Association, 1989 [currently under revision] ($15; WCAC, 6201 Fifteenth, N.W., #640, Seattle, WA 98107). *An indispensable resource for educators. Even though its focus is principally statewide, this is required reading for all school systems wishing to publish standard operating procedures for handling censorship complaints, book challenges, and the like.*

Weatherby, W.J. *Salman Rushdie: Sentenced to Death.* New York: Carroll & Graf Publishers, 1990. *A three-part, chronological look at Rushdie: Part I, his early years; Part II, the story behind* The Satanic Verses; *and Part III, the aftermath.*

Wertham, Fredric. *Seduction of the Innocent.* New York: Rinehart & Company, 1954. *An indictment of the crime comic books of the fifties, Dr. Wertham argues his case that they are a "pernicious influence . . . on the youth of today." Required reading for anyone interested in the history of comics in the U.S.*

Wildmon, Donald E., with Randall Nulton. *Don Wildmon: The Man the Networks Love to Hate.* Wilmore, KY: Bristol Books (308 East Main Street, Wilmore, KY 40390), 1989. *The story of Wildmon's holy war against television. This retelling sheds much light on Wildmon's perceptions of himself as a David fighting the Goliath of the television establishment.*

Acknowledgments

This book owes its genesis to Barry Hoffman, whose trenchant journal, *Gauntlet*, planted the seed for this compilation. Barry, who has fought the censorship battle on several fronts, always took time to help me in every way he could. Thank you, Barry. I couldn't have done this without your support.

I am likewise indebted to my book editor at Andrews and McMeel, Donna Martin, who gave the manuscript a careful reading and, by gentle suggestion, showed me how to tighten its focus and improve it in many ways, just as she had done for my two previous books. For this and many other reasons, she shares the dedication to this book.

I am further indebted to my other friends at Andrews and McMeel who, for the last two years, responded to my frequent phone calls and faxes for publications, information, and assistance. These kind angels include Patty Donnelly, Kathy Viele, and Dorothy O'Brien. Thanks, too, to Jean Lowe, who guided this book through production.

For assistance on the book above and beyond the call of duty, I wish to thank: Michael R. Collings, John E. Frohnmayer, Marcia Pally, Arthur J. Kropp, Gary Wood, Howard Wornom, Jr., Colleen Doran, William Margold, Dr. Carl Jensen, Christopher Finan, Skipp Porteous, Oren Teicher, and Janet Turnbull. Thank you, all.

The following organizations were especially helpful in providing information: Americans for Constitutional Freedom, Association of American Publishers, Institute for First Amendment Studies, Media Coalition, the National Coalition Against Censorship, the American Library Association, the American Civil Liberties Union, the Christian Coalition, Focus on the Family, the National Endowment for the Arts, the Washington Coalition Against Censorship, the American Booksellers Foundation for Free Expression, People for the American Way, The Institute for Creation Research, the Parents Music Resource Center, Morality in Media, and Project Censored.

Regrettably too numerous to mention by name, I also wish to thank all those who helped secure the necessary reprint rights for the pieces herein; I do appreciate your help.

I would be remiss indeed if I were not to acknowledge the considerable debt I owe to this book's illustrator, Kenny Ray Linkous. Working largely on his own, Kenny's dedication, enthusiasm, and professionalism for the book and its subject matter translated wonderfully in the powerful images that supplement the text. Thank you, Kenny.

Finally, I wish to thank my wife, Mary Beahm, who acted as the sounding board for this project from its inception. The silent partner in this project, Mary provided the necessary support, moral and otherwise, that kept me and this project on course. Thank you, Mary, for always being there for me.

Artist's Acknowledgment: The artist would like to give special thanks to Beverly Lembo.

About the Editor and Artist

George Beahm's first book, *The Vaughn Bode Index,* written when he was in high school and published the summer after college graduation, was published by a small publisher, Ned Brooks, who shares the dedication to this book. Following up with two more books on contemporary fantasy artists (*Kirk's Works,* published by Brooks's Heresy Press, and the unpublished *Corben's World*), Beahm subsequently self-published three books of general interest, then expanded into regional publishing, founding GB Publishing. Formerly a marketing director for a book publishing company and the U.S. distributor for a line of military books published in the U.K., Beahm has in recent years focused on writing non-fiction books for Andrews and McMeel: *The Stephen King Companion* (1989), *The Stephen King Story* (1991), and a revised edition of *The Stephen King Story* (1992). He is currently working on a book on basketball star Michael Jordan. With his new company, GB Ink, Beahm is self-publishing limited edition books. He and his wife, Mary, a high school English teacher, live in Hampton Roads, Virginia.

Kenny Ray Linkous is a self-taught artist whose first professional assignment was illustrating Stephen King's Philtrum Press edition of *The Eyes of the Dragon.* Linkous has subsequently rendered artwork for other book projects, including *The Shape Under the Sheet, The Stephen King Companion, The Stephen King Story, Stephen King: Man and Artist, Grimoire #1, Grimoire #2,* in addition to numerous magazines, including *Gauntlet.* Linkous was born and raised in Tams, West Virginia.

Copyrights Extension

1. "On Censorship" originally appeared in *Fates Worse Than Death: An Autobiographical Collage* by Kurt Vonnegut. Reprinted by permission of The Putnam Publishing Group for *Fates Worse Than Death* by Kurt Vonnegut. Copyright © 1991 by Kurt Vonnegut.

2. "Censorship in the Renaissance: A Paradigm for Today?" written especially for this volume, is copyright © 1993 by Michael R. Collings. All rights reserved.

3. Reprinted with permission of R.R. Bowker, a Reed Reference Publishing Company from *Banned Books, 3rd edition* © 1970, by Reed Publishing (USA) Inc. (pp. 130-134, Morris L. Ernst on Banned Books).

4. "Are There Limits to Free Speech?" by James A. Michener. Reprinted by permission of the William Morris Agency, Inc., on behalf of the author. Copyright © 1990 by James A. Michener. Originally published in *Parade Magazine*.

5. "Book Banning Blues: A New Chorus" by John F. Baker is reprinted from the November 23, 1990 issue of *Publishers Weekly*, published by Cahners Publishing Company, a division of Reed Publishing USA. Copyright © 1990 by Reed Publishing USA.

6. Reprinted with permission of R.R. Bowker, a Reed Reference Publishing Company from *Banned Books, 3rd edition* © 1970, by Reed Publishing (USA) Inc. (pp. 109-111, "Trends in Censorship").

9. "The Freedom to Read" by Anthony Schulte originally appeared in *The Meese Commission EXPOSED*, a Public Information Briefing on the Attorney General's Commission on Pornography, January 16, 1986. The essay is copyright © 1987 by the National Coalition Against Censorship.

10. "Dirty Books" by Art Buchwald appeared as a syndicated newspaper column in 1982 and is reprinted with the kind permission of Mr. Art Buchwald.

11. "Coda" by Ray Bradbury originally appeared in *Fahrenheit 451* and is reprinted by permission of Don Congdon Associates, Inc. Copyright © 1953, renewed 1981 by Ray Bradbury.

14. "Book Review, *American Psycho*" originally appeared in the *Washington Post Book World*, and has been revised and expanded for its inclusion in this volume. Copyright © 1993 by Douglas E. Winter. All rights reserved.

16. "Preface to *Nineteen Eighty-Four*" by Walter Cronkite is from *1984* by George Orwell. Copyright © 1949 by Harcourt Brace Jovanovich, Inc., renewed © 1977 by Sonia Brownell Orwell. Preface copyright © 1983 by Walter Cronkite. Used by permission of New American Library, a division of Penguin Books USA Inc.

17. Excerpts from *Orwell: The Authorized Biography by Michael Shelden* are reprinted by permission of HarperCollins Publishers.

18. "A Rushdie Chronology" is reprinted from the February 17, 1992, issue of *Publishers Weekly*, published by Cahners Publishing Company, a division of Reed Publishing USA. Copyright © 1992 by Reed Publishing USA.

20. "Interview: Salman Rushdie" conducted by Karsten Prager is copyright © 1991 by The Time Inc. Magazine Company. Reprinted by permission.

21. "A Folly Repeated" by Norman Mailer is reprinted by permission of the author and the author's agents, Scott Meredith Literary Agency, Inc., 845 Third Avenue, New York, New York 10022.

22. "The White House's Rushdie Brushoff" by Art Buchwald appeared as a syndicated newspaper column in 1992 and is reprinted with the kind permission of Mr. Art Buchwald.

23. The excerpt from "A Pen Against the Sword: In Good Faith" by Salman Rushdie originally appeared in *Newsweek*, and is reprinted with the permission of the author's agent, Wylie, Aitken & Stone.

24. "Artistic Freedom," a Briefing Paper published by the American Civil Liberties Union, is reprinted with permission. All rights reserved.

25. "Chairman's Statement: The National Endowment for the Arts" by John E. Frohnmayer, originally published in *The 1990 Annual Report,* is in the public domain.

26. "The Art Your Tax Money Buys" by John E. Frohnmayer, originally published in *The Washington Post* (April 13, 1991), copyright © 1991 by *The Washington Post* and is reprinted with permission.

27. "Raising Hell" by John E. Frohnmayer, a public address at the American Society of Newspaper Editors Conference held in Washington, DC, on April 10, 1992, is copyright © 1992 by John E. Frohnmayer and reprinted with his permission.

28. "Point: John E. Frohnmayer, Counterpoint: Phyllis Schlafly" appeared in the March 28, 1990, edition of *USA Today* and is copyright © 1990, *USA Today.* Reprinted with permission.

30. "To the Congress of the United States," an open letter by Pat Robertson under the letterhead of the Christian Coalition, appeared in the *Washington Post* (June 20, 1990), and is reprinted with permission.

32. "At Issue: Should Congress Restrict the Types of Art That Can Be Funded by the NEA? *YES* says Jesse Helms, *NO* says Wayne Lawson" is reprinted with permission from *Editorial Research Reports,* Vol. I, No. 20, May 25, 1990.

33. "John Frohnmayer on Tough Times at the NEA" is a *Newsweek* interview conducted by Daniel Glick under the title "The Nature of the Beast," which originally appeared in the March 16, 1992, issue. From *Newsweek,* March 16, 1992, and copyright © 1992, Newsweek, Inc. All rights reserved. Reprinted by permission.

36. "Cincinnati: City Under Siege" by Marcia Pally originally appeared in *Penthouse* (September 1990). Reprinted by permission of Penthouse, copyright © 1992, Penthouse International, Ltd.

37. "Interview: Dennis Barrie" originally appeared in *USA Today* (October 24, 1990) under the title "Public knows what's obscene, what isn't." Copyright © 1990, *USA Today.* Reprinted with permission.

38. "What Do Artists Want from Us?" by Irving Kristol originally appeared in *The Wall Street Journal* (August 7, 1990). Reprinted with permission of *The Wall Street Journal* copyright © 1990 Dow Jones & Company, Inc. All rights reserved.

39. "In Praise of Censure" by Garry Wills originally appeared in *Time* (July 31, 1989). Copyright © 1989 The Time Inc. Magazine Company. Reprinted by permission.

40. "The Naked Truth" by Dave Barry is copyright © 1992 and reprinted by permission of the author.

41. "Battle over the Books: Grave Impressions" was originally published as "A War of Words" by Jeff Meade, in *Teacher* (November/December 1990). Reprinted with permission from *Teacher Magazine.* Volume II, No. 3, November/December 1990.

42. "Don't Let Zealots Censor Kids' Books" was originally published as a *USA Today* editorial (August 28, 1990). Copyright © 1990, *USA Today.* Reprinted with permission.

43. "Local Pro-Censorship Group Formation" by Washington Coalition Against Censorship appeared in *School Censorship: An Emergency Response Manual* (January 1989), and is reprinted with permission.

44. "The Religious Right Must Guard American Values" is excerpted from *Listen America* by Jerry Falwell. Copyright © 1980 by Jerry Falwell. Used by permission of Doubleday, a division of Bantam Doubleday Dell Publishing Group, Inc.

45. "Diversity in Collection Development: An Interpretation of the Library Bill of Rights" and "Library Bill of Rights" are reprinted with the permission of the American Library Association.

46. "How Conflicting Values Result in Challenges" by Nancy Motomatsu and Jean Wieman, originally published in *School Censorship: An Emergency Response Manual,* is reprinted with permission from Washington Coalition Against Censorship.

47. "Some Specific Objections by Pro-Censorship Groups to Educational Materials" and "In the Eye of the Beholder" originally appeared in *School Censorship: An Emergency Response Manual,* and reprinted with permission from Washington Coalition Against Censorship.

Appendices